D1627830

Crises in World Politics
(Centre of International Studies, University of Cambridge)

TARAK BARKAWI • JAMES MAYALL • BRENDAN SIMMS
editors

GÉRARD PRUNIER
Darfur—the Ambiguous Genocide

MARK ETHERINGTON
Revolt on the Tigris

FAISAL DEVJI
Landscapes of the Jihad

AHMED HASHIM
Insurgency and Counter-Insurgency in Iraq

ERIC HERRING & GLEN RANGWALA
Iraq in Fragments—the Occupation and its Legacy

STEVE TATHAM
Losing Arab Hearts and Minds

WILLIAM MALEY
Rescuing Afghanistan

IAIN KING AND WHIT MASON
Peace at any Price: How the World Failed Kosovo

CARNE ROSS
Independent Diplomat

FAISAL DEVJI
The Terrorist in Search of Humanity—Militant Islam and Global Politics

JOHN BEW
MARTYN FRAMPTON
IÑIGO GURRUCHAGA

Talking to Terrorists

Making Peace in Northern Ireland and the Basque Country

HURST & COMPANY, LONDON

First published in the United Kingdom by
C. Hurst & Co. (Publishers) Ltd.,
41 Great Russell Street, London WC1B 3PL
© John Bew, Martyn Frampton and Iñigo Gurruchaga, 2009
All rights reserved.
Printed in India

The right of John Bew, Martyn Frampton and Iñigo Gurruchaga
to be identified as the author of this volume has been asserted
by them in accordance with the Copyright, Designs
and Patents Act, 1988.

A catalogue data record for this volume is available
from the British Library.

ISBNs
978-185065-967-9 *paperback*
978-185065-966-2 *casebound*

www.hurstpub.co.uk

CONTENTS

CONTENTS

ETA in Spain and the Basque Country: Rise, Decline and the Politics of Surrender

ACKNOWLEDGEMENTS

We have incurred countless debts in the writing of this book. While the views expressed herein and any errors contained in the text are entirely our own, there are many people to whom we owe thanks. First among these are Michael Dwyer and his staff at Hurst, Dr Dean Godson, Stephen Hayward, Sean O'Callaghan, Allen Roth and Professor Brendan Simms, who encouraged the project from its infancy. We are also indebted to those who read and commented upon all, or some of the manuscript, including Ruth Dudley Edwards, Professor Henry Patterson, Dr Simon Prince, Jonathan Scherbel-Ball, Jon Balasi Abando, Juan Aranzadi, Rafa Giménez, Marta Iturrioz and the reader, Dr Stephen Hopkins, of Leicester University. For guiding us towards interesting source material or allowing us to see previews of their own work, we are also grateful to Lord Bew, Lord Donoughue, Frank Millar of *The Irish Times*, Walter Oppenheimer, Ignacio Latierro, Robert Ramsay, and Professor Geoffrey Warner. Jonathan Bronitsky, Dr Sidney Elliot, Mick Forteath, Patrick Gregory and David Shiels provided us with fresh insights and important information, and Amanda Gurruchaga helped with graphics. The staff at the following institutions also provided much needed assistance: the National Register of Archives in Kew; the Cambridge University Library; the British Library; the Linenhall Library in Belfast; the Belfast Central Library newspaper archive; the Biblioteca Koldo Mitxelena in San Sebastián; and the library of the Instituto Cervantes in London (particularly David Carrión).

Those whom we interviewed—over a number of years and in many different contexts—were especially amenable and forthcoming, particularly Sir Brian Cubbon, Sir Nicholas Fenn, and Lord Trimble. Between us, we have had further interesting exchanges about aspects of the book with a long list of people from a variety of backgrounds: Lord

Mayhew, Hon. Professor Mitchell Reiss, Michael Barone, Owen Patterson MP, Jonathan Powell, Dr Dore Gold, Dr Richard Bourke, Dr Eugenio Biagini, Sir Kenneth Bloomfield, David Frum, Dr Eric Kaufmann, Dr Anthony McIntyre, Gerry Gregg, Martin Sieff, Gary Kent, Dr Ian McBride, Professor Michael Burleigh, Douglas Murray, Dr James Carleton Paget, Dr John Adamson, Professor Arthur Aughey, Eoghan Harris, Lisa Hyde, Dr Steven King, Henry Robinson, Melanie Phillips, and James Forsyth. To all of the above, we offer a heartfelt thank you. Undoubtedly, there are others not listed here whose indulgence we must request. For their hospitality and personal generosity in the course of researching the book, we are also indebted to Lord and Lady Wilson of Tillyorn, Dr Stan and Rebecca Perle, Michael and Susan McDowell and Professor Adrian Dixon and the fellows and staff of Peterhouse, Cambridge.

Finally, we would like to thank our close friends and above all, our families.

ABBREVIATIONS AND ACRONYMS

AAA	Anti-communist Apostolic Alliance—pro-state Spanish death squad that operated in the 1970s
ASU	Active Service Unit—IRA 'cell', consisting of eight members
ATE	Anti-terrorism ETA—pro-state Spanish death squad that operated in the 1970s
B Specials	Ulster Special Constabulary—controversial police reserve force in Northern Ireland, replaced in 1970 by the UDR
BVE	Basque Spanish Battalion—pro-state Spanish death squad that operated in the 1970s
CAIN	Conflict Archive Northern Ireland—http://cain.ulst.ac.uk/
DUP	Democratic Unionist Party—led by Revd. Dr Ian Paisley until May 2008
EE	*Euskadiko Ezkerra* (The Left of the Basque Country)—coalition of left-wing groups formed in 1977, with close involvement of members of ETA-PM
EH	*Euskal Herritarrok* (Basque Citizens)—name for electoral wing of ETA used from 1998 to side-step a legal ban on HB. In 2002, the party was reincarnated again as *Batasuna*
EEC	European Economic Community
ETA	*Euskadi ta Askatasuna* (Basque Homeland and Freedom)—nationalist paramilitary organisation, founded in 1959
ETA-*berri*	'New' ETA—short-lived Maoist splinter group from ETA, established in 1966–7

ETA-M	ETA Military—produced by ETA split in 1974, prioritising 'armed struggle' over any political involvement
ETA-PM	ETA Political Military—composed of the majority of members of ETA after the split with ETA-M in 1974, advocating a political party to represent violent Basque nationalism at the same time as the armed campaign
FARC	*Fuerzas Armadas Revolucionarias de Colombia* (Revolutionary Armed Forces of Columbia)—Marxist-Leninist guerilla organisation
FCO	Foreign and Commonwealth Office (UK)
Fianna Fáil	Largest political party in the Republic of Ireland
Fine Gael	Second largest political party in the Republic of Ireland
FRU	Force Research Unit—covert military intelligence unit of the British army
GAL	*Grupos Antiterroristas de Liberación* (Antiterrorist Liberation Groups)—a network of death squads sponsored by the Spanish government to fight ETA
Gardai (Síochána na hÉireann)	Irish Police force
GOC	General Officer Commanding—used to refer to most senior British army officer in Northern Ireland
Hamas (Islamic Resistance Movement)	Sunni Islamist terrorist organisation and political group based in the Palestinian Authority
HB	*Herri Batasuna* (Popular Unity)—an electoral coalition, formed in 1979 by parties and individuals inspired by ETA-M. It was subsequently known as *Euskal Herritarrok* and then simply *Batasuna*
Hezbollah (Party of God)	Shi'ite Islamist terrorist organisation and political group based in Lebanon
IICD	Independent International Commission on Decommissioning—set up by the British and

	Irish governments in 1997 to facilitate the disposal of paramilitary arms
IMC	International Monitoring Commission—set up following the British and Irish governments' 'Joint Declaration' of 2003, to monitor paramilitary activity
INLA	Irish National Liberation Army—left-wing Irish republican paramilitary organisation formed in 1974
Iparretarrak (ETA Northeners)	a branch of ETA formed by extreme Basque nationalists in France
IRA	Irish Republican Army (Provisional). Irish republican paramilitary organization, created in 1969–70, out of a split within republicanism. Linked to (Provisional) Sinn Fein
KAS	Socialist Patriotic Coordinator—underground network which aimed to unite the various strands of radical Basque nationalism, including ETA-PM
MI5	Military Intelligence (Section 5)—the British internal security service
MP	Member of Parliament (Westminster)
NICRA	Northern Ireland Civil Rights Association
NIO	Northern Ireland Office
NORAID	Irish Northern Aid Committee—Republican support group based in the United States of America
NRA	National Register of Archives in Kew, London (British State Papers)
OECD	Organisation for Economic Co-operation and Development—international organisation of thirty countries that accept the principles of representative democracy and free-market economy
'Official' IRA	Irish republican paramilitary organization, created in 1969–70, out of a split within republicanism; part of the 'Official' republican movement
OFPRA	French Office for the Protection of Refugees and Stateless People

PD	People's Democracy—radical Marxist student organisation, prominent in Northern Ireland in 1968–9
PP	*Partido Popular* (Popular Party)—the main conservative political party in Spain
PNV	Basque Nationalist Party—founded in 1895. Its name translates as *Euzko Alderdi Jeltzalea* in Basque or *Partido Nacionalista Vasco* (PNV) in Spanish
PSNI	Police Service of Northern Ireland—established in 2001 as the successor to the RUC
RAF	Royal Air Force
'Real' IRA	Dissident Irish republican paramilitary organization, created in 1997, by those unhappy with Sinn Féin's acceptance of the Mitchell Principles on non-violence
RUC	Royal Ulster Constabulary—Northern Irish police force, succeeded in 2001 by the PSNI
PSOE	*Partido Socialista Obrero Español* (Spanish Socialist Workers' Party)—one of the largest and longest established parties in Spain
SAS	Special Air Service—British army unit specializing in covert operations
SDLP	Social Democratic and Labour Party—a 'constitutional nationalist' Northern Irish political party, formerly led by John Hume
Sinn Fein	Irish republican political party, led by Gerry Adams. It was created 1969–70, after a split within republicanism. It is linked to the 'Provisional' IRA
SIS	Secret Intelligence Service (also known as MI6)—Britain's external intelligence agency
Taoiseach	Irish Prime Minister
TUAS	'Tactical Use of Armed Struggle'—Title of the 1994 Irish republican document that outlined the rationale for the first IRA ceasefire
UCD	*Unión de Centro Democrático* (Union of Democratic Centre)—short-lived coalition of a number of parties formed in 1977 by

	Adolfo Suárez during Spain's transition to democracy
UDA	Ulster Defence Association—loyalist paramilitary organisation
UDI	Unilateral Declaration of Independence
UDR	Ulster Defence Regiment—an infantry regiment of the British Army formed in 1970 to replace the B Specials
UFF	Ulster Freedom Fighters—loyalist paramilitary organisation (generally considered to be a part of the UDA)
UN	United Nations
UPN	*Union del Pueblo Navarro* (Union of the Navarran People)—a political party linked to the PP in the regional parliament of Navarre in Spain
UUAC	United Unionist Action Council—an umbrella organisation that united those involved in the failed loyalist strike of 1977
UUP	Ulster Unionist Party—the mainstream 'moderate' unionist party in Northern Ireland, formerly led by David Trimble
UUUC	United Ulster Unionist Council—an umbrella organisation that united those unionists opposed to the Sunningdale Agreement in 1974
UVF	Ulster Volunteer Force—loyalist paramilitary organisation
UWC	Ulster Workers' Council—a loyalist workers' organisation set up in 1974 in opposition to the Sunningdale Agreement
ZEN	Special Zone North plan—an inter-locking programme of investment in security, legal reforms and political initiatives to counter ETA, established by Felipe González's Socialist government from 1982

INTRODUCTION

THE SEARCH FOR A MODEL
OF CONFLICT RESOLUTION

Secretary of State One: If you want them to change their mind, you have to talk to them. They won't do it very willingly because they don't trust you, but yes, you have to talk to terrorists...

Secretary of State Two: My belief is you have to be ruthless about killing the guys at that sharp end and do some extremely deep thinking about taking away the base that sustains them ... you can't, you won't succeed without doing both.[1]

(*Talking to Terrorists*, a play by Robin Soans, 2005)

Governments talk to terrorists. This is a statement of fact rather than a critique; it is an acknowledgement of reality rather than a value judgement.[2] Indeed, the broader question of how democratic states deal with the challenge of terrorism—both domestic and international—has risen to the very top of the political agenda in recent years. There are many who counsel that governments should never engage in dialogue with those who are prepared to use violence to achieve their goals. At the same time, the uncomfortable truth is that many governments have done this in the past and that more are likely to do the same in the future. Taking that as a given, it is more important than ever to achieve an understanding of how, why and when such talking occurs and—by focusing on those instances where it has taken place—to understand the consequences of such actions. That is the purpose of this book.

In recent years it has become increasingly fashionable to use the peace process in Northern Ireland as a 'model of conflict resolution'. The presumed 'lessons of Ulster', where the Irish Republican Army

1

(IRA) ended its three-decade campaign of violence, are now regularly deemed to be applicable to other areas of conflict around the world.[3] Since the Belfast Agreement of Easter 1998, innumerable leading statesmen, policy-makers and commentators have sought to make policy prescriptions for other regions on the basis of the Northern Ireland experience. To a great extent, this is both understandable and justifiable. In an international arena littered with problems of ethnic and religious tension, violence perpetrated by non-state actors and, above all, the growing spectre of political terrorism, the apparent end of one of the longest-running conflicts in the world provides a welcome point of contrast.

Since the return of devolved institutions to Northern Ireland in May 2007, it has been generally agreed that the peace process there has finally been brought to a conclusion. The obstacles and political crises that emerged in the aftermath of the ground-breaking Belfast Agreement of 1998 are thought now to have been overcome. The apparent 'end of history' in Ulster has prompted widespread reflection. Thus, the former Secretary of State for Northern Ireland, Peter Hain, told the Chatham House think tank in London in June 2007:

After all the horror and bigotry of the past, since the Good Friday Agreement of 1998 progress in Northern Ireland has been an inspiration to other parts of the world that the journey towards lasting peace can be completed.

'If one of the longest running conflicts in European history can be resolved', he told his audience, 'then there is hope for even the most bitter and seemingly intractable disputes across the globe'.[4]

In line with the maxim that 'success has a thousand fathers', the transformation of Northern Ireland from controversial terrain to a form of good news politics is largely now complete. Viewed for decades as a provincial backwater, politically retarded by historically-rooted sectarian hatreds, the peace process has catapulted Northern Ireland to the front-rank of world-wide 'success stories'. In 2003, former US President Bill Clinton asserted that the peace agreement in Northern Ireland was 'as good as it gets'.[5] Five years on, during her attempt to win the Presidential nomination of the Democratic Party in 2008, Hillary Clinton cited her experience of bringing communities together in the country as a prime example of her international expertise.[6] Not to be outdone, Barack Obama, who defeated her to the nomination and went on to be elected the new US President, released a statement celebrating the Belfast Agreement on its ten-year anniversary.[7] On the other side of the political divide, Republican candidate John McCain told the Irish-American Presidential Forum in Pennsylvania that Northern Ireland's political progress was 'inspirational' and asserted that the establishment of devolution in May 2007 'captured a political courage the previous generation could have scarcely imagined'.[8] In April 2008, meanwhile, the leading US political commentator David Frum, reflecting on the growing tendency to internationalise the Northern Ireland model, mooted that the implications of the Ulster analogy might become 'the true ballot question' in the 2008 presidential election: 'Is it time for the US to stop fighting Islamic terrorists—and start negotiating with them? Time to quit dismissing their vision of the future as unacceptable—and to start treating it as debatable?'[9] While the election itself was ultimately shaped by other issues, the question that Frum posed is likely to increase in importance over the next four years and beyond.

Earlier in 2008, the release of a detailed insider account of the Northern Irish peace process written by Jonathan Powell, Chief-of-Staff to the former British Prime Minister, Tony Blair, precipitated a fresh wave of discussion as to the precise meaning of the Northern Ireland experience. Powell himself, while arguing that the peace process there was '*sui generis*', simultaneously declared that there were 'lessons to be learned'.[10] The most important of those that he identified were as follows:

- In Northern Ireland, politicians were prepared 'to take political risks in order to achieve peace.'[11]
- In the end, 'it was inevitable that peace could only be made by the DUP and Sinn Fein on the principle of "Nixon goes to China"—it is only the extremes who can build a durable peace because there is no one left to outflank them.'[12]
- Overall, 'the most important change of all [as compared to what had previously occurred in Northern Ireland] was in the attitude of the British government, which became prepared, after many years of trying to ignore the problem of Northern Ireland, to devote considerable time and attention to it.'[13]
- 'One of the lessons that comes most starkly out of the Northern Ireland experience is the importance of maintaining contact. It is very difficult for governments in democracies to be seen to be talking to terrorists who are killing their people unjustifiably. But it is pre-

cisely your enemies, rather than your friends, you should talk to if you want to resolve a conflict.'[14]

- 'Talking should not be seen as a reward to be held out or withdrawn.'[15]
- 'It is always an error to set a precondition to a negotiation.'[16]
- 'It is best to leave the issue of weapons to the end of a peace process.'[17]
- 'There was one thing more than any other that kept jumping out at me, and that was the importance of having a functioning process and keeping it going regardless of the difficulties... You have to keep the process moving forward, however slowly. Never let it fall over.'[18]
- 'If there is one lesson to be drawn from the Northern Ireland negotiations, it is that there is no reason to believe that efforts to find peace will fail just because they have failed before. You have to keep the wheels turning... there is every reason to think that the search for peace can succeed in other places where the process has encountered problems—in Spain, in Turkey, in Sri Lanka, in the Middle East, in Afghanistan and even, in the longer term, with Islamic terrorism, if people are encouraged to talk.'[19]

At the crux of the case laid out so comprehensively by Powell was the idea that unfettered 'dialogue' offers the only way out of what seem to be intractable conflicts. Governments should initiate such dialogue with all parties concerned, so the argument runs, without preconditions. In other words, the core emphasis is on bringing in the 'extremes', because only by so doing, can lasting peace be achieved.

In making this argument, Powell is far from alone. Many others have contributed to the construction of a discourse associated with the Northern Ireland peace process, that views other violent conflicts around the world through the prism of Ulster. Most striking in this regard have been the recent suggestions that the British government and 'the West' in general, should consider talking to al-Qaeda. As early as 2002, Peter Mandelson, the former Secretary of State for Northern Ireland and close ally of Tony Blair, argued that the United States, in pursuing its 'War on Terror', should reflect on how the British fought terrorism in Northern Ireland, opting to 'negotiate with the IRA through its political wing rather than to defeat it'.[20] It was a call further echoed in 2004, by his predecessor as Northern Ireland Secretary, the late Mo Mowlam, who suggested that the United States should actively seek talks with al-Qaeda.[21] 'Bombing will put Osama bin Laden's back up', she also commented, 'If you have to have a policy of force, for God's sake have a policy of talking and building alongside'.[22]

This is a view to which Powell has also subscribed. In an article for *Prospect* magazine, in which he responded to criticisms of his memoir, he again reiterated the importance of 'talking to your enemy', just as the British had done with the IRA. 'To argue that al Qaeda or the Taliban are different and that therefore you cannot talk to them,' he argued, 'is nonsense.'[23] 'It's very difficult for democratic governments to do—talk to a terrorist movement that's killing people', he also told *The Guardian*, but 'if I was in government now...I would want to find a channel to al-Qaeda'.[24] These comments were subsequently endorsed by Sir Hugh Orde, the Chief Constable of the Police Service of Northern Ireland (PSNI) in May 2008. When asked if Britain should attempt to talk to al-Qaeda, Orde replied, 'If you want my professional assessment of any terrorism campaign, what fixes it is talking and engaging and judging when the conditions are right for that to take place'. After his interviewer sought clarification that the Chief Constable was indeed recommending that the government should be prepared to engage al-Qaeda in dialogue, he confirmed, 'Well that's the logic of ... I don't think that's unthinkable, the question will be one of timing'.[25]

Beyond the thorny question of al-Qaeda, there have been a wide variety of attempts to apply the 'lessons' of Britain's experience with the IRA and Northern Ireland to various other groups and locations. To take one example, it was reported in 2007 that yet another former Northern Ireland Secretary of State (Paul Murphy) and senior British civil servants had been advising the separatist and Marxist-Leninist guerrilla group, the Tamil Tigers, on how to engage with the government of Sri Lanka. There, Chris Maccabe, the joint head of the British-Irish secretariat and one of the first officials to cultivate links with the IRA, talked about the importance of continuous dialogue and establishing minor acts of trust (actions that were assumed to be integral to the British government's approach to the IRA).[26] Similarly, Dr Jehan Perera of the independent National Peace Council of Sri Lanka, has argued that one of the key lessons of Northern Ireland for the region is 'the spirit of inclusiveness'—suggesting that the Tamil National Alliance (considered to be the political proxy of the Tamil Tigers), should be brought into all-party talks, just as Sinn Fein were in Ulster.[27] In another Southeast Asian initiative, the former Ombudsman of the

PSNI, Nuala O'Loan, was appointed Ireland's first 'Roving Ambassador and Special Envoy for Conflict Resolution to Timor-Leste' in February 2008. Her mission, according to the Irish Minister for Foreign Affairs, Dermot Ahern, was to offer assistance 'in examining how the positive lessons from the Northern Ireland peace process can perhaps be translated into the context of East Timor'.[28]

It would seem that many of those who have participated in the politics of Ulster are eager to internationalise their experience. This even includes those who played a somewhat ambivalent role in the peace process there. In September 2007, a delegation of Northern Ireland politicians met representatives from Iraq's Shia and Sunni factions in Finland to advise them on the principles of peacemaking. The talks were chaired by the former IRA man and now Deputy First Minister, Martin McGuinness, and the delegation also included Lord Alderdice (the former speaker of the Northern Ireland assembly) and Jeffrey Donaldson, the unionist politician who made his name in opposition to the Belfast Agreement of 1998, having disassociated himself from the deal at the last moment. The purpose of the gatherings was to see if the attendees could agree principles on 'non-violence' (akin to Northern Ireland's 'Mitchell Principles'), which could be applied to the Iraqi political scene. 'The important lesson to learn', asserted Martin McGuinness, 'is that if people are serious about bringing about peace in their country, that can only be done through an inclusive negotiating process'.[29] It was announced in April 2008, that McGuinness was to lead an 'international peace mission' to Iraq later in the year. Jeffrey Donaldson, who was also involved in this latter initiative, explained that this was 'about building up a base to getting a wider dialogue going ... We are using our experience to help them with a plan'.[30] When reflecting on this episode, Padraig O'Malley, a professor at the University of Massachusetts in Boston and an expert in post-conflict reconciliation, commented that what the Northern Ireland analogy appeared to hold for those seeking a talks process in Iraq was as follows: 'There has to be room at the table for everyone, for those you hate, those you despise, those you wish to kill ... In the end you will find that indeed there are people who have been talking to elements of al-Qaeda'.[31]

Perhaps more importantly, as one commentator has observed, Ulster has become 'the defining national security experience for that generation of people who now have stewardship of British policy'.[32] There

6

was little surprise, for instance, when it was revealed in March 2007 that Jonathan Evans, the newly appointed head of MI5, had direct experience handling British agents on the streets of Belfast as a member of the Force Research Unit.[33] As the Bishop of London, Dr Richard Chartres, put it, speaking at a service in St Paul's Cathedral to commemorate those who had been killed or injured in Northern Ireland, 'in other theatres ... the lessons of Northern Ireland have entered the DNA of the British Armed Forces'.[34] The tendency to draw upon this formative experience has been evident in Iraq in the behaviour of certain branches of the American-led Coalition. In November 2007, it was claimed that senior British army officers who had served in Northern Ireland had set up a special unit in Baghdad (the Force Strategic Engagement Cell) with the task of making 'discreet engagements' with armed Sunni and Shia insurgents, many 'with blood on their hands'.[35] By the same token, General Petraeus, the Commander responsible for the US troop 'surge' in Iraq, has spoken of the way in which his British counterparts' experiences in Northern Ireland influenced his handling of Sunni tribes in Anbar province. In particular, Petraeus has recounted that British military figures explained how, in Northern Ireland, they had sat 'across the table from individuals whose lads had been thumping [their] men with pipes two years earlier'.[36]

However, it would be wrong to assume that a consensus has emerged among those responsible for counter-insurgency tactics, as to the precise 'meaning' of the Northern Ireland model. In fact, Petraeus's remarks came shortly after a public rift within the Coalition on this very issue. US military figures had expressed frustration at the British army's penchant for bringing Northern Ireland into debates on strategy in Iraq. 'It's insufferable for Christ's sake', were the reported remarks of one senior US military figure, having just heard a speech from Major General Jonathan Shaw (Britain's senior officer in Basra at that time): 'He comes in and he lectures everybody in the room about how to do a counter-insurgency. The guys were just rolling their eyeballs. The notorious Northern Ireland came up again. It's pretty frustrating'. Another US military source was recorded saying: 'This isn't Northern Ireland... They thought they had a pretty good model but Iraq is a different culture'.[37]

This issue was the source of further controversy when, on 5 August 2008, *The Times* newspaper led with revelations that the British Army had struck a secret deal with the al-Mahdi militia of Muqtada al-Sadr

7

in Basra. Under the terms of this accord, the two sides had agreed to abstain from attacks on each other; allegedly, this had prevented British forces from coming to the aid of their US and Iraqi allies during the battle for Basra in early 2008. According to senior British defence sources, the rationale behind the move had been the desire for IRA-style reconciliation in Basra: 'That is what we were trying, but it did not work'. The result was said to be that 'accommodation' had now become a dirty word. In the blunt assessment of one senior US military figure, all that British actions had revealed was the fact that, 'Cutting a deal with the bad guys is generally not a good idea'.[38] Speaking to *The Times* journalist who broke the story about the British accommodation in Basra, General Petraeus refused to criticise British strategy directly. Acknowledging that deals had been made, he stated that 'Sometimes the deals work out well, sometimes they don't work and when they don't you have to go back to rectify the situation'. Notably, however, when pressed on whether there were lessons from Iraq which might also be applied in Afghanistan, he stated: 'The biggest lesson that we've all relearnt—and I think we relearn it periodically—is that every situation is unique. Every situation has its own context, its own circumstances and the key, of course, is an accurate and nuanced understanding of the conditions of the situation and then the crafting of an approach that is appropriate for that context'.[39]

Evidently, then, not everyone has been entranced by the purported lessons of Northern Ireland.[40] Indeed, it has fallen to some of those with direct experience of Ulster's peace process—including those who were central to it—to sound a note of caution about the dominant narratives which have emerged since 1998.[41] Nonetheless, such reservations have largely been drowned out and the 'internationalisation' of the Northern Ireland 'model' shows no signs of abating. Thus, in Afghanistan too it would seem that British and Irish officials have advanced from mere theoretical advocacy of the model, to actively trying to initiate such an approach on the ground. This resulted in one British member of the UN and one Irish member of the EU being asked to leave the country in December 2007, after they were found to have initiated back-channel contacts with the Taliban, in contravention of President Karzai's stated policy of not talking to the group.[42] One of the expelled men, Michael Semple, an Irish passport holder who had previously worked as an adviser to the British mission in Pakistan, claimed his actions were 'totally in line with official policy to bring people in from the cold'.[43] Semple and the other expelled official were both natives of Northern Ireland and the former has explicitly claimed inspiration from the Ulster peace process.[44] Far from being rogue participants, it seems that both individuals were in fact acting within the parameters of British government policy. In March 2007, the then Defence Secretary, Des Browne, appeared to confirm that policy trajectory when he asserted, drawing explicitly on events in Northern Ireland, 'What you need to do in conflict resolution is to bring people who believe that the answer to their political ambitions will be achieved through violence into a frame of mind that they accept that their political ambitions will be delivered by politics'; the way to do this, he argued, was through lines of communication with certain biddable sections of groups like the Taliban.[45]

Indeed, across the Middle East, the notion that talking to terrorists is a pre-requisite for peace has attained greater traction than ever, partly in response to the increased status and influence of groups like Hamas and Hezbollah.[46] For those eager to inject a 'creative breakthrough' in the Israeli-Palestinian conflict, the lessons from Northern Ireland have been regarded as particulary pertinent.[47] The appointment of Tony Blair, the Prime Minister who took great personal interest in the Northern Irish peace process, as the Middle East peace envoy of the 'Quartet' in late June 2007, has bolstered this line of thinking. Critics of Blair's appointment pointed to the unpopularity of the former Prime Minister's foreign policy decisions in the Middle East. Others asserted that Blair had a proven record as a peacemaker, referring to his central role in Northern Ireland. 'Call me a wild optimist', Blair himself stated, 'but I do think there are lessons from Northern Ireland for the Middle East'.[48] The former Prime Minister expanded further upon what these 'lessons' might be when appearing before the House of Commons International Development Select Committee in June 2008. Although he reiterated the Quartet's position that there could be no talks with Hamas until it accepted certain preconditions, he claimed to 'totally understand' those who did urge such a move.[49]

Among those who have made the case for dialogue with Hamas is Conflicts Forum, a think tank fronted by the former British intelligence officer Alistair Crooke (also a former advisor to Javier Solana, in his capacity as EU representative for Middle East policy). Conflicts Forum has been prominent in urging western governments to engage politically with Hamas and other Islamist political movements, without a set of rigid pre-conditions.[50] One of its members, Gabrielle Rifkind, has argued in a policy paper for the Oxford Research Group that the West's current 'conditions-led' approach to Hamas is counter-productive. She has contended that in Northern Ireland 'a number of thorny issues' were postponed to a later date in order to facilitate initial negotiations between the British government and the IRA; in keeping with this logic, she has advocated a similar approach towards Hamas.[51]

This line of thinking is also espoused by 'Forward Thinking', a charity founded in April 2004 by William Sieghart and Oliver McTernan, which lists amongst its aims: 'to promote a more inclusive peace process in the Middle East'. As to what this means in practice, its mission objective is described as follows:

to promote a more inclusive peace process by engaging the religiously motivated Palestinian and Israeli political parties who have been previously excluded from 'track two' dialogue...The Initiative aims to promote an environment of constructive dialogue between Israelis and Palestinians, by implementing a series of unilateral dialogue activities among religiously motivated and conservative political leaders on both sides. The objective of the Initiative is to focus on bringing leaders who have hitherto been excluded from the 'dialogue community' into a process of internal examination of contentious issues outstanding between the sides, and to provide them with the tools and knowledge to engage in a constructive bilateral process...[52]

In reality, Israeli 'religious' factions have never been excluded from any dialogue, particularly when they have been members of an elected government (as had been the case until recently with the Sephardi political party, Shas, for example). Thus it is clear that the reference here to 'religiously motivated' parties 'on both sides', is mainly concerned with Hamas, whose entry into peace talks the organisation seeks to facilitate. Again, the echo here is of what is assumed to be the essence of the British approach in Northern Ireland: the inclusion of the 'extremists' in the search for peace.

It is an attitude also shared by Daniel Levy, a former Israeli peace negotiator, Director of the Prospects for Peace Initiative at The Century Foundation, and the son of Tony Blair's former Middle East envoy, Lord Levy. In July 2007, Levy told *The Sunday Telegraph* that, 'For any process to have sustainability, legitimacy, and to guarantee security, it will have to be inclusive, not divisive and to bring in Hamas over time'. In the Middle East, he added, 'Mr Blair, with his Northern Ireland experience, may understand this better than most'.[53] Sir Jeremy Greenstock, Britain's former ambassador to the United Nations and head of the Ditchley Foundation, has added his voice to this growing body of opinion. Writing in *Newsweek*, he claimed that Fatah had been 'drained of credibility as a negotiating partner' and made the case for 'engaging Gaza and Hamas'.[54] This is not a view restricted to the quasi-official foreign policy establishment in the United Kingdom. Former US Secretary of State for Defence, Colin Powell, has told *National Public Radio* in the United States that Hamas 'has to be engaged'.[55] Perhaps most intriguingly of all, Efraim Halevy, former head of Israel's Mossad intelligence agency, has said that Israel has to face up to a situation in which it should negotiate with Hamas.[56]

Such views are yet to receive official sanction from the British government. Despite suggesting that the United Kingdom would no longer be 'joined at the hip' to the United States in its foreign policy, Lord Malloch Brown, Gordon Brown's Foreign Office Minister, has drawn the line at negotiating with Hamas, on the grounds that it is 'threatening the annihilation of its neighbour'.[57] This was a position he repeated in early 2008, in a House of Lords debate on the Middle East:

To those who have pointed out that the peace process in Northern Ireland was heavily conditioned, I say that we still look for the commitment of groups such as Hamas and Hezbollah to peaceful progress in the region. We continue to call on Hamas to adhere to the quartet's principles of non-violence, recognition of Israel and acceptance of previous agreements and obligations, including the road map. We still consider that these principles are not unreasonable and remain the fundamental conditions for a viable peace process. A political dialogue is impossible so long as one party is dedicated to violence and the destruction of the other.[58]

Nonetheless, this approach has not been entirely discounted by senior British policy-makers. In his June 2007 Chatham House speech, in which he described Northern Ireland as an 'inspiration' for others, Peter Hain made specific reference to the Middle East and warned against the application of 'pre-conditions'. These could, he said, 'strangle the process at birth'.[59] In early 2008, Lord Judd, a Labour peer and former Labour Foreign Office minister, made the case again in a House of Lords debate on the Middle East:

As an observer of Northern Ireland from across the water, what I thought took tremendous courage—no one should underestimate what it took in that situation—was the willingness to start talking to the political representatives of the IRA. I think that the same is true of Hamas ... securing the guarantees for Israel's existence ... may have to be something that comes out of the process rather than laying it down in tablets of stone as an unnegotiated precondition

11

of any conversations or talks about how that objective can be achieved. More widely in the region it means involving Syria and, yes, trying to involve Iran.[60]

The debate on whether to engage with Hamas does not reflect traditional divisions between left and right. In July 2007, for instance, Michael Ancram, a Conservative MP and former Minister in the Northern Ireland Office—now a director of the Global Strategy Forum—argued that the British had 'danced with wolves' in the search for a settlement in Northern Ireland. The government had, he asserted,

opened communications with the IRA, which even as we did so was killing our soldiers and maiming and murdering civilians. We did so because we had rightly concluded that there was no answer to 'the Troubles' that did not encompass and eventually include Irish republicanism... The primary lesson of Northern Ireland was that while you might militarily contain national terrorist movements you could not defeat them and more significantly you would never eradicate them. In the end you need to engage with them.[61]

In order to achieve peace in the Middle East, Ancram declared that the West must now start 'engaging' with Hezbollah and Hamas; and he has himself talked to Usamah Hamdan, Hamas' representative in Beirut.[62]

Thus, across the political spectrum, it would seem that a growing portion of parliamentarians are reaching this conclusion. In July 2007, a subcommittee of the House of Lords' European Union Committee, consisting of eleven members of Britain's upper chamber, released a report recommending that the EU avoid 'an undesirably rigid' approach in dealing with Hamas. A spokesman for the Foreign Affairs subcommittee said that, while pressure should be put on Hamas to recognise Israel and accept previous peace agreements, 'progress should not be scuppered because of this'. The report also stressed that any peace process should be inclusive, and once again cited Northern Ireland as a 'positive source of inspiration' in this regard.[63] Furthermore, in April 2008, the EU announced that it would establish a 'World Conflict Transformation Centre' in Derry, Northern Ireland, to help armed groups and paramilitaries from elsewhere study the history of the province, so as to encourage them to abandon violence.[64]

Yet, important questions remain. Much of the discussion about this 'model' is underpinned by a set of widely held assumptions about the origins and operation of the peace process in Northern Ireland. At the most basic level, understanding of the transition from war to peace there runs as follows:

1) In Northern Ireland, the British state faced an organised terrorist threat from the Provisional IRA that demanded a British withdrawal from the province. The British state tried to defeat the IRA through security policy only, but found that it could not do so; both parties became locked in a military 'stalemate'.
2) After three decades of stasis, the British government changed approach and decided to negotiate with the terrorists.
3) This made possible an 'inclusive peace settlement' that brought in the 'extremes' and ended the violence.

Typical of this is the verdict of one close American observer and participant in the Northern Irish peace process, who declared in 2007:

serious negotiations only became possible about twelve years ago, when the British government moved from a long-term strategic focus on security—which frequently led to actions that were provocative and counterproductive—to a discussion of legitimate grievances.[65]

The key lessons derived from this basic narrative are as follows:

1) The state should be prepared to talk to terrorists. Lines of communication should be maintained at all times.
2) Talks should not be predicated on rigid pre-conditions, because they discourage terrorists from taking up the process of dialogue.
3) In a conflict, a settlement can only be achieved by the accommodation of the 'extremes', even if this risks undermining 'moderates'.

Ironically, just as this analysis has become more pervasive and influential, it has drifted ever further from a detailed understanding of what occurred in Northern Ireland over the last forty years. There has, in some cases, been a tendency to transport platitudes and ill-defined terminology from one theatre of conflict to another, in an uncritical and inexpert fashion. In much of this, a holistic historical understanding of the core realities that underlay the search for peace in Northern Ireland has rarely been conveyed.

This book, then, is a response to a specific moment in the debate about the way democratic states respond to the challenge of terrorism. It aims to do several things. The first is to revisit the history of Northern Ireland in order to identify and challenge some of the more misleading commonplaces that have become associated with events there. A central question underpinning this endeavour is to ask whether there really are lessons that can be extrapolated from the British government's experience in Northern Ireland. And following on from that, to consider whether such lessons can have any relevance beyond a society of approximately one and half million people in a small corner of northwest Europe.

To begin to answer this latter question, the book also offers a narrative of the Spanish government's struggle against Basque separatist terrorism. Until recently, nowhere has the experience of Northern Ireland been evoked more frequently than in reference to Spain and the Basque Country. As Michael Burleigh has written, it is no coincidence that terrorists train their sights mainly, though not exclusively, against democratic states; operating in a cultural stream removed from democratic values, they seek to acquire through violence that which they cannot achieve through democracy.[66] Making a similar point, Maurice Goldring, in a recent study of Irish and Basque terrorist groups, concluded that both movements 'share with [Osama] Bin Laden a basic point: in the name of values taken as fundamental, a group of self-proclaimed men assume the right to destroy lives and goods to attain political objectives that they could not dream to attain by the traditional ways of democratic action'.[67] In addition, there are other similarities between the Basque separatist group, ETA (*Euskadi ta Askatasuna*, Basque Homeland and Freedom) and the IRA, which do not exist with other terrorist organisations. The creation of ETA as an armed group was, to some extent, inspired by the example of the original IRA in the first quarter of the twentieth century.[68] Both Irish and Basque terrorists have pursued an 'armed struggle' in the name of national independence, rather than just regional autonomy; both have pursued their goals by combining the actions of a secretive terrorist army with those of a public political front; and both have positioned themselves on the 'left' of the political spectrum, fighting against the alleged imperialism and oppression of central governments. It is instructive that the respective political wings of both groups—Sinn Fein and the various forms of Batasuna—have long maintained ties of 'solidarity', while there has also been some speculation in the past as to concrete 'terror' links between the two organisations.[69]

Moreover, the recent history of the Northern Irish and Basque conflicts has lent credence to the imagined synergy between the two. In 1998, only a few months after Ireland's peace accord had been concluded, ETA was at the forefront of a (ultimately unsuccessful) Basque nationalist 'peace initiative', modelled partly on the Irish example. On a number of other occasions over the course of the last three years,

ETA has again appeared to be consciously imitating the IRA. In March 2006 the organisation declared a 'permanent ceasefire', apparently ending a four-decade long violent campaign for Basque independence from Spain and France.[70] This was then followed by an announcement from the Spanish government that it would begin peace negotiations with ETA.[71] In an interview shortly after the ceasefire declaration, the Spanish Socialist Prime Minister Jose Luis Rodriguez Zapatero noted that ETA's cessation and its use of the word 'permanent' was highly redolent of the IRA ceasefire of 1994. Further, Zapatero also revealed that he had held conversations with Tony Blair and Irish Taoiseach Bertie Ahern on the matter—both of whom had urged him to always maintain a 'channel of communication' to ETA. *El País* published the interview alongside a lengthy article on 'the lessons of Ulster'.[72]

In an effort to encourage further parallels between events in Northern Ireland and those in the Basque Country, Sinn Fein leader Gerry Adams visited the Basque Country at the time of ETA's 2006 ceasefire to call for the 'lessons of the Irish peace process' to be observed in Spain.[73] The concepts of 'inclusive dialogue' and 'all-party talks'—so familiar in Northern Ireland—also became a feature of the Spanish political lexicon during this period. Many predicted that this latest phase of the Spanish peace process would evolve in a similar way to that in Northern Ireland. Father Alec Reid, a Belfast-based Redemptorist priest, who had played an important role in the IRA's decision to end its campaign, became a regular visitor to the Basque Country and a vocal promoter of a peace process along the lines of that in Northern Ireland.[74]

Yet, despite these attempts to foster a sense of shared experience, events in Spain have taken a markedly different path. The conservative opposition Popular Party (PP) condemned the decision of Zapatero to begin talks with ETA and accused him of having abandoned the bi-partisan consensus of the country's main political parties on this issue. Widespread opposition to Zapatero's strategy was registered on 10 June 2006, when an estimated 200,000 people marched through the streets of Madrid, demanding that the Spanish government halt the talks. Meanwhile, for its part, ETA was unsure how far down the Northern Irish 'road' it could, or would, travel. Thus, the embryonic Spanish peace process stalled, stuttered and then collapsed.[75] On 30 December 2006, ETA bombed a Madrid airport, killing two civilians. The group initially insisted that this action did not signal a return to a full-scale campaign and held out the prospect of further dialogue. But in June 2007 ETA officially announced an end to its 'permanent' ceasefire.[76]

Even at this point, however, the temptation to overlay a Northern Irish template on to events in Spain has not abated. After the Madrid bombing, as the Basque Socialist politician Jesús Eguiguren has recently claimed, both Tony Blair and Gerry Adams encouraged Zapatero to 'listen to ETA' and 'the government did so'.[77] On 29 January 2007, it was announced that the Basque President Ibarretxe had formed an international expert commission in Vittoria, headed by former Taoiseach Albert Reynolds.[78]

It is against the backdrop of such ongoing efforts to try to fit events in the Basque Country into a Northern Irish-shaped box that this book will examine the conflict there. It is one that both started while Northern Ireland was still at peace and has out-lasted the Ulster conflagration. The very fact that it has followed such a different path is itself informative and counsels against any attempt to draw facile comparisons. Already, Rogelio Alonso has challenged the manner in which the Northern Ireland model has been applied to the Basque problem since the late 1990s.[79] Any attempt to replicate Alonso's work would run counter to the purpose of this book. The aim here is simply to offer a historical and analytical account of what occurred in Northern Ireland over the last thirty years, alongside a similar account of events in the Basque Country during the same period (about which there has been surprisingly little written in the English language).[80] Such conclusions as can be drawn from these two disparate histories are predicated on the view that there is no single model which can be transported elsewhere. Crucially, there are aspects of both the Northern Irish and Basque cases that deserve serious consideration on their own terms— and there is an attempt to synthesise such key themes, in broad terms, in the conclusion of this book. But a comparative study would negate the central thrust of this work which is to capture the mosaic of contending variables that framed the conflicts in both regions, many of which have been lost sight of in recent accounts.

Finally, it is worth emphasising what this book is not. In attempting to distil what really happened in Northern Ireland and the Basque Country, the intention is not to provide a new model, with an equally rigid template and set of prescriptions for other conflict zones. Terrorism is not a generic phenomenon. In commenting on the IRA or ETA, this book cannot have half an eye trained on Hamas or Farc; for that reason, it is best left to experts on the Middle East or Colombia to discern what elements of the Northern Irish or Basque experiences are worthy of further analysis in their own regional, historical and political contexts.[81] To borrow a phrase from General Sir Mike Jackson's foreword to the British army's appraisal of its own operations in Northern Ireland, what follows 'seeks to stimulate thought and will have failed if whatever is written is slavishly and unthinkingly applied' to other areas of conflict, whatever the similarities.[82]

The left-wing French writer and former advisor to President Mitterrand, Regis Debray, once wrote that 'Nine out of ten political errors result from reasoning by analogy':

Just as an art lover's sensibility comes from comparing works, so people tend to react to current events by comparison with the past, something that helps them to reason but also causes gross idiocies ... The *analogizer* gets it wrong every time, but gives himself and us pleasure.[83]

Ultimately, however, this book acknowledges that 'reasoning by analogy' still persists. To that end, it is ever more important that those examples that are held up as being of educational value are properly understood.

THE BRITISH STATE IN NORTHERN IRELAND

BETWEEN DEMOCRACY AND TERRORISM

1

INTERVENTION AND OSCILLATION
BRITISH POLICY, 1968–1974

Background to the Crisis

'The Troubles' scarred Northern Ireland deeply over a period of thirty years and claimed approximately 3,500 lives. The origins of the conflict have been the subject of detailed historical inquiry.[1] It is now largely uncontroversial to note that Northern Ireland was a deeply flawed entity prior to the outbreak of violence in 1968–9. The population was divided between two distinct communal blocs: a Protestant-unionist majority who favoured the preservation of Northern Ireland's status within the United Kingdom and a Catholic-nationalist minority who wished to see the six counties of Northern Ireland absorbed into an all-Ireland state. Through the Stormont parliament on the outskirts of Belfast, the Unionist Party, which represented the interests of the Protestant majority, exercised political dominance for over fifty years. The application of Westminster-style, majoritarian democracy guaranteed that hegemony. By contrast, the bulk of the Catholic population, which held to the Irish nationalist view that the partition of Ireland had denied self-determination, was effectively excluded from power. Despite the formal adherence to democratic practices, therefore, a condition of inherent political inequality between the two communities existed in Northern Ireland.[2]

Northern Ireland was not an 'apartheid state'. But the result of unionist domination was the existence of some flagrant inequalities in certain localities—most famously, the city of Londonderry. In some areas, where the local population was majority Catholic, unionist-dominated councils indulged in the practice of gerrymandering, falsely

21

manipulating constituency boundaries in order to preserve their control. In some instances too, unionist local authorities were predisposed to rule in the interests of their own community, leading to inequities in the provision of employment, public housing and public services. That such socio-economic and political injustices existed in Northern Ireland before 1968 is undeniable; they were related to the unionist desire to retain political control of the province.[3] The regional parliament at Stormont—though not in itself the central bastion of discrimination and maladministration—failed to curb the worst excesses of prejudice against the minority community. As one insider-account of life within the pre-1972 Northern Ireland government succinctly puts it, 'The cardinal sins of the Stormont government were ones of omission rather than commission—principally and fatally their failure to deal with the shortcomings of local authorities'.[4] On top of this, the province had a history of sectarian antagonism which stretched back to the plantation of Ireland in the seventeenth century.[5] These were the ingredients that made social and political conflict likely in late 1960s Ulster. But that did not mean that the outbreak of violence in 1968–9 was somehow inevitable.

The unionist governing elite faced mounting pressure in this period. In response, an influential portion of that elite, under the leadership of Captain Terence O'Neill, Northern Ireland's Prime Minister from 1963, had come to recognise that some kind of reform was essential if Northern Ireland were to survive and prosper. With the intention of arresting economic decline in the province, O'Neill embarked upon a programme of 'modernisation', and sought to place the Unionist Party at the forefront of this process. In his first speech as party leader to the Ulster Unionist Council he asserted that his aim was to 'transform the face of Ulster'. The tactical concerns of unionism were a central component of O'Neill's thinking. The immediate prompt for his new approach was the challenge posed by the Northern Ireland Labour Party (NILP). In the late 1950s, the cross-confessional NILP had emerged as a potential threat to unionist dominance, particularly in the Greater Belfast area. There, it had achieved notable success in appealing to the Protestant working class.[6] In the first instance, therefore, O'Neill's reforms were focused on giving a boost to the Northern Ireland economy and thereby warding off the electoral threat from the NILP, as well as getting more money from the British state.

The limitations of this vision—regarding the underlying sectarian problems—were perhaps best encapsulated in O'Neill's statement that 'if you give Roman Catholics a good job and a good house, they will live like Protestants'.[7] His approach was informed by the belief that economic improvements would dilute sectarian tensions. 'As for the divisions in our society', he also remarked, 'I sometimes wonder whether we do much good by so frequently talking about them'.[8] Still, in his readiness to meet with the Irish Taoiseach (Prime Minister), Sean Lemass in 1965, O'Neill did offer a change of tone from previous unionist leaders.[9] Although he failed to show any serious interest in addressing the issue of political discrimination, his premiership did mark a watershed in the history of Northern Ireland—if only because it helped stimulate potent new political forces.

First, O'Neill's reformism, however limited, provoked vociferous and trenchant resistance from within the unionist community. It was at this time that the Reverend Ian Paisley emerged as an important oppositional figure.[10] Paisley's message, mixing vague socio-economic populism with stringent evangelical Protestant beliefs, spoke to those who felt that they had the most to lose from the alleged complacency of the governing Unionist Party. But arguably the most serious hostility to O'Neill came from within the Unionist Party and the Orange Order to which it was closely affiliated. As early as 1966, O'Neill had almost been removed as leader because of his 'presidential style' and perceived neglect of areas west of the River Bann. The Orange Order and more intransigent forms of unionism were stronger in those areas where Protestants felt under siege—demographically, economically, confessionally—from their Catholic neighbours.[11] While this reaction was grounded in the immediate context of the period—responding to problems such as high levels of unemployment—it had long-term antecedents in Ulster Protestant political culture. Unionism—simply taken to mean support for the maintenance of the Act of Union with the United Kingdom—encompasses a range of political opinions, but there had historically been a consistent strain within it had also been willing to challenge established authority. Writing in the second half of the 1970s, one scholar described this facet of Ulster loyalism as a highly confused political identity; its exponents were 'Queen's rebels'—professedly loyal, but periodically rebellious, with a contractarian view of political obligation.[12] They often set themselves against those unionists who held to a more explicitly civic form of unionism, based on an emotional attachment to the United Kingdom.[13] Those who tended towards more intransigent and volatile versions of unionism were galvanized by the apparent threat to their position, emanating from O'Neill's policies.

On the other side of the communal divide, meanwhile, O'Neillism also stimulated political forces that had already been emerging among the Catholic community in Northern Ireland. A key factor here was the rise of an increasingly aspirational, grammar school-educated Catholic middle class, many of whom had benefitted from the post-war welfare and education reforms of the British state. As the horizons of this group expanded, they became more willing to challenge injustices within the Northern Irish state. Growing awareness of an economic disparity between Protestants and Catholics helped drive the process of polarisation.[14] Working class Catholics were mobilised too and the desire for change fed into the creation of extra-parliamentary pressure groups such as the 'Campaign for Social Justice', which was established in 1964.[15] Unwilling to rely on the promise of slow and limited reform under O'Neill, these organisations sought to engage in grassroots agitation to highlight local abuses of power and increase the momentum for reform. Disparate local organisations were not the only force to put pressure on O'Neill; the Northern Ireland Civil Rights Association (NICRA) was formed in February 1967, initially with a predominantly Communist and Republican executive.

While the internal dynamics were changing within Northern Ireland, it was an external impulse which transformed the terms of the debate. As Simon Prince has argued, Northern Ireland was exceptional, but not unique in a global context of political radicalism, which included the student revolts of Europe and the civil rights movement in the United States. Inspired by these international events, other groups came into existence within Northern Ireland at this time too, such as the student-based 'People's Democracy' movement. This became increasingly prominent during a key period in 1968–9.[16] The rhetoric of the People's Democracy leadership was inflected with Marxisant discourse, as can be seen from an interview with its leadership in 1969. According to Michael Farrell, the foremost figure in the organisation, it was 'not just part of the Civil Rights movement, it is a revolutionary association'. For another prominent civil rights radical, Eamonn McCann, Northern Ireland was experiencing a 'pre-revolutionary situation'. What is also notable about this interview is that these radicals generally rejected the traditional republican notion that the core problem in Northern Ireland was the colonial interference of the British state. For McCann, this idea implied that 'Protestants are white sahibs ... Ulster is *not* a colonial state; it is in many respects, though not in ordinary respects, an ordinary bourgeois state'. Subsidies from the British government 'do not support a privileged layer of the population'; the Catholic working class 'have a lot of children and receive a lot of state benefits'. While he differed with McCann on strategy, Farrell concurred to the extent that he warned English 'comrades' against 'misunderstanding the Irish revolution as a simple national struggle against colonialism or a simple struggle of the Catholic peasants against the Protestant landlords ... it is much more complex than that ...'[17]

While this configuration of local forces, coupled with the injection of internationalist radicalism, set the stage for the onset of 'The Troubles'. Nonetheless, the descent into sustained violent conflict was not immediately obvious to participants. A civil rights march in Londonderry in October 1968 that degenerated into violence—much of it perpetrated by the forces of the Northern Irish state—is often taken as the moment when the conflict began. And yet, even as events 'came to the boil' in the second half of 1968, what was particularly striking about contemporary commentary was the belief that the situation was rescuable for O'Neill.

On 12 November 1968, an article by Roy Lilley in the liberal unionist newspaper, *The Belfast Telegraph*, which was supportive of O'Neill's reformism, had expressed the rather bleak view that unionism 'today is ill prepared for the challenges and demands' with which it was now 'confronted'.[18] But then, just as O'Neill appeared to be losing his grip, he responded on 21 November with the announcement of a comprehensive, five-point reform package that sought to reform the most egregious examples of unionist misrule. After some scepticism, this was followed by a successful televised speech on 9 December 1968, stating that Ulster was at the 'crossroads' and asking the civil rights movement to 'take the heat out of the situation' by coming off the streets, with the promise of more reforms to follow if this occurred.[19] This had the effect of bolstering O'Neill significantly and it seemed that he would ride out the storm. The *Belfast Telegraph* printed coupons offering support to the Prime Minister and 115,000 of these were signed and sent off by readers within days.[20] On 13 December 1968,

Percy Dymond, the London editor of the newspaper, reported the 'surprise' of the governing British Labour Party at O'Neill's success and quoted Paul Rose, one of the more vocal members of the 'Campaign for Democracy in Ulster'—a pressure group comprising Labour MPs and peers—who recommended that it was now time for the civil rights movement to 'go easy'.[21]

On 16 December, just over a month after the doom-laden predictions that unionism was 'ill prepared' for the challenge, the tone of *Belfast Telegraph* editorials had been transformed. 'Captain O'Neill', the Coupon success suggested, 'has won what many regard as a referendum on his policies almost as invaluable as a general election'. It was a 'personal triumph and expression of confidence in his brand of unionism and a repudiation of the old sectarian agenda'. The 'mass of the people', concluded the editorial in confident tone, now 'support liberal solutions to community problems'.[22] On 27 December, another editorial suggested that the politics of Northern Ireland may be returning to a state of 'normalcy'.[23]

Thus, O'Neill ended 1968 having apparently out-manoeuvred the hardliners within the unionist community. As a sign of his growing confidence, he duly sacked his controversial Home Secretary, Bill Craig—an unapologetic critic of the civil rights movement—on 9 December. So as news broke on 30 December 1968 of a proposed civil rights march from Belfast to Londonderry, the *Telegraph*, encouraged by the new dispensation, urged a tolerant line: 'The question to be asked is why any company of people should not able to march from one city to another'.[24] New agendas were at work however. The key organiser of the planned march was the young civil rights activist mentioned above, Michael Farrell. Farrell, along with his followers in the Young Socialist Alliance and People's Democracy, intended to use Ulster's own 'Long March'—modelled on the 1965 Selma-Montgomery rally in Alabama—to prevent a moderate accommodation between the civil rights movement and O'Neillite unionism. What Farrell and his supporters wanted was a ratcheting up of the pressure on the state. Indeed, even many members of People's Democracy had previously rejected the idea on the grounds that it was likely to inflame loyalist anger.[25] The Cameron Report on events in Northern Ireland, published on 12 September 1969 suggested that the march leaders sought to 'weaken the moderate reforming forces in Northern Ireland' and 'increase tension' by dint of what was viewed as a form of 'calculated martyrdom'. As Farrell had described in his interview with *New Left Review* in May-June 1969, 'We do not want reform of Northern Ireland, we want a revolution in Ireland'. For that reason, attacks on 'liberal unionism' and 'O'Neillism' became part of the strategy.[26] It was possibly because of this that the former secretary to the Cameron Commission later recorded that Lord Cameron himself often 'seemed more concerned about socialists than about extreme republicans or loyalists and reserved some of his harshest criticisms for the students of People's Democracy'.[27]

Perhaps emboldened by the seemingly positive turn in its fortunes, O'Neill's government took the fateful decision to allow the march to go ahead. Without doubt, banning it was a more than conceivable option, given the general disposition of the nationalist community at that moment. But this course was not chosen. Instead, it was announced that key decisions relating to the policing of the march would be made on the ground by officers of the Royal Ulster Constabulary (RUC). O'Neill's government thus placed its fate in the hands of those who had already been involved in ugly clashes with civil rights marchers in Derry in October 1968. Furthermore, even though an estimated one-third of RUC officers were used, the force did not have the levels of personnel to get the marchers through safely. On 1 January 1969, the march set off without the support of John Hume and other prominent civil rights activists who had decided that it was an unnecessary, provocative act. Four days later, when the march reached Burntollet Bridge near Londonderry, it was attacked by approximately two hundred loyalists (including some off-duty members of the security services). It was assailed again twice as it attempted to enter the city, prompting days of rioting.

Ultimately, Burntollet proved to be a decisive moment, from which neither the civil rights movement nor O'Neillism ever recovered. Whereas both of these had, to some extent, been in the ascendant in late 1968, they now succumbed to the reassertion of more familiar sectarian prejudices.[28] In the political realm, O'Neill's appointment of the Cameron Commission to investigate 'disturbances in Northern Ireland' had occasioned revolt from those sections of his party who had lost faith in his ability to end the crisis. Of particular significance was the resignation of O'Neill's Deputy Prime Minister and Minister of Commerce, Brian Faulkner, within days of the Commission's announcement. Faulkner, viewed by many as the 'darling' of the unionist right, cited the lack of 'strong government' as the reason for his departure. At the time, it was generally suspected that Faulkner was operating in concert with an anti-O'Neill conspiracy, yet this is denied by those who were close to him during the events in question. Rather, Faulkner—and others—had simply come to the conclusion that, while reform might be necessary, the current Prime Minister was not the man for the job. The result was a split within unionism, but one 'far more complicated' than was generally perceived; for 'it was not simply a split between 'progressives' and reactionaries'. Instead,

while it was true that among O'Neill's critics there was a fair number of thorough-going bigots, who looked on any measure in favour of the minority community as a 'betrayal'... there were many, inside the [Unionist] parliamentary party and throughout the country, who recognised that fundamental changes were a necessity, but who did not have confidence in O'Neill or the way he was going about matters.[29]

On 28 April 1969, after an election which strengthened his challengers within unionism, O'Neill resigned as Prime Minister. He was replaced by James Chichester-Clark.[30] From that point, the security situation became increasingly unmanageable, particularly in Londonderry, where defensive barricades were erected in the Bogside area. Clashes between the police and unemployed Catholic youths soon became everyday occurrences. Unionism was irreparably divided, the Stormont regime significantly tarnished; and from late 1969 onwards, opposition forces were increasingly monopolised by a re-born Irish Republican Army (IRA), which found its feet as violence spiralled out of control. 'Northern Ireland's '68', as Prince has written, 'was over'.[31]

The British state responds

Once the lid was blown off Northern Ireland in 1969, it seemed that nobody was able to put it back on again. Instead, the level of violence seemed only to escalate. In that year, there had been fourteen murders in the province. In 1971, there were 174 and in 1972, over 470. The conflict had, at its core, 'a local dialectic' of sectarian enmity, but it was one with which the British state became increasingly embroiled.[32]

For much of the 1960s, the Labour government of Harold Wilson had preferred to keep its distance, while expressing hope that a reform package might draw the sting of the civil rights movement, appeasing Catholics without antagonising Protestants at the same time. A convention had existed at Westminster since 1923, whereby MPs generally avoided asking questions which were in the competence of the Northern Irish government.[33] Some pressure for intervention had been exerted by the Campaign for Democracy in Ulster, but O'Neill had been successful in convincing Wilson that he was serious about reform. The British Prime Minister's instinct was to avoid being sucked into the 'Irish bog', despite the entreaties of the Nationalist Party leader Eddie McAteer for the pressure to be kept on O'Neill for reform after 1965.[34] Indeed, 'the tragedy', according to one formerly senior Northern Ireland civil servant, 'was that the really heavy guns of British governmental pressure were only brought to bear after the movement for civil rights in Northern Ireland ... began to run into serious trouble'.[35] The issue of whether earlier involvement on the part of Wilson would have made a greater impact remains a moot point.[36] Certainly, speaking in May-June 1969, the leadership of People's Democracy repeatedly rejected the prospect of Westminster intervention as a palliative to the situation. Farrell declared that 'we must reject the idea of Westminster intervening to secure reform in Northern Ireland'. McCann admitted that 'an awful lot of our supporters do see such an intervention as a means of solving the problems over which we have been agitating', but concluded that it was 'necessary to go to Westminster to demand the solution to these problems to show that Westminster is a farce, and that we will have to do it ourselves'.[37] Shortly after this, on 19 August 1969, Wilson did finally intervene but in circumstances that were unfavourable to such an endeavour, as the political situation had become increasingly precarious. He issued a 'Downing Street Declaration', declaring continued support for the Stormont administration, on the condition that it 'proceeded energetically with its programme of reforms'. The context for this belated message, however, was the deployment of British troops to Northern Ireland.

By the summer of 1969, the rapid deterioration of the security situation in Northern Ireland meant that the British government could no longer ignore events in the province. Major and sustained rioting in the cities of Londonderry and Belfast had brought the police force—the Royal Ulster Constabulary—to the brink of exhaustion. It was at this point that the decision was taken to deploy troops, in order to bolster the RUC—whose relationship with the Catholic community had effectively collapsed. The hope was to avoid enflaming the situation further by sending in the predominantly Protestant auxiliary force, the B Specials. The British Army's arrival on the streets of Northern Ireland in August 1969 has often been depicted as the seminal moment in the nascent conflict: the 'point of no return'. Once the troops were in place, it is sometimes assumed, an inevitable cycle of militarisation was set in train, as the Army was brought into conflict with the Catholic-nationalist population who turned in increasing numbers to a resuscitated IRA for defence. Yet, once again, the presumed inevitability of this sequence of events is not borne out by a closer analysis of events on the ground.

The allegedly immutable hostility of the Catholic-nationalist community towards the Army must be set against the warm welcome that was initially given to British troops, as they entered Catholic areas. As recent research has highlighted, this continued well into 1970 and, in some places, even after that time.[38] Initially, the arrival of an external force, interposing itself between the two communities was seen by many Catholic residents as by far preferable to the return of the local police force. The latter was drawn largely from the Protestant community and was held, by many Catholics, to have been culpable for the violence of the 1968–9 period. Scenes of Catholic housewives bringing cups of tea to young British soldiers thus became one of the abiding images of the early 'Troubles'.

The arrival of the troops on Northern Ireland's streets was in no way driven by a desire to see an end to the Stormont government on the part of the British state. Wilson had made this much clear in his Downing Street Declaration which had accompanied their deployment to the province. Rather, it was an *ad hoc* initiative designed to keep the two communities apart in some flashpoint areas that had seen the worst of the violent clashes. The plan had simply been for the Army to 'hold the line' between what were seen as two warring tribes, in order to allow a return to something not too far removed from the *status quo ante*, albeit with a greater emphasis on a continued process of reform to meet the demands of the civil rights movement.

In reality, however, a return to the *status quo* looked increasingly impossible. The manner in which the crisis unfolded—as violence filled the vacuum left by O'Neill's departure—served to generate a new and deadly force: the 'Provisional' IRA. To a significant extent, this was the product of a power struggle within the republican movement that bore only tangential relation to events in Northern Ireland. The determination of the existing IRA leadership around the Chief of Staff, Cathal

Goulding—a Dublin-born Marxist—to prioritise 'politics' (including participation in the civil rights movement) ahead of 'armed struggle', had provoked a backlash from 'traditionalists'. Over the course of the 1960s many of the latter had drifted away from the movement; those that remained had made clear their opposition to the Goulding approach. The communal violence of 1968–9 had crystallised the nature of this division within republicanism. Attacks on Catholic-nationalist areas by loyalist mobs allowed traditionalist republicans to argue that the Goulding leadership had failed to defend 'the people' because of its lack of focus on the situation in the north. The charge proved to be the catalyst for a split within the ranks. Those loyal to Goulding endured as the 'Official' IRA (which Goulding led until 1972), while the dissidents now broke away to form a new group, known as the 'Provisional' IRA.[39] Initially, it was unclear where the balance of power lay between the two organisations, but in subsequent years the 'Provisionals' would emerge as the majority shareholders within republicanism. To a great extent, this was a function of their self-professed determination to launch, as soon as they were able, a military campaign against the 'British occupation system' in Ireland.[40]

Above all else, it was this determination on the part of the Provisionals that was to be the single most important factor in making violence irrevocably part of the fabric of life in Northern Ireland. As Hennessey has described, much of the rioting that took place across Belfast in May, June and July 1970 was pre-planned by the Provisionals, with the direct intention of bringing the British Army into conflict with Catholic-nationalists.[41] Their intention was to poison relations between the two sides and thereby radicalise the Catholic community—turning it into a support base from which the new IRA could operate.

Indeed, this much is confirmed in an account of the period which was sympathetic to the republican cause. In an examination of the experience of the community of Ballymurphy, in west Belfast, it is noted that for 'Ballymurphy republicans', the months of rioting 'had served their purpose'.[42] 'By August 1969', records the same source, a young republican called 'Gerry Adams was in a leadership position in Ballymurphy'; and prominent at the centre of a 'disagreement on tactics and timing' and 'the tactical value of the rioting'.[43] As a central figure among the 'semi-autonomous Ballymurphy republicans', Adams and his supporters found themselves at odds with the new Provisional IRA leadership in the city, which preferred to subdue the riots. The group around Adams had 'decided that fighting the British was what they were for'. Adams himself was reported to have said:

Every man, woman and child was involved. They didn't fire a shot, but for months, the British Army had the hell beaten out of them. The women were humiliating and demoralising them. The kids were hammering them. You had the whole community organised right down into street committees, so that you had a sort of spider's web of regular co-ordination.[44]

Ed Moloney has remarked as to the bolstering effect that this hard-line position had on the future career prospects of the young Adams within the republican movement.[45] This was the application of classic insurgency tactics, articulated by the Brazilian Marxist, Carlos Marighela, in his *Minimanual of the Urban Guerrilla Warfare*. Through acts of provocation, the republican leadership sought to goad the state into a spasm of over-reaction, in order to undermine its moral legitimacy.[46]

For its part, the Army, having been tasked with maintaining law and order, had little choice but to respond to the rioting. The findings of the Hunt Committee—which had reported on the RUC in October 1969—had recommended that the force be disarmed and 'civilianised'.[47] In the wake of the report, the Chief Constable, Sir Arthur Young—who was assiduous in his determination to see its recommendations enacted—preferred to keep his officers away from riot control duties. Responsibility was thus delegated to the Army by default. Unfortunately, though, it displayed a marked heavy-handedness in the character of its conduct. As one of its officers, Colonel Michael Dewar, later recorded, the militarily tended to resort to, 'outdated riot-control techniques' drawn from 'far-flung corners of the Empire' and these were soon 'found to be inadequate and unsuitable'.[48] On the other hand, with the RUC seemingly hamstrung, the only other alternative was to abandon communities to rule by the mob—or more specifically, in the case of Catholic areas, to rule by the IRA. Of course, this was precisely what the latter hoped to achieve. 'If you get out of Ballymurphy', the Army were told in exchanges with the IRA in early 1971, 'we can control it without your assistance'.[49]

The fundamental problem of dispersing troops into a civilian population that increasingly resented their presence was epitomised by a series of high profile incidents that came to define this early phase of 'the Troubles': the 'Falls Curfew' of July 1970, when the Army sealed off the Lower Falls area of Belfast for 72 hours and fired CS gas at rioters (an incident remembered in republican circles as the 'Rape of the Falls'); the introduction of Internment without trial in August 1971; and 'Bloody Sunday' in January 1972, when Paratroopers opened fire on marchers in Londonderry, killing 14 unarmed civilians. The former IRA prisoner, Anthony McIntyre, has argued that such incidents served as the most effective recruiting sergeant available to the new IRA.[50]

With the benefit of hindsight, the Army's own official appraisal of its operations in these years—Operation Banner—demonstrates an awareness of the extent to which it contributed to the escalation of the crisis. During the conduct of house-to-house searches in Belfast in July 1970, for instance, the Army admits that its behaviour, although 'intended as taking a hard line against violence, it did not in practice discriminate between those perpetrating violence and the rest of the community'. As a result, it concludes: 'The search...convinced most moderate Catholics that the Army was pro-loyalist. The majority of the Catholic population became effectively nationalist, if they were not so already. The IRA gained significant support.'[51]

Even more controversial was the introduction of internment without trial on 9 August 1971. It has long been supposed that Brian Faulkner, who succeeded James Chichester-Clark as Prime Minister of Northern Ireland in March 1971, was an ardent advocate of internment and had enthusiastically pushed for its introduction since coming to power.[52] However, this view has recently been challenged by the account of Robert Ramsay, who headed Faulkner's Private Office throughout 1971. According to Ramsay, 'no-one was more acutely aware than Faulkner of the cost which would have to be paid in terms of adverse reaction in British and foreign public opinion; and even more importantly, he knew the risks of the likely effect that the move would have on his relations with the minority community'. For this reason, the Prime Minister 'agonized about it for weeks' and only arrived at the decision to introduce internment because he felt there was little other option. Ramsay recounts the meeting between Faulkner and the Army General Officer Commanding (GOC) Northern Ireland, Harry Tuzo, together with the RUC Inspector General, Graham Shillington, in which that key decision was taken. The immediate background was the marked escalation of violence over the summer of 1971, by which 'the terrorists were seen to be very much in the ascendancy'. During the meeting,

33

The GOC, reviewing the security situation, could only hold out the hope for major success through improved intelligence in the very long run... But, as for the foreseeable future, he had 'no more shots in the locker'. Shillington agreed with that assessment. 'That leaves us only internment', said Faulkner. 'I have the gravest of reservations about the chances of success of such a step, as you probably have yourself, and I am not recommending it, but I have nothing else to offer', was the reply.

Internment, then, was judged, at best, a necessary but extremely high-risk evil. And while Ramsay freely concedes that 'the outcome was a failure' he also notes that 'to call it a mistake pre-supposes that there were alternative courses of action available... I am convinced that no such alternatives existed'.[53]

What the foregoing also demonstrates is the fact that the Army itself did not push for the introduction of internment; on the contrary, many within its senior ranks were opposed to the policy. In particular, the GOC, Harry Tuzo, remained firmly against the introduction of internment throughout 1971 and only acquiesced because of his recognition that something had to be done to stop the violence, concluding that there was no other viable choice.[54] Nevertheless, once the decision had been taken at the political level, the Army gained responsibility for its implementation. Conventional wisdom now holds that what became known as Operation Demetrius was an unqualified disaster. Initially based on outdated intelligence and used exclusively against the Catholic population, internment was hugely damaging to British credibility. The early ineffectiveness of the operation, for example, was signalled by the fact that within days of its commencement, a well-known leader of the Provisional IRA in Belfast, Joe Cahill, ostentatiously delivered a press conference in the city.[55] For this reason, internment is often cited as a lesson for modern states of 'what not to do' when dealing with a terrorist threat—on the basis that 'limiting civil liberties does not guarantee security'.[56]

Once again, the Army's own record of its policy in Northern Ireland largely follows this line, stating that internment was 'in practice an operational reverse'.[57] Arguably, however, the Army's summary of this and other events, seems surprisingly inclined to repeat well-rehearsed narratives about the cumulative effects of its actions. The reality was a little more complex. The pioneering recent work of Geoffrey Warner, based on a rather closer examination of freshly released military papers from the time of the Falls Road curfew, has suggested that this event 'was not as crucial a turning-point in the Troubles as many claimed' and 'marked only a stage in the evolution of Catholic opinion'. Warner does not deny that 'the behaviour of some of the army units during the house searches was hardly designed to win hearts and minds'. But he also insists that the bitter rivalry between the Provisionals and the Officials—who were particularly strong in the Lower Falls—played 'just as important a part in the course of events as unionist exasperation and the overreaction' of the Army.[58] In much the same way, Thomas Hennessey has demonstrated that internment was not, in purely military terms, a complete failure. Initial errors were rectified and the operation yielded major intelligence advances, allowing the security forces to make significant inroads against the Provisional IRA.[59]

While acknowledging the simplicity of the narrative, however, there is no doubt that the use of internment did have a deeply damaging impact on the political mood of the province. For Catholic-nationalists, the suspension of due legal process represented a further regression from the aims of the civil rights movement. Its one-sided application to Catholics seemed to confirm the unionist-dominated nature of the Northern Irish state. Protests against the measure included the withholding of council rents, strikes and resignations by Catholic officials. Already, the newly-formed Social and Democratic Labour Party (SDLP), which was backed by the Irish government, had withdrawn from participation in Stormont entirely. This had ocurred after the security forces had killed two men in Londonderry during rioting in July 1971.[60] Now, the last possibility for an accommodation between constitutional Catholic-nationalists and the unionist regime appeared to vanish. For nationalists on both sides of the border, Irish unity reappeared on the agenda as something to be pursued as the only 'real' solution to the crisis.[61] Meanwhile, bolstered by new recruits, the IRA insurgency gathered pace. In 1971, before the introduction of the policy, there had been thirty-four conflict-related deaths in Northern Ireland; in the five months after it, down to the end of the year, one hundred and fifty others died.[62]

In terms of the domestic and international perception of what the British state was doing in Northern Ireland, internment was a festering sore. Over the following years, worse was to come as details emerged of the ill-treatment of some detainees. One particularly damaging revelation was that eleven of the approximately 350 suspects taken in the first 'wave' of internment, had been singled out as 'guinea pigs' for 'in-depth interrogation'.[63] This entailed prisoners being subjected to the so-called 'Five Techniques' during the course of their incarceration (which included being forced to: wear a hood at all times; stand spread-eagled against a wall; listen to 'white noise'; and go without food and sleep). Such methods had previously been employed in Britain's colonial dependencies, but the disclosure of their use in a part of the United Kingdom proved highly embarrassing for the government. Indeed, the Wilson government was forced to announce publicly a moratorium on such practices.[64] Subsequent court cases saw British behaviour placed under ever-closer inspection, which was again highly detrimental to Britain's reputation. In 1976 the European Commission on Human Rights found Britain guilty of having breached the European Convention on Human Rights, 'in the form, not only of inhuman and degrading treatment, but also of torture'.[65] While two years later the European Court of Human Rights ruled to drop the accusation of torture, it too found Britain guilty of 'inhuman and degrading treatment'.[66]

Yet, while the security services must necessarily take a significant portion of the blame for the various blunders of this period, it is important to emphasise that Army mistakes were more a symptom of higher-level hesitancy. Government policy exhibited a lack of clearly defined direction and it failed to respond to events with the requisite agility. Again, to quote from the Army's assessment of its performance in Northern Ireland, the nature of the challenge changed rapidly in the first few years of its deployment. 'The first period, from August 1969 until perhaps the summer of 1971 was largely characterised by widespread public disorder'. Marches, protests, rioting, and looting were seen as 'the main issues' in this initial phase. Then, from the summer of 1971 until the mid-1970s, the army faced what might best be described as a 'classic insurgency', though this then 'merged into the phase characterised by the use of terrorist tactics'.[67]

In response to these developments, the British government often appeared confused and wholly reactive. This ensured that the Army's operations were conducted in the context of a strategic vacuum. Westminster failed to give a decisive lead to those confronting matters on the ground; rather, some policy initiatives seemed only to make matters more muddled. For example, in the view of one civil servant, the original decision of the Wilson government to appoint the then GOC Northern Ireland, Lieutenant Sir Ian Freeland, as 'Director of all Operations' in Northern Ireland in 1969 (over and above the Northern

Ireland Parliament and the RUC), 'stood on its head all the doctrine and precedent about military aid to the civilian power'. In so doing, the government fell 'spectacularly between two stools', according to the scathing verdict of Ken Bloomfield:

it had failed to take into its own hands complete control of the situation, or to assert or exploit the authority of the Army before 'civil rights' had been over-taken by dissidence, a growing threat of terrorism and incipient civil war... We were soon to see the pernicious consequences of long-term British apathy, succeeded by belated intervention, an unhappy interregnum of divided author-ity, and the absolute abandonment of precedent in the involvement of the Army in the aid of the civil power.[68]

The Conservative government of Edward Heath that replaced Wilson's Labour administration after the British General Election of June 1970 scarcely fared better than its predecessor. It too had little in the way of a coherent strategic vision for responding to the problems in Northern Ireland; if anything, Heath and his fellow ministers were even more determined than their Labour counterparts to avoid deeper entanglement in the affairs of Ulster. Robert Ramsay, who served in Brian Faulkner's administration at Stormont, attests to the 'alarming ignorance' of the Heath Cabinet in relation to Northern Ireland. In a sign of things to come, he recalls conversations with the then Defence Secretary, Lord Carrington, in 1971–2, in which the Minister was 'fuzzy about the difference between a terrorist and a freedom fighter' and asserted, 'At the end of the day, we had to do business with Jomo Kenyatta, as one day we will have to with the IRA leadership'.[69] In the immediate term, the result was merely a diffident and vacillating policy that translated negatively on to the streets of Northern Ireland. In the words of a former senior army officer,

back then we were operating blindly, with little thought to political 'cause and effect'. The game plan was developing quite literally on a day-to-day basis as we tried to deal with the immediate challenges we faced.[70]

By the time 'Bloody Sunday' arrived on 30 January 1972, Heath's gov-ernment was clearly floundering and found itself, in its own estima-tion, in the 'last chance saloon'.[71]

In the aftermath of that calamitous event, the British government was forced to embrace the one outcome it had consciously sought to avoid: full-scale British political re-engagement with Northern Ireland. This occurred in March 1972, with the decision to suspend

37

the Stormont parliament and administer 'Direct Rule' of the province from Westminster. The imposition of Direct Rule had come too late to avert the crisis and significantly, it had been long preceded by the decision to send British troops into Northern Ireland in August 1969. As Hennessy has argued, 'It made sense to avoid Direct Rule in 1969. It did not in 1971'.[72] His argument—and that of others—is that the British government could have intervened much earlier than it did, to deal with the burgeoning conflict. Instead, though, the Stormont regime had been maintained—but, in the words, of one prominent civil servant, on an increasingly 'client basis'.[73] With regards to the latter, Robert Ramsay too has pointed to the way in which the British government slowly undercut the Northern Irish Parliament and the efforts of Brian Faulkner to engage with the SDLP. Of particular significance, he claims, was the 'Liaison Office' that the government had established at Laneside House, outside Belfast in County Down. Staffed by many with connections to the intelligence world, Ramsay notes that this established a direct channel between the SDLP (and others) to the Westminster government, by-passing Stormont entirely. The result was that 'representations which would normally have come to [the Northern Ireland] government were now passing to London, via Laneside'. Moreover, he observed sarcastically, many of those operating this channel came armed with 'useful' experience from having served in Lebanon, 'a country which had achieved an outstanding success in having a trans-communal power-sharing government'. 'Such was the wisdom of Laneside' is Ramsay's scathing verdict.[74]

Yet even as the Heath government appeared to becoming ever-more involved in the Northern Irish crisis, it refused to grasp the nettle of full intervention. It was for this reason that Faulkner continued to believe that Direct Rule would not be introduced; as late as February 1972 he was given face-to-face assurances by Heath himself that this was the case.[75] It was only belatedly, when apparently faced with the total collapse of the province, that the government concluded that it no longer had any choice but to intervene directly. Still, Direct Rule was never intended to be a long-term solution; the government hoped that it would be a temporary expedient. Yet, as Harold Wilson had feared, it proved even more difficult to get out of the Irish bog than to get into it. With direct control of the province from 1972, came a weighty and unwanted responsibility that tested the governments of no less than six British Prime Ministers, some of them to breaking point.

Talking to Terrorists I

In part, the imposition of Direct Rule was both a response to, and a consequence of, the British government's failure to settle upon any coherent long-term strategy for responding to the crisis in Northern Ireland. Furthermore, even after March 1972, the state's engagement with the province seemed to be bedeviled by a near-absence of policy. This contributed to an almost millennial atmosphere within Northern Ireland—the sense that 'anything was possible' and everything was 'on the table'.

Particularly significant, was the apparent willingness of elements of the British state to 'talk with the terrorists' in an effort to end the crisis. It was Harold Wilson, as leader of the opposition in March 1972, who first demonstrated this by his decision to meet privately with leaders of the Provisional IRA, while on a visit to Dublin on the eve of Direct Rule.[76] The IRA called a unilateral 72-hour ceasefire to facilitate the talks; and Wilson used the cover of meetings with various Irish political leaders to set up the encounter, which was held in the house of a member of the Irish Labour Party. The Provisional IRA delegation consisted of the Dublin-based republican Daithi O'Conaill, together with John Kelly and Joe Cahill from Belfast. During the meeting, Wilson was told that the IRA wanted the British government to commit itself to a 'phased and orderly withdrawal' from Northern Ireland; for his part, the former Prime Minister sought to get an extension of the ceasefire. In the end, in the words of one of the republican participants, Joe Cahill, 'There was damn all came out of it. It was just a talking shop, really'.[77]

Nevertheless, in acting as he had, Wilson had broken a key taboo for the British political establishment. In this way, he paved the way for the Conservative government's William Whitelaw, who had been appointed the first Secretary of State for Northern Ireland under Direct Rule, to hold secret talks with the leadership of the Provisional IRA. After preliminary contacts, the IRA asked for a meeting between the two sides in early summer 1972. On 12 June, Whitelaw rejected the proposal. However, after a large IRA bomb had destroyed Londonderry's Guildhall on 13 June 1972, the republican leadership allegedly visited John Hume's home in the city and asked him to try to contact Whitelaw again. It was to their surprise that Whitelaw now agreed. On 20 June, they met an MI6 officer called Frank Steele and civil servant Philip Woodfield to discuss arrangemens. On 26 June, the IRA announced a 'bi-lateral truce'.[78]

On 7 July 1972, six leading IRA figures assembled in Londonderry, from where they traveled in a minibus (its windows blacked out by tape) to a pre-arranged pick-up point. They were then taken by Army helicopter to RAF Aldergrove, near Belfast International Airport. Among the negotiators were top IRA figures Sean MacStiofain and Daithi O'Conaill, the two most senior southern-based republican leaders. The entourage also included a twenty-two year old Martin McGuinness, already a leading IRA figure in Londonderry (at that stage, on the run from the authorities), and Gerry Adams, a 'rising star' in the Belfast republican firmament. Adams had been released from prison specifically for the occasion—as one of the IRA's preconditions for the truce. Also present were other high ranking IRA men from Belfast, Ivor Bell and Seamus Twomey, and Myles Shelvin, a lawyer from Dublin who was to act as their legal representation. Eager to dispel the notion that the Provisionals were entering the ceasefire from a position of weakness, MacStiofain had ordered all IRA units to continue to bomb and kill right up to the moment it came into effect.[79] An army sergeant was shot in the Short Strand area of Belfast just five minutes before the deadline and two British soldiers were taken hostage as an insurance policy on the morning of the flight.[80]

On their arrival in England, the republicans were collected by a fleet of limousines and driven to the house of Paul Channon—Whitelaw's Junior Minister—in Cheyne Walk, London. Martin McGuinness later described how he 'couldn't help be anything but impressed by the paraphernalia surrounding the whole business'. Unlike Michael Collins, when he had come to London to negotiate the Anglo-Irish Treaty just over fifty years previously, the members of the IRA's team each turned down the offer of a drink from their British interlocutors. Thereafter, as the two sides got down to business, it quickly became apparent that the republicans had no strategy for the meeting, beyond reiterating their most basic demands. There was little hope for sustained negotiation. 'The only purpose of the meeting with Whitelaw was to demand a British declaration of intent to withdraw', McGuinness later recalled. The delegation left, 'quite clear in our minds that the British government were [sic] not yet in a position whereby we could do serious business'.[81]

In Whitelaw's eyes the meeting became a 'non-event' but others were less sanguine about its long-term implications.[82] For Brian Faulkner, the last Prime Minister of Northern Ireland before Direct Rule from London was imposed, news of the IRA's truce was deemed to be '397 lives, 1,682 explosions, and 7,258 injuries too late'. Moreover, he greeted with shock the revelation that, 'probably the most wanted men in the United Kingdom, men who had for several years been master-minding the murders of British citizens, were flown to London in an RAF jet at public expense for talks with British Cabinet Ministers'. Not only was this deemed to be 'the logical conclusion of the policy of appeasement which direct rule had initiated', but also it was judged to represent 'pragmatism gone mad'. Faulkner's argument was that, how-ever honourable the government's intentions, the decision to talk with the IRA was ill-conceived. In particular, he drew attention to what he saw as the absence of 'negotiable objectives' on the part of the IRA. Against this background, Faulkner contended that the government had demonstrated either 'an appalling ignorance about the nature of the organisation with which it was dealing', or 'a willingness to consider some of the demands'. Faulkner, who believed Whitelaw to be an hon-est man, preferred to believe the former interpretation.[83] Still, his assessment of the episode is indicative of how mainstream unionism was likely to view the decision to meet with the IRA.

Moreover, it was clear that several IRA leaders had drawn similar conclusions as Faulkner—but assumed the British government's behav-iour actually stemmed from a readiness to meet republican demands. As Martin McGuinness had observed, the British were 'not yet' ready to do this, but it certainly seemed plausible to many republicans that they would be at some point in the future. The IRA, it appeared, had been projected into a position of political importance because of its millitary campaign—sidelining constitutional nationalists in the proc-ess. As the ceasefire ended, MacStiofain announced that the campaign would resume with the 'utmost ferocity and ruthlessness'.[84] Conse-quently, the July 1972 meeting—which occurred in the context of a bitter and apparently escalating IRA insurgency—fuelled the republi-can sense 'one last push' might be enough to force the British govern-ment to reconsider its position in Northern Ireland. Just two days after the London encounter, the IRA staged a confrontation with the army and ended their truce. And on the 21 July, they exploded twenty-two bombs in Belfast in the space of seventy-five minutes, killing nine and injuring another one hundred and thirty on what became known as 'Bloody Friday'.

At this point, the British Army responded to the intensification of the IRA threat with a bold manoeuvre. Taking advantage of a dip in republican support following Bloody Friday, it implemented 'Operation Motorman', re-establishing control of the various 'no-go areas' that had grown up in Belfast and Londonderry over the previous two years.[85] On the same day as Operation Motorman was launched, the IRA struck again with a series of no warning car bombs that claimed nine lives in the village of Claudy, County Londonderry.[86] And in late 1972, the organisation's leadership took the decision to launch an 'England campaign'—to bring the IRA's war to the British mainland. Those within the leadership who had previously opposed such a move—people like Daithi O'Conaill—now endorsed it as likely to increase the pressure on the British government.[87]

In addition to this escalation in republican violence, the 1972 talks provoked further suspicion and distrust in the Anglo-Irish relationship, which was already reeling from the aftermath of Internment and Bloody Sunday (after which a an angry crowd of thousands had burnt down the British Embassy in Dublin).[88] The Irish government felt that such contacts merely prolonged the violence, by encouraging the IRA to believe that the British would eventually be prepared to negotiate a settlement with them. Despite its criticism of British policy, the Irish government was terrified that a withdrawal of British troops would lead to a vacuum of power and perhaps even a civil war on Irish soil in which they would have to intervene.[89]

Ominously, it was also in this context of constitutional instability that the long-feared Protestant loyalist 'backlash' gathered momentum. Evidence as to the possibility for such a development had already been seen the previous year with the rise of organised paramilitarism in loyalist areas. The perception that they could not trust even their own government for protection against the IRA's offensive had became commonplace among sections of the loyalist community. Hardliners organised themselves into paramilitary and vigilante groups. Among them was the Ulster Defence Association, which was to become a brutal fixture on the Northern Irish political scene. Attacks such as the bombing of McGurk's Bar in Belfast, which claimed fifteen lives in December 1971, had given signal to the violent potential arising out of this phenomenon.[90] By the same token, the first murders of Catholics to be claimed by the 'Ulster Freedom Fighters' in February 1972 was a further indication of the direction in which loyalism was headed. It is worth pointing out that periodic cycles of violence had been a recurring feature of Ulster political life in previous generations.[91] But on those past occasions, order had normally reasserted itself within days or weeks. In this case, however, loyalists were arranging themselves in killing squads, whose structure mirrored that of the IRA. More moderate unionists such as Brian Faulkner—who now faced a power struggle within their own community—argued that the arrival of these organised Protestant murder gangs on to the political scene 'coincided with the collapse of confidence among the unionist population in the will of the Westminster government' to deal with the threat posed by the IRA.[92]

The immediate result of all of this was that 1972 marked the worst year of the conflict, with more lives lost in that year than in any other. Indeed, July-August 1972—the period after the British government had held its meeting with the Provisional IRA—proved to be the single most bloody month of the 'the Troubles'. The decision to engage in dialogue with the terrorists had been a reflection of the desperation that marked government policy prior to this point. 'For the future', Whitelaw later recorded, 'I had learnt a lesson which taught me the dangers and risks of dealing with terrorists'.[93] When Faulkner saw Whitelaw shortly after the truce had broken down, he claimed that Whitelaw accepted that a new phase of policy had now arrived and that the government 'now realised that the IRA would have to be beaten'.[94]

Towards a new approach: building the moderate alliance

Against this inauspicious background, the British government sought to change tack. The focus was now placed on political innovation and constitutional change, as offering a possible solution to 'the Troubles'. The Permanent Secretaries of the Northern Ireland Office (the dedicated branch of the British civil service), operating under the aegis of the 'Future Policy Group', began to put together various 'What if' papers that examined an array of possible future scenarios.[95] A Green Paper, *The Future of Northern Ireland*, emerged out of this process in October 1972, only a matter of months after Whitelaw's attempted negotiation with the IRA. This document contained some of the key

43

cornerstones of subsequent British policy: support for the 'principle of consent', whereby Northern Ireland's constitutional status could only be altered with the support of a majority of its citizens; a refusal to countenance any return to majority rule in the province; and a recognition that any deal would have to involve a significant 'Irish dimension'. In addition to this, the Green Paper also looked to the re-establishment of proportional representation for elections in Northern Ireland, in order to ensure a voice for those from either community who found themselves in a minority in certain areas of the province. While their efforts were well-intentioned, the frenzy of constitutional activity in which the British civil service was engaged in 1973–4, had little in the way of solid foundations. The process going on in the corridors of Whitehall bore little relation to events within Northern Ireland. As was soon to become apparent, shifting strategy was the easy part; attempting to find a settlement to the crisis which enjoyed cross-community support was a much more difficult endeavour.

In the wake of the Green Paper, the government conducted a 'Border Poll' on 8 March 1973, to 'determine' the constitutional question. Yet, while the poll recorded a large majority in favour of Northern Ireland remaining within the United Kingdom, this was rather offset by the fact that under 600,000 people voted. The political leaders of the Catholic-nationalist community had urged their supporters to boycott the poll.[96] Undeterred by this, the government resolved to press ahead with the search for a new agreement. With the albeit-flawed affirmation of Northern Ireland's collective will to remain 'British' out of the way, the government proceeded to publish a *Northern Ireland Constitutional Proposal* White Paper that encompassed much of the earlier Green Paper's framework.

Support for the propositions contained within the White Paper was found among Brian Faulkner's Unionist Party (though there was also a sizeable unionist opposition movement), the centrist Alliance Party of Northern Ireland and the SDLP. In December 1973, these parties came together with the British and Irish Governments to sign the 'Sunningdale Agreement'—an accord so-named after the site of the Civil Service Staff College (now the National School of Government) in Berkshire, where it was signed. There, it was agreed that a cross-party executive would be established to govern Northern Ireland (comprising six members from the Unionist Party, four from the SDLP and one from Alliance). In addition, it was agreed that a 'Council of

Ireland' would be set-up to forge greater co-operation between north and south.[97]

Twenty-five years later, in a memorable phrase, the former deputy leader of the SDLP and Deputy First Minister of Northern Ireland, Seamus Mallon, described the Belfast Agreement of 1998 as 'Sunningdale for slow learners'.[98] At face value, he would appear to have a point. In terms of the impulses that underlay the two Agreements, both were built on the coming together of moderate unionists and moderate nationalists within Northern Ireland, under the tutelage and encouragement of the British and Irish governments, in the hope that an accommodation could be reached. Moreover, the constitutional machinery established by the two accords was very similar. Both contained proposals for the creation of an elected Northern Ireland assembly. And both envisaged that this assembly would give rise to a power-sharing, cross-community Northern Irish executive. More controversially, both Sunningdale and the Belfast Agreement provided for cross-border institutions that would bring northern and southern Ireland closer together, even as the application of the 'consent principle' ensured that Northern Ireland could not be led into a united Ireland unless a majority of its population so wished.

Why then, did the Sunningdale Agreement fail? At the most basic level, Sunningdale—as understood by the British government—represented an attempt to adjust the constitutional basis of Northern Ireland so that it took account of the 'root causes' of 'the Troubles'. In the words of one official, it was an attempt to answer the '$64,000 question': how to achieve a 'satisfactory position for the Northern minority and effective protection for them against any Unionist oppression' in the event of a return to devolved government.[99] It was thus designed to encourage unionists into a power sharing arrangement with nationalists within Northern Ireland, while also offering the latter an 'Irish dimension' as an acknowledgement of their distinct identity. Through these inter-locking structures, it was thought that the inequality that had blighted the province for fifty years could be rendered obsolete.

Crucially, though, this view of Sunningdale was not shared by all parties to the agreement. In particular, it is far from clear that the SDLP and the Irish government saw it in such prosaic terms. The former, according to one of its members, Paddy Devlin, looked to Sunningdale as likely to 'produce the dynamic that could lead ultimately to an agreed single state for Ireland'.[100] Equally, it was not clear what

45

the Irish government had conceded, in return for a more substantive say in the affairs of Northern Ireland. For instance, there was no willingness in Dublin to address the controversial issue of the Republic of Ireland's territorial and jurisdictional claim over Northern Ireland—as embodied in articles two and three of the Irish constitution. These were to remain a constant source of anxiety for unionists, who viewed them as the manifestation of the Irish state's irredentist attitude towards its northern neighbour. This perception was scarcely eased by the fact that the Irish government was forced, by a High Court challenge to its policy, to publicly restate its claim on Northern Ireland in January 1974.[101] Unionists could see little evidence that constitutional nationalism had forsaken the more strident line that it had adopted in the period after internment and Bloody Sunday.

In the meantime, Brian Faulkner had struggled to bring his Unionist Party with him in supporting the original constitutional proposals enshrined in Sunningdale. Unionism had not yet adjusted to the end of Stormont and the effective implosion of the Northern Ireland state. In a short period of time, it was being asked to swallow a number of particularly 'bitter pills'. The most obvious among these was the discarding of majority rule, in favour of institutionalised power-sharing that would guarantee Catholic-nationalists permanent executive power within Northern Ireland. More alarming still was the 'Council of Ireland', which remained remarkably ill-defined at the time when the Sunningdale Agreement was signed. While it suited nationalists to talk up its remit, these claims intensified unionist fears. There was a growing suspicion that the Council would, in the alleged words of one SDLP member, 'trundle' unionists into a united Ireland.[102]

The panic over the Council of Ireland precipitated a further fracturing of unionism. In the face of mounting opposition, Faulkner was forced to resign as Unionist Party leader in January 1974, to be replaced by an opponent of the deal, Harry West. Meanwhile, popular unionist opposition to Sunningdale coalesced under the umbrella of the United Ulster Unionist Council (UUUC). When Edward Heath decided to call a snap General Election in February 1974, in the wake of his problems with mainland industrial militancy, the UUUC won eleven out of the twelve seats available in Northern Ireland. It also secured three times as many votes as Faulkner's newly founded Unionist Party of Northern Ireland (UPNI).[103] Over the same period, the level of loyalist violence effectively increased three-fold—and even seeped south of the border, culminating in the simultaneous Dublin and Monaghan bombings of May 1974 that claimed thirty-two lives and injured hundreds.[104] The same month, Faulkner, who had limped on as Chief Minister in the hamstrung assembly, was finally forced to resign in the face of a general strike led by the Ulster Workers' Council (UWC). The power-sharing executive was then wound up, ending the short-lived Sunningdale experiment. In the aftermath, Robert Armstrong, Harold Wilson's Principal Private Secretary, noted on 31 May 1974, 'it is pretty clear that the prospects of any realistic power-sharing are ruled out unless, as tempers cool, there is a change of heart on the scale which is almost too much to believe ... the Emperor has no clothes'.[105]

Overall, the long-term legacy of Sunningdale was certainly not one of outright failure. For one thing, the institutions were never in existence long enough for power-sharing to be entirely discredited as a flawed system. In addition, even as the prospect of power-sharing receded in the foreseeable future, the Sunningdale experience had planted various intellectual seeds among those who were prepared to consider what an eventual settlement for Northern Ireland might look like. During the period of flux that followed the collapse of Sunningdale, some local politicians were prompted to think outside of normal parameters; and some began to consider the problem in fresh ways. Thus, the Constitutional Convention of 1975—a discussion body involving local parties that was set up to fill the vacuum which followed the fall of Sunningdale—can now be seen as something of a crucible of new ideas. Of course, the fact that there were so many conflicting ideas within that body virtually ensured that it achieved little in terms of practical politics. Nonetheless, some of the ideas discussed at the Convention did have a longer shelf-life than others and these later reappeared in modified form. For example, the future First Minister of Northern Ireland, David Trimble, emerged during the Convention as someone willing to countenance voluntary power-sharing with the SDLP. Trimble displayed a flexibility that did not seem to fit his persona as a member of the hard-line Vanguard Unionist Party that had supported the anti-Sunningdale UWC strike.[106] More broadly, there were some signs of cooperation between the Ulster Unionists and the SDLP, even during this unpromising period.

The fallout from Sunningdale brought the recognition of several rather less palatable home truths for the British government. Many of these slowly seeped into the consciousness of the state apparatus. The first and most potent lesson of this period was that the Protestant-majority within Northern Ireland constituted a serious potential obstacle to any deal which they felt jeopardised their constitutional position within the United Kingdom. In May 1974, when the predominantly Protestant workforce at Ballylumford power station in County Antrim—which controlled the electricity supply for Belfast—was persuaded to join the UWC strike, the country was effectively brought to a standstill. It was therefore clear that, even if power-sharing was the only possible solution to the problems of Northern Ireland in the long-run, it could not provide an immediate panacea. This explains why the Secretary of State for Northern Ireland, Merlyn Rees, was adamant that the government should avoid costly new political initiatives in the aftermath of Sunningdale. 'We should not take initiatives ourselves', he wrote, 'but we must be prepared to respond to local political movements to make sure that agreements in principle are steered into practical constitutional form'.[107]

By the same token, the intransigence of the IRA—and its refusal to give up 'armed struggle' until its aims had been achieved—was something which Sunningdale had not even attempted to address. On the one hand, government officials may have argued that the creation of a power-sharing, cross-community government might have undermined support for the IRA among the Catholic community. But this underestimates the ferocity, ideology and confidence of violent republicanism at this time. The IRA, buoyed by its previous successes, was certain that it could force the British out of Northern Ireland—and acted accordingly.

Overall, the Sunningdale initiative was clearly indicative of a new disposition and serious thinking from within the governmental apparatus. The Agreement that was produced was, in many ways, visionary and it left a lasting mark on the political landscape of Northern Ireland. At the same time, trust and confidence in both the British and Irish governments were clearly at an all-time low within the province. The British state had turned its energies and best minds to providing a constitutional arrangement to remedy the problems that had beset the province since the 1920s, but it failed. The site of Sunningdale in Berkshire was, for many, a symbol of just how far removed the processes of statecraft and inter-governmental politics had become from realities on the ground.

The Pendulum swings back: Talking to Terrorists II

It is easy to underestimate the sense of drift that infected the British state in the post-Sunningdale period. In 1975, *The Times* correspondent in Northern Ireland, Robert Fisk, produced a book describing how the British had been brought to their knees by the UWC strike.[108] Moreover, this was a period of wider instability in British politics, characterised by industrial strife, financial crisis and colonial decline. This combination of difficulties had helped bring about the defeat of Edward Heath's Conservative Party at the 1974 General Election and the return to power of Harold Wilson and Labour. Yet, the new government appeared to have little immediate sense of how best to respond to Ulster. It was under Wilson that the Sunningdale initiative finally collapsed—much to the disgust of the Prime Minister himself, who publicly lambasted the ungrateful unionist 'spongers' in the UWC who opposed the accord.[109]

The reality was that Northern Ireland was viewed as an unwanted headache and one which seemed increasingly impossible to solve. This much is made clear from official government documents from the period, which reflect the sense of defeatism and intellectual exhaustion that permeated the highest echelons of the British state. In the three years since the imposition of Direct Rule, Conservative and Labour Governments had cast around for a 'silver bullet' to solve the crisis, oscillating between markedly divergent positions. In the wake of Sunningdale, thinking on Northern Ireland now appeared more rudderless than ever.

As in 1972, a policy vacuum allowed the notion of 'talking to terrorists' to once more re-enter British calculations. To some extent this was unsurprising. Even though the government had been damaged by the 1972 talks' episode, the precedent of making contact with the IRA had been established. Furthermore, only nine days after the collapse of the July 1972 ceasefire, Harold Wilson had sought another meeting between himself and republican leaders. To this end, he had informed the Prime Minister, Edward Heath and Willie Whitelaw of his intentions and neither raised any objections. The rendez-vous was then arranged. Whereas in March 1972, Wilson had traveled to Dublin to meet with the IRA, this time he invited them to his country retreat in Buckinghamshire. For the republicans, Joe Cahill was again present— this time accompanied by the fellow Belfast republican, Tom O'Donnell and the lawyer, Myles Shelvin. The meeting, though cordial, proved unproductive. Wilson had pushed for a new truce, but the IRA representatives once more adhered to a hard-line. In the later assessment of Cahill, 'Again that meeting did not amount to anything'.[110]

Nevertheless, despite the failure of this latest overture, two channels of communication between the IRA and the British state were kept open from that point onwards. On the one hand, there were 'indirect' contacts, by which unofficial figures—often with no connection to either the government or the Provisionals—relayed information between the two sides. On the other hand, there were the more 'direct' communications cultivated by employees of the British state (though the extent to which these individuals were always acting with higher authority has been disputed).[111] These 'official' channels were principally operated by successive Secret Intelligence Service (SIS) officers, Frank Steele (who had been the intermediary during the 1972 truce) and Michael Oatley. As has recently been disclosed, one of these ran via the Londonderry businessman, Brendan Duddy.[112] Another passed through the Catholic priest, Father Denis Bradley.[113] Together with another unnamed individual, these men formed 'the link' that gave the British state direct access to the republican movement.[114] Of them, it would seem that Duddy emerged as by far the most fruitful access point; he was henceforth known only as the 'the Contact' and dealings with him took place on what British officials referred to as a 'non-attributable' basis. A note marked 'Top Secret and Personal', from Lord Bridges, Harold Wilson's Foreign Affairs Secretary, to the NIO in November 1974 revealed that the Prime Minister was 'content that officials continue these very, very secret contacts' with the IRA.[115] Yet, the question of who knew what and when, within government, remains unclear—apparently, not even Wilson's Northern Irish Secretary of State, Merlyn Rees, knew of such channels initially.[116]

From the perspective of the government, the contacts were regarded as valuable for a number of reasons. First, they helped the government piece together the IRA's 'corporate position' in the period after the abortive 1972 negotiations. Thus, while the Secretary of State was informed by Vivian Simpson—a former Labour Member of the Stormont Parliament—that the Provisionals blamed the government and the Army for the breakdown of the truce that year, the organisation made it clear through unofficial intermediaries that it was still 'prepared to have both a truce and a ceasefire' in the future.[117] The exchanges, though, were not always warm. The Secretary of State was also sent a message to the effect that the Provisionals believed 'the British Army could never win and Provisional units could strike wherever they wanted'. By way of response, the Provisionals were told, through intermediaries, that 'Unlike the Mau-Mau in Kenya', they did not have enough support in the country to achieve their ends.[118]

Another function of the contacts was that they allowed the government to build up a picture of the internal dynamics within the republican movement. While the latter sought to project an image of unity to the outside world, the work of intermediaries could provide a greater sense of the tensions that existed with the IRA. This opened the possibility—not necessarily one that was fully explored—that the Provisionals might be pulled in different directions by government policy. In this way, it allowed the government to identify persons with whom they might 'do business'. After he held meetings with Father Denis Faul of Dungannon and Father Patrick Conning of Dublin in April 1973, for example, Michael Oatley was able to make clearer assessments about where different republicans stood. The southern leadership figure, Daithi O'Conaill was thus said to be 'anxious for peace and a move to politics', whereas the Belfast-based IRA commander, Seamus Twomey, was described as 'the most intransigent'. Interestingly, serious consideration was given to the role that a young Gerry Adams might play in the evolution of the movement:

Adams (with whom they were both very impressed as being much more intelligent and idealistic than his companions) might readily be persuaded to the same point of view [as O'Conaill] if we could only produce some formula or arrangement which he could offer to his men.[119]

In similar vein, in 1974, some informants seemed to suggest that there was a 'less hard line faction in [the IRA] Army Council' that wanted encouragement 'to move into politics'. To this end, the IRA was said to have sought reassurance that Sinn Fein candidates would not be prosecuted.[120] On another occasion, the government noted that while the republican movement was in some danger of falling into the 'hands of teenagers or ... International Socialist/Trotskyist influences...a substantial body within Sinn Fein favours the alternative of political actions'.[121] It was perhaps as part of a conscious effort to foster this political tendency that the Secretary of State, Merlyn Rees, took the decision to legalise Sinn Fein, the political wing of the IRA, in 1974.[122]

Alongside 'intelligence-gathering' contacts and hopeful vistas, from the middle of 1974 the government embarked upon a renewed attempt at more meaningful, quasi-official talks with the IRA. This evolved out of the Oatley-Duddy line of communication (of which Rees was now informed). For its part, the readiness of the IRA leadership to engage in the enterprise stemmed from a variety of motives. On the one hand, the IRA's fortunes had declined after the high-point of 1972. The prophesied 'year of victory' had failed to materialize and instead there had been a marked reduction in the level of the violence in Northern Ireland. The reality was that the policy of internment—despite a disastrous start—had in fact taken a toll on the organisation. This was allied to other important developments in the British state's counter-terrorism apparatus. In particular, the British Army had made important advances in the intelligence war (even as it still suffered the occasional reverse), which had vastly improved its ability to take on the IRA. The result was that by 1974, republicans were under a great deal of pressure—especially in Belfast. There, senior and influential figures such as Ivor Bell, Gerry Adams and Brendan Hughes were all arrested over the course of that year.[123] Such was the rate of attrition that by some estimates the average 'life-span' of the Officer Command-ing (OC) the IRA's Belfast Brigade was reduced to just six weeks.[124] According to one informed account, republicans faced serious financial problems at this time—in terms of their ability to fund an ongoing campaign—and 'the IRA was almost unable to function militarily because of security-force arrests of active volunteers'.[125]

Despite this success, the British began to wind down the use of internment. The introduction of the Northern Ireland (Emergency Pro-visions) Act in 1973 had led to the creation of the 'Diplock' courts, presided over by a single judge and no jury, to try those accused of 'scheduled offences'. Henceforth, this was to provide a less objection-able legal framework for the battle against the IRA—at least in com-parison to the use of detention without any form of trial at all. But as one senior IRA figure later wryly acknowledged in conversation with another, the fact was that the British were abandoning internment just s it was really working to devastating effect.[126] It was this British success that ensured that the leading figures in the Belfast IRA—Seamus Twomey and Billy McKee, who both sat on the organisa-tion's Army Council—were prepared to countenance a ceasefire.[127] Neither of them particularly desired it, but both believed that the group was in desperate need of respite; and it was this consciousness of the IRA's true position in late 1974 that persuaded them to endorse a cessation.

This is not to say that the IRA leadership viewed a possible ceasefire as simply an exercise in 'damage limitation'. On the contrary, they were also more than aware of the extent to which British policy on Northern Ireland appeared to lack direction after the collapse of Sunningdale. As the senior republican, Ruairi O'Bradaigh later observed, this had thrown 'British policy totally into the melting pot... [it] swept the decks clean. It was back to the drawing board'.[128] The irony was that the loyalist UWC strike of 1974 seemed to have done more damage to the British presence in Northern Ireland than the republican movement could ever have hoped to inflict in the same time-frame. The intellectual and physical fatigue that afflicted the British state at this time—nowhere more obvious than in the person of Prime Minister Harold Wilson himself—encouraged senior figures in the IRA to believe that British withdrawal was a genuine possibility. In O Bradaigh's judgment, 'every solution was up for consideration'.[129] Or as an IRA statement put it in August 1974:

The Pilate-like washing of hands will be ceremoniously carried out and will be endorsed by the mass of the British people... A dignified withdrawal is then possible with little loss of face and considerable financial benefit to the British taxpayer.[130]

This belief was not necessarily discouraged by the IRA's British interlocutors. The precise terminology used in discussions between the two sides remains a source of some controversy, yet whether references were made to 'structures of disengagement' or simply British 'withdrawal', the government was anxious not to disabuse the IRA of the apparent seriousness of what was on offer.[131]

This was the context for the IRA ceasefire of 1974–5. Towards the end of 1974, talks had been held between members of the IRA and six Protestant clergy in Feakle, County Clare, in the Irish Republic.[132] Though the clergymen were operating independently from the state their actions were effectively a by-product of the growing willingness of the British state to engage in dialogue with republicans. And while no official agreement was reached, both sides produced a response to the talks and agreed to explore matters further. The IRA declared a temporary ceasefire in late December 1974, which was subsequently extended into January of the following year. In February 1975, the truce was then prolonged indefinitely.[133] In parallel with these moves, in January 1975, Merlyn Rees authorised talks between government officials and the IRA.

The IRA's appraisal of the situation was informed by two considerations: first, an appreciation of the group's overall military weakness; and second, optimism that the British were wobbling and that political success was within reach. For this reason, the IRA leadership of the time endeavoured to pursue talks from a position of strength. Over the course of 1974—even as contacts between republicans and the British progressed through intermediaries—the Provisionals turned their hand to accelerating their bombing campaign on the mainland under the guiding hand of Brian Keenan.[134] In February of that year, a bomb placed on a coach detonated while the vehicle was on the M62 near Bradford, killing eleven people. Then in June 1974, the cities of London, Manchester and Birmingham were all hit by a spate of attacks. Worse was to come in the autumn. October brought the bombing of public houses in Guildford and Woolwich, an act that claimed seven lives; and then, in November, two further attacks on public houses in Birmingham killed twenty-one and injured over one hundred and sixty others.[135] The scale of the carnage from the latter incident brought a brief suspension of operations, but the IRA leadership made clear that it was not finished. Immediately prior to the commencement of the ceasefire on 22 December 1974, Aldershot train station was attacked, as was the Belgravia home of the former Prime Minister, Edward Heath.[136] More ominously, there was widespread alarm within the British security services that the IRA would target the London tube network in the run-up to Christmas with 'no-warning' bomb attacks. Daithi O'Conaill had encouraged this belief by telling an intermediary that operations of this nature had indeed been planned.[137] In other words, the IRA was determined to ensure that any peace initiative would neither be construed as a sign of weakness, nor allow the pressure to be taken off the British—pressure that they believed was forcing the British government towards an exit from Northern Ireland.

From the outset, the nature of the IRA's 1974–5 'ceasefire' was never clearly defined. On the one hand, it was clearly meant to entail a moratorium on direct IRA attacks on the security forces. Yet, as it was implemented it actually brought an increase in violence within Northern Ireland. Much of this was sectarian in nature and the first six months of 1975 brought a surge in such incidents.[138] Moreover, as a wider symptom of instability, there was also a marked increase in the intra-factional feuding within republicanism, as paramilitary power struggles intensified. The latter saw a clash between the Official IRA and the Provisionals, which left several men dead in Belfast.[139] In total, more people were killed during the first nine months of the IRA's 'truce', than in the same period the previous year.

From August 1975, even the limited reduction of IRA activity that the truce had brought about appeared to have ended. Attacks on security forces resumed and the organisation's notorious 'Balcombe Street Gang' brought a wave of terror to the streets of London.[140] As far as the wider death-toll was concerned, meanwhile, 1975 proved to be one of the worst years of 'the Troubles', with 247 violent deaths and many more injuries. In the same way that the character of the IRA's ceasefire was shrouded in ambiguity, so too was the strategy of the organisation's leadership for the talks that took place. A 'Top Secret' document, passed from Merlyn Rees to Harold Wilson in November 1975, captured the British government's sense of this. '[The] Contact' (presumably, Brendan Duddy), had reported the IRA's confidence that it could agree terms with the loyalists for a 'six-county Ulster', independent of the United Kingdom, but not merged into a united Ireland (Intelligence reports also suggested that IRA members had been meeting their loyalist counterparts in Holland). Republicans believed that everything was in place; all they felt they needed from the British, according to 'the Contact', was 'a private indication of intent to withdraw from Ireland'. If such an indication was forthcoming, it was claimed, the IRA would then be prepared to call off its campaign for good.[141]

In the meantime, the IRA sought to extract limited concessions from the British government as the price of its ceasefire. One such 'gain' was the initial scaling down of security force activity in Catholic-nationalist areas. This was followed by the creation of 'Truce Incident Centres' in Enniskillen, Armagh, Londonderry, Newry, Dungannon and Belfast, in order to monitor the cessation.[142] Not only did this endow republicans with a public presence in 'their' communities, but also it seemed to suggest some level of permanent cooperation between the Provisionals and the security forces. This brought bitter complaints from the representatives of constitutional nationalism, who maintained that the centres effectively granted the IRA a free rein in Catholic-nationalist areas. In similar fashion, unionists complained that leading IRA members seemed to have been given immunity from arrest (as appeared to be evident from the fact that someone like Seamus Twomey, the organisation's then Chief-of-Staff, was able to deliver the main oration to the republicans' 1975 Easter Rising commemoration in Belfast and not be apprehended).[143] The Irish government too expressed serious reservations about British government policy. Not only was it deemed to be undermining moderate nationalists, such as the SDLP, but from their perspective it also seemed to be strengthening an armed conspiracy that was bent on subverting the fabric of the Irish state.[144]

Nevertheless, in spite of these tangible benefits for republicans, the ceasefire was failing to fulfill their expectations. Already in March 1975, IRA representatives were complaining to their British interlocutors that, 'Negotiations on the three basic demands of the Republican Movement... have not made any worthwhile progress'.[145] A month later, the Cabinet Committee on Northern Ireland was being informed that the primary focus for republicans seemed to be 'not so much on attempting to shore up the ceasefire', but on winning the blame game when it collapsed, as seemed increasingly likely.[146] By October 1975, the British were gearing themselves up for 'a return to full-scale violence'. 'The brutal fact', with which an increasing number of British officials were coming to terms, was that 'we cannot expect to satisfy extreme Republicanism by any arrangement which would be satisfactory to us', let alone 'responsible Irishmen' in the Republic. The only conclusion, according to the British Embassy in Dublin, was that the organization had 'to be opposed not appeased'.[147]

To this end, the intermittent talks between British representatives and senior republican figures began to be wound down. By November 1975, 'Top Secret' documents were reflecting the British government's assessment that the IRA was 'getting desperate'. On the one hand, it was said, they were 'aware of the lack of support in urban Catholic areas of Northern Ireland for a return to all-out violence'; on the other, the leadership was said to face 'loud rumblings of discontent in the ranks' of the organisation in Belfast and Londonderry.[148] That same month, amid renewed IRA violence, the 'Truce Incident Centres' were officially closed down, offering the clearest indication that the government now judged the ceasefire to be over.

From the perspective of the British state, two interpretations of the truce emerged. The first, which supports the view of the IRA leadership that engaged in the truce, was that the British government was seriously considering withdrawal. That this idea had been floated at the highest levels of government is clear. According to some of those involved, it was the subsequent abandonment of the 'withdrawal' policy that caused lasting damage, by ingraining deep suspicion of British negotiators within the IRA, which lasted two decades.[149] The second view of the ceasefire, which both the government and republican critics of the truce came to believe, was that the British had never seriously entertained the prospect of withdrawal. Merlyn Rees, the Secretary of State who had sanctioned official contacts with the IRA, has since claimed that he only maintained the 'truce', despite continued violence, in order to buy time to implement a series of changes in security and counter-terrorism policy.

The most realistic interpretation lies somewhere between the two. The fact is that there was little unity of purpose across the various arms of the British state dealing with Northern Ireland during the Wilson years. It is now known, for instance, that Harold Wilson's personal pessimism over the situation brought a new round of flirtation with the idea of withdrawal in official circles. Even before winning the General Election of 1974, Wilson had been pointedly ambiguous about where his party stood in relation to the status of Northern Ireland.[150] In May 1974, in the wake of the UWC strike, he had entertained discussion of a 'Doomsday' scenario of withdrawal—only to be told by Robert Armstrong, his Principal Private Secretary, that the likely consequences included the, 'outbreak of violence and bloodshed, possible unacceptability to moderate Catholics, ditto to the Republic, the United Nations'. In the view of people such as Armstrong, such a solution 'leaves more questions unresolved than it answers'; though even he was prepared to admit that it was 'one possible scenario' and he said he had 'a feeling that Parliamentary and other pressures may drive us to pretty early consideration of it'.[151]

Armstrong's measured response to Wilson's 'Doomsday' document constituted a 'counsel of caution' to the increasingly frustrated Prime Minister. Yet Wilson was not alone in his views. His highly able policy adviser, Bernard Donoughue, clearly shared the sentiments. 'Robert Armstrong is ... worried by our consideration of withdrawal from Ulster', Donoughue recorded in his diary, noting also that 'the machine' (by which he meant the civil service), was preparing a 'counter-offensive' against the government on the issue. In an entry for May

1975, Donoughue stated his conviction that 'we will have to withdraw from Northern Ireland at some point within 5–10 years'; what is more, a year after the UWC strike, Donoughue also believed that Merlyn Rees was coming round to the same conclusion.[152]

What becomes evident, then, is the extent to which the British state was not the monolithic entity that republicans believed. Indeed, it might even be said that its lack of internal coherence on this issue presents a striking picture of 'amateurishness'. On the one hand, 'the machine' attempted to pull the government back from the brink. On the other, intelligence officers—apparently operating independently from 'the machine'—seemed to predicate their communications with the IRA on the basis of the confused and reactive sentiments emanating from Downing Street. As the investigative journalist Peter Taylor has uncovered, the possibility of withdrawal was certainly being communicated to the republican movement by their British interlocutors throughout the truce talks. At a meeting in April 1975, for example, Ruairi O'Bradaigh and Billy McKee were told that the republican movement and the government could work together to allow 'the structures of disengagement', to grow naturally in Northern Ireland. A couple of months later, in June, republican minutes of another meeting attest to IRA representatives being told by their British counterparts 'very firmly that [the] Brits were going'.[153] The question therefore arises of whether the republicans were delusional in their assessment, or whether they were being lied to by the British government. The most likely explanation is again, a mixture of both, with the IRA leadership displaying a degree of credulity regarding British government intentions, even as the latter's representatives 'on the ground' sought to put the best possible gloss on developments. The latter may even have extended to a tendency for the British representatives to exceed their brief—staking out positions that may have been floated in Downing Street, but never came close to implementation.

Drift: the final months of the Wilson Premiership

During his final few months as Prime Minister at the beginning of 1976, Harold Wilson (who was replaced by James Callaghan in March), revealed the extent of his exhaustion and frustration with the issue of Northern Ireland. In a reworking of his 'Doomsday' document of 1974, he scripted an 'Apocalyptic Note for the Record', intended for 'limited circulation'. It was dated 10 January 1976, after a particularly brutal start to the year and a succession of horrific sectarian murders. In the memorandum, Wilson argued that the British government had to 'face up to a situation where Northern Ireland becomes ungovernable', either because 'terrorism amounting to civil war supervenes' or if industrial action, 'directed to constitutional pre-emption occurs on a scale where the civil power becomes impotent'.[154] The collapse of Sunningdale still haunted him. Despite the ferocity of the IRA insurgency, Wilson continued to view the intransigence of the Ulster Protestant community as the insurmountable problem in Northern Ireland.

More eccentrically, he attempted to anticipate their next move by recourse to the example of Rhodesia. There, in 1965, the white government of Ian Smith and his Rhodesian Front party had made a Unilateral Declaration of Independence (UDI) from the United Kingdom government, while professing continued loyalty to Queen Elizabeth II. The move was an attempt to sidestep London-driven attempts to push the colony towards an acceptance of black majority rule. Ten years later, with little in the way of serious evidence, Wilson suggested that the prospect of an Ulster loyalist UDI was something that the government had to take seriously, even though such a move 'would be a damning verdict on the claim to the name "loyalist"'. In the event that it happened, the Prime Minister claimed that this might present the government with an opportunity to extract itself from the province.[155]

Wilson's document was an expression of exasperation rather than a carefully thought out policy statement but it was symptomatic of a more fundamental problem; the Prime Minister's attitude towards Ulster loyalism risked becoming a self-fulfilling prophecy. Since 1970, loyalists had seen 'their' government at Stormont dismantled and replaced by Direct Rule, only for those charged with operating Direct Rule to flirt with abandoning the province entirely. Wilson's ambiguity on the question of Britain's commitment to Northern Ireland, which was something of an 'open secret', was only likely to increase the unionist impulse for disobedience. Indicative of this was the assessment of Airey Neave, the Tory shadow Secretary of State for Northern Ireland and a figure normally sympathetic to the unionist cause. After a meeting with local unionists in 1976, he reported that unionist politicians were considering increasingly wild and anachronistic constitutional solutions to the current impasse (one suggested that the office of Secretary of State be abolished in favour of a 'Lord President of Ulster', who, as the Queen's representative, would select a Prime Minister of the province).[156]

Notwithstanding Wilson's reflections, the notion of British withdrawal at no point became the settled objective of the British state. Most officials had come to believe that the drawbacks of such a policy would likely outweigh the benefits. As one internal Foreign Office memorandum concluded:

Leaving aside any moral considerations about our obligation to the democratic majority in Northern Ireland and the bloodshed which would follow a 'withdrawal'... it is in our own interests, selfishly defined, to stay in the province.

To do otherwise, it was argued, risked not only violent upheaval within Northern Ireland, but also a 'collapse of [government] authority in the South, leaving the field open to extremists, even to the extent of some sort of extreme left wing take over'. In the worst case scenario, it was imagined that this could lead to 'the establishment of a sort of Portugal [which had just experienced a left-wing revolt] on our doorstep'.[157]

Herein lay an irreducible problem, which had often been ignored during Wilson's periodic flirtation with the idea of withdrawal. The fact was that the IRA was as much, if not more, of a danger to the integrity of the Irish state, than it was to British sovereignty. In the event of a British withdrawal, the prospect of the Provisionals gaining a greater foothold in Ireland, raised a number of serious concerns, among them the 'overflow of violence, even as far away as Cork'. As one report concluded:

British observers may sometimes be tempted to regard extreme republicans in the North as potential politicians struggling to change the nature of squalid terrorist organizations ... in the eyes of the Dublin government, the IRA are an armed conspiracy bent on subverting the very fabric of the state.[158]

The reality was that the Irish government was incapable of dealing with the political, military and financial vacuum that this would leave. If the British withdrew from Northern Ireland, suggested senior civil servant Frank Cooper, the Irish government 'would be horrified and might well run off to the UN'.[159]

The truth of this analysis was verified by the later recollections of the Irish Foreign Minister of this period, Garret FitzGerald. FitzGerald has reflected on his own eagerness to prevent a British withdrawal. He describes how he sought out Henry Kissinger in Washington, to seek reassurances that he could rely on 'US assistance in persuading Britain not to embark on a course of action that could be so fraught with dangers not just to Northern Ireland but to the whole of Ireland, and conceivably even ... to the wider peace of north-western Europe'.[160] Throughout 1975, British officials described how they had been subject to 'a steady stream of enquiries and admonitions' from the Irish government as to their objectives, in which FitzGerald was painted as an increasingly frantic figure.[161]

As the British state ruminated on such considerations in the aftermath of the IRA's 1974–5 ceasefire—and it became clear that withdrawal was little more than a 'fantasy' that could never be enacted—a reappraisal of policy gathered momentum. It was a reassessment inspired largely by an awareness of Britain's lack of freedom to manoeuvre. For Merlyn Rees, for example, the only logical option, albeit one embraced reluctantly, was that the British commitment in the province had to be 'long-term'. Those that advocated withdrawal, he decided, were 'ignoring its implications':

Ulster is part of an island whose problems have defeated us for centuries; the Boyne, the Lagan and the Bann are not the Zambezi, the Nile or the Ganges... Northern Ireland does not pose a classical colonial question.[162]

Even as the British government was arriving at such conclusions, it was evident that an extended stay for British troops in Northern Ireland was a far from welcome prospect for many. Shocked by the sheer viciousness of the violence in Northern Ireland, mainstream British opinion had swung significantly in favour of withdrawal. On 9 December 1975, a Gallup poll showed that 64% of people in Britain wanted the troops 'out', compared to 55% in 1974 and 34% in 1972.[163] Yet, the government was coming to the realization that things were not that simple. Without any reliable, stable partner—and the prospect of the international censure that was likely to follow any 'cut and run' approach—alternative paths were severely limited.

On 12 December 1975, Merlyn Rees composed a memorandum, which communicated his view of the Northern Ireland situation to his Cabinet colleagues:

There is no chance of an immediate solution at a stroke. There is no chance of some instant solution. Understanding and patience are the keys. Our immediate aims must be the limited ones of keeping the temperature of political debate as low as possible; of seeking to bridge the difference between the two communities by degrees ... without any kind of drama on which extremists feed.[164]

By the spring of the following year, Rees had successfully entrenched this new approach. In May 1976, the Cabinet Committee on Northern Ireland was informed how, 'as the mirage of British withdrawal which sustained them through 1975 fades, [the IRA] will be capable of increasingly atrocious acts of violence'.[165] In response, Rees had chosen to implement a 'Long Haul' strategy. His calculation was that such a strategy might cause the IRA to 'lose heart', by demonstrating that they had neither the initiative, nor the attention, of the government. As one official observed, 'they think, rightly so far, that these things have been going their way'.[166] That was about to change.

2

THE LONG WAR
1975–1990

Settling in for the Long Haul: from Rees to Mason

Between 1969 and 1975, the IRA had drawn strength from what it saw as a lack of resolve on the part of the British state. For much of that period, successive governments had responded to the crisis in Northern Ireland with a mixture of panic, reaction, concession, force and experiment; but rarely with a long-term strategy. Moreover, the Provisional IRA could claim to have achieved certain key objectives. The old Stormont Parliament had been removed—in a development which was believed to have exposed the true 'colonial' nature of Northern Ireland's existence. In addition, the British government had been induced to hold talks with the republican movement on more than one occasion: negotiations that appeared to hold out the prospect of British withdrawal and a move towards Irish unity.

And yet, there also became visible the broad outlines of a new approach on the part of the British state, which was informed by the mistakes of the late 1960s and early 1970s. At the political level, any prospect of a unilateral British withdrawal had been withdrawn from the table. The government resolved that a consensus would have to be established among the people of Northern Ireland if new institutions were to be built for the province. It was recognised that while the state might provide a framework for a solution to 'the Troubles' (in terms of constitutional 'bottom-lines' and efforts to improve security) it was fundamentally for the people of the province (through their political representatives) to agree on how they wished to be governed. As government officials wrote in 1976, 'Power sharing cannot be imposed ...

the history of Northern Ireland has shown that any party representing a sizeable group within the community has the power to bring ordered government to an end'.[1] As Merlyn Rees later noted,

The dream of a united Ireland will long remain a dream. A devolved government in the North is the only basis on which the people in the two parts of Ireland will one day talk to each other. The hope of finding a successful solution lies with the Northern Irish people, not with outsiders in Dublin and London talking by proxy.[2]

Faced with this shift, the Irish government expressed concern that the British approach to Northern Ireland could become 'too passive'. In response, British officials claimed to share the Irish objective of 'power-sharing' as a long-term British aim, but insisted that this was a phrase they wished to avoid in the near future, on the grounds that it had 'acquired specific undertones and meant the [failed] 1974 form of Executive'. The Irish were told that there was 'nothing weak about deliberate inactivity'.[3]

This presumed 'inactivity' on the part of the British state prompted Brian Faulkner to conclude,

Westminster, having had its finger's burnt over its high-profile involvement in Sunningdale, rushed to the other extreme and adopted a 'sort yourselves out, it's nothing to do with us' attitude.[4]

Yet, while this may have been the impression garnered within Northern Ireland, the reality was more complex; the corollary of the move away from attempts at constitutional innovation were changes in security policy, to meet the challenge posed by the IRA. These had begun as far back as 1972–3, but they now increased significantly as the British state responded to the logic of Merlyn Rees' commitment to a 'long haul' presence in Northern Ireland.

The Northern Ireland (Emergency Provisions) Act of 1973 that created the 'Diplock' Courts had indicated the direction in which security policy was headed. This had been followed in late 1974 (in the aftermath of the Birmingham bombings) by the Prevention of Terrorism Act (PTA) that allowed for suspects to be detained for seven days without charge and for 'undesirables' to be excluded from the British mainland.[5] The IRA's 1974–5 ceasefire brought further changes in approach. During that truce, the British had presented the phasing out of internment as a concession to the IRA in the hope that this might persuade it to prolong its cessation; yet, in truth, the government had little desire to continue the policy anyway. In the view of Merlyn Rees, its use 'bedeviled relations between the government and the minority community and created sympathy for terrorists which conviction by the courts [does] not'.[6] For this reason, on 30 October 1975, Rees wrote to the Prime Minister to tell him that he was planning to release any remaining detainees by Christmas of that year, as part of a 'restoration of the normal processes of law and order'.[7] The abolition of internment did not mark a softening of the government's approach to terrorism. Rather, it was entirely consistent with the new emphasis on securing criminal convictions for those involved in paramilitary violence using the 'Diplock' courts. Merlyn Rees confirmed as much with his announcement in November 1975 that 'special category status' for paramilitary prisoners—previously introduced by William Whitelaw in 1972—was to be ended. From 1 March 1976, anyone found guilty of 'scheduled offences' (relating to terrorist crimes) was to be treated as a criminal, no different from any other.[8]

Integral to this effort to arrest and convict more known republicans, the RUC, re-fashioned as a more professional and modernised police force, was pushed to the front-line of Northern Ireland's conflict again.[9] In this endeavour, it was to be joined by the locally-raised Ulster Defence Regiment (UDR)—a branch of the Army, which had been created in 1970 to fill the security gap left by the standing down of the controversial B Specials a year earlier. With the exception of certain republican 'heartlands', such as South Armagh's 'Bandit Country', or North Armagh's 'Murder Triangle', the regular British Army was now largely withdrawn from view.[10] By October 1976, for instance, the general assessment as to the division of labour among the security services was as follows:

The Army [are] adjusting to the growing emphasis on normal policing; and the RUC [are] taking more of the initiative and obtaining results … But… The RUC, while being encouraged to assume a more prominent role, should have the assurance of continuing support by the Army, and the Army, in turn should be in no doubt of the continuing importance of the part they [have] to play.[11]

The arena of conflict was also shifting, partly because the truce had attenuated the IRA's operational capacity where the insurgency had once been strongest. While the IRA 'retain a dangerous military capability in the urban areas of Belfast and Londonderry', Merlyn Rees told the Prime Minister, the organisation's leaders were equally aware that 'if they use it in an all-out return to violence they may do themselves more harm than good unless they succeed in provoking us into security policies which would rebuild their support'. For this reason, 'pre-emptive' action against the IRA was ruled out, on the grounds that it would require 'a very high level of home searches and personal checks in the Catholic areas' and a return to 'detention', which 'solved nothing in the past and will solve nothing now'.[12] While Operation Motorman and the policy of 'sitting heavily' on Londonderry had yielded limited success in 1972, wary eyes were being trained on renewed IRA activity in the border areas, such as South Armagh.[13] It was identified that the main thrust of insurgency 'is at present in the rural areas where they can operate from safe bases in the Republic—particularly along the South Armagh border'.[14] While the army was to continue its work in 'the bandit country of South Armagh', therefore, it was to be 'thinned progressively in urban areas'.[15] In the latter, the job of countering the IRA was to be left predominantly to the RUC.

The RUC made use of the new anti-terrorist legislation to arrest IRA members and extract confessions at specially-designated holding centres at Castlereagh in East Belfast, Strand Road in Londonderry and Gough Barracks in County Armagh. These confessions were then accepted as admissible evidence by the judges presiding over the 'Diplock' Courts (despite controversy over the methods used to obtain them). Anyone found guilty was dispatched to the newly built, high-security, Maze prison just outside Belfast, where they were held as ordinary criminals. For many within the Catholic community, this new security apparatus, dubbed the 'conveyor belt', was regarded as little else than a reincarnation of the old regime. The holding centre at Castlereagh, in particular, soon developed a particularly sinister reputation, with allegations of the maltreatment of prisoners.[16] Nevertheless, for all the criticism it attracted, what the security machinery illustrated was the fact that the state was better equipped to deal with the problem of violence and insurgency than it was in 1968–9.

'Criminalisation' and the establishment of 'police primacy' (or 'Ulsterisation' as it was more frequently known), constituted two-thirds of the new public security policy adopted by the British government. Completing the trident was the push for 'normalisation': an overarching effort to return the province to a state of normality. Taken together, as John Newsinger has highlighted, 'criminalisation, Ulsterisation and normalisation', represented a decisive shift towards what might be called an 'internal security strategy'.[17] In Cabinet Committee discussions on Northern Ireland in 1976, the focus was increasingly placed on 'proceeding against terrorists through the due process of law and the courts'. Through the 'primacy of the Police' and 'the reduction of the Army to garrison status and its withdrawal to barracks', the government felt it could avoid 'the traps constantly set up for us by the Provisionals', by which the latter sought to 'alienate the Catholic community' further from the British state.[18]

With the 'internal security strategy' in place, a new intelligence offensive was launched against the IRA. In this too, the police had primacy (through RUC Special Branch), although the Army did continue to play a role, especially through the deployment of specialist units such as the 22nd Special Air Service Regiment (the SAS), the Force Research Unit (FRU) and 14 Intelligence Company. The Wilson government had given notice to this reality with its headline-grabbing decision to deploy the SAS in South Armagh in January 1976, in the wake of a particularly vicious bout of sectarian killings at the start of the year.[19] At the time, the Prime Minister wrote to his Irish counterpart, Liam Cosgrave, justifying the move in the following terms:

The Spearhead Battalion has started to move today over to Northern Ireland and will be deployed in South Armagh. We need to catch a relatively small number of people on both sides, and no effort will be spared. I wanted you also to know that we propose soon to dispatch part of the special air service [SAS] who are trained particularly for surveillance and are particularly well suited for the problem we face ... I am certain that we shall need to step up our co-operation on the border and we are indeed grateful for all the help that has been given to us in the past months and for the excellent results that the Gardai have achieved. It is a sad start to the new year but we are utterly determined to bring matters in Northern Ireland to a happier state.[20]

Much controversy was to surround the role of the SAS in the province over the following two decades. Many Irish nationalists viewed the unit's deployment with a great degree of uneasiness, and it enjoyed a mythic reputation in some quarters.[21] The British Embassy in New York, for example, reported that, among Irish-Americans, the SAS often provoked comparison with the 'nefarious activities of the CIA'.[22] When eight SAS men were arrested on the wrong side of the border on 6 May 1976, the incident generated a crisis in Anglo-Irish relations which lasted for the rest of the year.[23] The British struggled to convince their counterparts that the affair was an accident, with 'a touch of the Keystone cops about it'.[24] This became even more difficult when it emerged that two of the men were dressed in the uniform of the parachute regiment, six in civilian clothes and with eleven weapons between them, including daggers and sawn off shotguns.[25]

To a significant extent, however, the deployment of the SAS was a knee-jerk response to the public outcry at the spiralling sectarian violence. And while certainly eye-catching, those in charge of strategy were eager to play down its wider import. Airey Neave, the Conservative MP and shadow Secretary of State for Northern Ireland, had been greatly excited about the potential role that the SAS could play in the conflict. In response, though, senior army officials told him that 'it was important to realize that the job of dealing with terrorists in the border areas was very much a long haul one'.[26] In some respects, the role of the SAS was a tangential aspect of a broader security policy (though one which was to become increasingly important in the early to mid-1980s). If anything, the unit's high-profile introduction into south Armagh in early 1976 actually went against the grain of the policy that had been put in place incrementally over the previous few years; it was a distraction from the new emphasis on 'criminalisation, Ulsterisation and normalisation'.

While it was Merlyn Rees who put in place the key elements of the British state's new apparatus in Northern Ireland, the new security policy was to become most closely associated with his successor, Roy Mason, a tough-talking Yorkshireman who had gained a reputation as a hard-liner.[27] Already, as Secretary of Defence, it had been Mason who had pushed for the 'Spearhead Battalion' to be dispatched to the province.[28] After his appointment as Secretary of State for Northern Ireland in September 1976, he came to embody the new government approach that prioritised security first and foremost. Like Rees, Mason had concluded that the whole constitutional issue should be 'put on the back burner' until, 'we had created the right atmosphere to make progress'. It was, he believed 'futile to barge in with great plans and programmes and plans for constitutional change'.[29] Since the imposition of Direct Rule in 1972, successive governments had, he argued, 'desperately tried to reach some kind of political accommodation with the warring factions in Ulster', but 'with little success'—as demonstrated by the failure of both the Sunningdale Agreement and Rees' constitutional 'Convention' (which was wound up in March 1976).[30]

Bernard Donoughue, a policy advisor at Downing Street, advised Jim Callaghan that Mason was excessively hostile to republicanism and, indeed, the Irish Republic itself.[31] But the new Secretary of State's preference for a steadying period of Direct Rule—with no constitutional experiments—also provoked a challenge from loyalist politicians, among whom, the Revd. Ian Paisley was again conspicuous. In May 1977, Paisley and his allies called for a new general strike in protest against British policy—this time under the aegis of the United Unionist Action Council (UUAC). The government, Paisley claimed, was not doing enough to combat IRA terrorism and for this reason, majority rule should be reinstated. In an effort to rally his supporters, Paisley appeared to stake his political future on the success of the strike. 'If it fails', he told a crowd in his County Antrim constituency, 'then my voice will no longer be heard'.[32]

In the event, the crisis was averted, although an official review of the episode suggests that it was 'a close run thing'.[33] Unlike in 1974, more moderate unionists refused to join the strike. And following a crucial meeting at Stormont, Mason managed to convince a majority of the Protestant workers of Ballylumford power station (the same men who had played a crucial role in supporting the UWC strike) that his efforts against the IRA were both serious and delivering results. In a secret ballot, 286 voted against another strike, as opposed to 171 who declared themselves in favour. The lights therefore stayed on and Mason had, narrowly, survived the test; Paisley had been overcome, though he did not, as he had hinted, retire from politics.[34]

While all this was going on, Mason was, by his own estimation, intent on 'harrassing the IRA with as much vigour as was possible in a liberal democracy'.[35] 'We are squeezing the terrorists like rolling up a toothpaste tube', he told the *Daily Express* in 1977: 'We are squeezing them out of their safe havens. We are squeezing them away from their money supplies. We are squeezing them out of society and into prison'.[36] Interviewed in *The Guardian* in September 1993, Martin McGuinness was asked which Secretary of State had most impressed him, to that point. 'The only one who impressed anybody was Roy Mason', he asserted, adding the qualifying statement: 'He impressed some of the Unionists, because he beat the shit out of us'.[37] In 1977, it was reported that a new slogan had appeared on the Falls Road: 'Stone Mason Will Not Break Us'.[38]

And yet, there was more to Mason's approach than the simple application of hard power. As he himself later commented, 'A vigorous security policy is certainly necessary in the war against terrorism; but it isn't enough'. Rather, he reflected:

'I never believed that normality could be restored to Northern Ireland simply through more arrests, more roadblocks, more army patrols and the rest. If we were to wean people—particularly the impressionable young—away from the culture of violence, we absolutely had to provide them with some hope for the future'.[39]

The 1976 Quigley Report had pointed to the poor state of the economy within Northern Ireland and Mason was influenced by its recommendation for heavy subsidisation. With unemployment, in particular, a source of concern (11.4% of the local workforce was unemployed), the years that followed saw a massive expansion of the Northern Irish public sector.[40] The Secretary of State was determined to tackle 'unemployment, poor housing, sectarian bigotry... all the things that [give] the terrorists the chance'. To this end, the importance of regenerating the province economically became a regular theme for Mason during his time in office, alongside his emphasis on the need for security.

According to Ed Moloney, Mason 'nearly defeated the IRA'.[41] Others have been less impressed with his record as Secretary of State for Northern Ireland, arguing that his tenure in the role did not constitute as much of a watershed as is often assumed. Instead, it is argued, Mason remained within the limits of Rees' established policy; his main innovation, on such a reading, was simply tougher rhetoric.[42] There is some truth to this argument, but there is one important distinction to be made and it concerns the issue of the government's policy on 'talking to terrorists'.

When the Irish Taoiseach, Liam Cosgrave, met Harold Wilson on 5 March 1976, he insisted that the British should not seek dialogue with the paramilitaries to fill the political vacuum within Northern Ireland. If the government was intent on reducing its contact with the constitutional parties, Cosgrave argued, it was essential that this was matched by a refusal to engage with those involved in terrorism. The Irish Prime Minister, though, was rebuffed. According to Garret FitzGerald, Merlyn Rees had insisted that contacts with the IRA and other paramilitaries were 'too valuable to be broken off'. As a result, says FitzGerald, the Irish government 'remained concerned about contacts with Sinn Fein', even after Wilson had left office.[43]

Thanks to the release of British State Papers under the Thirty Year Rule, it is clear that Mason did made an explicit break from this policy. A document from Mason to the Prime Minister, James Callaghan, dated 9 February 1977, outlined the terms of the new departure.

Callaghan, it was noted, had previously agreed to a proposal made by Rees on 29 July 1976, 'that we should distance ourselves from the intermediary we had used in these talks (Contact) and reduce the rate of payment to him'. Thereafter, a deliberate policy was adopted, which left 'Contact to make the running'. The British government restricted its payment to him 'to the minimum necessary'. On 31 December 1976, Contact had received the last of his quarterly payments for that year and Mason now signalled his intention to 'make a clean break with him', because he no longer had any intention of dealing with the IRA. On 30 January 1977, 'Contact' was told that Mason's 'considered opinion' was that his role, 'as an intermediary had ceased to have any relevance and should be brought to an end'. 'Contact' replied that he thought the policy 'mistaken' and said he believed that 'sooner or later we shall have to engage in a further dialogue with the leaders of Provisional Sinn Fein'; nevertheless, 'Contact' accepted the Secretary of State's position.

In addition to the foregoing, Mason also disclosed that he had been

taking discreet steps to close the office at Laneside from which the Political Affairs Division of the NIO (in which the officers in touch with Contact served) operated and to move the Division itself into more normal accommodation on the Stormont Estate.

The rationale for the move, according to Mason, was to restore greater confidence in the government:

closure of the office should have a generally beneficial effect since it is associated in the public mind with the NIO's past talks with paramilitaries on both sides of the community.[44]

In line with this, Mason had pointed to his determination not to engage with the paramilitaries during his meeting with a deputation from the Ballylumford power station in 1977.[45]

Mason ruled out any re-establishment of the channel of communication with the IRA in the future. As he himself put it, 'I do not myself envisage that we shall in future wish to engage in any talks with the leadership of Provisional Sinn Fein, either open or covert'. 'If we did', he concluded, 'I am clear that there would be no shortage of potential intermediaries and that our future needs will not be adversely affected by making a break with Contact now'.[46] This break was deemed by Mason to be essential, in order to give the new security apparatus a chance to make an impact. In keeping with this, the State Papers for the following year confirm that the British rejected what they believed to be yet another 'credible channel of approach by the PIRA', a 'fishing expedition' exploring the chance of further negotiations. In March 1978, with 'the Contact' out of the picture, a new intermediary (with links to Amnesty International) passed a message to the British government, purportedly from the IRA, 'to the effect that it was time to talk and end the present violence'. Callaghan, after consultation with Mason and a senior official at the NIO—who believed the organisation was 'testing the water entirely without any commitment of any sort'—agreed that the intermediary was to be given 'no inclination whatsoever that we are interested in this'.[47]

An overview of the State Papers for this period also suggests that British officials felt they were succeeding against the IRA. The organisation, it was observed, 'maintained their capacity to inflict great damage' with incendiary attacks, but the 'attrition of terrorists' had increased.[48] Moreover, there were signs that the British state had begun to adjust its sights as to what it sought to achieve in its battle with the IRA. Conversations between the Army and the Foreign Office suggested that 'although no level of violence can be regarded as "acceptable", there would always be some violence in Northern Ireland which we should perhaps call "normal"'.[49] In this way, a policy that sought the 'containment' and 'slow defeat' of the IRA, rather than an immediate victory, emerged.

Again, to assume that this was the only dynamic at work in this period would be to oversimplify matters. The reality, as Mason's Under-Secretary Brian Cubbon has since described, was that there was no single narrative dictating the course of events. Rather, events played out in a 'maelstrom' of political circumstances, in which the existence or otherwise of a direct line to the IRA—whether active or not—represented 'about two per cent of the action'.[50] Cubbon's assessment fits neatly with Martin Dillon's 1988 verdict on the conflict—that there was no grand theory but 'numerous pieces to the jigsaw', as well as 'many parts which have not yet been discovered'.[51] That not withstanding, Mason's decisive approach to the IRA challenge helped produce a marked reduction in the levels of violence within Northern Ireland on his watch. The death toll for 1977 was 116—a third lower than that for 1976.[52] The fall in levels of violence might have begun under Mason's predecessor Merlyn Rees, who set the direction of policy; but it was Mason who saw it through to its logical conclusion.

The IRA responds: 'The Long War'

The extent to which the IRA was weakened under first Merlyn Rees and then Roy Mason, forced the organisation to contemplate a major rethink of its own approach. Just as the British state had opted to settle in for the 'long haul', so republicans now sought to do likewise with the shift to a 'Long War' strategy.

Reports from the British Army's Northern Ireland Headquarters and other sources had suggested that a process of re-organisation was already being undertaken during the truce of 1974–5.[53] This process was accelerated after the return to violence towards the end of that year. It was driven by a group of young, militant IRA leaders, drawn predominantly from the urban 'cockpits' of Belfast and Londonderry; foremost among them were allegedly Gerry Adams, Ivor Bell, Brendan Hughes, Martin McGuinness and Brian Keenan. Many of these people had been in prison when the ceasefire had been called and were there-fore untainted by its failure. From this position they launched a wither-ing critique of the IRA leadership that had called the cessation. That leadership was caricatured as southern-dominated (which, in truth, was not the case) and out of touch with realities on the ground in Northern Ireland.[54] At the same time, the IRA's involvement in inter-necine feuding with the 'Official IRA' was highlighted, as was the organisation's part in unashamedly sectarian killings. On both counts the morale and public image of republicanism was held to have been severely damaged. In sum, the truce was deemed to have brought the IRA to the brink of disaster.[55]

What had become clear to the young dissidents was the extent to which the old vistas of 'one last push for victory' were no longer ten-able. For this reason, they argued, republicans needed to commit them-selves to a 'long war' of attrition to break the will of the British government to remain in Ireland. To this end, the IRA now abandoned the effort to maintain a 'people's army' existence, such as it had styled itself during the early 1970s. The 'conveyor belt' security system of the British—whereby arrest was followed in relatively short order by inter-rogation, confession, conviction (at the 'Diplock' Court) and then sentencing—was judged to have shown the unsustainability of such romantic notions. What was required instead, the 'young Turks' claimed, was a more closed, secretive structure—one more akin to the 'classic' terrorist organisation.[56] This 'secret army' was to be based around small cells of radicalised volunteers (Active Service Units).

In an effort to counter the regularity with which IRA members would 'break' under interrogation, much more emphasis was to be placed on indoctrination and anti-interrogation techniques.[57] The organisation's 'Green Book' was created at this time as a 'cross between a political manifesto and training manual', with volunteers required to study it before admission into the IRA.[58]

Within each Active Service Unit, meanwhile, the intention was that only the leader would know the identities of the other members; and he would also be the only person in contact with the higher echelons of the organisation. With regards to the latter, a 'permanent leadership' was to be put in place, divided between a Northern Command (responsible for the 'war zone') and a Southern Command (in charge of logistics and training). This leadership, divorced from actual operations and thereby protected from arrest, was to oversee the 'complete fusing' of the political and military aspects of the IRA's 'struggle'; a struggle that was to be waged relentlessly against the British state until it issued a declaration of intent to withdraw from Ireland. There would be no more ceasefires.[59] The leaner, self-sustaining IRA would instead fight on until it achieved its objective, regardless of the vagaries of community support—though that support was simultaneously to be sought by a revitalised Sinn Fein. Through its engagement in active, everyday politics, the political party would 'republicanise' the people in Catholic-nationalist areas and establish a support network out of which the IRA could operate. A 1977 keynote speech by a senior republican, Jimmy Drumm, at the graveside of the ideological father of Irish republicanism, Wolfe Tone, signalled the new departure:

We find that a successful war of liberation cannot be fought exclusively on the backs of the oppressed in the 6 counties, nor around the physical presence of the British Army... We need a positive tie in with the mass of the Irish people who have little or no idea of the sufferings in the North... We need to make a stand on economic issues and on the everyday struggles of the people.[60]

One republican present on that day has recalled watching the discomfort on the faces of the old republican leadership as these words were read out.[61]

The importance of the IRA securing the support of the people—even as it withdrew from public view—was brought home to the republican proponents of change after an incident in late 1976, when an IRA volunteer inadvertently killed three young children in Belfast. The deaths spawned a movement of civil protest against the continued violence—

the 'Peace People'—that briefly attracted the support of tens of thousands and attained international recognition. Though the moment passed (with the credibility of the 'Peace People' undermined by concerns over the ambitions of its leaders), the episode had demonstrated the danger of IRA volunteers being seen as little more than criminals and gun-men.[62]

In December 1977, the then IRA Chief-of-Staff, Seamus Twomey was arrested by Irish police in Dun Laoghaire near Dublin. A 'Staff Report' that had been produced by IRA GHQ earlier that year was found in his possession. It contained the fullest single explanation of the changes that were by then under way inside the IRA. The report noted:

The three-day and seven-day detention orders are breaking volunteers, and it is the Republican Army's fault for not indoctrinating volunteers with the psychological strength to resist interrogation. Coupled with this factor, which is contributing to our defeat, we are burdened with an inefficient structure of commands, brigades, battalions and companies. This old system with which Brits and Branch are familiar has to be changed… We must emphasise a return to secrecy and strict discipline. Army men must be in control of all sections of the movement. We must gear ourselves towards long-term armed struggle based on putting unknown men and new recruits into a new structure. This new structure shall be a cell system… Sinn Fein should come under Army organisers at all levels… Sinn Fein should be radicalised (under Army direction) and should agitate about social and economic issues which attack the welfare of the people… It gains the respect of the people which in turn leads to increased support for the cell.[63]

In the years that followed the 1974–5 ceasefire, the young northerners advocating this 'long war' strategy slowly established their control over the IRA. And as they convinced people of the merits of their arguments, the character of the organisation changed. A leaked intelligence report by the British Army's Brigadier James Glover, in November 1978, confirmed that the authorities were aware of the shift. In his memorandum Glover noted that:

PIRA's organisation is now such that a small number of activists can maintain a disproportionate level of violence. …Our evidence of the calibre of rank and file terrorists does not support the view that they are merely mindless hooligans drawn from the unemployed and unemployable. PIRA now trains and uses its members with some care. The active service units are for the most part manned by terrorists tempered by up to ten-years operational experience… They are continually learning from their mistakes and developing their expertise. We can therefore expect to see increased professionalism and the greater exploitation of modern technology for terrorist purposes.[64]

Unsurprisingly, when Sinn Fein got hold of a copy of this internal Army report, it jubilantly published it in full in its newspaper, *Republican News*.[65] It seemed to confirm the success of the movement's reorganisation.

Nonetheless, almost inevitably, many aspects of the grandiose plans for the rejuvenation of the IRA's campaign were not realised. The late seventies saw Sinn Fein make little headway in its effort to make 'active republicanism' a popular political force. On the military side, meanwhile, the notion of discrete, unidentifiable 'Active Service Units' continued to belong to the realm of theory. In many rural areas, such as south Armagh, the new structures were simply not implemented. Even in urban environments, the close-knit nature of Catholic communities made it impossible for IRA members to remain anonymous. Moreover, of more serious concern for the republican leadership was the fact that the new formation actually made it easier for the British authorities to concentrate their resources against the smaller, ultimately more manageable, IRA. In this regard, the changes, while possibly saving the IRA from the perilous position in which it found itself after 1975, were also a tacit admission of weakness on the part of republicans. Over time this weakness would resurface in insurmountable form.

Borders and Statecraft: Anglo-Irish Relations

In developing an 'internal security strategy', the British government was, to some extent, demonstrating a willingness to 'go it alone' on Northern Ireland. Such unilateralism was born of the realisation that the Republic of Ireland was not necessarily—at that time—the most reliable of partners. Successive British governments had, since the start of the Troubles, been uneasy with the IRA's capacity to utilize cross-border routes, both as lines of supply for attacks in Northern Ireland and as means of escape in the aftermath of operations. There was a perception in London that the IRA was afforded an undue degree of freedom within the Republic of Ireland's territory. The assumption was that an Irish government, ruling over a state that was itself born out of an IRA insurgency against British rule (in 1919–21) and which continued to hold a territorial claim on Northern Ireland (as embodied in articles two and three of the country's constitution) found it ideologically difficult to challenge whole-heartedly an IRA that held to an analogous creed.

For its own part, the IRA's calculation had long been that it was best to avoid full-scale confrontation with the Irish authorities. As a result, the organisation's General Order No. 8, which forbade military action 'against 26 County forces under any circumstances whatsoever' was, for the most part, strictly enforced. The IRA sought to cultivate a 'sneaking regard' among a section of the Irish people, for its campaign against British rule in Northern Ireland, on the grounds that it was fighting the 'unfinished revolution' of fifty years earlier. Much to the disquiet of successive British governments, there were fears that in this respect, the organisation had enjoyed some success. While both the Irish government and the vast majority of the Irish population were a long way from actively supporting the IRA campaign, the British felt that their opposition was not all it might have been. There was, for instance, no question of British security forces being allowed to cross the border in pursuit of IRA activists. This possibility was judged to be too awkward domestically for the Irish government, as the SAS debacle of 1976 had proved.[66] The British were thus forced to look to the Irish themselves to deal with the IRA threat—though, initially at least, they had little confidence that this would be done with the necessary rigour.

Cracks in the Anglo-Irish relationship had already been visible in the aftermath of the introduction of internment in 1971–2, when the Irish government had drifted towards a more stridently pro-Irish unity stance. This had continued during the Sunningdale process, despite the fact that the Irish authorities were co-authors of the Agreement. Sunningdale's provision of an 'Irish Dimension' to sooth nationalist concerns had not been matched by an unambiguous acceptance of the principle of consent by the Irish government. In January 1974, the British Prime Minister, Edward Heath, had complained that Irish ministers seemed to be giving the impression that Northern Ireland 'was now part of the Republic'.[67] Later, Merlyn Rees, after becoming Northern Irish Secretary of State in the Labour government that replaced Heath's Conservative administration, was also critical of the Republic's 'wishful thinking' on this issue.[68]

The endurance of this Anglo-Irish divergence was somewhat surprising given that the Irish government of the mid-1970s appeared, at first glance, to be predisposed to a better relationship with its British neighbour. The Fine Gael-Labour coalition headed by Liam Cosgrave that won the February 1973 Irish General Election seemed far more receptive to British concerns than its Fianna Fail predecessor—the latter traditionally associated with a more vehement anti-British policy. Notably, the coalition contained the Labour politician and leading Irish intellectual, Conor Cruise O'Brien, who was known for his articulate and relentless attacks on the IRA. Other reasons for long-term optimism included the UK and Ireland's common entry into the European Economic Community (EEC) on 1 January 1973. Henceforth it seemed inevitable that the two states would forge ever closer ties as the 'two parts of Ireland and Britain were all moving forward into a new relationship'.[69]

It was perhaps because of these factors that some within the permanent British state claimed to detect a shift in the approach of the Irish government. By the mid-1970s, the British government was willing to acknowledge that since 1972, there had been some improvement in security cooperation, including a willingness to consider reciprocal legislation and greater co-ordination between Gardai and the RUC. Admittedly, such developments were held to have been 'stimulated by fear that the situation in the North might get out of control or that violence on a large scale might be imported into the south'. But they were judged no less significant for that. Cabinet Committee papers from the period reflect an awareness of the fact that while popular attitudes towards cooperation with the British remained 'ambivalent' in Ireland, the position of the Coalition government was one of 'unambiguous hostility towards terrorism'.[70] Furthermore, there was a belief in some quarters that the Republic was showing signs of a 'psychological retreat from unification as a practical goal'.[71]

At the same time, however, the Fine Gael-Labour coalition government in Dublin was perceived to be acutely weak domestically. On this basis, questions were raised within the British government as to its viability, as a long-term partner for peace. 'One has to be careful when speaking of Southern Irish opinion to distinguish the government from the people as a whole', warned one British official in the summer of 1975, 'especially as at the moment the Government scarcely represents even a parliamentary, let alone a popular majority'.[72] Compounding this problem were the serious economic difficulties then facing the Irish state. 'For the moment', advised a Foreign Office briefing for the Cabinet Committee on Northern Ireland in July 1975, 'the Irish government have enough internal problems on their own hands—notably, in attempting to deal with even more massive inflation and unemployment than we ourselves are suffering'.[73]

For its own part, the Republic's government was far from oblivious to British anxieties as to its position. On the contrary, it was hugely sensitive to allegations that Irish cooperation on security issues was half-hearted or below par. In his memoirs, Garret FitzGerald, Irish Minister for Foreign Affairs in the mid-1970s, made a point of defending his government's record on security cooperation. In particular, he argued that only 3% of the terrorist incidents that took place north of the border had a connection with the south. He also pointed to Irish legislative innovations to combat terrorism, such as the Criminal Law (Jurisdiction) Act, which came into being at the end of May 1976. The whole purpose of this measure, according to FitzGerald, was that it should be used 'to put away any IRA men in the south'.[74]

Such encouraging developments as there were, however, were over-shadowed by evidence that the IRA continued to derive advantage from its southern Irish logistical base. In January 1976, for example, Reports from the British Embassy in Dublin recorded that Irish police had uncovered how two factories in County Cavan were being used by the IRA 'out-of-hours' to manufacture 'potentially hundreds of missiles'. What was 'particularly embarrassing for the Irish authorities' on this occasion was that one of the factories had actually been set up under the sponsorship of the Irish Industrial Training Authority.[75]

While this kind of episode clearly caused discomfort for the Irish government, the situation was exacerbated immeasurably by the assassination of the British Ambassador in Dublin, Christopher Ewart-Biggs, on 21 July 1976. The Ambassador was killed along with a twenty-six year old civil servant, Judith Cook, as his official car hit an IRA landmine near his residence—an operation widely held to be the handiwork of the senior militant, Brian Keenan.[76] Further disaster was only narrowly avoided: the British Secretary of State, Merlyn Rees, would also have been in the car had a late vote in the House of Commons not detained him in London that day.[77] The driver, Brian O'Driscoll and Brian Cubbon, the Permanent Under Secretary of State at the NIO, were also in the car, but survived with injuries.

Nevertheless, the murder of Ewart-Biggs did prove to be something of a turning point. Brian Cubbon describes how he received a moving letter from Garret FitzGerald as he recovered after the attack, stating that they were engaged in a fight against a 'common foe'.[78] And soon after the Ambassador's death, some British officials concluded that the best response to the killing was to use it as an opportunity 'for pressing the Irish to improve their performance in security and associated fields' and to call for a new initiative 'on the information side, possibly jointly in some measure with the Irish Authorities, and particularly in the Republic and the US, to bring home to people the true nature of the terrorist threat'.[79] By the end of August 1976, there had been a break-through in the effort to agree a common security package. The Irish now promised to push through new legislation that included tougher sentences for terrorist-related offences (such as possession of firearms and explosives). Dublin also pledged to introduce extended powers of detention, more in line with the British authorities' ability to hold sus-pects for seven days, as established by the 1974 Prevention of Terror-ism Act. The eventual Irish bill actually went further than the existing British law in that it allowed the detention of those suspected of assist-ing terrorist activities, rather than being solely applicable to those directly involved in them.

In spite of this, the British government still continued to express reservations about the shortcomings of their Irish counterparts on security matters. It was alleged that the Dublin government was relying upon evidence of ongoing violence in Northern Ireland in order to justify the new measures, rather than making an all-encompassing case against the IRA. It was felt that the immediate stimulant for the secu-rity package was the murder of a British Ambassador on Irish soil— but this was being ignored.The Dublin government was thus judged to be 'sheltering behind [British] misfortunes as the excuse for introduc-ing legislation which they need in the South to defeat a common enemy'.[80] The fact that the British were later concerned about whether or not the suitcases of Ewart-Biggs and Cubbon had been tampered with by the Irish security services after the IRA's attack reveals much about the continually fractious nature of the inter-governmental relationship.[81]

That there was still much to be done was made plain during discus-sions of the Cabinet Committee on Northern Ireland in late 1976, which concluded that in spite of the new Irish legislation, 'there had been no significant change in the extent of cross-border cooperation with the Irish government on security matters'. The situation was described as follows:

The Irish continued to display much willingness in principle to co-operate. But they were often also reluctant to accept the need for improvement in present arrangements; in practice co-operation tended to go only so far as the Irish thought necessary on a strict interpretation of their own interests; and its effectiveness depended on the outlook of local Garda commanders.[82]

A security assessment of the Republic of Ireland from the same period underlined the enduring tensions between the two states. 'Because of the complex-ridden relationship between Britain and Ireland', it was argued, 'there are some areas of security activity about which we are well-informed but others about which the Irish are particularly cagey with us'. It was acknowledged that 'economic, geographic and personal links' between the two states remained very close, but it was also noted that the relationship was 'complicated by keen if distorted memories of Irish history, by Irish concerns to assert their independence against an over-influential neighbour, and by the problem of Northern Ireland'. The goal of reunification was said to be little more than 'a pious hope' for the majority of the Irish people, but it was also conceded that on this matter 'extreme Republicans can exploit the vein of ambivalence in a large section of the Irish population'. In sum, the document pointed to a 'friendly disposition towards the British people as individuals', among the Irish, coupled with a continuing 'extreme sensitivity towards HMG, and, above all towards the British army'.[83]

Thereafter, despite the victory of Fianna Fail in the 1977 Irish General Election, British analysts of the Irish state argued that there was 'a fair chance' that the new Taoiseach, Jack Lynch, would have 'a free hand to operate pragmatically in the immediate and short-term', provided that he simultaneously retained a rhetorical commitment to Irish unity.[84] Nonetheless, the cool nature of the British state's overall relationship with the Republic of Ireland in 1977 was made evident in the fact that the British said they were prepared to 'discuss' some issues with the Republic, 'rather than... consult them' on the formation of policy.[85]

Thatcher and Haughey: First Openings and Another Failure for Devolution

27 August 1979 proved to be one of the bloodiest days in Northern Ireland's thirty year conflict. First, Lord Louis Mountbatten (the Queen's cousin and the man who had overseen the transition to independence in the Indian sub-continent) was killed along with three others by a booby-trap bomb on his boat, as it sailed into Donegal Bay,

near County Sligo. Hours later, the British Army suffered its worst ever loss in a single attack when eighteen soldiers (drawn from the Parachute Regiment and the Queen's Own Highlanders) were killed by two huge bombs near Warrenpoint, County Down. At Warrenpoint, the devices had been staggered to detonate one after another and those who had laid the bombs had predicted with brutal accuracy where the soldiers who survived the first explosion would run for cover. No sooner were they entrenched in their would-be 'shelter' than the second blast occurred, with devastating results.

For the IRA, the events of that day represented a mighty blow against their enemies in the British security forces. The former republican prisoner, Anthony McIntyre, has recalled the effect of the news on the wings of the Maze prison, where the majority of the IRA's incarcerated members were held. According to McIntyre, he and a fellow prisoner were puzzled by the decision to target Mountbatten who 'didn't strike us as a senior figure in the "British war machine"'; yet there was no such emotional ambivalence as far as the soldiers were concerned—particularly the 'Paras':

Our comrades had delivered a blow to the most murderous regiment to visit Ireland since the Black 'n Tans. We were delirious with joy. Seven years earlier the Paras had visited a war crime on an unsuspecting civilian population. Now it was pay back time. It seemed then we were unstoppable—our day had come.[86]

Within British establishment circles, by contrast, news of that day's events brought dismay and consternation. A particular cause for concern was the unavoidable truth that the territory of the Republic of Ireland had again proven integral to an IRA attack. In the case of Mountbatten this was self-evident—he had been in Irish territorial waters on his annual holiday to the country. At Warrenpoint too there had been an extra-territorial dimension. Immediately following the explosions, the surviving soldiers had come under heavy fire from IRA men positioned across Carlingford Lough, also in the Irish Republic. Furthermore, subsequent investigations revealed that the bombs themselves had been detonated from the Irish side of the Lough. Thus, for the newly elected Conservative government of Margaret Thatcher, the Warrenpoint and Mountbatten attacks confirmed the failure of British efforts hitherto to achieve rigorous and effective security co-operation with their Irish neighbours.

The response of the incoming Thatcher administration to this stark reality was complicated by the fact that Airey Neave, the man to whom Thatcher had previously turned on all Northern Irish issues, had himself been killed on 30 March 1979. Neave, who had earned a reputation as an anti-devolutionist, who favoured a robust security policy and the closer integration of Northern Ireland with the UK, was killed by an Irish National Liberation Army (INLA) car bomb, as he drove out of Westminster. Deprived of the man who would almost certainly have been the new Secretary of State for Northern Ireland, the Prime Minister had appointed a relative unknown to the position: Humphrey Atkins, or 'Humphrey Who?' as one newspaper headline greeted him in Northern Ireland.[87] While Atkins was not regarded as a great adherent to the Neave vision, the Conservative Party election manifesto for the May 1979 General Election did indicate a continued preference against devolutionist experiments.[88]

Soon, however, Atkins made the decision to depart from Roy Mason's approach of the previous three years. The new Secretary of State was of the opinion that a fresh attempt to achieve a devolutionary settlement to the conflict was what was required; a belief partly encouraged by the international pressure on Britain over Northern Ireland. The latter was something that the SDLP, increasingly under the influence of John Hume, had sought to foment ever since the collapse of Sunningdale. Hume had become deeply disillusioned with prospects for an 'internal settlement'. An ardent critic of Mason's decision to adopt a joint security and economic focus, to the detriment of the search for a political solution, Hume sought the internationalisation of the Northern Irish conflict, believing that outside intervention could open up new possibilities—not in terms of British withdrawal as traditionally conceived, but through a recasting of Anglo-Irish relations.[89] He had particularly concentrated his efforts on the United States, working alongside the Irish government's Department of Foreign Affairs to cultivate powerful allies within Irish-America. Their aims were two-fold: to reduce support for the IRA (as expressed through such groups as NORAID, which provided a steady stream of funds to republican coffers from its inception in 1969); and to boost the influence of constitutional nationalism. With regards to the latter, they scored a spectacular success with the decision of the US State Department to halt a shipment of handguns to the RUC, in protest at the 1979 Bennett Report (which found evidence that some prisoners had been ill-treated at police interrogation centres in Northern Ireland). The move—an extraordinary expression of US disapproval for British policy—came after a high profile campaign led by the 'Four

Horsemen' of Irish America: 'Tip' O'Neill, then Speaker of the House of Representatives, Senator Edward Kennedy, Senator Daniel Moynihan and Hugh Carey, then Governor of New York. It seemed to confirm the growing importance and authority of the Irish diaspora in the United States.[90] Senior figures within that diaspora clearly agreed with Hume's analysis that a renewed search for a political solution in Northern Ireland was required. Two years earlier, in August 1977, the 'Four Horsemen' had successfully persuaded President Jimmy Carter to deliver a statement in which he promised US government assistance to Northern Ireland in the event that a political settlement was reached.[91] In the years that followed, the Americans continued to be outspoken in their criticism of what they saw as the British government's refusal to pursue actively a resolution.[92]

The result of this pressure—and Thatcher's own developing sense that 'security could [not] be disentangled from wider political issues'—was Atkins's new devolutionary initiative.[93] In October 1979, the Secretary of State announced that he would convene a conference between the main parties in Northern Ireland to discuss a possible way forward. Significantly, the venue for Atkins' announcement was the Association of American Correspondents in London, an indication of the conscious appeal to a transatlantic audience.[94] Yet, the initiative was beset by difficulties from the start. The government White Paper discounted any discussion of an 'Irish dimension', which immediately provoked uncertainty as to whether the SDLP would participate. Amid internal divisions, the party's leader, Gerry Fitt (who wished to take part) resigned, to be replaced by the more 'green' John Hume (who opposed involvement under the stated conditions).[95] As a result, Atkins was forced to pull back from the outright exclusion of the Irish dimension—a move which persuaded the SDLP to play a part in discussions. Even then, prospects for success looked bleak because the Official Unionist Party, led by James Molyneaux, refused to join in. Molyneaux had succeeded Harry West as party leader in 1979 and was an avowed integrationist. Through his friendship with Airey Neave he had hoped to see Northern Ireland assimilated more closely into the United Kingdom; and even after Neave's death he believed the government might steer such a course. For this reason, he denounced the Atkins conference as a 'gimmick' and eschewed participation—in the hope that its failure would encourage the government down an integrationist path.[96] Interestingly, the smaller unionist party—Ian Paisley's more devolutionist DUP—did not share Molyneaux's reservations and participated in the talks that began in January 1980. Despite this, few held out much hope that these talks would achieve anything and there was little surprise when the conference was officially terminated in November 1980.

The collapse of this latest effort to reconstitute devolved government for Northern Ireland prompted a re-think on the part of Thatcher—but not in the way that James Molyneaux had hoped. In light of the failure of the parties to reach a consensus on the way forward she increasingly looked to a fresh approach, which would operate 'over the heads' of the fractious local politicians. This perception dove-tailed with the belief that there needed to be a new drive to engage the Irish Republic in security co-operation against the IRA, with the result that the British government now sought to build closer relations with the Irish state.

In this endeavour too there were obstacles. Not least in this regard was the fact that the Fine Gael-Labour coalition government had been defeated at the June 1977 Irish General Election. The return to power of Fianna Fail—the party that espoused a more traditional brand of Irish nationalism—scarcely seemed to augur well for those seeking to draw the British and Irish states closer together. This was particularly so after Jack Lynch resigned as the leader of Fianna Fail and Taoiscach in December 1979, to be replaced by the apparently more radical figure of Charles Haughey. A key dimension of the flamboyant Haughey's appeal to his party's grass-roots had been his willingness to articulate an uncompromising nationalist line in relation to Northern Ireland. Moreover, his credentials on the issue were strengthened by the fact he had earlier been sacked by Lynch as Minister for Finance in May 1970, because of his alleged role in trafficking arms north of the border to support the IRA (though at a subsequent trial, Haughey and his fellow accused were found not guilty).[97] Thereafter, Haughey had maintained a rhetorical commitment to the cause of irredentist Irish nationalism.

Neither was it just the rhetoric on the Irish side of the border that seemed to offer little encouragement for a warming of ties between the Irish and British states. Haughey's apparently unreconstructed approach was mirrored by Thatcher's strident reassertion of British national pride and support for the Union. Allied to this was her resolute opposition to Irish involvement in the affairs of Northern Ireland. As she declared to the House of Commons in May 1980, 'The future of the constitutional affairs of Northern Ireland is a matter for the people of Northern Ireland, this government and this parliament and no one else'.[98]

In spite of this less than promising background, though, Thatcher and Haughey came together in the aftermath of the failed Atkins conference to usher in a new departure in Anglo-Irish relations. A first meeting between the two leaders in May 1980 in London had already heralded a warming between the two sides. A statement released subsequently had promised 'new and closer political co-operation between the two governments' on the issue of Northern Ireland and referred to the 'unique relationship' between the two countries.[99] Then, in December 1980, Thatcher and Haughey met for a return summit in Dublin. This was later hailed as 'historic' because of the changing atmosphere it appeared to demonstrate, with Thatcher becoming the first British Prime Minister to visit Dublin since partition. In the wake of the summit, the two governments commissioned studies by a joint Anglo-Irish Committee to examine 'possible new institutional structures, citizenship rights, security matters, economic co-operation and measures to encourage mutual understanding'. The two Prime Ministers agreed to devote their next meeting to 'special consideration of the totality of relationships within these islands'.[100]

In the event, the new dispensation proved short-lived. Even as the Thatcher-Haughey summits were being held, events 'on the ground' in Northern Ireland were developing in such a way as to transform the political horizon. Decisive here, was the decision of republican inmates in the Maze prison to go on hunger strike in their effort to secure *de facto* 'political status', after its withdrawal by Rees. Not only did this subject the new Anglo-Irish *entente cordiale* to fresh strain, but it also inaugurated fresh contact between the British government and its Irish republican adversaries.

The Hunger Strikes: Talking to Terrorists II

From the moment of its inception, the government's criminalisation policy, with regard to convicted republican prisoners, had met with fierce opposition. The first man to be sentenced under the new approach in September 1976, Ciaran Nugent, had refused to wear the designated prisoners' uniform—arguing that he was a political prisoner and as such, entitled to wear his own clothes.[101] Famously, Nugent was reputed to have declared, 'If they want me to wear a uniform, they'll have to nail it on my back'.[102] In place of the requisite clothing, Nugent was simply given a blanket to wrap around his body; in so doing, he launched the 'blanket protest' against criminalisation. In the years that followed, hundreds of other republican prisoners followed Nugent's lead. At the same time, the campaign against the penal system escalated, both inside and outside the prisons. From the spring of 1976, the IRA began targeting prison warders; eighteen were killed over the following four years.[103]

Ironically, in 1977, some hope was expressed by the Cabinet Committee on Northern Ireland that the problems over special category status had 'probably been overcome'.[104] In reality, however, the crisis was only just beginning. Within the jails, the 'blanket protest' had, by the middle of 1978, evolved into both a 'no wash' and then 'dirty' protest. The latter, arising out of the refusal of republican prisoners to leave their cells, which in turn meant that the warders refused to clean them, saw piles of faeces build up within the small rooms. This was then smeared on the walls by the inmates in an effort to breakdown the smell.[105] Despite such extreme measures—and the publicity they generated (with prominent figures like the Catholic Archbishop of Armagh, Tomas O Fiaich, decrying prison conditions)—the prisoners were unable to shift government policy.[106] Thus, by the summer of 1980, the IRA leadership inside the Maze had decided to adopt the most radical instrument available to them: a hunger strike. This began in late October 1980, when seven republican prisoners, led by the IRA's OC in the prison, Brendan Hughes, refused food and demanded the implementation of 'five demands':

1. The right not to wear prison uniform.
2. The right not to do prison work.
3. The right to associate freely with other prisoners.
4. The right to a weekly visit, letter and parcel and the right to organize educational and recreational pursuits.
5. Full restoration of remission lost through the protest.[107]

Taken together, the demands, if accepted, would have amounted to the recognition of 'political status' by the British government.

The immediate British response to the hunger strike was one of blunt intransigence. Thatcher declared: 'I want this to be utterly clear— the government will never concede political status to the hunger strikers or to any others convicted of criminal offences'.[108] This position continued to be articulated by the goverment thereafter. On 4 December 1980, for instance, Atkins delivered a statement to the House of Commons in which he again insisted there could be no concessions.[109]

Nevertheless, there was evidence that the hunger strike was winning support for the republican cause within nationalist Ireland. Where once the campaign for political status had gained the backing of only a few hundred people, thousands were now turning out to support the hunger strikers.[110] The image of self-sacrifice had tapped into the deepest well-springs of Catholic-nationalist consciousness. An appeal which evoked Catholic martyrology had appeared to confirm the veracity of the celebrated maxim of Terence McSwiney, a member of the original Sinn Fein, who had died on hunger strike earlier in the century: 'It is not those who can inflict the most, but those who suffer the most who will conquer'.[111]

In the face of the mounting crisis in mid-December 1980, the British government was presented with an avenue that appeared to offer a way out. Brendan Duddy—the 'Contact'—re-activated his channel of communication with Michael Oatley and suggested that the IRA leadership might be willing to accept a compromise settlement.[112] As per the most recent account, Oatley in turn contacted the Permanent Secretary of the NIO and informed him that a resolution to the dispute might be possible. This message was then passed on to the Prime Minister and, notwithstanding her hard-line public stance, Thatcher approved the dispatch of Oatley to Belfast with an offer of a deal on 18 December.[113] In the meantime, an outline of the proposed compact was given to the IRA's prison leadership, which was placed under added pressure by the fact that one of the hunger strikers—Sean McKenna—was close to death. In the words of Leo Green, one of the hunger strikers,

As I remember, it was an explanation that what we had set out to achieve in terms of the Five Demands would become available. In terms of the actual wording, I don't remember, but I certainly believed that it meant that we would have been allowed to wear our own clothes and there would have been no more compulsion to do prison work.[114]

On this basis, the decision was taken to end the hunger strike, without the prisoners having seen the actual document containing the offer from the British government. As it turned out, that document proved to be extremely vague. The new OC of IRA prisoners inside the Maze prison, Bobby Sands (who had taken over from Brendan Hughes when

Hughes went on hunger strike) was reported to have described it as containing 'absolutely nothing concrete'.[115] And after the initial euphoria had passed, during which many prisoners felt they had achieved victory, a sense of betrayal set in. In particular, the continued denial of the demand that prisoners should be free to wear their own clothes was bitterly resented. This was taken to be symbolic of the authorities' enduring desire to stigmatise IRA prisoners as 'ordinary' criminals. For this reason, a further hunger strike became all but inevitable.

By taking the decision to launch a second hunger strike, the prisoners involved and the wider republican leadership were under no illusions about the likely outcome. According to Richard O'Rawe, a senior IRA prisoner who served as the hunger strikers' Public Relations Officer (PRO) during the second protest, Gerry Adams had offered a stark assessment of the prisoners' prospects for success, even prior to the first hunger strike: 'Margaret Thatcher, the British Prime Minister, would definitely let men die'.[116] If that had been the case then, there was little reason to doubt that it would have changed in the interval. O'Rawe also claims that the man who would lead the second hunger strike, Bobby Sands, was only too aware of this.[117]

On 1 March 1981, Bobby Sands commenced the second, ultimately fatal, hunger strike by republicans in the Maze prison. Unlike the previous occasion, there was no use of 'block' tactics, whereby a group of prisoners began the process simultaneously. Instead, they joined the protest one-by-one, with Sands followed after a couple of weeks' interval by the next man, thus establishing the sequence. The attitude of Sands and his fellow hunger strikers was unyielding. After the confusion surrounding the collapse of the first hunger strike their approach was simple: victory, or death. For Sands, and nine other prisoners, their fate was the latter. But not before they had generated a political earthquake. On 5 March 1981, the independent nationalist MP for Fermanagh-South Tyrone, Frank Maguire, had died. In the subsequent by-election, other nationalist candidates were persuaded to stand aside in favour of Sands, who then defeated the Official Unionist Party candidate, Harry West, by 30,492 votes to 29,046, on an 87% turnout.[118] It was a truly startling victory for republicans that vividly captured the mobilisation of nationalist Ireland behind the hunger strikers. Neither was it an isolated event. In June 1981, two other republican prisoners, Kieran Doherty (who was also on hunger strike) and Paddy Agnew (who was not) were elected in the Irish General Election—victories that helped deprive Charles Haughey of a Dáil majority.[119] The notion that Sands and other IRA prisoners could be dismissed as 'mere' criminals appeared harder than ever to substantiate when set against the background of such electoral triumphs, notwithstanding Thatcher's continued assertion that 'Crime is crime is crime, it's not political'.[120]

Sands' death on 5 May 1981 unleashed an outpouring of anger and indignation across nationalist Ireland. While Thatcher informed the House of Commons that, 'Mr Sands was a convicted criminal. He chose to take his own life', black flags were hung in predominantly Catholic-nationalist towns in Northern Ireland and an estimated 100,000 people attended his funeral.[121] In the days and months that followed, the province was convulsed by riots as people who would not normally have supported the IRA protested the apparent willingness of Thatcher to 'let' the hunger strikers die. For her part, meanwhile, the Prime Minister declared that, 'Faced with the failure of their discredited cause, the men of violence have chosen in recent months to play what may well be their last card'.[122]

After four men had died on the strike (Sands, Francis Hughes, Raymond McCreesh and Patsy O'Hara), the Dublin-based Irish Commission for Justice and Peace (ICJP) had attempted to act as a mediator between the prisoners and officials at the NIO. This was followed by a statement from the IRA leadership inside the Maze on 4 July 1981, which set out their position in rather more conciliatory tones than had previously been the case.[123] As indicated by Richard O'Rawe, this emollient statement was a product of desperation on the part of the hunger strikers, who feared that the British would simply not move. Moreover, O'Rawe and the IRA's prison OC, Bik McFarlane—the men responsible for running the protest—had previously decided that if the British had shown no sign of movement after the first four deaths then they would halt the strike, before a fifth man died.[124] As that fifth man, Joe McDonnell, approached death at the end of June-start of July, McFarlane was apparently readying himself to call off the protest. In a communication ('comm') with the IRA leadership outside the jail on 28 June, he said he was giving 'consideration to terminating the hunger strike and salvaging something from Brit concessions'.[125] A further 'comm' confirmed this:

we should seek a way out of this situation, saving lives and as much face as possible. If it doesn't appear that the Brits will be forthcoming with a feasible settlement, then we should get in before public opinion swings against us, forcing us to halt after say six or seven deaths, which would be a disaster.[126]

It was this growing pessimism that formed the background to the 4 July statement; British intransigence had forced the prisoners to contemplate the unilateral termination of the hunger strike.

It was at this moment, however, that the British government, for all its uncompromising rhetoric, again showed itself ready to engage in behind-the-scenes negotiations to try and end the hunger strike. Peter Taylor claims that, in the aftermath of the prisoners' 4 July statement, 'the Contact'—now known to be Brendan Duddy—reopened a line of communication with the British government; though according to Taylor, 'The Contact [Duddy] presumably dealt with another British official as it seems that Michael Oatley was out of the country'.[127] This latter information is somewhat contradicted by the account of Richard O'Rawe, who claims to have been told that the 'Mountain Climber' was involved (the 'Mountain Climber' being Oatley's *nom de guerre*).[128] Whatever the identities of the people involved, the result was that an offer was made to the IRA by the British authorities and Danny Morrison was allowed into the prison to explain it to the hunger-strikers. By Taylor's account:

The government was prepared to issue a public statement outlining agreed concessions, on the understanding that it would bring an immediate end to the hunger strike: all prisoners in the North would be allowed to wear their own clothes, regardless of the nature of their offences; visits and other such privileges would be agreed; prison 'work' would be fudged; and there was a vague offer to restore a proportion of lost remission.[129]

This, it would seem, was acceptable to the prisoners. But, according to O'Rawe, the IRA leadership outside the prison decided to reject the deal and instead hold out for a second offer. This 'dangerous game' of 'brinkmanship' failed, though, when Joe McDonnell died earlier than anticipated on 8 July 1981.[130] Five days later, Martin Hurson became the sixth man to die in the protest. O'Rawe maintains that responsibility for the deaths of these two men lay with 'the outside leadership [that]...took the decision to play brinkmanship with Joe McDonnell's life'.[131]

In spite of these latest deaths, one final attempt was made to negotiate an end to the protest. Peter Taylor claims that the IRA leadership was sent a lengthy message by the government on 17 July 1981, which proposed that a 'genuinely "new" regime' would be established in the prisons after the end of the strike.[132] O'Rawe reports a similar offer, but claims it was received a couple of days later.[133] Either way, the terms of the deal again fell short of what the hunger strikers required—particularly on the issues of work and freedom of association—and consequently, it was rejected.

Ultimately, the hunger strike was brought to an end through the efforts of Father Denis Faul, a Catholic priest and known critic of the IRA. Faul by-passed the IRA leadership and the organisation's prison hierarchy and instead looked to the families of the hunger strikers to bring the protest to a conclusion. With no end in sight and only more death on the horizon, his arguments eventually prevailed. In late July, the mother of Paddy Quinn intervened to save her son's life after he had slipped into a coma. Others followed suit and on 3 October 1981 the hunger strike was finally called off altogether.

On the face of it, the prisoners had been defeated. Two days later, the new Secretary of State for Northern Ireland, James Prior (who the previous month had replaced Humprey Atkins in the post) announced several concessions, but these fell some way short of the full 'five demands'. Nevertheless, as with the introduction of internment a decade earlier, the most significant consequences of the hunger strikes lay in the political realm; here, the balance sheet for the republican movement looked far less negative. The wave of emotion that had attended the death of ten IRA and INLA prisoners had allowed Sinn Fein to secure its first Westminster MP in the modern era. After the death of Bobby Sands, his election agent, Owen Carron, had run for the vacant seat and won it in August 1981, on an increased majority.[134] Carron's success would scarcely have been possible, but for the fact that the hunger strike was still ongoing at the time of the by-election. Indeed, it is this fact that has led Richard O'Rawe to suggest that this was the real reason the IRA leadership rejected the deals put forward by the British government to end the hunger strike in July 1981.[135] It is a highly controversial suggestion and one that has been dismissed by many, including O'Rawe's immediate superior during the 1981 hunger strike, Brendan McFarlane.[136] Whatever the truth of such claims, what can be said with certainty is that the hunger strikes sustained the entry of Sinn Fein into modern, electoral politics in the years that followed. What is more, the communal response of Catholic-nationalists also reflected the growing polarisation between the two communities in Northern Ireland. In this context, the level of violence within the province climbed once more, with 117 deaths during 1981, as compared with 86 the previous year.[137] And against this backdrop, hopes for a solution to Northern Ireland's 'Troubles' seemed more remote than ever.

Towards the Anglo-Irish Agreement, 1981–5

In the face of the turbulence that accompanied the hunger strikes, the Irish Taoiseach Charles Haughey had re-embraced a more recognisably 'republican' brand of rhetoric. Whether this was out of conviction, or political expediency is a moot point. But this tougher rhetoric was particularly evident after his decision to call a General Election for June 1981, which, after the election of two republican prisoners, brought the fall of his government and its replacement by a new Fine Gael-Labour coalition administration under Garret FitzGerald. Unsurprisingly, Haughey was vocal in blaming Thatcher's 'intransigence' for his defeat. When he then returned to power for nine months in February 1982 at the head of a Fianna Fail minority administration (after the collapse of the coalition government over a budgetary dispute), he showed little of his previous willingness to soften his position on Northern Ireland. Indeed, Haughey instead invited the prominent SDLP politician, Seamus Mallon, to join the upper chamber of the Irish parliament, the Seanad, in a clear nod towards the creation of 'all-Ireland' structures. He also appeared anxious to bolster his anti-British credentials, adopting a neutral stance and refusing to support the European Union's sanctions on Argentina during the Falklands War of 1982.[138]

It was perhaps because of this recrudescence of unreconstructed Irish nationalism in Dublin that Margaret Thatcher acquiesced in another tilt at achieving devolution within Northern Ireland. James Prior had viewed his appointment as Secretary of State for Northern Ireland as something of a snub from a Prime Minister who disagreed with his more patrician 'wet' Toryism: 'She wanted to get rid of me from London, I think'.[139] Nevertheless, he resolved to try to bring things forward and took great interest in a proposal that originated with the Conservative Party's backbench Northern Ireland committee. This looked towards a mechanism of 'rolling devolution'. Under this scheme, a Northern Ireland assembly was to be elected which would, initially, have merely a scrutinising role, holding civil servants to account. At the same time, it was also to act as a forum for constitutional discussion. If it could generate 'cross-community' consensus on the need for certain powers to be devolved to the assembly, then Prior undertook to transfer the powers in question. The formula was simple. In the words of one study: 'the greater the agreement, the more power would be transferred'.[140] Once more, though, the absence of support for the project effectively guaranteed that it was a stillborn initiative. The Prime Minister herself was less than enthused by the proposals; by Prior's own admission she had let it be known that she thought the endeavour worthless.[141] She also admitted to the strongly unionist MP Ian Gow, a close advisor, that she thought the policy 'rotten'.[142] Within Northern Ireland, meanwhile, the SDLP refused to participate in the assembly when it was convened in October 1982—thereby removing the possibility that a cross-community consensus might be constructed.

Still, Prior's assembly proved to be a defining moment in the history of the conflict because it ushered in a new era in the political landscape of Northern Ireland. It confirmed the arrival of Sinn Fein as a serious electoral force within the province. Hitherto, the party had boycotted elections on the grounds that it did not recognise the 'partitionist' bodies involved. Since the mid-1970s, however, the republican leadership had begun to reconsider this prohibition on political activity—in the context of the shift to a 'Long War' strategy and the need to secure support for the IRA's campaign. The outpouring of emotion that had surrounded the hunger strikes merely intensified the belief within a section of the leadership that a sizeable proportion of the Catholic-nationalist community was prepared to support Sinn Fein. Thus, the decision to embrace electoral politics, even as the IRA's military campaign continued, was taken; the new policy described by the senior republican, Danny Morrison, as one that would see the movement proceed with the 'Armalite in one hand and the ballot box in the other'.[143] In the election to Prior's assembly, Sinn Fein secured 10.1% of the vote and five seats in the body. Several months later, the party captured over 13% of the vote in the British General Election and Gerry Adams won the seat for West Belfast.

The rise of Sinn Fein raised a horrifying prospect in the minds of the British and Irish governments: the potential eclipse of the SDLP as the majority representatives of Northern Ireland's Catholic-nationalist community by the political wing of the IRA. In the event that such a situation came to pass, few envisaged a peaceful and stable outcome in the province at any point in the near and medium-term future. What emerged thereafter—albeit in stilted and far from predictable fashion—was a fresh change in the direction of British policy. This was driven partly by default and partly by the desire of both the British and Irish governments to arrest the electoral growth of Sinn Fein. To this end, the pendulum now swung back towards a renewed drive to achieve an Anglo-Irish accommodation at governmental level. According to the senior Northern Ireland civil servant, Ken Bloomfield, the calculation behind the new departure was as follows:

Anything resembling a Cabinet in Northern Ireland would have to embody both the nationalist and unionist elements, and it followed from this that any route blocked by either interest would prove a cul-de-sac. Faced by the propensity of one party or another not merely to veto progress but to withhold participation from negotiations to achieve it, one could expect from time to time a strong desire to present local parties with a fait accompli achieved behind their backs or over their heads, if need be in direct negotiation between the British and Irish Governments.

The return to power of the Fine Gael-Labour coalition led by Garret FitzGerald in November 1982 dramatically increased the likelihood that such a 'direct negotiation' between London and Dublin could be successful. During his brief spell as Taoiseach between July 1981 and February 1982, FitzGerald had overseen the establishment of the Anglo-Irish Inter-governmental Council after a summit with Thatcher. Furthermore, as Minister for Foreign Affairs during the mid-1970s, FitzGerald had been forthright in his vehement opposition to the IRA. After 1982, he made clear his anxiety at the prospect that Sinn Fein might over-take the SDLP. To prevent such an outcome, he was prepared to significantly modify the outlook and role of the Irish state. As one of the British officials who later dealt with the Fine Gael leader noted,

Dr FitzGerald was prepared drastically to lower Nationalist sights on Irish unification in the interests of promoting stability in Northern Ireland and halting the political advance of Sinn Fein. This meant trying to reconcile Nationalists to the union rather than breaking it...

From the British perspective, therefore, FitzGerald appeared to be the ideal man with whom Thatcher could 'do business'; and from the second half of 1983 there was an upsurge in talks between the two Governments.[144]

Even then, the path towards Anglo-Irish accommodation was a far from linear and smooth one. In March 1983, in an apparent tack towards a more recognisably nationalist approach, FitzGerald's government had announced the creation of a New Ireland Forum to discuss the future of Northern Ireland. Representatives were invited from all non-violent, 'constitutional' parties on the island of Ireland; Sinn Fein, because of its support for the IRA, was not invited (the unionist parties, predictably refused to attend, as did the Alliance Party of Northern Ireland). The initiative had been undertaken partly at the behest of SDLP leader John Hume, who had become convinced of the need for a common approach among Irish nationalists. Yet, when the Forum delivered its report a year later, it served only to provoke a new mini-crisis in relations between the British and Irish governments. The Forum had laid out three possible options for resolving the conflict: Irish unity; the establishment of joint authority over Northern Ireland by the Republic of Ireland and Britain; or a federal or confederal arrangement. In keeping with his personal shift to a more hardline rhetorical stance, the Fianna Fail leader, Charles Haughey, had insisted that the report express a clear preference for a unitary state and an end to partition. The response from Thatcher, though, was unceremoniously abrupt. At a press conference at Chequers in November 1984, after a meeting with FitzGerald, she ran through the Forum's proposals, dismissing each in turn with a terse, 'that is out'.[145]

Though this riposte was criticised as both ungenerous and unnecessarily offensive, it was in part a product of the environment in which both governments were operating. The discussion of constitutional matters was proceeding against a backdrop of heightened republican violence. This included a number of devastating attacks perpetrated by the IRA. In July 1982, for example, IRA bomb attacks in London's Hyde Park and Regent's Park had claimed the lives of eleven soldiers. A year later, in December 1983, the group bombed the Harrods department store, killing eight Christmas shoppers.[146] Back in Northern Ireland too the bloodshed continued—and not solely from the IRA. In December 1982, the INLA had perpetrated one of the most brutal attacks of the conflict when it bombed the 'Droppin Well' Bar and Disco in Ballykelly, County Derry, killing seventeen people. Finally, October 1984 brought the most high-profile attack of all, when the IRA bombed the Grand Hotel in Brighton—an operation that nearly took the lives of Thatcher herself and most of her Cabinet. With Thatcher's 'out, out, out' response to the Forum report following less than a month later, her brusque manner on that occasion perhaps becomes more explicable. Still, as with the Warrenpoint and Mount-batten murders of five years previously, the Brighton attack also pressed home the need for a new and more meaningful push on Anglo-Irish security co-operation if the IRA campaign was to be truly inter-dicted. 'We were', according to a leading Northern Ireland civil servant who was critical of the subsequent Agreement, 'about to witness a strange phenomenon: the conversion of a triple negative into an affirmative'.[147]

On 15 November 1985, the British and Irish governments announced the signing of what became known as the 'Anglo-Irish Agreement'. Whereas Thatcher had previously stated that, 'no commitment exists for HM government to consult the Irish government on matters affect-ing Northern Ireland', she had now agreed to do precisely that.[148] The Agreement provided for the creation of an Inter-Governmental Confer-ence with a permanent secretariat residing at Maryfield in Belfast. This Conference was tasked with discussion of a wide range of issues—across political, legal and security spheres—and as such, gave the Irish government an enduring say in the affairs of Northern Ireland. The *quid pro quo* for this was the closer co-operation, particularly on secu-rity matters, that was envisaged between north and south, and the restatement of the 'consent principle' regarding the constitutional posi-tion of Northern Ireland.

The Agreement fell a long way short of creating a dynamic towards Irish unification. Neither was there the establishment of 'joint author-ity' between the British and Irish governments over Northern Ireland; article one confirmed that any change in the status of the province would only come about with majority consent. Interestingly, the then Secretary of State for Northern Ireland, Douglas Hurd, has revealed that the Foreign Office (FCO) and Foreign Secretary 'would have liked to move a little further towards joint authority', whereby the Irish and the British would have an equal share of influence over the province:

The Foreign Secretary, Geoffrey Howe, was prepared to go a long way to meet the Irish. Contrary to the conspiracy theories held by Unionist politicians, he never argued or authorised his officials to argue that the ultimate objective should be a united Ireland. He was, however, prepared to contemplate a sys-tem of joint authority by which the Irish and British governments would gov-ern the Province, with a strong degree of devolution to local politicians working together.[149]

In the event, the alleged views of Howe and certain elements in the FCO did not prevail (it should also be said that a former British Ambassador in Dublin expressed surprise to the authors when shown this passage and does not believe that it necessarily reflected the attitude of the FCO as a whole).[150]

Any effort to assess the success or failure of the Anglo-Irish Agreement faces the difficulty of trying to ascertain what it was that it set out to achieve. Here, the disparities in various official accounts of the accord do much to cloud the issue, and identifying unity of purpose across all strands of the British state was certainly a challenge. Not only were the NIO and the FCO 'uneasy bedfellows' at this time, with the former reported to be sceptical of the Agreement, where the latter was enthusiastic, but also the close involvement of Number 10 added a further dimension.[151] On top of this, the American President, Ronald Reagan—with whom Thatcher enjoyed a warm relationship—appears to have played an important role in convincing the British Prime Minister to accept the deal. Indeed, Ian Gow MP—previously a close supporter of Thatcher who resigned from the government over the issue—believed that the pressure to sign the Agreement had come from the United States, via the Foreign Office.[152]

Among the various overlapping objectives set for the Agreement by its various proponents, five in particular are worth mentioning. First, the Agreement was designed to institutionalise Anglo-Irish relations and thereby move them into a new, more harmonious era. It was hoped that there would be no return to the 'megaphone diplomacy' of times passed.[153] Second, the British government in particular hoped to change the international perception of Northern Ireland's 'Troubles'—especially in the United States. The problems that followed from the conflict being seen as one of Britain's making—or even just one in which Britain had proven itself the most truculent, unyielding player—had been made plain by the US State Department's decision to suspend gun sales to the RUC. A major initiative such as the Agreement offered a shift in international public opinion and the substantial rehabilitation of the British government's image.

The third main aim invested in the Agreement by many was that it would halt the electoral rise of Sinn Fein and insulate the SDLP from the threat of revolutionary republicanism. As has been noted, the danger that Sinn Fein might establish political hegemony over the Catholic-nationalist community of Northern Ireland was one that animated the Irish government especially. By giving something to the SDLP— showing that constitutional nationalism could succeed—it was hoped that they would be better equipped to resist the challenge of Sinn Fein. Moreover, on this basis, a fourth aim that some, particularly the SDLP, saw for the Agreement, was the possibility that it might pave the way towards a more stable future within Northern Ireland. For those who held to such a view it was their hope that a deal could henceforth be concluded between constitutional nationalism and moderate unionism over new institutions to govern the province. The final goal of the Agreement, which would affect everyone involved, was the expectation that it would lead to an improvement in security. Opponents of the measure within Conservative circles believed that this was a key motivation for Thatcher:

Howe and his co-adjutors smuggled the agreement past her on the utterly spurious grounds that it would help bring the Dublin government into intense co-operation with Britain on the suppression of terrorism.[154]

With regards to the first of these objectives, it is clear that the Agreement did shift Anglo-Irish relations on to a new footing. It signalled a growing rapprochement between civil servants and diplomats on both sides that would survive over the coming years, even following the return to power of Charles Haughey in 1987. It did not put an end to 'megaphone diplomacy' between the two countries, which reasserted itself, for example, over extradition cases in the late 1980s. Nonetheless, Sir Nicholas Fenn, British Ambassador to Dublin in the post-Agreement period, describes how warmer individual relationships were cultivated between the representatives of the two states.[155] Moreover, as far as the wider reputation of the British government was concerned, the Agreement reinforced the sense that it was actively committed to the search for peace. The most important audience here had always been the United States and it was clear from the outset that the accord received American blessing. Not only had Reagan impressed on Thatcher the positive benefits of signing the Agreement, but it was also followed by an injection of US and other international money into Ireland in an effort to promote peace.[156]

On the other hand, the notion that the Agreement could halt the rise of Sinn Fein was, to a significant extent, based on an alarmist misreading of that party's electoral potential. Its successes in the immediate wake of the hunger strikes during 1981–3 had certainly been dramatic, but the reality was that its expansion had already been demonstrably halted in both 1984 and 1985, before the Anglo-Irish Agreement. In the European election that was held in the former year, Sinn Fein's candidate, Danny Morrison, was comprehensively outpolled by the SDLP's John Hume. In local elections in 1985, the vote of the SDLP held up and Sinn Fein failed to make any major advances (indeed, its share of the vote fell back on the figure it had achieved at the 1983 British General Election). There was thus every reason to believe that the nationalist political spectrum within Northern Ireland had stabilised prior to the Agreement. The leading electoral analyst at that time was Dr Sydney Elliott at Queen's University, who had helped to prepare the White Paper on the border poll at the time of Sunningdale and was well-known to have produced the most subtle accounts of the voting dispositions of both communities—particularly with regards to second and third preference voting intentions. If anything, Elliott's analysis of the local election results also showed a considerable stabilisation of Catholic opinion. The majority of SDLP voters, Elliott noted at this time, leant more towards the moderate Alliance Party, than Sinn Fein, as their second choice. Tellingly, although senior British officials did eventually consult Elliott about his findings, this was not done until after the Anglo-Irish Agreement.[157]

This must be placed alongside consideration of the fourth definable objective of the Agreement, which pertains to conditions within Northern Ireland: whether or not it could be used as a platform for the more stable governance of the province and even, looking further ahead, lead to the creation of a cross-community devolved administration. Among mainstream Catholic-nationalists, the Anglo-Irish Agreement was immediately hailed as an important development. It was seen as a key step towards tackling the problem of nationalist 'alienation' in Northern Ireland. It certainly was seen as a triumph for the SDLP which, under John Hume, had increasingly pushed for the redefinition of Anglo-Irish relations at inter-governmental level, as a foundation for the resolution of Northern Ireland's conflict. Hume argued that the Agreement represented a willingness on the part of the British government finally to face down the unionist 'veto'. The government's open demonstration of its readiness to listen—on an enduring basis—to an 'Irish' perspective was believed by Hume to have created genuine equality within Northern Ireland between the two 'traditions'. The British state had, he argued, finally shown its neutrality in relation to

Northern Ireland. In so doing, it had made a new political framework possible—one which would, in turn, allow for reconciliation and an end to conflict. To this end, Hume looked to the emergence of a 'new' form of moderate unionism that would be prepared to 'cut a deal' with his party. He even predicted that negotiations would be under way by the end of the following year, which would lead to the establishment of a cross-community power-sharing government on this basis.

Hume's vistas, of course, relied on the willingness of unionism to accept the Anglo-Irish Agreement as a fundamental 'base line' for political life in Northern Ireland. It was here that the analysis broke down. The Anglo-Irish Agreement provoked an outburst of fear and anger among unionists, with lasting repercussions. Most of the latter, including moderates, viewed the deal as, at best, a 'diktat' and, at worst, a staging post towards joint sovereignty and eventual Irish unity. The assurances as to the sanctity of the 'consent principle', as contained in article one, were offset in unionist minds by the failure of the Irish government to change its constitution to remove what they saw as the irredentist claim on Northern Ireland. As at Sunningdale, unionists asked what sacrifices the British had asked for from the Irish government as part of the compromise; the response they received did little to convince them that the traffic was not all one way. Indeed, the accord was also seen as emblematic of the growing imbalance in the way in which Northern Ireland was run. Whereas the Irish government had shown itself happy to act as the guarantor and advocate for Northern Ireland's Catholic-nationalist community, the failure of the British state to fulfill a similar role for Protestant-unionists increased their sense of isolation. As Ken Bloomfield put it:

The Irish government clearly entered into the talks process as the champion of nationalist Ireland. The British government was not, and could not be, the champion of the unionist interest in Northern Ireland. The consequences of this disparity were to be quite apparent on the face of the ultimate Agreement, which entrenched the Irish government as the accepted guarantor of nationalist interests, without any balancing reassurance to unionists.[158]

The sense of unionist isolation, outrage and dislocation in the wake of the Agreement, described by Arthur Aughey in his book *Under Siege*, had profound long-term implications.[159] The feeling that Protestants could not rely on the British state fed into the upsurge in loyalist paramilitary violence at the end of the 1980s. Historically, unionism was a calmer, more rational force, during those periods of its history when it felt connected with the establishment in London.[160] During the run-up to the Agreement, the political leadership of unionism had maintained the complacent assumption that a deal would not be done without their being consulted upon it. Consequently, when the Anglo-Irish 'diktat' of 1985 was revealed, it prompted the allegation that the Official Unionist Party leader James Molyneaux had displayed a servile trust in the Conservative government, only to be duped.[161] The result was a lasting suspicion of joint British-Irish initiatives, which was to become apparent again in 1993, 1995 and 1998.

Days after the Agreement was announced the new Secretary of State for Northern Ireland, Tom King (who had replaced Douglas Hurd in this role in November 1985) was set upon by an angry mob as he attempted to enter Belfast City Hall to attend a function.[162] Over 100,000 people subsequently attended a vast 'Ulster says No' rally in the centre of the city. In December, the crisis worsened as all fifteen unionist MPs at Westminster resigned their seats and attempted to turn the resulting by-elections into a referendum on the Agreement. In the event, the move back-fired somewhat: the unionist vote did increase slightly, but a seat was lost to the SDLP. Still, this did not bring an end to unionism's opposition to the accord. Consequently, a 'Day of Action' was held in March 1986—an effort to recreate the success of the Ulster Workers' Council strike that had brought down the Sunningdale Agreement in 1974. However, this too failed to derail the Agreement, which had been specifically designed by British and Irish officials to be impervious to the kind of loyalist mass action that had secured the collapse of Sunningdale.

Long term, while they could not topple the deal, unionists showed little willingness to work within its parameters. It was this that was to prove so deleterious to the notion that it could serve as a platform for the construction of a more stable cross-community government, as initially envisaged by John Hume. Not until the early 1990s would the leaders of mainstream unionism be prepared to engage in constitutional dialogue with the SDLP—and even then, only in a context no longer shaped by the Anglo-Irish Agreement. Hume's predictions as to the emergence of an ameliorative, softer form of unionism in the wake of the Agreement proved unrealistic. What is more, his own disillusionment at this reality led him in new directions. In the late 1980s—with cooperation between the local parties looking increasingly unlikely—the SDLP moved away from its conventional emphasis on power-sharing; instead, its strategic inclination shifted towards the pursuit of greater inter-governmental cooperation between London and Dublin, set within the context of further European integration. In the early 1990s, the party moved further away from the previous focus on a deal with moderate unionists. Hume now began to prioritise the goal of bringing republicans 'in from the cold' as a precursor to any settlement. In early 1988, he had entered direct talks with Sinn Fein, indicating the trajectory upon which constitutional nationalism was now headed. This approach was expanded upon in the decade that followed.

The significance of all this, then, is that the depth of unionism's hostility to that accord was such as to ensure that it could never work as planned, with several unintended consequences. Among these was the fact that the post-Agreement period coincided with a sharp upsurge in loyalist violence. Of course, the accord alone cannot be held responsible for this; other factors internal to loyalism played an important part (notably, the rise of a younger, more militant, generation of para-military leaders). But the Anglo-Irish Agreement did prompt a marked change in the political atmosphere of the time and underscored the belief among loyalists that they must preserve their own position, rather than simply relying on the British state. Thus, whereas loyalist paramilitaries had killed only five people in 1985, within a decade they were 'out-murdering' the IRA.[163] Moreover, for the first time, organised loyalist violence was now directed against the state itself. In the aftermath of the Agreement, for instance, the homes of over 500 RUC officers were attacked in a concerted campaign of intimidation.[164]

The scale of this unionist/loyalist 'backlash' did much to ensure that the fifth and final objective of the accord would be unrealisable. Uppermost in the mind of the Prime Minister when she had given her support to the Agreement was the hope that it would deliver a security dividend. The key initiative arising out of the accord for Thatcher was to be the creation of a 'Joint Security Commission' and the idea of 'reciprocity' in this sphere between the two states. She did not share the belief that the deal in any way derogated from British sovereignty; rather she felt that the Irish were only being given the right to put forward ideas and proposals relating to Northern Ireland. With regards to the latter, the Agreement committed the British government to working towards devolution, but this had been at the forefront of British policy since at least 1979. 'The real question', she asserted, emphasising her central theme, 'was whether the agreement would result in better security'. Above all, 'we hoped for a more co-operative attitude from the Irish government, security forces and courts'.[165]

Another senior member of Thatcher's Cabinet—the Chancellor of the Exchequer Nigel Lawson—reflected in similar fashion on what he saw as the central conundurum of the Agreement: whether, 'the domestic political cost would be far outweighed by the military benefits that might be expected to come from greater co-operation from Washington in preventing the supply of Irish American money and weapons to the IRA' and whether greater co-operation would be forthcoming from the Irish government. At the time, he claims to have had 'no doubt' that the accord would become a 'political liability' and he believed that this pessimistic reading of the Agreement proved accurate: 'the subsequent black comedy of attempts to persuade the Irish courts to extradite terrorists did not make me any less sceptical'.[166]

As a result, while security cooperation did seem to improve, it did not occur to the extent that the British government had hoped. More generally, the period following the Agreement was characterised by 'a rising trend of violence, particularly against personnel in the security forces, and cross-border co-operation was still not effective'.[167] According to the British Army's own appraisal of 'the Troubles', as late as 1988, ten of the sixteen IRA Active Service Units were operating south of the border.[168] Continued atrocities, such as the 1987 Remembrance Day bombing which killed eleven in Enniskillen in County Fermanagh, seemed to suggest that things were getting worse, rather than better. Admittedly, the IRA 'surge' at this time had little to do with the Agreement (and was instead a function of the organisation's success in importing fresh arms and munitions from Libya). Nonetheless, it fed into the perception that the Agreement had failed to fulfill its promise.[169] Shortly after the Enniskillen attack, Charles Morrison, a Conservative MP, told a friend how the Prime Minister had privately admitted that 'she [has] no solution to the Irish problem, no glimmer of light—the first time he had heard her admit defeat on any issue'.[170] A major increase in loyalist violence merely underlined the problem in the most brutal possible fashion. 'It slowly became clear', Thatcher later concluded, 'that the wider gains for which I had hoped from greater support by the nationalist minority in Northern Ireland or the Irish Government and people for the fight against terrorism were not going to be forthcoming'. Her response to this realisation was to change tack again and revert to an earlier approach: 'My reluctant conclusion was that terrorism would have to be met with more and more effective counter-terrorist activity; and that in fighting terror we would have to stand alone, while the Irish indulged in gesture politics'. On this basis, she arrived at a further conclusion:

In dealing with Northern Ireland, successive governments have studiously refrained from security policies that might alienate the Irish government and Irish nationalist opinion in Ulster, in the hope of winning their support against the IRA. The Anglo-Irish Agreement was squarely within this tradition. But I discovered the results of this to be disappointing.[171]

3

THE PEACE PROCESS

Towards an end to violence

The early 1990s in Northern Ireland witnessed the onset of two apparently conflicting—and somewhat paradoxical—developments. First, the province seemed to draw ever closer to the precipice of all-out communal civil war. The pressure being exerted on the IRA by the security forces meant that republicans increasingly struggled to inflict serious strategic damage to the state. Instead, a growing proportion of its operations appeared to be overtly sectarian in character. Already, notwithstanding the rhetoric of Irish republicanism, the IRA's campaign was perceived by many unionists to be no less sectarian than that of the loyalist paramilitaries. The fact that the vast majority of those deemed 'legitimate targets' were drawn from the Protestant community seemed only to corroborate such a view. Moreover, in certain localities—such as rural Fermanagh—where Protestants were in a minority, the local unionist population had long felt themselves to be facing a republican campaign of 'ethnic cleansing' to drive them from their land.[1] As the IRA's 'war' entered its third decade, the inherently sectarian character of many of its activities seemed only to become more patent. In a 1988 interview with *The Observer*, Gerry Adams had come close to admitting as much, when he acknowledged that the British had effectively managed to 'reduce the violence to Irish people killing each other'.[2]

Attempts by the IRA to introduce innovations in its military strategy in this period led it into a series of damaging blunders that did little to further the republican cause. In October 1990, the organisation introduced the 'human bomb' tactic to Ireland, when IRA volunteers held hostage the family of Patsy Gillespie, a civilian worker at a local British

107

Army base, while forcing him to drive a 1,000lb bomb to a security check-point at Coshquin, near Londonderry. Unlike today's 'human bombs'—the stock in trade of modern Islamist terrorism—Gillespie did not choose 'martyrdom'; it was selected for him by the IRA. As the vehicle he was driving approached the check-point, the bomb with which it had been fitted was detonated by remote control, killing five British soldiers along with the driver. In the aftermath, the Catholic Bishop of Derry, Edward Daly, captured the sense of public revulsion in both communities, describing it as, 'a callous, cynical, crude and horrible deed'.[3]

Sentiments of this kind posed a serious challenge to the political ambitions of the republican leadership. Moreover, despite the murder of five soldiers in this instance, such 'successes' were becoming increasingly infrequent. In 1990, the organization killed ten soldiers in total; in the whole of the following year, it claimed only half that number.[4] Forced to look elsewhere to sustain its campaign, the IRA shifted focus to comparatively softer targets—principally, off-duty RUC and UDR men—though again, this merely fuelled the perception that republicans were primarily engaged in an assault on the Protestant community.

As the sectarian war intensified, loyalist paramilitaries became increasingly prominent actors. Ironically, the government's effort to uncover possible instances of 'collusion' between elements of the security forces and loyalist death squads in the late 1980s had unintentionally contributed to a surge in loyalist violence. The arrest of the older, more cautious generation of loyalist leaders opened the way for a new generation of militants to come through. This was the era of Johnny Adair and his notorious UFF 'C-Company', which operated out of the Shankill Road in Belfast. With men such as Adair free to pursue their avowed aim of 'taking the war to the IRA', the result was a significant spike in loyalist killing.[5] 1991 was the first year since 1974–5 when the numbers of those dying at the hands of loyalists approached parity with those being killed by republicans. During 1992, the gap narrowed even further, while in 1993 and 1994, for the first time during 'the Troubles', loyalist killings actually outnumbered those committed by republicans.[6]

Significantly, although much of this surge in loyalist activity was baldly sectarian—the majority of victims were innocent Catholics—it also impacted on high level republicans. Between 1989 and 1993, the UFF and UVF killed no fewer than twenty-six members—or relatives of members—of the IRA and Sinn Fein.[7] The IRA struggled to adapt to this new dimension in the conflict. Their response was a policy of 'targeted assassination' against the loyalists which also proved to be deeply problematic. Symptomatic of this was the attempt to murder the UFF leadership with a bomb attack on a fish-and-chip shop on Belfast's Shankill Road in October 1993. When the device detonated prematurely it killed nine Protestant civilians, as well as the bomber. Contrary to IRA intelligence, the leadership of the UFF had not been in the building. Loyalist paramilitaries responded with a wave of brutal attacks, taking the lives of sixteen Catholics in the course of the following month. In one gruesome incident on the evening of Halloween, hooded gunmen burst into a pub in the small village of Greysteel, shouted 'trick or treat' and machine-gunned the occupants.[8] Even in the context of Northern Ireland's thirty-year 'Troubles', the violence of late 1993 represented a new low for the province.

And yet, less than a year after the Shankill and Greysteel atrocities, in August 1994, the IRA—which only a few years previously had declared there would be 'no more ceasefires' until it achieved victory—announced 'a complete cessation of military operations'.[9] Shortly afterwards, the loyalist paramilitaries followed suit, adhering to their professed claim that, 'if they [the IRA] stop, we'll stop'.[10] Four years later, the peace process came to successful fruition as parties from across the political spectrum in Northern Ireland—with some important exceptions—acceded to the 'Good Friday' Agreement of Easter 1998.

With hindsight, there were more layers to the conflict than were immediately obvious in the early 1990s. Chief among these was the fact that the IRA's organisational capacity had been eroded considerably. As the 1980s drew to a close, many commentators remained convinced that the IRA continued to be 'a potent guerilla force' and argued to the effect that 'the indications are that there is little real understanding in London of Irish nationalism and the current strength of its military wing'.[11] In retrospect, however, it would seem that a combination of war weariness, the loyalist backlash and the growing effectiveness of the security forces in infiltrating and interdicting the IRA's campaign was having an impact upon republicans. It is true that the British had been unable to achieve a decisive military victory over the IRA, but their policy of containment and attrition had undoubtedly taken a toll. Between 1983 and 1992, for example, the British security services—particularly the SAS—were responsible for shooting dead 35 IRA volunteers.[12] The majority of these were killed in pre-laid 'ambushes'. The most notorious of these occurred in Loughgall, Co. Armagh, in May 1987, when an IRA attack on the village's RUC station was met with a deadly SAS-led response that saw all eight IRA volunteers involved in the operation killed (the group's biggest single loss during the conflict).[13] Significantly, the republicans who died on that occasion were drawn from what were widely held to be amongst the most militant sections of the organization. This fitted into a broader pattern, which has led at least one informed commentator to conclude that it was 'more or less open season... as far as the SAS and British intelligence were concerned' with regards to the most belligerent divisions of the IRA, such as that based in Tyrone.[14]

Meanwhile, aside from such high profile incidents, the security services were also engaged in a highly sophisticated 'intelligence war' against the IRA. The extent of infiltration of the latter organisation may not be known for many years. But a series of revelations, such as those surrounding Denis Donaldson and Freddie Scappaticci, seem to suggest that it was extensive, even at leadership level. Scappaticci, for instance, has been identified as a long-serving British agent within the IRA, code-named 'Stakeknife' (though he denies it).[15] Further, the centrality of Denis Donaldson to the Sinn Fein machine is beyond question.[16] In both cases, the men involved were 'career agents', which is to say they were people who were in place for a considerable length of time. According to the Army 'whistle-blower', 'Martin Ingram', Scappaticci was recruited as far back as 1978. Donaldson, in his public confession, admitted to having been 'turned' in the eighties.[17] By this estimation, the two men survived undetected for the greater part of two decades at the heart of the republican movement. While republicans maintain that these were isolated examples, the suspicion remains that other, equally senior 'agents' continue to reside within the republican movement to this day.[18]

Thus, although the IRA still posed a deadly threat into the 1990s, its capacity for 'war' seems to have been gradually curtailed. In the estimation of former RUC Detective Superintendant Ian Phoenix, by 1994, eight out of ten operations planned by the IRA's Belfast Brigade were being thwarted by the RUC.[19] No British soldier died on duty at the hands of the IRA in Belfast after August 1992 and the last major commercial bombing in the city was in May 1993.[20] In Northern Ireland's capital, always a key crucible of the conflict, the IRA was apparently being brought to a stand-still, prompting a growing realisation within its leadership that the 'armed struggle' had reached a point of deadlock.[21] In the words of Sean O'Callaghan, 'Adams and McGuinness had looked down the road and seen slow defeat staring them in the face.'[22] While it was likely that a low intensity campaign could continue for many years, mere survival did not constitute success. As the republican strategist Danny Morrison put it, writing from his prison cell in October 1991, 'I think we can fight on forever and can't be defeated. But, of course, that isn't the same as winning or showing something for all the sacrifices'. The logic of this situation, he concluded, was that republicans might have to take 'hard decisions' in the near future.[23] Republican horizons were being transformed; just under five years earlier, in November 1986, Morrison had predicted that there would be a united Ireland by the year 2000.[24]

The political sentiments of Northern Ireland's nationalist community fed into this reappraisal. While Sinn Fein had achieved some success during its early forays into electoral politics, its levels of support seemed to have reached a plateau. By the late 1980s, Sinn Fein's share of the vote had settled around the 11% mark, not too far from the figure achieved when the modern party first began to contest elections in 1982. Support for the SDLP stood at almost twice that level. In 1992, Sinn Fein lost the 'jewel' in its political 'crown' when Gerry Adams was defeated in West Belfast by the SDLP's John Hendron in the British General Election of that year—a result that prompted much soul searching within the party.[25] The confident assertion of a decade earlier, that it was possible to combine the Armalite and the ballot box, appeared ever more open to question. Many now asked whether Sinn Fein's vote had reached a natural 'ceiling'.[26]

Perhaps more important still, politics in Northern Ireland had a momentum which operated independently of Sinn Fein and the IRA. The appointment of Peter Brooke as Secretary of State for Northern Ireland in 1989 had been followed by a thaw in relations between the unionist parties and the British government, after the years of antagonism which had followed the Anglo-Irish Agreement. By 1991, this thaw had advanced far enough to allow inter-party talks between the SDLP and the unionist parties to take place.[27] With Sinn Fein excluded, because of the ongoing IRA campaign, there were concerns within the republican movement that a deal could be reached which would increase the political marginalisation of republicanism, just as its military strategy seemed to have run out of momentum. Again, Danny Morrison offers confirmation of this; reviewing the episode from prison, he felt the republican response to the Brooke talks, 'gave the impression that we were panicking'.[28]

It was at this point that the viability of the republican movement's political strategy—and its foray into electoral politics—once more became a matter of internal debate.[29] The clearest exposition of this was provided by an article entitled 'Bitter Pill' that Morrison wrote from prison in April 1992 (but which was never published by Sinn Fein). The recent election results, Morrison noted, were 'very bad for Sinn Fein, very bad for the IRA and for the struggle'. In light of them, he predicted that there might be a 'temptation' for republicans to 'abandon even their limited faith in politics and place all their trust in armed struggle'. Such an 'emotional reaction', he insisted, would be a 'gross mistake'. The IRA was, he asserted, in a situation 'out of which it cannot simply bomb its way'. Instead, it had to, 'raise the quality of its campaign', or 'consider the alternative'. Citing the example of the Sandinistas (the Nicaraguan liberation movement that had recently lost an election, but decided to go into opposition, rather than return to violence), Morrison declared that,

The pragmatism of the head had to take precedence over the principle of the heart. Some day we shall be faced with the same choice. We should never allow the situation to decline to the extent that we face such a decision from the depths of an unpopular, unseemly, impossible-to-end armed struggle or from the point of brave exhaustion—another one of the 'glorious defeats' with which our past is littered.'[30]

The message was clear. Republicans, in Morrison's view, needed to 'cash in' their chips and end the IRA's armed struggle while they could still claim something from the spoils. Against the backdrop of the organisation's declining fortunes this logic began to assert itself ever more forcefully.[31]

Talking to Terrorists IV

During the late 1980s and early 1990s, partly as a product of republican soul-searching, various lines of communication were established between the republican movement and various other actors in the conflict. First, Gerry Adams had been attempting to initiate a dialogue with other Irish nationalists—through the Belfast-based Redemptorist priest, Father Alec Reid—from as early as May 1987. In that month, as Ed Moloney has revealed, the *Irish Press* journalist Tim Pat Coogan delivered a letter from Reid, which bore Adams' imprimatur, and was addressed to the Fianna Fail leader (and recently returned Taoiseach), Charles Haughey.[32] A similar letter was also sent to the SDLP leader, John Hume, in Londonderry.[33] It called for the construction of 'a common nationalist policy of aims and methods for resolving the conflict and establishing a just and lasting peace'.[34] The suggestion was that this could act as a 'realistic alternative' to the 'armed struggle' and thereby 'persuade the IRA to end their campaign'; the construction of this 'alternative method' would show them, it was claimed, that 'the use of force was no longer necessary to achieve justice for the nationalist community'.[35]

For the moment, persistent doubts over the circumstances in which the IRA would actually call a ceasefire ensured that the kind of 'pan-nationalist alliance' envisaged in the Reid letter was unlikely.[36] Nevertheless, the process by which the republican leadership sought to engage with the other representatives of Irish nationalism had begun. Haughey's unwillingness to sanction 'face-to-face' meetings with Gerry Adams—as sought by the Sinn Fein leader—saw him delegate responsibility for such a venture to John Hume (though Haughey retained an input through his special adviser, Martin Mansergh, who was appointed the Taoiseach's 'point man' on dialogue with the northern parties). This set the stage for the talks Hume's party held with Sinn Fein in 1988. Though these had achieved little, other than demonstrating how far apart the two nationalist parties were in terms of ideology and approach, Hume endeavoured to remain in contact with Adams from that point onwards.[37] Increasingly, the SDLP leader came to believe that only by bringing republicans 'in from the cold' could a lasting peace settlement be achieved in Northern Ireland. This impulse towards the creation of an 'inclusive' peace process meant that Hume was prepared to co-operate with Adams on an effort to construct a new alliance between the forces of Irish nationalism in the first years of the new decade; for Sinn Fein, it represented a route out of political isolation.[38] In 1990–1, Gerry Adams approached John Hume with the proposal that they reinvigorate their past contacts and work at the enterprise afresh. The focus for this now was to be the drafting of a new 'joint declaration', articulating the nationalist position, to be sent to both the British and Irish governments. Hume hoped that this document, if adopted by the two governments, might give enough to satiate IRA demands and thereby persuade republicans to end their 'armed struggle' and embrace a non-violent approach.[39]

Alongside this intra-nationalist dialogue, meanwhile, a new departure occurred in relations between the British government and Sinn Fein. Again, Moloney has established that a conduit between the two sides had been in operation as early as 1986, with Father Alec Reid again acting as intermediary.[40] Adams had used this to pose a number of questions to the government regarding the nature of the British position in Ireland and the likely parameters for a settlement. In reply, the Sinn Fein leader received a lengthy document that, according to Moloney, stands as the 'philosophical fountainhead' of the peace process. This rejected the republican movement's colonial analysis of events in Northern Ireland and argued that Britain had 'no political, military, strategic, or economic interest in staying in Ireland'.[41] The root of the conflict was said to be 'the divisions between the people of both traditions'. IRA violence was said to be 'holding back the day' when those divisions could be healed. By contrast, the British government declared its role to be that of a 'facilitator', hoping to encourage dialogue between unionists and nationalists. To this end, it was, 'prepared to withdraw from the central area of historical, political, religious and cultural conflict and from the central forum of political debate... so that... the people of the nationalist tradition and the people of the unionist tradition can engage freely, independently and democratically in... political dialogue and in agreement-making'.[42] In the event that such dialogue reached agreement, the British government promised to 'respond with the necessary legislation'. However, it was adamant that, while a republican outlook was an entirely valid one, talks aimed at a solution could only take place among non-violent parties:

We accept that the republican tradition within the nationalist community should be represented at the peace conference table but we cannot and never will accept that the Provisional IRA and the Sinn Fein party should be represented there while they continue to use the tactics of violence.[43]

In this way, therefore, the British government outlined to the republican movement its stance on a number of key issues. There was a direct proclamation of certain 'base-line' positions, with the British interested to see how the IRA would respond. The fact that the 'armed struggle' continued at this time offered the clearest signal as to the tenor of that response. Indeed, it was this that curtailed the Father Reid-centred contacts in 1987–8 (the discovery of an apparent conspiracy to murder the Secretary of State overseeing the exchange, Tom King, prompted him to conclude that republicans were not then interested in peace).[44]

In subsequent years many of the themes covered in the exchange were publicly enunciated. The most striking example of this came in November 1990, when the Secretary of State for Northern Ireland, Peter Brooke, gave a keynote speech. The objective of Irish unity, he noted, was perfectly legitimate—if pursued by democratic, peaceful means. But it was neither acceptable, nor achievable, if pursued through coercion. That this should be so, he insisted, was a function of what he held to be the true nature of the 'British presence'—'the reality of nearly a million people living in a part of the island of Ireland who are, and who certainly regard themselves as British'. On this reasoning, Brooke argued, 'Partition is an acknowledgement of reality, not an assertion of national self-interest'; rather, 'The British government has no selfish strategic or economic interests in Northern Ireland'.[45] Brooke's description of the British state's rationale behind its presence in the province was hardly revelatory but the comments generated interest because they were clearly aimed at the republican movement.

As has been shown, there was, in itself, nothing new about the British government sending messages to, or talking with, the representatives of violent republicanism. On the contrary, it had done so at various points during 'the Troubles'. This much was confirmed by Sinn Fein when news of further contacts between the two sides emerged in late 1993. In a document the party released giving its own version of what had taken place, it emphasised that a 'line of communication' had been in existence between republicans and the British government for over two decades; however, it had 'not been in constant use'.[46] This was a direct reference to the Londonderry-based 'link' that comprised Brendan Duddy, Denis Bradley and another individual. Though Bradley had dropped out of the 'link' since the late 1970s, he had, by this point, rejoined it. Moreover, Duddy, in particular, appears to have kept open an unofficial channel of communication with the British Intelligence officer, Michael Oatley.[47] According to Sinn Fein's chief negotiator Martin McGuinness:

After the Hunger Strikes the line of communication was dormant until mid 1990. Even though the line of communication was dormant the contact remained in touch with the British government representative and occasionally with me.[48]

This conduit was confirmed in mid-to-late 1990 when Oatley, with his retirement approaching, arranged for his successor to inherit access to 'the link'. The result was an October 1990 meeting between Oatley and McGuinness that was also attended by Duddy, 'the Contact'.[49]

It was at this point—as Margaret Thatcher's tenure as Prime Minister was drawing to a close—that some within the permanent British state considered resurrecting the policy of 'talking to terrorists'. Notwithstanding the Father Reid-inspired contact between Adams and Tom King in 1987–8, Thatcher had largely adhered to a hard-line approach to republican violence. This, coupled with her robust public line during the hunger strikes, had earned her the lasting enmity of many within republican circles.[50] For her part, the feeling was mutual. Thus, there was a widespread perception by this stage that any moves towards reinvigorating these conmmunications would have to post-date her departure from office.

Accounts of what subsequently took place diverge. According to Sinn Fein, the impetus for re-engagement came from the British state; it was the latter that came to republicans seeking to talk. This question—of who came to whom—might seem something of an irrelevance in the context of the broader trajectory of events of this period. However, the implication of the republican claim is that it was the British who definitively shifted position. The accompanying narrative runs as follows: in a situation of military 'stalemate', it was the British government that recognised it could not defeat the IRA and so instead opted to negotiate with their erstwhile enemies. This was a notion repeated in the English press when news of the communications became public; sources reinforced the view that there could be no 'winner' in this 'Mexican stand-off'.[51] Such an interpretation, though, stems from a fundamental misunderstanding of what had occured.

It may be the case that the October 1990 meeting involving Oatley, McGuinness and Duddy was pushed for by Oatley, with the Secretary of State for Northern Ireland, Peter Brooke, giving approval for the encounter to go ahead.[52] Indeed, Brooke was also aware that Oatley's successor—a fellow SIS officer known only as 'Fred'—established contact with the 'link' in June 1991.[53] But rather than representing a genuinely innovative policy development, this meeting can be understood as ushering in a shift in style, rather than substance. The permanent

British state was giving notice that there would be a return to the *status quo ante* Mason and Thatcher. It was indicating that the 'line of communication' remained open, and that it was ready to listen. In other words, the government was signalling that, in the event that the IRA was ready to bring its campaign to a halt, the British would endeavour to provide it with a 'soft landing'. As Jonathan Powell's account of the period makes clear, shortly after this point, the IRA gave notice that this was an option it was prepared to consider: 'early in 1991 [Duddy] told Oatley that the IRA might now be ready to discuss a political way forward'.[54] It was for this reason that the subsequent behind-the-scenes contacts were allowed to move forward. The government (now under John Major, who replaced Thatcher as Prime Minister in November 1990) was prepared to open the door that led to negotiations, but it was up to republicans themselves to walk through it.

The content of the subsequent exchanges between republicans and the British government, as revealed by Sinn Fein's own account, exudes this philosophy throughout. On the one hand, the government attempted to emphasise to republicans that the effort to achieve a solution to the conflict would not solely be determined by the IRA. Significantly, one of the documents passed to Sinn Fein in April 1992, was an assessment of the inter-party talks then being conducted under the aegis of the new Secretary of State for Northern Ireland, Patrick Mayhew, from which republicans were excluded. That missive reported that the atmosphere of the talks had improved and they had 'entered an entirely new stage'.[55] It also included the outline of a solution, based on the three 'strand' formula that would ultimately provide a template for the Good Friday Agreement of 1998. With these foundations in place, the document noted that, 'events could begin to develop very quickly'. In its own commentary on this memorandum, Sinn Fein described it as being infused with 'unfounded optimism' and contrasted it with other more pessimistic analyses of the talks.[56] Still, the point cannot have been lost on republicans; other dynamics were in play, which could lead to them being left behind, isolated from the political process.

On the other hand, the government was careful to emphasise that there were alternatives for Sinn Fein. Time and again, the point was made to republicans that they would be permitted to enter the political process. Crucially, however, their participation depended on their capacity to meet certain pre-conditions: namely, an end to IRA violence and an acceptance from republicans that there could be no predetermined outcome to any such peace process. In October 1992, for instance, Sinn Fein was given the draft of a speech to be given by Patrick Mayhew in Coleraine, in which he underlined that Sinn Fein was 'not denied current involvement in democratic institutions', while reiterating that its 'relationship with the campaign of violence' made things difficult. Even more explicitly, Mayhew then stated that, 'An Irish republicanism seen to have finally renounced violence would be able, like other parties, to seek a role in the peaceful political life of the community'.[57]

It was against this backdrop that the back-channel communications threw up one of the most controversial incidents of the peace process. In February 1993, the British government was passed a message purporting to be from Martin McGuiness. It read: 'The conflict is over but we need your advice on how to bring it to a close.'[58] When news of British-republican communications entered the public domain in late 1993, the government immediately claimed that the McGuinness communiqué had been the spur for contacts with the IRA. Republicans, by contrast, claimed that the message was 'bogus' and had been 'written by the British government'.[59] The issue was complicated by the fact that the government was subsequently exposed as having lied over the duration and character of the behind-the-scenes talks; far from beginning in February 1993, there had been exchanges going back to 1990. Moreover, various inaccuracies and errors in the government's account of those communications further increased the suspicion that it had deliberately falsified its testimony on this key matter.

The truth would appear to be that the British government's representative—'Fred'—had indeed been given such a message and, believing it to be genuine, he had passed this on to the government.[60] But the message had not originated with McGuinness. Denis Bradley later admitted to the journalist and author, Liam Clarke: 'I made it up, but I made it up on the basis of what I knew their real position was. Any mediator worth his salt will push things along from time to time but you can't do it too often'.[61] Bradley's confession has meant that recent accounts of the peace process have tended to downplay the importance of the 'McGuinness message'. Yet, this is to ignore its fundamental significance: namely, that it reveals the basis on which the British government of John Major subsequently chose to intensify its engagement with republicans. Thus, the head of the NIO, John Chilcott recalls:

The Prime Minister asked us quite explicitly, was this message authentic? Did it come from McGuinness, was McGuinness speaking for the IRA leadership? What we told him, having worked it through and done some digging, was that yes, it was authentic, it was from McGuinness and it was spoken with authority.[62]

Regardless of its actual lack of authenticity, the various arms of the British state believed the message to be true and proceeded on that basis. Mayhew sent a minute to Major urging the Prime Minister to take the message seriously but cautiously.[63] In other words, the government did not view the exchanges that followed as a 'coming together' of two equal combatants who were locked in a 'military stalemate'; rather, its understanding was that the IRA had finally realised it could not win and was seeking a way out of the conflict.

For this reason, the Prime Minister convened a special Cabinet Committee comprising himself, the Secretary of State for Northern Ireland, Patrick Mayhew, the former Secretary of State, Douglas Hurd, the Home Secretary, Kenneth Clarke and the Attorney-General, Nick Lyell.[64] This Committee resolved that the government was duty bound to follow up the message and an immediate, holding response was sent to the effect that the 'seriousness' of what had been said was both understood and appreciated. The government promised to 'reply further as swiftly as possible'.[65]

Nevertheless, even now, in its eagerness to explore the apparent breakthrough, the government did not lose sight of the parameters it had set for a peace process that was to involve republicans. On 19 March 1993, the government sent a nine paragraph document to Sinn Fein which constituted its substantive response to the IRA's 'offer'. Talks involving republicans, it was maintained, could be forthcoming: 'The British government has no desire to inhibit or impede legitimate constitutional expression of any political opinion'.[66] But crucially these talks could only occur after an end to violence. Furthermore, only if it was shown that the IRA's campaign had been 'genuinely brought to an end' could 'progressive entry into dialogue' take place. The same document also stressed that there could be no 'predetermined outcome' to any talks process. It freely acknowledged that a united Ireland could be one resolution to the conflict; however, it emphasised that this could only occur, 'on the basis of the consent of the people of Northern Ireland'. In other words, there could be no 'declaration of intent to withdraw' from Northern Ireland by the British government, in advance of negotiations—a long-standing demand of republicans. The aim was for an 'agreed accommodation, not an imposed settlement'.[67]

The republican response appeared unequivocal: the day after the message had been received the IRA exploded a bomb in Warrington in the north of England, injuring scores of people and killing two young children.[68] In spite of this, 'Fred', at the urging of Brendan Duddy, took part in a face-to-face meeting with senior republicans Martin McGuinness and Gerry Kelly. It remains unclear whether or not this encounter was authorised by his superiors. Damagingly for the government, it later emerged in the press that a meeting took place just two days after the Warrington attack.[69] Either way, it would appear that 'Fred' now delivered a message that went much further than anything prior to that point—or indeed, anything that came subsequently. By Sinn Fein's account of the meeting, McGuinness and Kelly were told,

Mayhew had tried marginalisation, defeating the IRA etc. That's gone ... Mayhew is now determined. He wants Sinn Fein to play a part not because he likes Sinn Fein but because it cannot work without them. Any settlement not involving all of the people North and South won't work. A North/South settlement that won't frighten unionists. The final solution is union. It is going to happen anyway. The historical train—Europe—determines that. We are committed to Europe. Unionists will have to change. This island will be as one.[70]

On the surface, this statement—recorded in Sinn Fein's official account, which was generally assumed to be more accurate than the version provided by the British—would appear to be highly significant. For it lends credibility to the notion that the British state had signalled to the IRA that a united Ireland was 'on the table' in the event of peace—and it was this that helped convince the republican movement to embrace a non-violent path. In Peter Taylor's 2008 television documentary, *The Secret Peace Maker*, Brendan Duddy confirmed that the British interlocutor had indeed made this assertion.[71] Crucially, Duddy also revealed that 'Fred' had added a qualification: that no British government would abandon the unionists. There are two possible explanations for these different narratives. The first is that Sinn Fein's account of these discussions was not as accurate as has subsequently been believed. The second and perhaps more likely, is that the qualification had simply failed to register on the republican radar, because of the significance that they invested in the main part of 'Fred's' analysis. If this is the case, it would seem to support the view that the republican movement was not so much cynically selective in its use of this information, as wilfully deluded by some of its content.

Furthermore, while this statement was always likely to capture the attention of a movement which still held that the British acted like a colonial overlord, it was, by and large, speculative. More important, in terms of how to proceed in the short-term, was the fact that 'Fred' also went on to outline a situation in which republicans could enter 'delegate' talks with the British government after a mere two-week ceasefire. When set against the tenor and substance of other British government communications with the republican movement over this period, the content of this exchange seemed to represent a remarkable departure. Thus, there is some suspicion that 'Fred', in his anxiety to keep the process going after the Warrington attack, may have significantly over-stepped his brief. If this was indeed the case, his interlocutors had no idea that this was so; on the contrary, McGuinness later recalled his own sense of being 'quite convinced from my contacts with this person that he was a bona fide representative of the British government'.[72] A recurrent flaw in republican strategy had been to assume that their enemy, the British state, always acted with unity of purpose.

Whatever the truth underpinning the actions of 'Fred', with the benefit of hindsight it seems likely that the IRA leadership drew a more damaging lesson from the message as he relayed it: its bombing offensive—particularly on the British mainland—was weakening British resolve. This offensive, which had been ongoing since 1989 had included a series of high-profile attacks: the murder of ten Royal Marines in Deal in September 1989; the murder of Conservative MP, Ian Gow in July 1990; the mortar attack on Downing Street in February 1991; and the bombing of the Baltic Exchange in April 1992. The March 1993 Warrington attack had been merely the latest in a series of similar acts of violence (an almost identical device had been left in Camden Town, London, the previous month, killing one and injuring many more).[73] And after the meeting that republicans held with 'Fred', they saw little reason to abandon that approach. Thus, April 1993 brought another huge bomb in the City of London that killed one man and caused hundreds of millions of pounds worth of damage. Further assaults on the UK's capital followed in autumn of the same year.[74]

In the meantime, republican representatives held to an uncompromising position in the back-channel communications with the British government, who grew impatient with their unforthcoming responses.[75] Central to this was the attempt to side-step the crucial issue of whether violence would be ended on a permanent basis. In an effort to make things as easy as possible for the republican leadership, the British had signalled that any IRA cessation could be 'unannounced' at first, so long as it came with private assurances that the violence was truly over. At this point, republicans were reluctant to move as far on this issue as the British required. Thus, while Sinn Fein subsequently made much of a purported offer from the IRA of a two-week suspension of its campaign in May 1993, the message that accompanied that offer stated simply, 'we have proceeded to this stage, without assurance. We wish now to proceed without delay to the delegation meetings'.[76] Republicans, it was claimed, were 'prepared to make the crucial move' and in line with this Sinn Fein had 'sought and received a commitment which will permit you [the British government] to proceed'.[77] What was omitted was any indication that the 'suspension' (and the terminology used here is significant) would be anything more than a hiatus in the ongoing violence. Neither was there a willingness to give any form of 'assurance'—whether private or otherwise—on even a limited cessation of violence. Instead, the formal 'basis for entering into dialogue' that Sinn Fein also delivered at this time, stated 'we do not seek to impose pre-conditions nor should pre-conditions be imposed on us'. Here was a line which would resonate long after, even beyond Northern Ireland: 'Pre-conditions represent obstacles to peace'.[78]

From the perspective of the British government, the crucial obstacle to progress remained the lack of clarity on the issue of the IRA's campaign. That is not to say that the government did not contemplate an acceptance of the IRA's two week ceasefire offer. Evidently it did, and this much was relayed to Sinn Fein by 'Fred'—again, in what may have amounted to him exceeding his brief (with the result that an account of the internal Downing Street debate is included in Sinn Fein's record of this period).[79] In the end, though, the government decided that the proposed length of cessation was simply not long enough. As it clearly stated in its formal response to the 'ceasefire offer' in July 1993,

Recent pronouncements [from republicans]... seem to imply that unless your analysis of the way forward is accepted within a set time, the halt in violence will only be temporary. This is not acceptable.

What the government was indicating—in the starkest terms—was that it could not allow republicans into talks without an emphatic statement—comprising actions as well as words—that this was a new departure. To underscore the message, this and previous communications also pointed to the problems caused by 'events on the ground'—a clear reference to IRA violence.[80] The government, it was stressed, 'cannot conceivably disregard them'; 'unfortunate headline events' (for example, major bomb attacks, such as that on London's Baltic Exchange in April 1993) made 'bold steps' (any move towards dialogue) almost impossible.

This was the bottom line. The issue of violence—and more particularly, whether or not it would be permanently halted—remained absolutely central to the exchanges between the British government and republicans during the 1990–3 period. And ultimately, it was British uncertainty over IRA intentions that led to the collapse of those talks amid mutual recriminations. As one of the final messages sent by the British government to Sinn Fein noted, a key sticking point remained the fact that republicans had not confirmed that a 'lasting end to violence does not depend on [their] analysis being endorsed as the only way forward'.[81] In other words, the government continued to fear that the IRA might call a halt only temporarily, to facilitate Sinn Fein's entry into talks, before resuming its campaign as before—either during the talks, or in their aftermath if republicans failed to achieve what they wanted. It was the inability of the republican leadership to provide unambiguous clarification on that point that precipitated the failure of the secret communications in 1993.

The Battle over Preconditions

Ultimately, this breakdown meant that there was to be no simple trajectory from 1993 to the Belfast Agreement of 1998. At the same time, the very fact that such alternative channels of communications had existed, did at least suggest a recalibration of republican strategy, expanding the range of possible future outcomes. Although Sinn Fein's dialogue with the British government had reached an impasse, talks with Hume and the SDLP had intensified in the interim. The existence of this dialogue was publicly confirmed on 24 April 1993—the day the IRA bombed Bishopsgate in the City of London—when Adams and Hume finally released a joint statement. In it they asserted that there could be no 'internal solution' to the conflict and that 'the Irish people as a whole have a right to self-determination'.[82] This was balanced by the acknowledgement that 'not all the people of Ireland share that view or agree on how to give meaningful expression to it'.[83] Even so, the strongly nationalist tinge to the language was clear in what represented the first public expression of the 'Hume-Adams' process.

123

A draft of a proposed inter-governmental joint declaration, produced by Hume and Adams, was later passed to the Taoiseach, Albert Reynolds (who had succeeded Haughey in early 1992). Despite his misgivings as to its viability, Reynolds in turn passed it to the British government in July 1993.[84] The reaction of the British Prime Minister, John Major, was as Reynolds had predicted:

I had a look at it and it was just awful. ... It had everything in it that we couldn't possibly accept—we couldn't be persuaders for Irish unity, we needed changes to Articles 2 and 3 of the Irish constitution, we weren't at all keen on pan-Irish authority over things that were legitimately the responsibility of the United Kingdom.[85]

On top of all this, the 'Hume-Adams' document also envisaged a commitment from the British government that it would withdraw from Ireland within a certain 'timeframe'.[86] This negation of the 'consent principle'—that the future of Northern Ireland could only be decreed by the decision of a majority of its inhabitants—settled any remaining doubt as to whether the document might prove acceptable. Major decisively rejected it as constituting a way forward. After receiving a personal letter from Reynolds imploring him to keep it on the table, Major replied to the effect that 'Hume-Adams' was 'a kiss of death' on the fragile process.[87]

Still, the British government was not oblivious to the opportunity contained within the 'Hume-Adams' process. It was clear that the more that republicans associated themselves with 'peace', the more public pressure they were likely to generate upon themselves to match words with actions. There was an element of self-fulfilling prophecy about the 'Hume-Adams' process and it was this that the government now sought to maximise. For this reason, it sought to build on the 'process' that had begun, but to invest it with new content. Over the summer and early autumn of 1993, work began on re-writing the putative joint declaration to bring it into line with the parameters for ending the conflict, as defined by the British state.

The process was disrupted, however, by ongoing IRA violence, such as the Shankill road bomb of October 1993 (particularly as Gerry Adams was pictured carrying the coffin of one of the bombers, who had died in the attack).[88] In the aftermath, the Irish as well as the British government decided that any initiative bearing the imprint of 'Hume-Adams' was a non-starter. The result, as Albert Reynolds' close aide Sean Duignan was to put it, was that 'Hume-Adams' had to be declared, 'dead in order to keep it alive'.[89] In keeping with this impulse, the two governments issued a statement following a meeting in Brussels in late October 1993 that definitively ruled out the adoption or endorsement of the 'Hume-Adams' proposals. Meanwhile, London and Dublin determined to seize the initiative themselves, supplanting 'Hume-Adams' with a publicly stated agreement of their own shared position.

The product of this enterprise was the 'Downing Street Declaration' of 15 December 1993. It was finally settled upon after tough negotiations in which, according to Reynolds, he had 'chewed [Major's] bollocks off', while the British Prime Minister 'took a few lumps outta me'.[90] Communication between the IRA and the government had stuttered to a halt in 1993 but, ironically, it was the collapse of this channel—rather than its continued existence—which provided the context for this new initiative: a seminal moment in the formation of the peace process in Northern Ireland. The Declaration looked explicitly to the creation of 'a new political framework' on the basis that,

The British government agree that it is for the people of the island of Ireland alone, by agreement between the two parties respectively, to exercise their right of self-determination on the basis of consent, freely and concurrently given, North and South, to bring about a united Ireland, if that is their wish.[91]

In this way, it set in stone the two central pillars of the British government's position: on the one hand, its lack of strategic interest for remaining in Ireland; on the other, its commitment to the principle of 'consent' for Northern Ireland. The latter was pointedly emphasised by John Major in the House of Commons when he declared, 'the Declaration provides that it is and must be for the people of Northern Ireland to determine their own future'.[92] As far as the British government was concerned, this was the *sine qua non* of any resolution to the conflict.

In speaking as he did, the Prime Minister sought to reassure unionists, aware of the danger that the Declaration might spark a new wave of anxiety on a par with that precipitated by the Anglo-Irish Agreement of eight years earlier. In the tense negotiations between the British and Irish government officials which led to the Declaration, Irish officials claimed that the British had attempted to change the text completely. In the Irish analysis, the British were, 'at the very least, trying to buy time to appease Jim Molyneaux, the Ulster Unionist Party leader'.[93] As a British government insider noted at the time, with reference to the 1985 deal, 'We were very keen not to be in that territory again'.[94]

In response to the Declaration, Ian Paisley's hard-line reaction was in keeping with his previous pronouncements. In 'this dark hour of treachery', he declared, the British government had 'sold Ulster to buy off the fiendish Republican scum'.[95] In contrast to Paisley's invective, though, the leader of the Ulster Unionist Party, James Molyneaux, did not reject the Declaration out of hand. Unlike in 1985, the Prime Minister of the day had been careful to keep Molyneaux abreast of key developments in the run-up to the Declaration. Thus, immediately prior to the exposure of the government's secret communications with the IRA in late 1993, Molyneaux had been informed of what had taken place. Then, during the drafting of the Declaration itself, the unionist leader was shown early versions of the document and allowed to contribute to its formulation.[96] The emphasis was on ensuring that it was not seen as a new 'diktat' that could catch the mainstream leaders of unionism by surprise. As a consequence, Molyneaux's reaction to the Declaration was one of composed caution; this, coupled with Major's reassurances, helped ensure that the loyalist response was relatively muted compared to 1974 and 1985–6.

In fact, behind the scenes, the loyalist paramilitaries were inching towards a ceasefire of their own in this period. Just as the British state had established 'behind-the-scenes' contacts with the republican movement, so the Irish government had allowed an informal line of communication to grow up between itself and the loyalist paramilitaries. This involved a Dublin trade unionist, Chris Hudson, who had had a chance encounter with UVF leaders in 1993 and subsequently maintained the relationship. As Jim Cusack and Henry McDonald have detailed, Hudson kept the Irish government informed of his dealings, via Fergus Finlay, special adviser to the Irish Foreign Secretary, Dick Spring.[97] Simultaneously, a Presbyterian Minister, the Reverend Roy Magee, was engaging in private dialogue with the UDA-UFF leadership, challenging them to end the violence. Archbishop Robin Eames, the Anglican Archbishop of Armagh and the Primate of All Ireland, was also brought in on that process and acted as an intermediary, relaying the loyalist position to both the London and Dublin governments. The essence of this position, as relayed by the Hudson and Magee-Eames channels, was 'Prepared for Peace, Ready for War'; indeed, these very words had been daubed on a loyalist mural in Belfast.[98] Thus, Hudson recalls being told by the UVF leadership that they wanted peace, but were also prepared to take their campaign south, possibly with indiscriminate, no-warning bomb attacks in Dublin. For its own part then, the Irish government had a security incentive not to yield too far to the pan-nationalist position. Among loyalists, revelations about the extent of the IRA's contacts with the British government caused some consternation. But, as Peter Taylor has described, the prospect of an intensified loyalist backlash was dampened by Archbishop Eames who—after travelling to Downing Street and speaking personally to John Major—was able to reassure loyalists that no secret deal had been made with the IRA.[99]

With the confidence of unionism and loyalism bolstered with regards to the intent of the British state, the Downing Street Declaration attempted to set the terms for republican involvement, with a restatement of the government's terms for peace negotiations. Article nine of the Declaration stated:

The British and Irish Governments reiterate that the achievement of peace must involve a permanent end to the use of, or support for, paramilitary violence. They confirm that, in these circumstances, democratically mandated parties which establish a commitment to exclusively peaceful methods and which have shown that they abide by the democratic process, are free to participate fully in democratic politics and to join in dialogue in due course between the Governments and the political parties on the way ahead.[100]

While there was to be some ambiguity as to how the commitment to 'exclusively peaceful methods' could be demonstrated, this established the principle that parties tied to violence could not simultaneously 'participate fully in democratic politics'. Here was a public restatement of what had been articulated by the British government through the back-channel communications of previous years, to which the Irish government had also subscribed. In the absence of violence, the governments had pledged that republicans would not be ignored; but neither would they occupy the central role in any negotiation process. Instead, the sole criteria for inclusion were to be the possession of a democratic mandate, together with a commitment to purely democratic methods. As the Irish government mandarin Martin Mansergh later reaffirmed, the 'requirements [for Sinn Fein to come into the process] were stated clearly' in paragraph ten of the Declaration.[101]

Unsurprisingly, therefore, the Downing Street Declaration constituted a major challenge to republicans. If the 'Hume-Adams' process was symptomatic of their effort to secure a peace process on their terms, the Declaration produced by the two governments marked the comprehensive failure of that endeavour. In other words, the momentum of 'Hume-Adams' had been turned back against republicans. Expectations of an IRA ceasefire had been raised by 'Hume-Adams', only for the process to change track. Now, in agreeing to a ceasefire on the terms of the Downing Street Declaration and the principle of consent, the IRA would effectively be acceding to a reality against which it had fought for thirty years. A review of the republican position at this moment captured the difficulty. On the one hand, there had been little improvement in the overall prospects for the IRA's campaign (despite the bombing campaign in England). On the other, Sinn Fein was now exposed to the vagaries of a political process with which it had tentatively become involved. If republicans were seen to walk away from the fledgling peace process, they were likely to face opprobrium and greater marginalisation.

Faced with this dilemma, there were two aspects to the republican response. First, they played for time. Given the scale of the ideological compromises involved, outright acceptance of the Declaration was impossible. The republican leadership therefore successfully used requests for 'clarification' of the document's meaning in order to delay a formal rejection of it.[102] By the time that rejection duly materialised (at a specially-convened Sinn Fein conference in June 1994) it was soon overtaken by the second prong of the republican response to the Declaration. This entailed a half acceptance of one precondition (a halt in IRA violence), in an effort to manoeuvre around those that remained (such as the demand for a permanent renunciation of violence and formal acceptance of the consent principle).

The manifestation of this was the IRA's announcement of a 'complete cessation of military operations' on 31 August 1994. Both at the time and subsequently, this was portrayed as the act of a republican movement that was turning decisively away from violence and *de facto* accepting the Downing Street Declaration. In reality, it was a purely pragmatic response from an organisation that still thought in terms of long-term strategic goals. The recognition that the traditional military campaign of the IRA had failed to achieve its objectives had forced a reappraisal. Yet this did not involve a rejection of violence in principle. On the contrary, the intellectual rationale for the ceasefire was defined by the 'TUAS' document that the republican leadership produced over the summer of 1994. The acronym by which this document was known was entirely indicative of the philosophy underpinning the subsequent cessation: it stood for the 'Tactical Use of Armed Struggle' (not, as was initially believed by some, Totally UnArmed Strategy).[103]

The British government's awareness of this—the result, it would seem, of the intelligence services' extensive penetration of the republican movement, particularly in Belfast—ensured that it reacted cautiously to the IRA ceasefire.[104] As John Major declared, 'I am greatly encouraged but we need to be clear this is intended to be a permanent renunciation of violence. If it is, then many options are open. ... Let words now be reflected in deeds'.[105] This question, of the 'permanence' or otherwise of the cessation, now emerged as the central issue on the political agenda. This was, after all, merely an extension of the dispute that had dominated the British government's backchannel communications with republicans over the previous four years. Immediately prior to the ceasefire, the NIO Minister, Michael Ancram, had reaffirmed that this remained the fundamental issue of concern: 'We are not prepared to enter into any form of dialogue, including exploratory dialogue, with those who support violence until there has been a permanent renunciation and cessation of violence on a credible basis'.[106] When the IRA then called its campaign to a halt, the Secretary of State, Patrick Mayhew, made it emphatically clear that the British government's apparent obsession with 'permanence' was, 'not just a piece of pedantry or nitpicking about a particular word'.[107] Instead it was matter of 'absolute essential importance' that such talks and negotiations 'as may take place in future shall not take place under the implied threat that violence, which after all has gone on for so long, could be taken up again and renewed and resumed if people don't behave during those discussions in a way which was congenial to the IRA'.[108] This was a long way from 'peace at any price'.

Six weeks later, on 13 October 1994, the Combined Loyalist Military Command (CLMC)—an umbrella group formed three years earlier to co-ordinate the activities of the UDA-UFF, the UVF and the smaller paramilitary group, the Red Hand Commando—announced that their members had been ordered to 'universally cease all operational hostilities'. In an unexpected gesture of repentance, the CLMC statement had also spoken of the loyalist paramilitaries' 'abject and true remorse' for the death of 'all innocent victims' over the previous twenty-five years.[109] Indeed, it has since been suggested that the loyalist cessation could have occurred several months earlier but for a series of republican actions targeted directly against loyalists. The latter later dubbed this a 'summer of provocation' and responded with a number of sectarian atrocities.[110] As Henry McDonald has noted, in the weeks leading up to the IRA ceasefire at the end of August, republicans had intensified their attacks on loyalists, including bomb attacks on pubs frequented by UDA members in Belfast. According to the late David Ervine, head of the loyalist political front, the Progressive Unionist Party (PUP), speaking shortly after the loyalist ceasefires in October: 'The Provos wanted to strut the world stage as peacemakers while we, the bloodthirsty loyalists, were still killing people'.[111]

On 21 October 1994, John Major declared that he would make a 'working assumption' that the IRA cessation was permanent and cleared the way towards talks between government representatives and Sinn Fein.[112] Yet he did so in an atmosphere in which some form of weapons handover was beginning to be discussed as a possible alternative to an IRA statement confirming permanence. Earlier that same month, the Prime Minister had told the House of Commons that, 'Armaments—especially Semtex and detonators, perhaps more than guns—are a crucial issue that will have to be dealt with as we advance the process'.[113] The shooting dead by the IRA of a postal worker, Frank Kerr, in Newry several weeks later—the first major violation of the ceasefire—seemed merely to corroborate Major's point. In late November 1994, the leader of the Irish Labour Party and erstwhile Irish Foreign Secretary, Dick Spring, noted that peace could only be achieved by the 'decommissioning of all the means of destruction'.[114] The following month, Michael Ancram asserted that a failure to resolve the arms issue would create a 'substantial barrier' to Sinn Fein's full involvement in all-party talks.[115]

Towards the Agreement

For the moment, this growing focus on weapons decommissioning appeared to register little with republicans. Instead, they remained adamant that, in the words of Sinn Fein strategist Mitchel McLaughlin, any insistence on a handover of IRA weaponry would 'invite this very fragile consensus to collapse'.[116] The republican leadership seemed determined to circumvent the decommissioning/permanency issue and to use the popular support and momentum arising out of the ceasefire to drive forward the political process over the temporary impasse. The high-point for this strategy came in February 1995, when the British and Irish governments released an outline for a possible negotiated settlement. The 'Frameworks for the Future' documents proved to be highly controversial, particularly because of leaks prior to their official release, which tended to heighten unionist concern over the character of the proposals. *The Times*, for instance, predicted that these would be 'considerably more green than the Ulster Unionists have expected' and also subsequently declared that they brought, 'the prospect of a united Ireland closer than it has been at any time since partition in 1920'.[117]

Despite such fears, however, the truth about Frameworks proved to be far more prosaic. As the *Belfast Telegraph* noted at the time, the documents actually offered 'something for everyone'—and what any individual chose to focus on was very much in the eye of the beholder. Unionists could thus, if they wished, 'regard the strong North-South dimension as a slippery slope to Irish unity'. Indeed, it was precisely on this basis that republicans welcomed the document, pointing to the potentially powerful and 'free-standing' nature of cross-border bodies. Yet, as the *Belfast Telegraph* also observed, just as the Frameworks proposals could be seen as the thin end of the wedge of Irish unity, they could just as easily be seen as 'a means of copper-fastening partition for generations to come' by their focus on 'agreement and consent'.[118] Similarly, the proposed north-south institutions, by which republicans set such store, could, in the words of one academic study, be viewed as little more than a 'bureaucratic fantasia' designed to appeal to Sinn Fein, but built on 'some very modest realities'.[119]

In many ways the importance of the Frameworks documents lay not in what they were, but in what they represented. For republicans, they marked a clear improvement on the Downing Street Declaration and one that they hoped then to build on in further talks. They saw them as a kind of beach-head for further negotiations in which republicans believed that a settlement might evolve in a yet more 'green' direction, to the point where it might plausibly be portrayed as having ushered in *de facto*, joint British and Irish authority over Northern Ireland. In this context, it is perhaps significant that Gerry Adams had, as far back as July 1993, hinted that such 'joint authority' might be an acceptable outcome for republicans.[120]

For unionists, by contrast, the Frameworks proposals were regarded as a significant turn for the worse. Just as with the Anglo-Irish Agreement ten years earlier (and unlike the Downing Street Declaration), the unionist leader, James Molyneaux had not been consulted and his leadership of unionism came under renewed scrutiny. Attacks on him from critics of the peace process, such as Paisley (who had described it as a 'one-way street to Dublin') gained momentum.[121] Worse was to follow, as Molyneaux's party lost a hitherto 'safe seat' in a Westminster by-election to a staunch opponent of the peace process. By September, he had resigned, to be replaced by the Ulster Unionist MP for Upper Ban, David Trimble, who though elected on an apparently hardline platform, proved to be a much more complex political figure.[122]

In response to the obvious disquiet and upheavals within unionism, the British government took stock of its position. The perception grew that unionism had been pushed too far. Nevertheless, the British government had not retreated from the pre-conditions it had set for Sinn Fein's entry into the political process. Thus, while meetings between Sinn Fein representatives and government officials had taken place—leading to further exploratory dialogue over the summer of 1995—this had not been followed by the launch of meaningful negotiations. The government stuck to the view that 'substantive' or 'significant' progress on the weapons question was essential, if republicans were to demonstrate a clear commitment to purely democratic methods.[123] Again and again, John Major returned to this theme.[124] His position was clear: 'A just peace and one that is fair to all sides... must be a peace that is constructed away from the shadow of the gun'.[125] In this respect, the furore surrounding the Frameworks proposals served to obscure a deeper truth about the fledgling peace process: the preconditions' quarrel had not been resolved.

In March 1995, on a visit to the United States, the Secretary of State, Sir Patrick Mayhew, laid out what subsequently became known as the 'Washington 3' criteria. These were three inter-locking provisions, to which republicans would have to adhere, if Sinn Fein were to enter all-party talks. Foremost of these was the demand for the commencement of (at least some) weapons decommissioning. In response, republicans were unbending in their assertion that this was impossible; as an IRA spokesperson declared, 'there is absolutely no question of any IRA decommissioning at all, either through the back door or the front door'.[126] In June 1995, Martin McGuinness famously stated that there was 'not a snowball's chance in hell of any weapons being decommissioned this side of a negotiated settlement'.[127] By September 1995, Gerry Adams was describing 'the placing of preconditions on the road to dialogue' as a 'formula for disaster' and stating that, if the government did not shift position 'then the peace process, or this phase of the peace process, is doomed to collapse'.[128]

Throughout 1995, republicans argued that the growing preoccupation with decommissioning was a new precondition on progress, a post-dated innovation which had been inserted by the British after the IRA's ceasefire. In an interview with the *Irish Times* in June 1995, for instance, Gerry Adams claimed that it was 'never mentioned' prior to the 31 August 1994 cessation.[129] A month later, in the same newspaper, Adams repeated this claim and contended that the British government had known that there would have been no ceasefire, if the question of arms had been a major issue. All that had been required for Sinn Fein to enter all-party talks, he averred, was an end to IRA violence.[130] As to why the British should now be insisting on weapons decommissioning, the suggestion from republicans was that John Major's Conservative government had become more hard-line in order to secure unionist support at Westminster, where it enjoyed only a narrow House of Commons majority. Certainly, as Paul Dixon has argued, the requirements of parliamentary arithmetic may have contributed to the British government playing 'something like the supporting role' for unionists that the Irish had always played for nationalists, after years of destabilising ambiguity.[131] Tied to this was the republican insinuation that both unionists and the British government were attempting to achieve by stealth, what the security services had failed to accomplish militarily: an outright defeat of the IRA.[132]

What all of this ignored was the fact that decommissioning had been discussed prior to the IRA's 1994 ceasefire. Quentin Thomas—the senior civil servant who led the post-ceasefire meetings with Sinn Fein—has been quoted to the effect that Major, Ancram and Mayhew had experienced 'a strange psychological flip' on this issue and were determined to show 'that they were not patsies'.[133] Nonetheless, decommissioning had not simply emerged from nowhere as a British stalling tactic. The Irish Foreign Minister, Dick Spring, had told the Irish Parliament in December 1993 (during a debate on the Downing Street Declaration which was announced the same day),

We are talking about a permanent cessation of violence, and we are talking about a handing up of arms, with the insistence that it would not be a case of 'we are on a temporary cessation of violence to see what the political process offers'.[134]

Six months later, Spring had reaffirmed this position.[135] Moreover, republicans themselves were only too aware of the likelihood that the decommissioning question could become a stumbling-block. In an interview he gave to the *Irish News* in January 1994 (some eight months before the ceasefire), Adams had heavily criticised the British government on precisely these grounds.[136] Even in late 1994, Sean Duignan, the press secretary for the Irish Prime Minister Albert Reynolds, recorded how 'Martin McGuinness spoke frankly about the need to dispose of armaments' in Reynolds' office: 'We know the guns will have to be banjaxed', he had conceded.[137] The suggestion that the demand for decommissioning was an *ex-post-facto* creation of either the British state or unionism does not stand up to scrutiny.

Nevertheless, it is striking that republicans found considerable support for their stance from the rest of nationalist Ireland. In April 1995, for example, John Hume declared that there was 'no excuse' for further delay in the launching of all-party talks. In the same way, the former Taoiseach, Albert Reynolds (who had been forced to resign for domestic political reasons in November 1994) also now emerged as a prominent voice in favour of the immediate commencement of such talks. In an interview with *The Observer*, Reynolds argued that the British had 'miscalculated' over decommissioning. Even more striking was his implicit suggestion that in the event of continued deadlock, a return to violence by the IRA could be understandable: 'if they went back to the armed conflict people won't blame them because they have shown good faith'.[138] While not going as far, the Irish Foreign minister, Dick Spring, had clearly shifted position as well, by the autumn of 1995. In September he declared,

To make the decommissioning of weapons a precondition for entry into negotiation, as opposed to an important goal to be realised in that process, ignores the psychology and motivation of those on both sides in Ireland who have resorted to violence and the lessons of conflict resolution elsewhere.[139]

Soon after, the Taoiseach himself, John Bruton—not known for his sympathy for the republican cause—also appeared to back his Foreign Minister's stance and called for a beginning to meaningful dialogue between all the parties.[140] Bruton's remarks brought a swift riposte from John Major and the ensuing row was testament of the extent to which the two governments had diverged over the decommissioning issue.[141]

The effort to square the circle between the apparently incompatible positions of the British and Irish governments led to the adoption of a 'twin track' approach to the political process in late November 1995 (just prior to the visit of US President Bill Clinton to Belfast). On the one hand, preparations would begin for all-party talks, with the 'firm aim' of launching these before the end of February 1996.[142] Alongside this, an international body was created, under the stewardship of former US Senator George Mitchell, to consider the way forward. When the idea for just such an entity had first been suggested earlier in the year, it was reported that Sinn Fein had told Irish government officials there would 'bodies in the streets' if the plan went ahead.[143] On that occasion, the suggestion was that republican doubts had prompted the Irish government to back away from the proposals; by November, however, it appeared to have given its support to the scheme in an effort to resolve the decommissioning standoff.

The report subsequently produced by the Mitchell Commission concluded that decommissioning would not occur prior to all-party talks. It therefore recommended that a weapons handover might be pursued 'in parallel' with such talks. On this basis, John Major's acceptance of the report was interpreted, in some quarters, as a significant climbdown by the British. Yet, the truth was not nearly as straight-forward as that, for Mitchell provided a much broader framework for taking forward the talks process. Crucial here was the fact that those wishing to be involved in formal dialogue would have to affirm their 'total and absolute commitment' to six fundamental principles of democracy and non-violence:

a. To democratic and exclusively peaceful means of resolving political issues.
b. To the total disarmament of all paramilitary organisations
c. To agree that such disarmament must be verifiable to the satisfaction of an independent commission
d. To renounce for themselves, and to oppose any effort by others, to use force, or threaten to use force, to influence the course or the outcome of all-party negotiations
e. To agree to abide by the terms of any agreement reached in all-party negotiations and to resort to democratic and exclusively peaceful methods in trying to alter any aspect of that outcome with which they may disagree.
f. To urge that 'punishment' killings and beatings stop and to take effective steps to prevent such actions.[144]

In addition to this, Major also adopted Mitchell's suggestion that an 'elective process' be held in order to 'contribute to the building of confidence' ahead of talks. In so doing, the government effectively endorsed the view of the new Ulster Unionist Party leader, David Trimble, who had argued that elections were an indispensable precursor to any dialogue.

The Mitchell Principles—and indeed, the report as a whole—represented the latest effort to move the peace process forward, while retaining certain core provisions. If the requirement of decommissioning had been a way of sidestepping the demand that the IRA declare a 'permanent' end to violence, the Mitchell report was, in turn, about manoeuvring the peace process around the decommissioning issue—finding a way to get the republican leadership off the 'hook' that they had put themselves on with their repeated assertions that equated decommissioning with surrender. The proposed solution was the conduct of decommissioning in parallel with talks, with those involved in talks deriving their mandate from the electoral process. As David Trimble has since described, the pack had been shuffled but the fundamentals— pre-conditions and a framework for future negotiations—remained in place, albeit in a different order.[145] In a context in which republicans were unable to say that the ceasefire was 'permanent' and decommissioning had been equated with surrender, adherence to the Mitchell Principles was to serve as the entry point to negotiations for those with a democratic mandate.

The fact that Trimble's imprimatur underscored the election proposal contained within Senator Mitchell's report, no doubt contributed to the hostile reception it received in many nationalist quarters. The SDLP leader, John Hume, accused the Prime Minister of playing 'politics' with people's lives and of trying to 'buy votes' from Unionist MPs in order to stay in power. Republicans, meanwhile, accused Major of having 'binned' the Mitchell report and said the British had 'effectively dumped the twin-track process'.[146] Again, the emphasis was on apparent British duplicity and the introduction of new obstacles to all-party talks. It was this line of argument that was subsequently used to explain the end of the IRA's ceasefire just over two weeks later when the organisation detonated a huge bomb at Canary Wharf in London in February 1996; the abandonment of Mitchell, it was argued, provided the immediate *causus belli* for the resumption of republican violence.

Once again, however, the underlying reality was very different. First, with regards to the timing of the IRA's 'return to war', plans for this had been laid long before Mitchell produced his report. Indeed, it might have happened earlier, but for the visit of the American President, Bill Clinton, to Northern Ireland in late 1995. The desire of republicans not to alienate their American support base effectively ensured that they were unwilling to countenance renewed violence prior to his visit. More fundamentally, the notion that the IRA resumed its campaign in order to defend the honour of Mitchell and his report has to be subjected to critical scrutiny. For one thing this is because the report itself went down very badly among grass-roots republicans. For another, as has been described, the government had not abandoned Mitchell. Far from disposing of Mitchell's recommendations, the government had largely endorsed his model.

The result was the calling of elections to a Northern Ireland Forum in June 1996. When the time came for that body to meet, Sinn Fein found itself 'locked out' of the Forum because of the resumption of the IRA's campaign in the intervening period. Here, it is worth challenging the widely held view that the IRA successfully forced their way back into the political picture with the Canary Wharf attack. According to Fergus Finlay, former advisor to Dick Spring, the reality was very different. If they had waited just another two weeks, to the end of February, 'they'd have had a firm date for the start of all-party negotiations, and they'd have had it in a way that would have made it impossible for Major to avoid sharing the table with them at the opening of these negotiations'. Instead: 'Once Sinn Fein had put themselves beyond the pale yet again, the search for mechanisms of inclusion became endlessly complicated'.[147]

One way of viewing the eighteen month return to 'armed struggle' by the IRA is as a final attempt by republicans to determine the basis upon which talks aimed at ending Northern Ireland's conflict would occur. However, the objective political realities still had not changed for the IRA during the months of cessation. It was going back to a campaign that had previously been failing and which had scarcely been assisted by the period of its ceasefire. Thus, the return to conflict was directed not at the attainment of republican goals, in any meaningful sense. Instead, it was one last effort to overcome the government's preconditions for peace talks. At the start of the 1990s, republicans had called for 'inclusive dialogue' to be held without any preconditions, even so much as a ceasefire. The Downing Street Declaration had confirmed that this was simply not an option and emphasised that any participants to a talks' process would have to renounce violence permanently. In response, republicans had called a cessation, but attempted to side-step the question of whether this marked a 'permanent' end to violence. The controversy over decommissioning and now the Mitchell Principles had established that this was not possible either. Consequently, Sinn Fein was allowed to enter the talks in September 1997 only when the IRA had 'restored' its ceasefire and Sinn Fein had subsequently announced that it accepted the Mitchell Principles.

In the spring of 1997, election results in both Britain and Ireland combined to change the atmosphere surrounding the peace process. In May, Tony Blair's 'New' Labour Party ended eighteen years of Conservative government, when it won a landslide victory in the British General Election; in June, Bertie Ahern led Fianna Fail back into government in the Republic of Ireland in coalition with the Progressive Democrats and independents. Both developments appeared to favour the republican movement. South of the Irish border, the return to power of Fianna Fail, which tended to uphold a more traditional form of Irish nationalism than its Fine Gael rival, appeared to bode well for republicans—all the more so, given that Ahern had previously been vocal in calling for dialogue with republicans, even in the absence of weapons decommissioning.[148]

Meanwhile, the triumph of Tony Blair's Labour Party was also viewed in a promising light by the republican leadership. For one thing, Blair's massive Westminster majority meant many expected him to enjoy a freedom of manoeuvre not open to his Conservative predecessor (republicans had attributed the sluggish pace of events between 1994 and 1996 to the latter's precarious parliamentary position and Major's need for unionist support). Added to this was the fact that the British Labour Party had traditionally favoured Irish unity 'by consent' and was generally considered to be less sympathetic to unionist concerns. Even more pertinently, Blair had made it plain soon after taking office that his preference was for an inclusive peace. Republicans would have a place in all-party talks, he declared, provided that the ceasefire was restored and they committed themselves to exclusively peaceful means.[149] After the IRA had ended its first ceasefire with the Canary Wharf attack, both the British and Irish governments had emphasised that any new cessation would have to be 'permanent' and there were various discussions about the period of decontamination that would be required before Sinn Fein was admitted to negotiations.[150] Yet, Blair had unmistakably discarded such notions, stating publicly on 25 June 1997 that republicans would quickly be allowed to enter into all-party talks after a restored ceasefire.[151]

Nonetheless, while these events represented a shift in the mood music of the peace process, there was actually little change in the core position of the British state. Prior to taking office, Blair had, in an interview with Frank Millar of the Irish Times, emphasised his break with the 'unity by consent' policy which had once guided Labour's approach to Northern Ireland.[152] As Dean Godson has described, Blair had also taken the time to establish a good relationship with David Trimble, which left the latter convinced of the Labour Party leader's commitment to an unadulterated conception of the principle of consent for Northern Ireland.[153] Moreover, the prerequisites for a republican entry into the talks' process, as staked out by the future Prime Minister, differed little from those of John Major. By the end of 1996, Major, in an effort to achieve a restored IRA ceasefire before he left office, was seeking to dilute his own tougher post-Canary Wharf stance.[154] Major's inclination was to return to the preconditions laid out by Mitchell and that he himself had previously accepted.[155] Blair's approach was entirely in keeping with this. True, the effect was that both Blair and Major appeared to be indicating that republicans would not be penalised for the resumption of violence; the same pre-conditions pertained to their entry into substantive talks as had been applicable immediately prior to the Canary Wharf bomb. Still, this did not amount to an absence of preconditions. As Tony Blair had stated in a pre-General Election article for the Irish Times, what was required was a 'genuine ceasefire', coupled with explicit republican acceptance of the 'Mitchell Principles'. Only in such circumstances, Blair averred, would Sinn Fein be allowed to 'take its place at the talks table'.[156] Furthermore, the Prime Minister subsequently indicated that the talks would proceed, with or without republicans: 'The settlement train is leaving, with or without Sinn Fein. If it wants to join it is absolutely clear what it has to do'.[157]

In the event, republicans opted to fulfil the conditions and participate. The IRA announced the 'unequivocal restoration' of its cessation in late July 1997. In response, the government declared that Sinn Fein would be allowed to enter the talks process six weeks later, provided that the party's leadership announced its acceptance of the Mitchell Principles. On 9 September, Sinn Fein duly endorsed the Principles (though a minor crisis was created when the IRA subsequently claimed that it was not bound by that endorsement—a notion rejected by the British government) and on 15 September 1997, full-scale talks began.[158] In so doing, republicans were taking advantage of a shift in atmosphere with the arrival of Blair and 'New' Labour, rather than a definitive shift in the substance of British state policy.

The talks that republicans now joined were far from open-ended; rather, the key parameters for negotiation were already in place. Thus, while it was technically possible for the government (and republicans) to argue that everything was 'on the table' (with Sinn Fein putting the case for Irish unity), the reality was that the central building blocks for any settlement had long been established. Blair himself had taken care to emphasise the most important of these during a visit to Northern Ireland soon after his election success—one principally designed to ease unionist concerns over republican involvement in negotiations. In a speech given to the Royal Ulster Agricultural Show at the Balmoral Show Grounds in Belfast, Blair articulated his position on Northern Ireland in forthright terms:

My message is simple. I am committed to Northern Ireland. I am committed to the principle of consent... A settlement is to be negotiated between the parties based on consent. My agenda is not a united Ireland... Northern Ireland will remain part of the United Kingdom as long as a majority here wish... Northern Ireland is part of the United Kingdom because that is the wish of a majority of the people who live here. It will remain part of the United Kingdom for as long as that remains the case. This principle of consent is and will be at the heart of my Government's policies on Northern Ireland. It is the key principle.[159]

The event and location for Blair's words had been carefully chosen. In the words of his new Secretary of State for Northern Ireland, Marjorie ('Mo') Mowlam, the government was determined to reach out to the 'heart of unionism'.[160]

Unsurprisingly, republican reaction to Blair's address was less than enthusiastic. Gerry Adams, for instance, subsequently described it as a 'very, very, very bad start' for the Labour Party leader.[161] The one bright spot for them was that Blair had confirmed that Sinn Fein could enter talks if a new IRA ceasefire was forthcoming. Still, Blair had quite clearly signalled the basis upon which those talks would be held.

Of equal significance was the fact that he had symbolically demonstrated that the concerns of the unionist majority in Northern Ireland would be uppermost in the search for any settlement; there was to be no sidelining of that majority in the quest for a deal with republicans. This impulse was reinforced by a further 'building block' that had been put in place long before the 1997 talks: the notion that any agreement had to be backed by 'sufficient consensus'. This concept, initially borrowed from South Africa, had been settled as early as 1992, in the talks overseen by Sir Patrick Mayhew and it remained non-negotiable after that point.[162] The idea of 'sufficient consensus' meant that unanimity on the part of all parties was not needed in order to achieve a settlement. Rather, it was 'sufficient' to have the support of the two governments, and a majority of unionists and a majority of nationalists. Not only did this invest the majority centre-ground of the political spectrum with the greatest influence, but also it ensured that no one organisation could exercise a veto on any agreement. As Fergus Finlay put it, 'We were bogged down on one primary issue "sufficient consensus" ... Simple majorities were not enough ... Blocking mechanisms could end up acting as IRA vetoes ... So it was vital to come up with a set of rules that would allow progress to be made, but without anyone's vital interests being trampled on'.[163]

In the context of 1997, the relevant majorities within the respective communities were determined by the results of the elections held to the Northern Ireland Forum in 1996. On the unionist side, the Ulster Unionist Party of David Trimble, with the support of the smaller loyalist parties, the PUP and the UDP, could achieve this requirement. Equally, the SDLP—which at that time still had more electoral support than Sinn Fein—could deliver the nationalist community's backing for a deal. The real balance of power, therefore, lay with the moderate 'centrists' in the UUP and the SDLP. The 'extremes', while welcome to join the process, could not dictate its outcome. Consequently, by removing themselves from the political process in July 1997—in protest at the prospect of the admission of Sinn Fein to the talks—the DUP were unable to bring the talks down. In fact, David Trimble— countering the notion that the DUP exit weakened the hand of unionism—has suggested that Paisley's departure made it easier for him to negotiate a deal.[164] Even more important, as the DUP walked out and Sinn Fein walked in, the latter were acceding to a process which they could not control.

141

It was not just the basic framework for negotiation that was already in place by September 1997; it was, in fact, already possible to discern the outline of a possible settlement. As has been noted, the Good Friday Agreement of 1998 bore a striking resemblance to the 1973–4 Sunningdale Agreement. In the two and a half decades between the respective accords there had been important additions and reformulations, but the underlying template was the same. The Brooke-Mayhew talks of 1990–2 had confirmed this approach. These discussions had enshrined a negotiating process that operated along 'three strands' and looked to the construction of mutually-dependent, inter-locking institutions that catered to different aspects of the population's identity and political inclinations: a locally elected assembly to govern Northern Ireland (strand one); some form of north-south body to facilitate cross-border co-operation with the Irish government (strand two); and a new British-Irish understanding that consolidated the east-west relationship and placed the island of Ireland within its wider, British Isles context (strand three). This set-up had already been brought into existence long before the commencement of all-party talks in September 1997. The fact was that the peace negotiations were, from the outset, built on an edifice that was independent of republican involvement, however desirable that involvement might have been.

The negotiations that began in September 1997 and ran through to April 1998, then, had a self-fuelling logic and momentum that were unconstrained by any Sinn Fein veto. The truth of this was made self-evident at a critical moment in the process in late 1997, when the British government became eager to produce a document to structure the final stage of talks. When the parties adjourned for Christmas, a key point of disagreement was whether or not there should be a devolved assembly for Northern Ireland. The unionist parties saw this as the cornerstone of any proposed settlement. Republicans, by contrast, were vehemently opposed to such an entity, which they saw as an entrenchment of partition and a reincarnation of the pre-Direct Rule regime. Only the previous year, the republican leadership had declared that people could, 'be sure of this—Sinn Fein will be no part of a return to Stormont'.[165] According to David Trimble, Sinn Fein's Chief Negotiator, Martin McGuinness, had spoken of there being 'blood on the streets' if any eventual agreement included some form of assembly for Northern Ireland.[166]

At that point in time, it should be noted, the prospect of a return to violence by the IRA appeared to be a real one. The IRA's renewed ceasefire was only a few months old and the fact that one truce had broken down appeared to serve notice that the same thing could reoccur. As if to confirm this, in November 1997 newspapers had reported the words of a senior member of Sinn Fein, Francie Molloy, who had allegedly said that if Sinn Fein failed to achieve its objectives in talks, then republicans would 'go back to what we do best'.[167] Against this background, there must surely have been a temptation for the British government—determined to secure a peace settlement that included republicans—to try to abandon plans for an assembly.

Despite this, the response of the British state—in the form of the 'Heads of Agreement' document of January 1998—was unequivocal: the concerns of Sinn Fein would not be prioritised ahead of the 'sufficient consensus' principle and the 'three strand formula'. 'Heads of Agreement' made it quite clear that a Northern Ireland assembly would be the essence of any deal. Moreover, this was to be set into a broader institutional context that was far from congenial to republicans. The 'cross-borderism' envisaged in the settlement was thus to be limited and 'sensible'. Simultaneously, the conception of what was attainable in 'strand three' had evolved considerably, with a new 'Council of the Isles' also provided for, in order to strengthen east-west links. On a personal level, this latter aspect of the nascent deal represented something of a triumph for the Ulster Unionist Party leader, David Trimble, who had set much store in the creation of such a body.[168] It confirmed that the establishment of a governing assembly in Northern Ireland could be linked to the Labour Party's restructuring of the United Kingdom more broadly. Events in the province could be set alongside legislative devolution in Scotland and Wales (as well as ultimately abortive plans to create 'regional parliaments' across England). New institutions arising out of any peace settlement did not have to symbolise Northern Ireland's position as a place apart within the United Kingdom. Rather than being seen as the thin end of a wedge to drive the province out of the Union, any agreement could instead be seen as entirely consistent with what Gerry Adams himself described (in a phrase that carried more truth than he perhaps intended), as a wider 'renegotiation' of the Union.[169]

In terms of what 'Heads of Agreement' revealed about the peace process, it emphatically reaffirmed that it was the constitutional parties that formed the moderate majority that set the agenda; and the implications of this for republicans were clear. As one commentator noted at the time, 'Where does Sinn Fein fit into all this? Rather worryingly, at the moment Sinn Fein does not appear to be fitting in at all... [Heads of Agreement] has knocked firmly on the head Sinn Fein's dreams of "rolling over" Mr. Blair'.[170]

The Good Friday Agreement

It was against this background, then, that the process arrived at the final week of talks in Easter 1998. Once again, what is striking about the most recent accounts of that final week is that the dynamic remained largely consistent. Although the political pendulum swung back and forth, from hour to hour, when the deal became imperilled the British government tilted towards what they regarded as the key consideration: keeping the unionists on board.

Over the weekend of 4–5 April 1998, the British and Irish governments had between them agreed a 'blueprint' for the agreement. This included an extensive remit for possible north-south co-operation covering three annexes and some fifty subject areas. On this basis, it seemed that the Irish government had successfully improved what was on offer for Irish nationalism from the settlement in the last stages before the deal was struck. Yet the corollary of this was that the anxieties of unionists had once again been stirred. The chairman of the talks process, George Mitchell, had anticipated this, even as he presented the 'draft paper' to the parties on Monday 8 April. 'I knew instantly that the Ulster Unionists could not, and would not, accept this agreement', he subsequently recalled.[171] So it proved, with the UUP rejecting the document and the party's deputy leader memorably stating that he would not touch it 'with a 40-foot pole'.[172]

At this point, Tony Blair took the crucial decision to go back to the Irish government to 're-open' negotiations on what was thought to be a settled document. According to the Prime Minister's closest aides, there had been a realisation within British circles that Trimble had been pushed too far. At a critical moment, Blair and his colleagues displayed an awareness of the imbalance which had bedevilled attempts to find a settlement for many years: the Irish government had essentially been negotiating on behalf of the SDLP and Sinn Fein, while the British government had not done likewise for the UUP.[173] On the crucial matter of north-south bodies, the British now essentially agreed to 'row in' behind the unionist position. To this end, in the words of

Blair's Chief-of Staff, Jonathan Powell, the Prime Minister told the Irish government 'that they had to amend the text on North/South matters radically and that there could be no progress elsewhere until this was unblocked'.[174] The Taoiseach was told that if this was not done, then the British government would abort the talks and blame Dublin for their collapse.

Alistair Campbell's diary entry for 9 April confirms that Blair and his advisers judged this to be the key psychological pressure point on their Irish counterparts. 'When the Irish came in, I suggested to TB that he "turn off the charm tap" and he start to get a bit heavier', wrote Campbell. The key British government negotiators duly warned Ahern that he would be 'crucified if we fall apart over this'.[175] Even before the final round of negotiations had begun, Ahern had stated that it would be very difficult for Dublin to turn down a deal with unionism.[176] Faced, therefore, with this British u-turn, partly carried out at the behest of David Trimble, Bertie Ahern agreed to re-negotiate strand two of the document—much to the delight of the Ulster Unionist leader who reportedly announced, 'I have just witnessed the ritual humiliation of an Irish prime minister'.[177]

In the end the scope for 'cross-borderism' contained within the emerging agreement was dramatically curtailed. The number of 'annexes' detailing north-south co-operation was reduced from three to one, while the number of designated areas for potential cross-border co-operation fell from 49 to 12 (of which only six were eventually enacted). This aspect of the accord was subsequently described by one of David Trimble's biographers as the unionist leader's 'greatest triumph'. Indeed, it would seem that Trimble himself even wondered if the scale of his victory might not be too great; so much so that the republican leadership might prove unwilling to endorse the deal.[178] In these final days, Sinn Fein's chief negotiator, Martin McGuinness, had indeed appeared to suggest that republicans might reject the putative settlement, publicly warning the British government to 'avoid the temptation to go for the Unionist position'.[179] Behind closed doors, the message was even starker, with McGuinness allegedly delivering a veiled warning to Tony Blair: 'Believe me, this is not a threat, but they could return to violence'.[180] As the tone of the republican movement's commentary on the negotiations became more negative—both publicly and privately—there was a belief in some quarters that they would not commit to any deal. Alistair Campbell recorded his sense that the Irish government were 'spooked' by Sinn Fein's growing opposition.[181] Tony Blair too, according to Campbell, felt that 'Sinn Fein were pulling the plug because they didn't want a deal'.[182] In a last ditch effort to alter the trajectory of the talks, Sinn Fein produced a lengthy list of some 78 areas of 'concern' over what was emerging.[183] In light of their determination to keep republicans 'on board' the two governments (but particularly the Irish) attempted to address Sinn Fein's queries. As the Taoiseach, Bertie Ahern, later recalled:

What did go on that night was that it looked as if Sinn Fein were not going to be part of it. I sat down with Martin McGuinness and Gerry Adams, taking all the questions they raised—there were reams of them about everything and anything. We had the entire Irish team working for hours on end, in the most detailed fashion we could, with them feeding all those replies back to me as I went back through for hours on end into the night. I painfully went through every single one of those with them, arguing as passionately as I could for the benefits of doing a comprehensive deal.[184]

As Ahern's account reflects, this process was about persuading republicans to accept what was already on the table, in terms of the constitutional framework of the settlement. Sinn Fein's unhappiness with the central terms of the emerging agreement did not prompt serious renegotiation, as had been the case in response to unionist concern. The account of the critical last round of negotiations by Martin Mansergh, Bertie Ahern's close advisor, corroborates this version of events. He states that the 'essential dynamic was that no party wanted to be blamed for failure', including the Irish government, and that 'the British Government went to extraordinary lengths to accommodate and support David Trimble'. When he woke up on the final day of the talks, he was surprised to find that Sinn Fein had dropped their 78 demands.[185]

Ultimately, Sinn Fein appeared to recognise their limited room for manoeuvre, to the extent that the threatened walk-out did not materialise. Notwithstanding Trimble's feeling that his last minute negotiating triumph may have made it impossible for Sinn Fein to 'sign up', he is also alleged to have told one of his advisers during the final week of negotiations that the party would participate in a settlement.[186] For this reason, much of Sinn Fein's energy in the final hours of the talks was focused, not on constitutional aims, but on matters of more immediate concern, particularly the question of when paramilitary prisoners would be released.[187] In the context of an agreement in which Sinn Fein had lost out on the major constitutional issues underpinning Northern Ireland's conflict, it was vital to the republican leadership that it could offer tangible, concrete benefits to its grassroots supporters. The expeditious release of IRA prisoners was one such decisive sweetener, on which the governments were prepared to concede ground. The proposed timeframe for the release of all paramilitary prisoners was thus reduced from the original three-year period to full completion within two years.[188]

The last issue to be debated in the negotiations was that which had figured so prominently in earlier stages of the peace process and had still not been satisfactorily resolved: decommissioning. After they had prevented the feared unionist walk-out, the governments' desire to keep republicans 'in' and secure an 'inclusive' settlement now became more of a consideration. It was perhaps for this reason that they proved receptive to Sinn Fein's pleas that they downgrade their requirements on this issue. Of crucial long-term significance, an original stipulation, which emphasised that there would have to be IRA decommissioning prior to Sinn Fein participation in a new Northern Ireland executive, was watered down.[189] The relevant section of the Agreement was thus couched in ambiguous terms:

All participants accordingly reaffirm their commitment to the total disarmament of all paramilitary organisations. They also confirm their intention to continue to work constructively and in good faith with the Independent Commission, and to use any influence they may have, to achieve the decommissioning of all paramilitary arms within two years following endorsement in referendums North and South of the agreement and in the context of the implementation of the overall settlement.[190]

For the British government at this point, decommissioning was viewed as something of a side issue. Accordingly, the Prime Minister urged unionists to accept the above formulation on the basis that all their 'principal objectives' had been achieved; in the words of one close observer, he urged them to 'concentrate on the big picture'.[191]

Nevertheless, as it became clear that David Trimble and his party would not endorse the Agreement unless the strictures on weapons decommissioning were strengthened, Blair made one last effort to resolve unionist concerns. The result was a 'side-bar' letter from the Prime Minister to the UUP, in which Blair emphasised that his conception of how the Agreement would work was in line with that of the Ulster Unionists—which was to say that there was be no place in gov-

ernment for those who refused to hand over their weapons.[192] Armed
with this reassurance, David Trimble, having persuaded a majority of
his party colleagues to follow him, now felt able to endorse the
settlement.[193]

Shortly after 5pm on Good Friday, 10 April 1998, George Mitchell
spoke to the media, stating: 'I'm pleased to announce that the two
governments and the political parties of Northern Ireland have reached
agreement'. It was an agreement that had been achieved by the British
government's readiness—at key moments—to focus on the needs of
moderate unionism, as embodied by the Ulster Unionist Party. Furthermore, after initial reluctance, this was an approach that was decisively
backed by the Irish government of Bertie Ahern. In the making of the
Agreement, the government's impulse, as defined by Jonathan Powell
to 'build out from the centre with an agreement between the UUP and
the SDLP', had trumped the desire for an 'inclusive' settlement that
prioritised the needs of the extremes.[194] Consequently, even though
great efforts were made to bring Sinn Fein along with the settlement,
republicans were not permitted to define the parameters of the final
outcome.

The central impulse behind the accord was clear: Irish nationalism
and Irish unionism had agreed a historic compromise. Unionists had
conceded the principle of power-sharing within Northern Ireland and
accepted that there should be a cross-border 'Irish dimension' linking
north and south. In return, Irish nationalism explicitly accepted that
the 'consent principle' would govern the future of Northern Ireland.
Unlike the Sunningdale or the Anglo-Irish Agreement, the Irish state
was also seen to have made significant concessions to secure a settlement. Articles two and three of the Irish constitution, which laid claim
to Northern Ireland were thus altered to reflect these new realities,
while northern nationalists promised to operate within the political
framework of the province. Irish nationalism as a whole was *de facto*
and *de jure* accepting the democratic legitimacy of partition and the
existence of the Northern Irish state.

Moreover, unlike all the previous attempts to solve the Northern
Ireland crisis over the previous thirty years, popular endorsement of
the Agreement confirmed its political authority. Significantly, given the
scale of the departure from traditional conceptions of Irish nationalism, some 94% of the Republic of Ireland's population voted 'yes' in
the referendum to ratify the accord. The level of support among north-

ern nationalists was even higher, with over 96% of people supporting the deal as a whole. Unionist support for the Agreement proved far less overwhelming, with only a narrow majority of 53% voting 'yes' in the same referendum. Still, when combined with the results for nationalists in Northern Ireland it meant that the Agreement had been endorsed by some 71% of the province's electorate.[195] This confirmed that this was an accord forged on the political centre-ground that enjoyed the approval of a democratic majority within Northern Ireland. In comparison with Sunningdale, those charged with implementing the Good Friday Agreement possessed a critical advantage—related less to the content of the deal, than the context in which it was signed. The key difference between the two accords was that the 1998 vintage was 'more acceptable to a wider spectrum of political groups in Northern Ireland'.[196]

Post-Agreement

The defining feature of the post-Good Friday Agreement political landscape in Northern Ireland was to be the sense of unease that the unionist population felt with the accord, as manifested in the lukewarm support recorded for it by that community during the referendum. In part, this was a function of the deft *volte-face* performed by republicans in the immediate aftermath of the Agreement. The reality was that Sinn Fein had played very little part in constructing the institutional framework of the Agreement, and, as has been described, had threatened to walk away at the last moment. Yet, within hours of the talks' conclusion, the Sinn Fein President, Gerry Adams had begun the process by which republicans would claim 'ownership' of the settlement. It was a remarkable piece of political gymnastics. Adams and his party worked rapidly to establish themselves as the most ardent supporters of the Agreement, calling at every turn for its implementation and safeguarding against unionist regression.[197] In the zero-sum world of Northern Irish politics, one effect of republican enthusiasm for the Agreement was to foster unionist suspicion.

It was clear also that unionist discontent with the accord ran deeper than mere resentment at the contentment of their communal counterparts. As Trimble later described, 'unconditional prisoner release' and the failure to decommission 'caused the disenchantment'.[198] This was recognised by the British government in the run-up to the decisive referendum on the Agreement. In the weeks between the announcement of the deal on 10 April 1998 and the vote on 22 May 1998, the 'No' campaign made considerable progress on the unionist side. It was this that prompted Tony Blair to involve himself ever more closely in the 'Yes' campaign, culminating in the famous hand-written 'pledges' that he delivered to unionists, just two days prior to the referendum. The significance of these five commitments was that they both underscored Blair's understanding of what the Agreement was about and showed recognition of the key drivers of unionist dissatisfaction. As the Prime Minister declared:

I pledge to the people of Northern Ireland:
– No change in the status of Northern Ireland without the express consent of the people of Northern Ireland.
– Power to take decisions returned to a Northern Ireland Assembly, with accountable North/South co-operation.
– Fairness and equality guaranteed for all.
– Those who use or threaten violence excluded from the Government of Northern Ireland.
– Prisoners kept in unless violence is given up for good.[199]

Blair's dramatic intervention helped secure sufficient support within unionism for the Agreement and thereby ensured that it was endowed with cross-communal democratic legitimacy. Yet what is striking is the way in which the issues he identified came to frame much of the subsequent political agenda in Northern Ireland. As Blair's 'pledges' appeared to acknowledge, it was the immediate, tangible effects of the accord, as opposed to its constitutional provisions, that many unionists found objectionable. Far from serving as a springboard from which a sceptical unionist population would be convinced of the Agreement's merits, the referendum of May 1998 constituted the high water-mark of unionist support for the accord. Thereafter, anti-Agreement unionists moved into the ascendancy and David Trimble's brand of pro-Agreement unionism became ever more embattled.[200]

This shift in power within unionism was driven by a succession of events that attenuated that community's confidence in the Agreement. Within two years of the accord, unionists witnessed the release of all paramilitary prisoners linked to groups that endorsed it—even as the paramilitaries to which they belonged retained their arsenals of weaponry. At the same time, the police force that had worked to put those prisoners behind bars—the Royal Ulster Constabulary (RUC)—was subjected to far-reaching reform, by which it was transformed into the 'Police Service of Northern Ireland' (PSNI).[201] For many unionists these parallel developments symbolised the moral vacuum at the heart of the peace process as a whole. Even as the paramilitaries responsible for some 94% of conflict-related deaths in 'the Troubles' welcomed home their imprisoned comrades and eschewed decommissioning, unionists were confronted by the apparent 'destruction' of the RUC, which was itself responsible for less than 5% of the conflict's victims (although there were frequent allegations of collusion with loyalist paramiltaries).[202] Tellingly, Dean Godson, David Trimble's most-comprehensive biographer, has argued that the UUP leader's failure to exert sufficient influence on the sensitive issue of RUC reform was his biggest mistake, costing him the support of many middle-class unionists.[203]

Meanwhile, the decommissioning question remained unresolved, overshadowing the post-Agreement period. To some extent, the subject had, despite last minute exertions, received insufficient attention during the Agreement negotiations. Trimble himself has since acknowledged that the 'linkage' made in the Agreement between decommissioning and entry into government was not as strong as he would have liked in the accord; although he had made the judgement that it was not worth sacrificing the whole deal on that point alone.[204] This ambiguity left a legacy of unionist disquiet over what became known as the 'guns and government' question.[205] Would parties linked to paramilitary organisations be allowed to enter government without a handover of weaponry, or would the paramilitaries concerned first have to begin decommissioning? If the IRA refused to disarm, could Sinn Fein be kept out of the new Northern Ireland executive when its electoral mandate seemed to entitle participation? For unionists, 'government' could not come without the handing over of 'guns'.

Initially, this key demand was backed by other key players involved in the process. In February 1999, for instance, the Taoiseach, Bertie Ahern had told the *Sunday Times* newspaper that decommissioning would have to occur in advance of the setting up of a power-sharing executive.[206] Increasingly, however, David Trimble and his party came under pressure from the two governments to dilute their stance on this issue. According to Jonathan Powell, as early as September 1998, some people in both the Northern Ireland Office and Downing Street were suggesting that the British government should abandon its insistence on the need for decommissioning, prior to the creation of an executive.[207] A key moment then came in April 1999, after an abortive attempt to construct a deal that required decommissioning before the establishment of the executive. This notion was rejected by Gerry Adams as 'entirely unacceptable' who also claimed that it was likely to provoke a split within the IRA.[208] Thereafter, the British government appeared to abandon the idea that prior decommissioning was possible. By that summer, the Irish government too had altered position and was now urging unionists to 'jump first' and establish the executive without a weapons handover, on the understanding that this would follow afterwards. By October, a familiar figure had added his voice to those attempting to push decommissioning off the agenda. Michael Oatley, the former British intelligence officer, penned an article in *The Sunday Times* urging the government to 'Forget the weapons and learn to trust Sinn Fein'.[209]

Following lengthy rounds of negotiation during both 1998 and 1999, Trimble himself was persuaded to support the creation of the power-sharing executive on the proviso that this be followed, within a short-time frame, by IRA decommissioning. At the end of November 1999, the first executive was formed. At the same time, the UUP leader also issue a post-dated resignation letter, by which he would step down from his position as the First Minister of Northern Ireland—and thereby collapse the executive—if decommissioning did not follow within six weeks. In the event, the anticipated weapons' handover failed to materialise and the British government interceded by passing the Northern Ireland Act 2000. This provided for the 'suspension' of the Agreement's institutions, in the face of fierce opposition to such a move from both the American and Irish governments. Rather than see Trimble resign (with the danger that he would not secure enough unionist votes to be re-elected as First Minister), the government opted to place everything into 'cold storage' in the hope that a new accommodation could be reached that would bring full implementation of the Agreement.[210]

This was to set the pattern for subsequent events. In May 2000, Trimble re-entered government, having extracted a promise from the IRA that it would allow the inspection and regular monitoring of its arms dumps by independent observers. When this was not followed by actual decommissioning, a further period of suspension followed from July 2001. In October of the same year, the executive was re-established after the IRA conducted its first act of decommissioning, but a year later, amid ongoing concerns about IRA activity, the institutions were again suspended. Thereafter, much of the following year consisted of talks aimed at restoring the assembly and executive for a fourth time, until those negotiations collapsed amid acrimony in October 2003.

On each occasion, despite vociferous criticism from anti-Agreement unionists and sceptics, Trimble succeeded in maintaining the leadership of unionism, albeit by the narrowest margins in a succession of dramatic, yet decisive victories he secured at meetings of his party's ruling body, the Ulster Unionist Council (UUC). Trimble's hard-won triumphs suggested that a sufficient portion of the broader unionist family remained to be won over to the Agreement; continued uncertainty was a function of the apparently interminable effort to resolve the 'guns and government' question.

Ultimately, the piecemeal and stuttering nature of the republican movement's approach to this issue proved decisive. From the negotiations in 1998–9 to the appointment of an IRA interlocutor with the decommissioning body, to the inspection of arms dumps in May 2000, through to the institution of the so-called 'modalities' of decommissioning in August 2001 and then to the actual installments of decommissioning that took place in October 2001, April 2002 and October 2003, the same basic pattern held true. Republicans moved forward, only incrementally, only after sustained bouts of profile-raising negotiation and only in such a way as to enhance their own political prospects. Republican political strategy was allowed to set the agenda at every turn, at the expense of moderate voices in both communities. The sense of a deeper IRA commitment to decommissioning and the use of 'exclusively peaceful means', as a principle, was not forthcoming.

More importantly, this tactical feet-dragging took place against the backdrop of successive IRA infractions of its ceasefire. The moderate centre-ground had looked to the Good Friday Agreement to usher in a new, violence-free era in public life, in which the menace of paramilitarism would evaporate. Instead, they were presented with a succession of transgressions, albeit falling short of a return to all out war. In the four years after the Agreement, these transgressions included the following: the murder of the IRA Volunteer-turned arch critic of the republican movement, Eamonn Collins, in January 1999; the shooting of the IRA informer, Martin McGartland, in June 1999; the arrest of three members of the IRA accused of gun-running in Florida in July 1999; the murder of a Belfast man, Charles Bennett, the same month; serial republican involvement in large-scale rioting across Belfast; the arrest of three senior IRA members in Columbia accused of aiding the FARC in August 2001; suspicion of IRA involvement in a raid on Special Branch Headquarters at Castlereagh in Belfast in March 2002; and the exposure of an alleged IRA spy-ring operating at the heart of Stormont in October 2002. Along with a series of other lower-profile episodes, these incidents told of an IRA that remained markedly active in military as well as intelligence terms. Altogether, some thirty lives were lost at republican hands in the decade after the Agreement—a statistic that made a mockery of the explicit commitment, contained within both the Mitchell Principles and the Agreement itself—to abide by 'exclusively democratic and peaceful means'.[211]

Acts of completion

It was in the wake of the so-called 'Stormont-gate' spy-ring affair that Tony Blair was prompted to make his famous Harbour Commissioners' speech of October 2002. During that address, the Prime Minister acknowledged that post-Agreement politics had effectively become a series of 'trades' that had led to a fundamental loss of trust in the process. As Jonathan Powell later reflected: 'We had struggled for four years to implement the Good Friday Agreement by giving a few concessions to one side and then to the other... but... the process had become badly discredited and morally undermined. It no longer seemed based on principle'.[212] Blair now explained how 'the very thing republicans used to think gave them negotiating leverage, doesn't do it anymore':

...the crunch is the crunch. There is no parallel track left. The fork in the road has finally come... we cannot carry on with the IRA half in, half out of this process. Not just because it isn't right any more. It won't work anymore.[213]

What was required, the Prime Minister asserted, was not another 'inch by inch negotiation', but rather, 'acts of completion'. Central to such acts was to be a republican commitment to 'exclusively peaceful means, real, total and permanent.'[214]

As an articulation of the problems that had developed within the peace process in the effort to secure implementation of the Agreement,

Blair's speech was an open and accurate assessment. The Agreement was meant to have secured an end to the threat, as well as the active use, of violence within the political sphere; yet, increasingly it appeared as if the republican movement was exploiting the continued existence and activity of the IRA for political gain. The 'inch by inch' negotiations that characterised the effort to achieve the implementation of the Agreement had allowed republicans effectively to deploy the same card time and again, in return for a string of concessions.

As 'Sean Sexton' (an anonymous commentator with links to the Irish government) has noted, the dynamic was such that 'Political concessions won from the other parties were pocketed; political concessions won from the Provos had to be repurchased from them again and again'.[215] On the one hand, this boosted Sinn Fein, which could claim to be delivering further change for the nationalist people of Northern Ireland, in contrast to the SDLP, which was repeatedly criticised for having settled for too little in negotiations. This dynamic was integral to the haemorrhaging of political support away from the SDLP and towards republicans in this period. Moreover, the growing perception that the peace process amounted to little more than a 'one-way street' of concessions to the republican movement altered the balance of power within unionism. To some extent, this was only natural: the rise of the 'extremes' on one side of the communal divide was always likely to generate a mirror effect on the other. At the same time, the increasing strength of anti-Agreement unionism—and particularly the swing towards Ian Paisley's Democratic Unionist Party (DUP)—had an autonomous logic and momentum. It was the product of an altogether deeper problem. The governments had, at some point after May 1998, lost sight of the foundations upon which the Agreement was based. An awareness of the extent to which this was an accommodation forged on the centre ground, pivoting on the support of moderates, was slowly evaporating. In its place, a growing emphasis was placed on the notion that an 'inclusive' peace had been forged.

Rather than prioritise the needs of the moderate majority, the central focus increasingly became the need to keep everyone on board. As to why this should have occurred, the two governments—especially the British—continued to fear either an outright resumption of violence by the IRA, or a split within the organisation that would lead to a sizable number of republicans returning to 'armed struggle'. In particular, the concern the IRA campaign might be restarted was something that clearly had an impact on government thinking. According to David Trimble, Tony Blair continued to express anxiety on this issue, long after the whole notion of traditional republican 'armed struggle' had been irreparably damaged by first the Omagh bombing of August 1998 and then the terrorist attacks on America on 11 September 2001.[216]

Alongside this, the fear that there might be a major republican split became a key preoccupation for the government too; and one that was successfully played upon by the republican leadership. According to Jonathan Powell, at the very first meeting between Sinn Fein and the Blair government in 1997, the determination of both sides to secure the unity of the republican movement had been established.[217] Thereafter, it is clear that Gerry Adams and Martin McGuinness frequently raised the spectre of a split in republican ranks during negotiations. To give one example, after David Trimble had agreed to set up the executive in December 1999—on the understanding that decommissioning would follow—Adams had sent word that a handover of weapons was not possible because it would lead 'to the emergence of a new IRA'.[218] Such warnings from Adams and McGuinness became a feature of British government talks with Sinn Fein, as the latter attempted to extract further concessions.[219] As the former Secretary of State for Northern Ireland, Peter Mandelson, later recorded, the Sinn Fein leadership would always stress that 'they were modernisers and if you didn't maintain [them and] give success to the modernisers then power would pass back to the bad men'.[220] Indeed, as late as January 2006 Adams was claiming that his 'leadership would be finished' if republicans did not obtain a satisfactory result from ongoing talks.[221] Such claims ran entirely counter to almost all informed analyses of the internal republican balance of power. Ed Moloney, for instance, has argued that from late 1997-onwards (when dissidents left the Provisionals to form the Real IRA), the control of Adams and McGuinness over the republican movement was near total. And by 2000–1, that control had become almost absolute.[222] This view would certainly accord with the impression of republicans held by the Irish government during this time.[223] It is also echoed in the verdict of President Bush's Special Envoy to Northern Ireland, Mitchell B. Reiss, who asserts that the 'consensus of the U.S. and Irish governments was that Adams was in control of the movement and had been since the Good Friday Agreement, when two small breakaway groups formed separate dissident movements'.[224]

Notably, Blair has recently testified that he was given a near identical picture of the republican leadership by British intelligence services. He admits, though, that he chose to ignore it and instead follow his 'instincts', which told him that that leadership needed to be protected.[225] In so doing, he arguably displayed the same attitude that he demonstrated post-Agreement with regards to the relationship between Sinn Fein and the IRA. Jonathan Powell records how, 'On a number of occasions during the negotiation Tony would offer to meet the high command of the IRA to try to reason with them himself'.[226] One commentator has responded to this statement with incredulity: 'who did he think he was meeting when he was talking to Gerry Adams, Martin McGuinness, Martin Ferris and Pat Doherty? The four men represented a working majority on the Army Council?'[227] Indeed, it could be argued that in accepting the notion that a serious gap existed between Sinn Fein and the IRA, the British Prime Minister was disregarding the position he had staked out earlier during the September 1997 crisis over the Mitchell Principles (when the IRA had tried to distance itself from Sinn Fein's commitment to the Principles). 'No one should be naïve about the IRA and Sinn Fein', he had then said, 'The two are inextricably linked. One cannot claim to be acting independently from the other'.[228] In the years that followed the Agreement, it would seem that personal instinct rather than hard intelligence had prompted Blair to shift position and accept Sinn Fein's line on this issue.

In an article published in the spring of 2002, one academic commentator had already suggested that the tendency to tilt policy towards the republican movement risked creating 'a potentially fatal asymmetry in the peace process that benefits the fringes rather than the moderate centre'.[229] It has also been argued that as the threat of a direct terrorist assault on the British state diminished, the longer-term British desire for 'insulation from the tiresome vestige of the Irish Question' reasserted itself.[230] Former Secretary of State Peter Mandelson, a close ally of the Prime Minister, has suggested that Blair was too eager to agree to the republican 'shopping list', while ministers were asked to maintain the 'fiction' that they were not talking to the IRA when they met Sinn Fein.[231] According to Mandelson, 'one problem with Tony's fundamental view ... is that the process is policy'. This manifested itself in an approach defined by the attitude 'that so long as you are giving plenty of evidence that you believe in the process, even if you can do nothing else, that is sufficient policy'. In Mandelson's view, by regularly acceding to republican demands, Blair was failing to recognise that these were 'calculated to push the unionists off the other end of the table'.[232]

As Trimble and his party looked increasingly unable to control their own destiny in the face of this dynamic, unionist voters shifted towards those figures who had declared themselves opponents of the peace process from the outset. Although Trimble topped the poll in his own constituency and his party far from collapsed, Ian Paisley's DUP finally became the majority shareholder within unionism following elections to the Northern Ireland assembly in November 2003. A key element in this shift was rooted within the Orange Order. Eric Kaufmann has described how many Orangemen began to rebel against the traditional link between the Ulster Unionist Party and the Order, because of their concerns over the peace process. This contributed to the draining away of support for Trimble after the Good Friday Agreement, and the growing electoral success of Paisley, despite the fact that the latter has always had a strained relationship with the Orange leadership.[233] The decision to call the 2003 assembly elections—which Sinn Fein had demanded—had been a controversial one, given that the assembly was not currently sitting. Polling showed that a majority of unionists did not want elections in these circumstances. In the event, the results seemed to confirm the triumph of the extremes within both communities.

On the surface, it might have seemed that the DUP's victory heralded the final collapse of the pro-Agreement project, given that Paisley and his party had declared their inveterate opposition to the accord since 1998. The reality was that DUP objections to the agreement were not as fundamental as their rhetoric suggested. Even before their victory in November 2003, elements within the British and Irish governments had concluded that the best long-term prospect of a sustainable deal was for it to be predicated on the acquiescence of Northern Ireland's extremes. This belief was not universally adhered to. Notably, Tony Blair himself remained committed to preserving David Trimble as an essential pre-requisite of the Agreement's survival, long after many of his officials had begun to put out tentative feelers to the DUP. It was on this basis that he was prepared to intervene four times to suspend the institutions and twice postponed assembly elections that were scheduled to take place in spring 2003. However, Blair's Harbour

Commissioners speech of 2002—an attempt to bolster Trimble's position after polls had shown a worrying decline in unionist support for the Agreement—had been regarded by elements in the Northern Ireland Office as an unrealistic attempt to save a man who had almost certainly lost control of the leadership of unionism. The NIO were not alone in this regard. There were many voices, particularly within both the Irish government and the US State Department—who were receiving favourable noises from DUP Deputy leader Peter Robinson about his party's willingness to do a deal—who had arrived at the same conclusion.[234] Eventually, so too did the Prime Minister.

The Final Act?

After 2003, government policy shifted towards a new dispensation: to hang the future success of 'power-sharing' on ensuring that the 'extreme' parties were put centre stage. The possibility of a DUP-Sinn Fein accommodation was first broached in 2004 in the aftermath of the parties' electoral triumph. In February of that year, the British and Irish governments launched a 'review' of the Agreement in the hope that, to paraphrase one commentator, 'one man's review would be another man's renegotiation' (a reference to the DUP's pre-election pledge that it would 'renegotiate' the accord).[235] On that occasion, the faint prospect that a deal might have been reached, whereby the DUP would agree to share power with Sinn Fein, was undone by another spasm from militant republicanism. A little over two weeks into the review period, the Northern Irish police foiled the attempted abduction of a dissident republican, Bobby Tohill, from a bar in Belfast city centre. PSNI Chief Constable Hugh Orde identified the IRA as the culprits, a view subsequently endorsed by the Independent Monitoring Commission (IMC), which had been established the previous year to scrutinise the paramilitary ceasefires.[236] The Secretary of State for Northern Ireland, Paul Murphy, labelled it a 'serious breach' by the IRA and David Trimble, turning the tables on the DUP, withdrew his party from the review. Although the DUP did not leave the latest round of talks, any hope that they might deliver a break-through was effectively shelved.

After the summer—following European elections that confirmed the dominance of Sinn Fein and the DUP within their respective communities—a new round of negotiations was initiated in autumn 2004.

159

These talks, which began at Leeds Castle in southern England in September and continued in Belfast over subsequent months, were aimed at finally resolving the obstacles to the restoration of devolved institutions to Northern Ireland. In the wake of the Leeds Castle discussions in mid-September, the two Prime Ministers had released a joint-statement in which they declared, 'The governments believe that what is on offer now [from the IRA] is reasonable in its substance and historic in meaning'.[237] But the fundamental sticking point remained a familiar one. Over the course of 2004, the DUP had spoken of the need for visible weapons decommissioning and increasingly this had focused on the demand for photographs of the process. The refusal of Sinn Fein to accede to this 'Kodak Moment' led to the collapse of the talks in early December, despite a putative offer from IRA that it would end all its activities, complete decommissioning in the presence of two clergy witnesses and move thereafter into a 'new mode'.[238]

Sinn Fein claimed that it was the DUP's attempt to 'humiliate' republicans (to force them to wear 'sack-cloth and ashes' as Ian Paisley had put it) that had wrecked hopes for a deal. With regards to the latter point, there is undoubtedly some truth in the suggestion that the DUP was less than enthusiastic about the prospect of sharing power with Sinn Fein. At the same time, the party's insistence on the need for photographs could also be seen as an antidote to the 'constructive ambiguity' on this issue that had bedevilled the process for many years. As late as 28 October 2004—scarcely six weeks before the collapse of talks—the IMC had reported that the IRA showed no sign of 'winding up' its capabilities and structures and was continuing to recruit and train new members.[239] On top of this, attempts to resurrect the process were hit with the fallout from the massive multi-million pound robbery of the Northern Bank in Belfast on 20 December 2004, for which both governments believed the IRA to be responsible. The subsequent exposure of a sophisticated, cross-border 'money-laundering' operation—allegedly connected with both the bank robbery and known republicans—merely increased fears that far from 'going out of business', the IRA was instead building a major criminal organisation. It was becoming, according to one media report, the 'biggest crime gang in Europe'.[240] Such concerns reached new heights following the murder of a Belfast man, Robert McCartney in late January 2005. The determination of the dead man's partner and sisters to achieve justice for the murder generated a high profile campaign that focused yet more attention on the darker side of the republican movement's activity and the vice-like grip it exerted over some Catholic working class communities.[241] Sinn Fein's popularity in the United States dipped considerably as the McCartney sisters embarked on a much publicised visit to America. Their campaign received the support of, amongst others, Senator John McCain. At a St Patrick's Day event in March 2005, which Gerry Adams attended, McCain denounced the IRA as 'cowards'.[242]

These successive events had put the question of criminality at the top of the political agenda. This was particularly the case south of the border, where the Irish Justice Minister, Michael McDowell—a long-standing opponent of Sinn Fein—attempted to lance what he saw as the specious distinction between Sinn Fein and the IRA. McDowell alleged that both Gerry Adams and Martin McGuinness were members of the IRA's 'Army Council'.[243] In the same vein, the Irish Defence Minister Willie O'Dea declared that, 'We are no longer prepared to accept the farce that Sinn Fein and the IRA are separate. They are indivisible'.[244] This stance was echoed by the British government, which also now held Sinn Fein publicly to account for IRA transgressions. 'The obstacle... to a lasting and durable settlement in Northern Ireland', Blair affirmed, 'is the continuing paramilitary activity and criminal activity of the IRA'.[245]

On the part of Sinn Fein, bluster and angry defiance replaced the confidence and surety of tone that had characterised republicanism since 1998. In the wake of a statement from Bertie Ahern that Sinn Fein leaders had had prior knowledge of the bank robbery, for instance, Adams said the Taoiseach was 'talking nonsense' and challenged the authorities to arrest him if they had proof of this.[246] More startling was the decision of the IRA to issue what was widely interpreted as a threatening statement. This withdrew the organisation's previous proposals (made in the context of December 2004's failed negotiation) to complete the decommissioning process. The group lambasted the fact that it saw its 'initiatives' as having been 'attacked, devalued and dismissed by pro-unionist and anti-republican elements, including the British Government'. Republicans, it was said, would not 'remain quiescent' with what it called an 'unacceptable situation'.[247] A further IRA statement stressed the 'seriousness' of the situation and said the crisis in the peace process should not be 'underestimated'.[248] The fact that they thought such a statement would make an impact said much about their estimation of the British government.

The scale of the controversy surrounding IRA activity refused to recede and republicans were forced to alter course, as the stream of negative news coverage was harming Sinn Fein's political fortunes. During January and March 2005, newspaper polls showed that a sizeable majority of nationalists—both north and south of the Irish border—desired an unambiguous separation between the IRA and Sinn Fein.[249] Moreover, it was clear that public confidence in Gerry Adams and his party had been badly shaken. Not only did the approval ratings of the former dip markedly, but the electoral prospects of the latter seemed to have suffered a major setback. This was confirmed by the party's poorer than expected performance in a by-election just over a month after the McCartney murder in the southern Irish constituency of Meath.

This was the background for Gerry Adams' 'appeal' to the IRA in April 2005—in anticipation of the forthcoming British General Election—to 'fully embrace and accept' democratic means. The 'response', which came some three months later, saw the IRA announce (via a specially-released DVD) a formal end to its armed campaign:

All IRA units have been ordered to dump arms. All Volunteers have been instructed to assist the development of purely political and democratic programmes through exclusively peaceful means. Volunteers must not engage in any other activities whatsoever.[250]

This was followed in September of the same year by the completion of the decommissioning process, as overseen by the IICD and witnessed by two 'independent' clergymen acting as witnesses.[251]

Even at this moment, it is striking that the British government seemed unwilling to exercise the extent of its leverage to secure the full implementation of decommissioning. US Special Presidential Envoy Mitchell Reiss has described how it was only the firm hand of the Irish government which prevented the British from allowing a degree of ambiguity to return to the political agenda on this issue:

No. 10 had more room for maneuver than it realized. In July 2005, the IRA had finally agreed to decommission all its weapons. At the last minute, Adams called No. 10 to demand that some of the weapons not be destroyed so that the IRA could arm itself against possible attacks from dissident members. Unless this was allowed, he threatened, decommissioning would not proceed. The Blair government conceded, but wanted to check with Dublin. Irish Justice Minister Michael McDowell refused to acquiesce in the backsliding, despite enormous pressure. Powell told Adams of the problem, and Adams gave way. Decommissioning took place as planned.[252]

Thus, a combination of governmental pressure and republican strategic concerns set the scene for the republican movement's 'historic' departure. Without question, the electoral setbacks suffered by Sinn Fein (which included the 2005 British General Election when, in contrast to previous predictions, the seemingly inexorable rise of Sinn Fein was halted by a better than expected SDLP performance) had fed into the logic behind this new initiative. The credibility of republicans as 'peacemakers' and mainstream political players had been badly damaged in early 2005, particularly south of the border, where they had high ambitions. The republican leadership therefore sought to restore the respectability of Sinn Fein with a view to regaining the party's lost momentum. Central to this would be the return of the party to governance in Northern Ireland before the scheduled Irish General Election of 2007.

The DUP did not achieve the desired photographic evidence of decommissioning, although the issue had been effectively concluded. In recognition of the fact that its core support was deeply uneasy about the possibility of the party going into government with republicans, it insisted on a period of 'decontamination' before any DUP-Sinn Fein deal could be attempted. In April 2006, the British government attempted to inject a degree of urgency into events by announcing that the Northern Ireland assembly would be convened in May and its politicians given a deadline of 24 November 2006 to agree to the creation of a power-sharing executive. In response, the DUP revealed that it would hold an 'internal consultation' with its members on whether or not to share power with Sinn Fein. In October 2006, the two governments unveiled a new 'road-map' towards the restoration of the Agreement's institutions. The product of three days of intensive talks in Scotland, the 'St Andrews Agreement' gave a new target date of 26 March 2007 for the return of devolved government to Northern Ireland. A 'transitional assembly' was to come into being on 24 November 2006, with an election held in advance of the creation of a new executive on 7 March 2007.

In the months that preceded and followed the St Andrews' negotiations, the republican movement's attitude to the Police Service of Northern Ireland (PSNI), which had replaced the RUC, emerged as the final stumbling block. Previously, the question of whether Sinn Fein would give its full support to the PSNI had been seen as an important, but ultimately secondary issue. Even the abortive 'Comprehensive

Agreement' of 2004 had envisaged that Sinn Fein would enter a power-sharing executive without having endorsed the local police force. Yet, the growing concerns over republican 'criminality' meant that policing was now viewed as the key litmus test of republican intentions. As had been the case with previous preconditions, republicans were initially insistent that the demands being made of them on policing could not be met. Instead, they argued, the issue of their support for the PSNI should be postponed until the implementation of devolution and the transfer of policing and justice powers to the Northern Ireland assembly.[253]

Nearly ten years after the Belfast Agreement of 1998, the British government's priority was to see the deal completed, particularly as Tony Blair seemed to be nearing the end of his premiership. It fell to the US government—mainly through President Bush's Special Envoy to Northern Ireland, Mitchell Reiss—to take a tougher line and demand that Sinn Fein give its backing to the police. After the 2005 murder of Robert McCartney, republican fund-raising visas to the US had been suspended; their restoration was effectively made dependent on a Sinn Fein endorsement for the PSNI.[254] In late 2005 and throughout 2006, Reiss (who had also been a firm supporter of the ceasefire monitoring body, the IMC) was openly critical of Sinn Fein on this issue, sparking a public row with Gerry Adams.[255] In an interview with the *Irish Times*, the US Envoy emphasised the importance of 'giving the decent, law-abiding people in republican and nationalist communities the type of police service they deserve... it's about normality'.[256] In contrast, during 2006 the British government appeared ready to accept a lower benchmark for republicans. In a major speech in July, the Secretary of State, Peter Hain outlined a position that offered republicans significant room to manoeuvre:

It is not unreasonable that Sinn Fein should see a link between its official support for the institution of the Policing Board and devolution of policing and criminal justice... if the devolution point can be satisfied, republican support for the PSNI becomes as constitutionally logical as support for the Garda.[257]

Soon after, Hain wrote an open letter to unionists that appeared in the *Belfast Newsletter* that encouraged them to embrace renewed power-sharing in the Autumn on the basis of a positive report from the IMC. There was no mention of a Sinn Fein endorsement for the police.[258]

Ultimately, though, with it subject to damaging criticism in the United States and with an impending Irish election, there was more incentive for Sinn Fein to budge on this issue than there was for the DUP. Many of the latter's supporters still held to the belief that their party would never form an executive with republicans. On 28 January 2007, Sinn Fein held a special party conference to debate whether or not the party leadership would be empowered by its members to support the police. The results were overwhelming: over 90% backed the position taken by the Adams leadership, which had already given notice that it would endorse the PSNI if allowed to do so. Arguably, the margin of victory was yet another indication that the republican leadership was strong enough internally to push through even the most far-reaching changes in republican ideology.

With this hurdle cleared, the scene was set for the final denouement. In early March 2007, elections for a new Northern Ireland assembly were held and the DUP and Sinn Fein were confirmed as the two largest parties in Northern Ireland. This was followed by a development which turned the logic of thirty years of violent conflict on its head: an agreement between the DUP and Sinn Fein, two of the most intransigent players in the conflict, to share power in a new Northern Ireland executive. On 8 May 2007, Ian Paisley was sworn in as the new First Minister of Northern Ireland, with Martin McGuinness as his Deputy—from which point the two men apparently struck up a genuine rapport, to widespread bewilderment.

It has been claimed that this unlikely denouement has led to something resembling 'the end of history' in Northern Ireland, with elections now decided by 'butter, not guns'.[259] The executive continues to function, even after Paisley's retirement in May 2008 and despite continued tensions over the issues of policing and justice. There has been evidence of a stirring of opposition to the apparent rapproachment among hardliners within both communities, but this disillusionment would have to increase significantly if the dominance of both parties is to face a serious challenge. Meanwhile, there is, as yet, no substantive evidence to suggest that the moderates can recover the ground lost during the polarisation of the post-Agreement years, despite their promises to challenge the allegedly sectarian 'carve up' of political power.[260] It has now been confirmed that mainstream parties from the Republic of Ireland and the United Kingdom will organise themselves in Northern Ireland, potentially adding another dimension to local political life. But again, it remains to be seen whether they could make any significant inroads in the short-term. What seems more likely is a marked decrease in overall voting levels.

More broadly, several questions about the nature of the peace remain unanswered. What, for instance, will be the long-term impact on Northern Ireland of a political class so obviously divided between competing, communally-defined, power blocs?[261] What are the long term hopes for reconciliation between the two communities?[262] Can it really be that two ideologically opposed parties, with little common ground between them, provide a basis for lasting stability? As Stephen Farry has written, there is much to support the assertion that 'peace has come at the price of reconciliation'.[263] Perhaps more troubling is the question of whether this is the best version of a settlement that Northern Ireland could have hoped for; or does it in fact betray a fundamental poverty of ambition, derived from a profound misreading of the basis upon which peace was brought to Ulster in 1998?

As many of those associated with peace in Northern Ireland are in evangelising mode about their achievements, it is crucial that those achievements be put in historical context. As one Belfast political commentator put it, those who recommend Northern Ireland's 'template of power sharing' in other conflict zones often fail to point out that the basis of this template was established as early as 1973, in the form of the Sunningdale Agreement:

We almost never talk about how we got to the point where we were ready to agree to a deal that was, in its essentials, more than 30 years old ... And why do we not do that? Because to do so would shame those who delayed it, our slowest learners.[264]

ETA IN SPAIN AND THE BASQUE COUNTRY

RISE, DECLINE AND THE POLITICS OF SURRENDER

4

BIRTH, RESISTANCE AND THE ASSAULT ON LIBERTY

Origins

A decade before the eruption of Northern Ireland's 'Troubles', *Euskadi ta Askatasuna* ('Basque Homeland and Freedom', or ETA as it simply became known) was founded in 1959. The group's creators were young followers of Basque nationalism whose central tenets had been canonised in the writings and activities of Sabino Arana. A young and prolific author, Arana had, in 1895, created the *Euzko Alderdi Jeltzalea* (the 'Basque Nationalist Party', the 'Partido Nacionalista Vasco' or PNV in Spanish, by which it is generally known). His conception was that the PNV would be the embodiment of the 'Basque people': the modern bearer of national identity for what was held to be an ancient race.

For as long as anyone could remember, the Basques had inhabited an area that straddled the western Pyrenees Mountains. The difficulties of scientific research on Prehistoric times and a lack of written records until the late Middle Ages have made for much speculative interpretation on the early history of the Basque-speaking peoples. Recent investigations have suggested the formation of an Ice Age refuge in the area during Upper Palaeolithic times and this could explain the uniqueness of Basque, or *Euskera*, as the only European language that does not belong to the Indo-European family.[1] Historians are also reasonably certain that the formation of the first political institutions in the region occurred after the breakdown of the Roman Empire.[2] And there appeared an early dividing line separating the lands north of the Pyrenees from those to the south. Yet much remains unclear.

By the eleventh century the land populated by what might be termed the 'proto-Basques' had become part of the Kingdom of Pamplona, or Navarre. The Navarran Kingdom had been created in the eighth century by *muwallads*—Visigoths converted to Islam after the Arab and Berber invasion of the Iberian peninsula. Over the subsequent centuries, it expanded to include the land populated by the Basque-speaking peoples, as well as other territories. This was the only period in history in which all of what would later be considered *Euskal Herria*—the Basque Country—was encompassed within a single political unit. It was to prove a short-lived moment of unity.

From the twelfth century, Navarre came under increasing pressure from more powerful neighbours. Its declining position was demonstrated by the annexation and partition of much of its territory. By the beginning of the sixteenth century, the newly-united Spanish monarchy had incorporated all the lands of the old Kingdom of Navarre that lay south of the Pyrenees; while, in the north, the lands of the Duchy of Aquitaine had become part of France. In 1659, the Spanish and French kings agreed that their shared border would be defined by the line of the Pyrenean frontier; at its western end, this guaranteed that the 'Basque people' would be divided between the two countries. In later times, Basque speakers referred to this division as being between *Iparralde* in the north (comprising the provinces of Basse Navarre, Labourd

The modern-day 'Basque Country' comprising seven provinces divided between France and Spain

and Soule) and *Hegoalde* in the south (consisting of Biscay, Guipúzcoa, Álava and Navarre).

South of the Pyrenees, the process of assimilation into the Spanish state had seen Basque towns being granted *fueros*, or charters of rights, that bestowed relatively high levels of autonomy. At the same time, within the burgeoning Spanish Empire Basques played a prominent role as sailors or administrators in the court. A prosperous ship-building industry grew up in the towns around the Bay of Biscay, which seemed to point to the ever closer integration of the Basques with Spain, even as the old pastoral and farming ways were maintained in the mountainous areas. It is this duality that defines Basque history as described by Julio Caro Baroja, with an interest in 'technical evolution' and industry, co-existing alongside the wish to see 'some kind of natural integrity' for the Basque Country as a distinct territorial unit.[3]

The European-wide crisis at the end of the eighteenth century profoundly altered the economic and political life of the Basques. The loss of trade routes with America in the war against Britain dealt a devastating blow to the region's industrial base and the expansionary impulses of revolutionary France created particular tensions in the frontier areas. A dynastic dispute in Spain then degenerated into conflict between *Carlistas*—supporters of Don Carlos—and *Isabelinos*—supporters of Isabel. The former embodied the desire for the 'old order' under the flag of absolute monarchy, while the latter embraced the ideals of a new liberal state. Within the Basque Country, this division also pitted urban forces against their rural counterparts; the former siding with the liberals, the latter, who enjoyed much greater representation in the *fueros* assembly, with the traditionalist *Carlistas*. Two wars between these rival forces in the nineteenth century effectively put paid to the system of *fueros*. The Basque *Carlistas*—who had been particularly strong in Navarre, but also popular in the provinces of Biscay and Guipúzcoa—were defeated on each occasion. The result of their alliance with an aspiring absolute monarch who was himself hardly a firm believer in local autonomy—was that the four Basque provinces within Spain, where the old language of *Euskera* was now in decline, were fully politically integrated into the Spanish state, while retaining fiscal autonomy.

In the late nineteenth and early twentieth centuries, the onset of the industrial revolution brought new and dramatic changes to Spain's northern regions. The exportation of iron ore to Britain and the corresponding import of that country's new technologies brought wealth and demographic transformation. Between 1877 and 1900, the population in the province of Biscay, an area of little more than two thousand square kilometres, grew from just under 190,000 to over 310,000 people.[4] In Bilbao, it doubled. In towns further west, where major factories were established, the pace of immigration from other parts of Spain was even more rapid. In just two decades, the population of Baracaldo trebled; in Sestao, it increased nine-fold.

It was against this backdrop of demographic upheaval and rapid socio-economic change that Sabino Arana emerged to reconsider the 'lost history' of the Basque peoples. Drawing on the alienation felt by many Basques who, after the derogation of the *fueros*, had lost their autonomous political power, or who were, for the first time, conscripts in the Spanish army, Arana repudiated the liberal ideas of the centralising Spanish state. And he raised, on behalf of the 'aboriginal' people, the claim of an independent Basque state, for which he invented a name (*Euzkadi*), a flag and an anthem.

Arana's work was in keeping with other late Romantic movements based on putative anthropological research. It looked to a corpus of theories about the supposedly characteristic features of a Basque race. To this, he added an opposition to socialism and a focus on the importance of religion.[5] He founded the PNV on the day of commemoration for Saint Ignatius, founder of the Jesuits. There was in Arana's religion, as in that of Ignatius, both a strong allegiance to Roman Catholic doctrine and tinges of northern Protestantism. He therefore wrote about the seriousness of Basque faith in contrast to the alleged fickleness of southern immigrants, who were said to be prone to immorality. At the same time, he defended the separation between church and state and presented democracy as part of the pre-existing social make up of the Basques. As a result, a Catholic Church hierarchy that was more comfortable with the traditional parties of the right, viewed Arana and his party with suspicion.[6]

Nevertheless, the PNV gained popularity, first among the urban middle and lower-middle classes and then also amid the ranks of Basque industrialists. In the years after Arana's death in 1903, the party became a substantial political movement in the provinces of Biscay and Guipúzcoa—though it was often split between those who called for outright Basque independence and other more pragmatic members who argued (as had Arana himself) for the autonomy of the Basque region within Spain as a necessary first step. These factions struggled for control of the party in the first quarter of the twentieth century, as the changing Spanish political environment increasingly appeared to make Basque autonomy a realistically achievable goal.

After being forced underground during the dictatorship of Primo de Rivera (1923–30), the PNV re-emerged under the Spanish Republic (1931–36), as a powerful political force. The future of the party—like so much else in Spain at this time—was decided by the defining event of the period: the Civil War. This pitted an insurgent fascist alliance of the wealthy, the Catholic Church and a great proportion of the armed forces, against a government supported by the mass of the peasants, the working class in the country's industrial heartlands and a section of the middle classes attached to the values of the Enlightenment. In this great ideological rupture, the PNV, now headed by José Antonio Aguirre, initially had its feet on both sides of the divide. It defended private entrepreneurship and religious freedom, as did the right; but it supported political and social liberties with the left. Ultimately, however, its destiny was determined by its principal objective, Basque Home Rule, which could only conceivably be achieved through alliance with the Republic. Thus, a party whose motto—*Jaungoikoa eta Lagizarrak*—invoked 'God and the Old Laws', abandoned its earlier allegiance to the retrograde cause of the nineteenth century Carlists and, at the outset of the Civil War, embraced an alliance with Spanish republicans, socialists, communists and anarchists.

Already, in the elections of February 1936, the PNV had become the biggest party in the Basque region and the driving force behind the introduction of a 'Statute of Autonomy'. With the co-operation of the Republican government in Madrid, this statute paved the way for the first ever Basque government that united three Spanish provinces: Álava, Biscay and Guipúzcoa. This regional government came into being in the weeks that followed Franco's rising (which sparked the Civil War) in July 1936. Thereafter, the PNV supported the forces of the Republic and for eight months its government held out against an army composed variously of Navarran 'Carlists', insurgent army troops and Italian fascists. In the end, though, it was the notorious bombing of Guernica that broke Basque resistance and the regional government surrendered in June 1937. The PNV leadership fled—first to Spanish areas still under the control of the Republican government and later into exile.

173

From the start, Aguirre's Basque 'government-in-exile' looked for salvation from abroad. To a significant degree, this was unsurprising. Since its inception, the PNV had been alert to the potential power of foreign allies. The party's creator, Sabino Arana, had dreamt that the British Empire might embrace the Basque cause. Also, prior to his death he had spent time in prison for having sent a telegram to President Theodore Roosevelt, congratulating him on the US' decision to assist Cuba achieve independence from Spain in 1898. Aguirre now maintained this internationalist outlook. He hoped that America and the European powers would dislodge Franco from power and restore democracy to Spain, in the context of the global struggle against totalitarianism. To this end, he instructed the PNV intelligence service, which had branches to Spain, Europe, South America and Asia, to cooperate with the Allied war effort. In addition, he expelled the communist minister from his 'government-in-exile' and his party did not join with the communist-inspired guerrillas inside Spain.

Aguirre placed particular emphasis on the United States as a likely patron of the Basque cause. In 1942, he launched an appeal to the American people, in the epilogue to the English translation of his political memoirs,

Please pay attention, American reader... This war, the most terrible and cruel in history, will weigh more heavily on your shoulders than on any others. To win this war your country will have to spend more than any other in dollars, war materials, tears and blood. And, if you ask me why, I will tell you why: Just as once you astonished the world with your sky-scrapers and your ingenious inventions, so today you have been given the greatest and most noble role in history, saving mankind through saving liberty.[7]

Aguirre had good reason to believe that his call to the American people was being sown in fertile ground. In early 1939, when the Spanish Civil War was nearing its end, a poll showed that 87% of the US population sympathised with the Spanish Republic against the Francoist uprising.[8] The bombing of Guernica by the Luftwaffe had caused worldwide condemnation. This sense of outrage was aided by the impact of Picasso's painting, which had travelled from the Paris International Exhibition to London and then to America. Eleanor Roosevelt and the Secretary of the Interior, Harold Ickes, attended the preview of its first showing on American soil, at the Valentine Gallery, in New York. Elizabeth McCausland saluted Picasso in the *Springfield Republican* because in the painting 'he functioned not only as a son of Spain but as a citizen of the democratic world'.[9] Elsewhere, George Steer had reported the attack on Guernica as a correspondent for *The Times* and *The New York Times*, refuting the Francoist propaganda that blamed Republicans for the destruction of the town and the killing of some one hundred and fifty of its inhabitants.[10] 'The Basques were', wrote Steer, 'a small people... and they did not have many guns or planes, and they did not receive any foreign aid, and they were terribly simple and guileless and unversed in warfare; but they had, throughout this painful civil war, held high the lantern of humanity and civilisation'.[11]

In the years after 1945, Aguirre continued to pursue his internationalist approach. He felt that the new American superpower represented the values that were the very opposite of Franco's Spain: 'You are a new man, a symbolic fusion of all the races from the earth'.[12] In 1950, Aguirre wrote to President Truman, urging him to embrace the Basque cause:

The words and actions of your great president Roosevelt were, after God, our supreme light and hope. Today the words and actions of you, his illustrious successor, constitute again the strongest hope to those of us who fight for freedom and human dignity against its oppressors, Franco's fascists or Stalin's communists.[13]

But such sentiments and Aguirre's expectations were to be a casualty of the emerging Cold War environment. Rather than force Franco out, the Americans and their allies increasingly sought to bolster him as a bulwark against communism. Far from condemning the dictator, President Truman instead signed a bill that appropriated $62.5 million in aid to Spain. He also supported a motion at the UN, calling on it to abandon its censure of Franco's regime. Then in 1953, with the conflict in Korea having confirmed the new bi-polar division of the world into American and Soviet blocs, the US government signed the 'Pacts of Madrid' with Franco. Under the terms of these agreements, three American air bases and one naval base were to be established in Spanish territory, while the country received some $2 billion in economic and military aid.[14] That same year, Franco signed a concordat with the Vatican Holy See, under which Roman Catholicism was blessed as the official religion of Spain and the 'perfect society' of the church was exempted from taxes, granted a yearly assignment of public funds and provided with a central role in education, the media and public ceremonies. Six years later, President Eisenhower set the American seal on Franco's international rehabilitation when he visited Spain in 1959 and waved to the cheering crowds, as he was driven through the streets of Madrid.

All that Aguirre and his followers could offer in response were peaceful and largely muted objections. The Spanish republican parties were similarly defeated, divided and ineffective. And even the communists abandoned their token guerrilla campaign in the mountainous areas of Spain and instead promoted 'national reconciliation'. The prospects for Basque nationalists—as much as for the rest of the Spanish opposition—looked bleak. Yet it was this very sense of despondency that formed the background to the foundation of ETA, in the same year that Eisenhower made his Spanish sojourn.

The Urgency of Youth

The creators of ETA were the sons of the defeated members of the PNV and other republican nationalists. They were reacting to the failure and collapse of Aguirre's 'gentlemanly' diplomacy and the refusal of the West to intervene against Franco. As one of them wrote,

We, Basque nationalists of this generation, have only known the farcical 'vertical trade union' of Franco, his northern policy, his 'organic democracy', the claws of Eymar [a military prosecutor] and his henchmen, the monstrous confabulation of the bishops with the most abject and reactionary regime on earth and the quiet wait for the Yankees to impose free elections in the Spanish state...We now think that we have understood. And, contrary to what our elders do, we have decided to change course.[15]

Young nationalists came together to challenge the moderate stance of their fathers. And when looking at the quarrels of their parents' generation, ETA's founders identified with those who had aimed for full Basque independence. For them, the ills of the nation were a consequence of entangling the Basque cause with Spaniards of any persuasion. At the heart of their reflections was a major crisis of identity, brought on by the twin stimuli of exposure to non-democratic rule and the impact of further socio-economic change. With regards to the latter, just as Sabino Arana's ruminations on the nature of the Basque nation had been in part, a response to regional demographic change, so the post-1945 period had brought renewed upheavals that stimulated the fresh ideological ferment.

When ETA was established in 1959, the industrial heartlands of the Basque Country were benefiting from a Spanish economic upturn. The population of the region had already doubled, when compared to the level of half a century previously. By the time Franco died sixteen years later, it had trebled. In this context, fears grew that new waves of internal Spanish immigrants would create 'estrange[d] areas of population, a new alien Ulster inside the Basque Country'.[16] On top of this, there was the impact of Franco's repression. Since the end of the Civil War, *Euskera* had been suppressed and all manifestations of Basque nationalist identity vigorously proscribed. The simple act of putting up Arana's Basque flag or distributing leaflets that were critical of the regime was enough to earn someone arrest and imprisonment—usually with physical assault thrown in for good measure. Against this background, according to one young writer, the 'disappearance of the Basque people was an imminent danger': twenty years more of dictatorship, it was felt, 'and not even the memory of us would remain'.[17]

A sense of urgency therefore replaced the failed diplomacy of Aguirre's PNV and helped spur the creation of ETA. It was the product of a generation that had imbibed the old ideas about Basque nationhood and was determined to do something about it. In addition, the original members of ETA had read about national liberation movements in Africa and Asia. They debated Marxism and Maoism and identified especially strongly with the examples of the Israeli Irgun and the Irish Republican Army of the 1920s. To some extent, there was nothing new in this. In 1921, at the time of the Anglo-Irish Treaty, a member of a pro-independence faction within the PNV, Eli Gallastegi, had written: 'Basques, we must learn. There never was in the history of peoples a more exemplary case as this titanic struggle of seven centuries for the independence of the fatherland'.[18] Forty years later, Gallastegi's son, Iker, who had actually been raised in Ireland, took part in the meetings that led to the founding of ETA. Iker Gallastegi—and others like him—thought that only by recourse to violence would the 'ills' of the Basque people be remedied:

There cannot be peace between good and evil, between truth and lie, between justice and oppression, between freedom and tyranny. There will always be war between them until evil is mended, truth prevails, justice is done, liberty is reached. War is a terrible thing but it is not a bad thing. The causes of wars, those are indeed bad.[19]

Seven years after those words had been written, ETA's self-declared war against the Spanish state would claim its first publicly-recognised victims.

ETA *under Franco*

The road towards 'armed struggle' was a slowly travelled one for ETA's first activists. Early plans to bomb police stations were discarded. An attempt to emulate the guerrilla warfare in Indochina ended in farce after armed ETA members took up strategic positions in a remote village, only to leave shortly afterwards without firing a shot. In 1961, the organisation did succeed in derailing a train carrying members of the Falange—the official political movement within Franco's one-party system. But in Eibar its efforts to initiate a military campaign ended calamitously and an ETA member suffered serious injuries, when, after leaving a bomb in the offices of a newspaper, he realised that a cleaner had entered and returned to retrieve the device, only for it to explode in his hands. As this last episode showed, the group, at this stage, was determined to ensure that acts of violence were not directed against innocent civilians. Nevertheless, the first death for which ETA was responsible occurred in June 1960 (though it did not acknowledge it), when a bomb planted in a train station in the town of San Sebastián killed a 22 month-old baby.[20] It was scarcely an auspicious start.

On 7 June 1968, however, ETA claimed both its first publicly acknowledged victim—and martyr. That evening, a 24 year-old student of economics in Bilbao, Txabi Etxebarrieta, was travelling with a companion when their car was stopped by a traffic patrol of the Civil Guard (a Spanish police force), near the village of Aduna, in the province of Guipúzcoa. Etxebarrieta, who was also a leading figure in ETA, came out of the car and shot dead one of the policemen, José Pardines. A few hours later, Etxebarrieta was himself shot dead by police. The killings catapulted ETA into the media spotlight. And they sparked off a cycle of violence. Even prior to the death of Etxebarrieta, ETA's leaders had resolved to kill two police officers who were infamous for assaulting and torturing prisoners. Emotionally shaken by the death of one of their young and charismatic leaders, the group's members now implemented these plans. Though they failed in one instance, the result was that a member of ETA gunned down Police Inspector Melitón Manzanas in Irún, when he returned home after work on 2 August 1969.

The response from the authorities was swift and draconian, with a round-up of those suspected of having any link with the murder of

Manzanas. In December 1970, sixteen people were tried for the crime in a military court in Burgos. Among the accused were two priests and the Vatican could have demanded a private trial, as provided for under the terms of the 1953 Concordat that it had signed with Franco. It renounced this right, however, and as a consequence the entire proceedings of what became known as the 'Burgos Trial' were held in public.[21] The media, though controlled by the government, gave extensive coverage to the deliberations of the military court. In addition, two days before the trial was due to start, ETA helped to publicise the case further by carrying out the softest of kidnappings—that of the German consul in San Sebastián. He was later freed prior to the announcement of the inevitable 'guilty' sentences—a move which enabled ETA to present itself as an idealistic group, as capable of mercy as of murder. During the trial itself, the defendants and their lawyers successfully used the court to advertise their cause and discredit the tribunal. When in the dock, the accused publicly proclaimed their revolutionary convictions and declared solidarity with oppressed Spaniards across the country. The last of the accused, Mario Onaindia, even ended his contribution by singing the 'anthem of the Basque soldier', *Eusko Gudariak*—a symbolic echo of the lost Civil War from thirty years earlier.

On 28 December 1970—'Fools Day' in the Spanish calendar—the military court handed down nine death penalties to six people, alongside lengthy terms of imprisonment for the others. The regime may have hoped that the severe nature of the punishments would serve as a deterrent to further actions. It had, though, miscalculated the likely effects of putting so many young people together for three weeks in front of a *sumarísimo* tribunal, of the kind created specifically for the task by Franco's Army. Protests immediately followed in the Basque Country, Catalonia and in Madrid. Western European governments sent telegrams to their Spanish counterparts appealing for moderation. Pope Paul VI also called on Franco to show clemency. Under this intense international pressure and with the image of the regime already tarnished by the affair, Franco commuted the death sentences to life imprisonment two days later.

Yet, to a significant extent, the damage was already done. The 'Burgos Trial' had had an enormous impact on the Basque Country. Immediately prior to the court proceedings, ETA had been in a very weak state. It could count on few supporters and those on trial in Burgos were among the more militant of its members. But many now felt sympathy for the accused. They were held to be the embodiment of a newly rebellious and assertive youth—the Basque Country's answer to the student radicalism that had swept across Western Europe in the late 1960s. Moreover, ETA's activists were viewed as having struck a blow against Franco's dictatorial system by killing a policeman with a reputation for inflicting gross brutality on figures within the political opposition. In this way, a new generation of Basques became aware of both the existence of ETA and the cause of Basque nationalism.

Then, at the end of 1973, a bomb planted in a purpose-built tunnel in a wealthy area of Madrid blew the car in which the Spanish Prime Minister, Admiral Luis Carrero Blanco, was travelling, over the roof of a nearby building, some twenty metres high. The Prime Minister, his driver and his bodyguard were all killed in the attack. ETA's assassination of Carrero, Franco's most trusted servant, struck at the heart of the regime. Furthermore, it ensured that the organisation was regarded with new reverence. Hitherto it had appeared to kill unintentionally (as with the murder of the infant during the 1960 train station bomb), or without strategic direction (as in the case of Manzanas). Now, ETA had murdered Franco's right hand man. In the wake of the attack, the organisation welcomed a fresh stream of recruits into its ranks and the respect with which it was viewed reached unprecedented levels. Still, the Carrero murder was arguably the high point of ETA's fortunes. Its attempt to replicate that success with a second attack in Madrid ended in disaster in September 1974. The bombing of the Rolando cafeteria, close to the headquarters of the state security forces, left ETA's reputation for daring efficiency buried under the rubble, along with the bodies of twelve ordinary civilians—among them, waiters, teachers, housewives and students.

Meanwhile, the indiscriminate nature of the murder aggravated an increasingly fractious debate already under way inside ETA. Just as the history of Irish republicanism has long proven to be a discordant one, the potentially fissiparous nature of radical Basque nationalism had already become apparent. As early as 1966–7 a section of ETA members, inspired by Maoism, had splintered away to form the short-lived rival organisation, *ETA-berri* or 'new ETA'. A few years later, another split had followed at the group's sixth assembly, which saw the departure of those imbued with a belief in Trotskyism. Again now, in 1974, another split beckoned. This time it was to prove a more significant cleavage, with two substantial forms of ETA enduring thereafter: ETA Political-Military (ETA-PM) and ETA Military (ETA-M). Both were committed to pursuing the 'armed struggle' and both lent their support to an independent socialist Basque state. What separated them was their attitude to the character of the military campaign that was felt to be required. They also held conflicting views as to the appropriate role for political activity.

The leadership of ETA-PM, which enjoyed the support of a greater number of activists, consisted of those who thought that a more enlightened application of violence was needed. They also wanted to form a political party that could respond to the changing environment within Spain. By that time, Franco's failing health was widely known and many were beginning to contemplate the post-regime era. The leaders of ETA-PM thus wished to establish a political wing that could exploit any evolving political opportunities. Out of this emerged the entity that would become *Euskadiko Ezkerra* ('The left in Euskadi', or EE). By contrast, as its name suggested, ETA-M continued to put sole emphasis on the role of 'armed struggle'. Its leaders disdained the notion that there should be a full-scale political party (though they did create a political 'apparatus' within the army), on the grounds that there would inevitably be contradictions between 'political' and 'military' imperatives, as the party attempted to extend its appeal.

This split of ETA into two branches competing for hegemony produced a marked increase in violence. Targets for assassination included members of the Civil Guard and the National Police, people accused of being security service informants, and council leaders in Basque towns and villages. In this period, both ETA-PM and ETA-M operated across the border between Spain and France with something approaching impunity. It was in the latter country that their leaderships operated, apparently unhindered by French security forces. It was there too that new recruits were taken for training and to receive instructions. Overall, the French portion of the Basque Country became established as the logistical and financial base for violent Basque nationalism during this period. A report published by the Spanish intelligence service, Seced, in 1975, pointed out that, taken together, the two branches of ETA had killed 22 people in the three Basque provinces: none in Álava, 7 in Biscay and 15 in Guipúzcoa. When considering the factors that might explain this disparity across the provinces, the report's conclusions were clear:

What is there in Guipúzcoa that is not in Biscay and explains the double number of murders perpetrated by ETA? The answer is very simple: the French frontier...This is a reality, a big part of the blood spilled in Spain by ETA unavoidably stains all those in France that tolerate, promote or abet the murderers.[22]

Using the French hinterland, the two forms of ETA showed themselves able to conduct, for the first time, a sustained campaign of bombing, kidnapping and murder.

ETA in 'The Transition'

Franco died on 20 November 1975. In the immediate aftermath of his passing, uncertainty over the future direction of the country—which had been governed by personal diktat for nearly forty years—was compounded by memories of the civil war. The 'generalissimo' had given very few instructions to his appointed successor, Prince Juan Carlos, beyond a death-bed plea: 'Your Highness, only one thing I will ask you: please, preserve the unity of Spain'.[23] As a result, few knew what to expect in terms of constitutional change, though many hoped for a *transición* towards democratic governance.

The long dictatorship appeared to have created a stable political framework and the country had benefitted from the broader economic expansion of the western world. Between 1960 and 1974, Spain enjoyed a period of sustained, high economic growth which was became known as the 'Spanish miracle'. Work was available; and an enlarged middle class was keen to preserve the advent of consumerist society. Meanwhile, tourism had brought Spaniards into contact with other Europeans. In its last decade, the regime had opened its doors to the publication of foreign books and records. At home, a growing number of young people attended university. At the same time, there were more fundamental problems under the surface. Franco had left behind a Spain in which 40% of the country's National Income was owned by one tenth of the population—one of the least equitable levels of wealth distribution in the OECD.[24] Furthermore, the differential between Spain's GDP per head of population and that of the countries of Western Europe was the same as it had been in the 1930s. The oil price shocks of the early 1970s exposed the weaknesses of an economy that was heavily regulated, with little exposure to competition. This was particularly true in relation to the country's industrial sector—

located principally in the Basque Country, Barcelona and Madrid— which was intensive in the use of energy and manpower. Added to this economic crisis were the uncertainties caused by the onset of political change.

In the accession speech he delivered to Franco's 'organic' parliament, the new King, Juan Carlos I, described Franco as an 'exceptional figure', but also expressed his desire for 'new solutions' to promote a 'free and modern' Spain. Such solutions, he declared, could accommodate the country's 'regional peculiarities', while preserving 'the unity of the kingdom and the state'. With strong support from the United States and other European governments, Juan Carlos then set about implementing reforms, which were designed to lead Spain on a *transición* towards democracy.

Against the background of growing economic turmoil and after a short period of apparent stasis, the King appointed a former Francoist Minister, Adolfo Suárez, as Prime Minister in July 1976. The latter soon steered an Act of Political Reform through the 'organic' parliament, which was itself only too aware of its own lack of legitimacy. In effect, the parliament voted for its own extinction. The bill was subsequently backed by popular referendum, with some 94% of adult Spaniards voting in favour of it (on a high overall turnout of over 77% of the electorate—a success achieved in spite of a call from the still-banned opposition parties for a boycott of the poll). Under the terms of this new Act, a Congress and Senate were to be elected by universal suffrage. And seven months after the endorsement of the Reform Act, on 15 June 1977, the Spanish population elected deputies to a Congress (the 'Constituent Cortes'), tasked with drafting a new constitution.

All parties were free to present their candidates in elections to this body. Nonetheless, it was the party led by Adolfo Suárez, the Union of Democratic Centre (UCD) that emerged as the largest party. Formed from elements of the previous regime, groups linked to the Catholic Church and Social Democrat associations, the UCD took some 34.4% of the vote and secured 166 seats of the 350 available in the new assembly. The Spanish Socialist Workers' Party (the PSOE) came a close second, winning more than five million votes (29.3% of the total) and becoming the main party of opposition in the Congress with 118 seats.

In the new Congress, Suárez became the first democratically elected Prime Minister of post-Franco Spain. To carry forward the *transición*, he worked closely with the other major parties to produce a package of reforms (the so-called 'Pacts of Moncloa') and a legislative programme for the assembly. Work also began on writing a new constitution, the draft of which was finally produced in July 1978. Article two of the document declared the 'indissoluble unity of the Spanish Nation, common and indivisible fatherland of all Spaniards'; while article eight gave the armed forces the role of 'defending the territorial integrity and the constitutional order'. This potentially far-reaching role for the armed forces was introduced into the draft document with little debate among the writers, after one of them produced a secret missive sent by the heads of the military to the government, demanding just such a position for themselves.[25] It was an unpromising omen; and one that scarcely seemed to suggest that the old Francoist elites were willing to allow a more open, less centralised Spain.

Yet alongside this, the new constitution also provided for a 'Spain of the Autonomies'. In the first instance, the draft document responded to demands for autonomy among the country's 'historical nationalities'—in the Basque Country, Catalonia and Galicia. However, the efforts of nationalist parties in those regions inspired others to follow suit. As a result, the Spain that emerged became a state with seventeen autonomous communities—a profound transformation from inefficient, dictatorial regime, to highly de-centralised state. The autonomous regions were endowed with substantial powers and their representatives were given the right to defend local legislative initiatives in the national parliament in Madrid. Moreover, as far as the Basque Country was concerned, the draft constitution provided for the restoration of the provinces' lost fiscal autonomy. These provinces could now unite to form an 'autonomous region'; and the constitution even allowed for the possibility that Navarre might join the Basque autonomous region (a move that would unify the 'Spanish' portion of historical *Euskal Herria*), in the event that the province ratified such a measure by referendum.

The constitution was overwhelmingly approved in a referendum in December 1978. A year later, in 1979, a 'Statute of Autonomy', that provided for the establishment of a 'Basque Autonomous Community', comprising the provinces of Guipúzcoa, Biscay and Álava was enacted. Thereafter, the capital of the autonomous region was established in Vitoria-Gasteiz, the principal city of Álava. Nationalists were empowered to set the name of the country as *Euskadi*, its flag and anthem having been invented a century before by Sabino Arana. The Basque government was given a wide-range of powers, including control of health, education and a local police force. The founding statute made *Euskera*, spoken by only a quarter of the population, an official language, to be used in both the education system and the new public broadcasting body. A substantial decree of fiscal autonomy was also devolved to the new regional parliament. The Basque government would both set taxation and collect revenue—only agreeing later with the Spanish Treasury, for each five year period, the amount they had to pay for services provided by the central government.

As an attempt to resolve the aspirations of Basque nationalism, albeit within a Spanish framework, such provisions appeared comprehensive. But despite all of this, from the start of the reform period ETA-M refused to participate in the evolution of the *transición* at the mainstream political level. It instead cooperated with an underground network that aimed to unite the various strands of radical Basque nationalism—the so-called 'KAS' (Socialist Patriotic Coordinator). This alliance, which also incorporated ETA-PM, then produced a common negotiating programme—the 'KAS Alternative'—that included the following demands:

- Democratic freedoms
- An amnesty for political prisoners
- The better treatment of the working class
- Disbandment of security forces
- Recognition of Basque sovereignty and the right to create a state
- Immediate establishment of a Basque government with provisional autonomy for Álava, Guipúzcoa, Navarre and Biscay.[26]

Initially, the outright hostility with which ETA viewed the 'transition' was entirely in keeping with the more general sense of suspicion with which many Basques looked on the reforms. This ambivalence was made manifest at the ballot box. For instance, as has been described, the Reform Act that provided for the first democratic elections was endorsed by some 94% of all adult Spaniards, on a turnout of over 77%, but it received less than overwhelming support in the Basque Country. In Biscay, for example, a bare majority of voters (54%) participated in the vote; while in Guipúzcoa, only 45% of the electorate went to the polling stations. These were the lowest figures in Spain.

A similar story was evident when it came to voting on a new constitution in December 1978. Across Spain, this document attained widespread approval but once again the Basque Country proved to be an exception. This was mainly because of a major disagreement between the national government and the PNV over where sovereignty lay—with Spain or with the Basque Country. During the drafting of the constitution, the PNV's deputies had taken part in debates of the Constitutional Commission, but they were not represented on the final committee, which comprised only seven members (in the Constitutional Cortes, Basque and Catalan nationalists had formed a joint parliamentary grouping and it was a Catalan deputy who represented both on the committee). Despite this, the parties co-operated extensively and this enabled the PNV to present various amendments as the constitution was being framed. At this time, *Euskadiko Ezkerra* (EE)—the coalition formed around the party linked to ETA-PM—had urged the PNV to push for a recognition of the Basque right of self-determination. The PNV leadership, however, had judged this to be unachievable; instead, it focused on establishing the principle that underlay the historical *fueros*. They held this to be Basque sovereignty. The *fueros*, the PNV argued, were mutually agreed accommodations between sovereign Basque entities and the Spanish crown and as such were a manifestation of Basque sovereignty. For this reason, the PNV maintained, any decision to restore the *fueros* or equivalent rights, would mark an acceptance of Basque sovereignty. This line of reasoning, though, was rejected and the seven-man committee, while agreeing to restore the *fueros*, did so 'within the framework of the constitution'—which emphasised the primacy of Spanish sovereignty. A dramatic late effort to secure the Basque nationalist interpretation of the *fueros*, by dint of an EE-negotiated offer of a ceasefire from both branches of ETA (which was to come into effect in the event that an agreement was reached), also proved unsuccessful when the PNV felt unable to acquiesce in the proposition.[27] Subsequently, the PNV's failure to achieve its aims fostered a sense within the party that it had been cheated by Suárez. This, in turn, provoked a disillusion with the constitutional process and led the PNV to recommend that its followers not participate in the vote on the constitution. Both branches of ETA had similarly called for abstention. As a result, nearly 56% of the electorate abstained in Guipúzcoa and Biscay; 41% did so in Álava.

Nevertheless, broader Basque hesitancy over the transition eventually gave way to a *de facto* embrace of the country's new democratic and devolved structures. Here again the role of the PNV proved crucial. It is important to remember that this party constituted the original expression of Basque nationalism; ETA was born out of it, not vice-versa. Thus, even as many had admired ETA's violent opposition to Franco's dictatorship, the PNV had continued to be seen as the repository of democratic legitimacy. This was confirmed in the first all-party democratic elections of 1977.

Prior to those elections, ETA-M had convened a gathering in the Basque-French town of Anglet, to which all Basque nationalist groups were invited. There, they proposed the formation of a 'National Front' and urged all parties to boycott the upcoming electoral contests until a full prisoner amnesty had been promulgated by the Madrid government. The PNV refused to follow ETA's lead. As one of the representatives of the PNV recalled thirty years later:

people were anxious to participate. We had thought that we could keep voters under control, but the referendum of 1976 had shown that it was not possible. If we had not fought the elections, our space would have been taken by other ideologies.[28]

The PNV's decision to participate ensured that ETA-M's efforts to disrupt the poll—and thereby annul its claims to democratic legitimacy—failed. At the same time, the PNV emerged from the contest as the most popular party in the provincial constituencies of Biscay and Guipúzcoa. These successes paved the way for its later triumph in elections for the regional Basque Parliament in 1979, when the PNV secured 38.1% of the vote and 25 deputies and went on to form the first government of the Basque Autonomous Community.

Enemies of Liberty

Even as the PNV came to recognise the benefits of the new *status quo*, the attitude of the two branches of ETA to political developments remained one of implacable hostility. This was despite the fact that much of the KAS Alternative was being implemented, or was under consideration, within the context of the *transición*. The first two demands of this programme, for instance—the establishment of democratic freedoms and the promulgation of an amnesty for all political prisoners—resonated with all those opposed to Franco, and had a clear appeal across Spain. The democratisation of the Spanish state was being taken forward with tangible momentum. Meanwhile, the political parties that emerged at the start of the 'transition' had promised to push for a full amnesty of political prisoners in any new parliament. When elected, they did exactly what they had pledged. The PNV joined in the drafting of a wide-ranging bill and the Act was passed inside five months, with 296 votes in favour, 18 abstentions, one spoiled vote and just two against.[29] The first article of this new law left no room for doubt: individuals guilty of 'all actions with political intent', before the referendum of December 1976, were to be pardoned; so too were those who had engaged in 'illegal activities' between that date and the June 1977 elections, 'when it is perceived [there was] a motive to restore public liberties or vindicate the autonomy of the peoples of Spain'; and, finally, people who had carried out actions of a similar nature until the publication of the Act of Amnesty, if they 'had not meant serious violence against the life or integrity of persons' were also to be included.

The Act of Amnesty crystallized the implicit *'pacto de olvido'* or 'pact of forgetting' that existed among the protagonists of the 'transition'. It drew a veil over the crimes of Franco's followers—from those committed during the Civil War, to the execution of 50,000 prisoners at that conflict's end.[30] It was judged that to do otherwise was to risk serious civil disorder and even a return to the violence of the past. The reality was that the heads of the armed forces and the police—together with most judges, ministers and newspaper editors—all occupied their respective positions because of their collective Francoist past. Many had embraced the democratic changes reluctantly or only in part; some feared retribution at the hands of their former enemies. Thirty years later, Gregorio Morán would write that, 'The democratic transition elevated duplicity and cynicism to the rank of a public good'.[31] At the time, those involved saw matters in more pragmatic light. Leaders of the political opposition, encouraged by western governments, embraced the 'transition' and avoided giving any excuse to those, particularly in the armed forces, who were horrified by the return to mainstream politics of their old enemies. The 'pact of oblivion' allowed Spain to move ahead, even if it did mean saddling the country with a heavy load of unresolved memories.

It was perhaps this inherently pragmatic feature of the *transición* that guaranteed it would be deemed unsatisfactory by both branches of ETA. Imbued with a form of revolutionary maximalism that brooked no compromise—and acting against a backdrop of constitutional instability, in which utopian goals seemed achievable—they were unwilling to lower their objectives. Seven days before the Congress of Deputies voted on the Act of Amnesty, ETA-M murdered three people: the president of the provincial council in Biscay and two people accompanying him. In response, ETA-PM described the assassinations as a 'gratuitous action' and said that ETA-M simply wanted 'to recapture the limelight'; despite this, its own military wing continued to prosecute its self-declared 'armed struggle' against the Spanish state.

The third demand of the KAS Alternative, 'better treatment of the working class', was extremely vague. One of the fascistic aspects of the Franco regime had been the creation of a 'vertical' trade union, in which employers and employees could 'work together' for the good of the nation and overcome the ills of capitalism and socialism. In 1977, a law authorised the registration of free trade unions. Whether this met the requirements for the 'better treatment of the working class' as defined within the KAS Alternative, was unclear. But again, neither branch of ETA appeared ready to engage with the reform process that was being carried forward; nor did they offer any significant commentary on labour reform. Instead, the literature produced by both forms of violent Basque nationalism continued to describe their respective organisations as the vanguard of the 'Working Basque People', even though their economic agendas rarely seemed to consist of more than an ill-defined populism and outright rejection of the *status quo*.

Other aspects of the KAS Alternative, meanwhile, were, from the start, unrealisable. The fourth demand of the document, for example, was for the 'disbandment of security forces'. At this time, the police were divided into three sections: a civilian branch dedicated to the investigation of crime and two armed formations—the Armed Police and the Civil Guard. These latter two operated on a military structure and were run respectively by the departments of Interior and Defence. Both were the subject of much criticism from opposition parties, several of whom had also called for their abolition. Yet, it was always highly unlikely that out-and-out disbandment of the police was a serious option in a country enduring the turbulence arising out of major political reform, as was Spain in this period. In the Basque Country alone, for instance, it would have meant security was *de facto* left in the hands of the two branches of ETA—at the very moment that they were engaged in a murderous campaign of unprecedented intensity against the nascent democratic state. It was perhaps in recognition of this that in later versions of the KAS Alternative, ETA-M modified its

189

demand for the disbandment of the police forces, instead calling for them to be withdrawn from the Basque Country. However, this was scarcely a more realistic demand, as it still required the Spanish state to do the unthinkable and cede control of the territory to ETA.

The last two demands of the KAS Alternative were: on the one hand, recognition of Basque sovereignty, including the right to create a state; and on the other, the immediate establishment of a provisional Basque government in the provinces of Álava, Guipúzcoa, Biscay and Navarre. Here, ETA was attempting to lay the groundwork for Basque independence by unifying the 'historic' provinces of Spanish *Euskal Herria*, drawing on the historical legitimacy of pre-Franco Spain. Yet, the 1936 Statute of Autonomy had not included Navarre. Attempts to include the province had failed when Navarran Carlism and Basque nationalism parted ways and they joined opposite sides in the Civil War. It was true that deputies elected for these four 'Basque' provinces in the post-Franco elections of June 1977 had immediately grouped together to set out plans for a new autonomous entity. But Navarran deputies and senators subsequently left the group, opting instead for full restoration of their own autonomy, which had survived partially under Franco. In so doing, they were supported by the UCD and the PSOE. Thus, the most that the rest of the Spanish political class would assent to, with regards to the fifth and sixth demands of the KAS Alternative, was self-government—not independence—for the remaining three Basque provinces and the right of Navarre to join the Basque Autonomous Community, if its inhabitants so wished. Moreover, as has been described, PNV efforts to ensure that sovereignty lay with a future Basque parliament, rather than with Madrid, had failed during the drafting of the 1978 constitution. The subsequent passage of that constitution in a referendum that saw a majority vote in favour of it in the Basque Country, despite PNV and ETA calls for abstentionism, confirmed that failure. It was this that pushed the PNV into accepting limited measures of autonomy and the party postponed the objective of outright independence into the indefinite future.

In stark contrast to this pragmatism on the part of the PNV, violent Basque nationalism adopted a very different path. Rather than acknowledge the realities and the limits of what could be achieved during the *transición*—and to seek to strengthen the path of reform—radical Basque nationalism instead opted for all-out confrontation with the Spanish state. The two branches of ETA demanded the creation of an independent socialist Basque Country—and were prepared to use force to attain it. Consequently, the years of the 'transition' saw these organisations 'compete' for the business of terrorism within Spain and the Basque Country. Where ETA-M concentrated mainly on killing policemen and members of the armed forces, ETA-PM bombed tourist resorts in Spain, as well as airports and train stations in Madrid. Both groups appeared to make a virtue of killing civilians at random. Prior to the death of Franco, the various branches of ETA had killed seventy people in eighteen years.[32] In 1978, the first full year of the democratic national parliament, they murdered sixty-seven. In 1979, they killed eighty people. And, when Basques voted for the first time ever in their history to elect a Basque Parliament, in 1980, ETA-M and ETA-PM together murdered some one hundred people—the highest number of victims for a single year in the history of ETA.

As has been described, the transition towards democracy was being played out alongside a serious economic crisis. When the first democratic elections were held in Spain in 1977, inflation was running at 44.7% and foreign exchange reserves appeared to be running out.[33] Inside three years, the country's external debt trebled to $12 billion as the state appeared to face imminent economic collapse. Between 1978 and 1983, some twenty-four banking institutions had to be rescued by the Spanish central bank, with estimated private banking losses equivalent to 16.8% of the country's total GNP.[34] Against this backdrop, unemployment rose, the level of Spanish GNP per capita did not improve over the first decade of restored democratic governance and the country's overall standard of living actually fell in comparison with that of the twelve countries of the European Economic Community (EEC). The economy even reached a point where it was estimated that fully a quarter of the population were earning a living in the black economy.[35]

The industrial sector in the Basque Country was hit particularly hard by this burgeoning economic crisis—just at the moment when the region's 'baby boom' generation was reaching adulthood. Within the Basque provinces, the population aged between 15 and 35 years old increased by some 53% between 1960 and 1980.[36] Thus even as many young Basques gained their first experience of democratic liberty, they were also faced the prospect of being unable to find work. Simultaneously, the sense of confusion that characterised the *transición* encouraged a certain ideological promiscuity. Many saw little incongruity in the simultaneous idolisation of retrograde Carlist priests of the nineteenth century alongside the heroes of the modern far left such as Che Guevara. The result was that both ETA-M and ETA-PM found fertile ground for recruitment and this enabled them to take their violent campaigns to new levels.

With that said, responsibility for the violence that afflicted the Basque Country, and indeed Spain more generally, during this era, did not rest solely with those groups opposed to the state, such as ETA. Often, the security forces acted in a heavy-handed, even brutal, manner, and with little sense of accountability. To give but one example, in July 1978, the police entered the bullfighting ring in Pamplona to make arrests, because members of the public had displayed a banner demanding a further prisoner amnesty. The operation resulted in one fatality, with many more injured—an outcome that provoked fierce rioting and the subsequent cancellation of the famous fiesta of San Fermín. Yet, no one was ever brought to trial for the actions of the police that day.[37] Nor was this an isolated incident of police brutality. It was frequently alleged that suspects arrested and taken to Basque police stations were being tortured during interrogation. In one infamous incident in Almería in the south of Spain in 1981, three young men from Santander were arrested, tortured and finally shot dead. A unit of the Civil Guard had judged them to be members of ETA and acted (as they saw it) accordingly; in fact, they were not even Basques.

Elsewhere, suspected members of ETA and innocent civilians alike were targeted by state-sponsored death squads that hid behind various flags of convenience: the Anticommunist Apostolic Alliance (AAA); Antiterrorism ETA (ATE); the Spanish Armed Groups; the Warriors of Christ the King; and the Basque Spanish Battalion (BVE). Several of these groups emerged in 1974, but only became more active in the following year, just prior to the death of Franco, amidst the growing sense of constitutional instability. Arguably, their most high-profile victim was the leader of ETA-M, José Miguel Beñarán, who had personally taken part in the assassination of Prime Minister Blanco Carrero in 1973. Beñarán was murdered by a bomb placed under his car, in 1978, in the south of France. Still, such 'prestigious' victims for the death-squads were rare. The reality was that the targets in this campaign of terror were highly diverse and most commonly comprised individuals, bookshops, Basque language schools and bars. Particularly troubling was the fact that the groups appeared to act with an impunity granted by authorities that were, at best, apathetic, and at worst, in collusion with them. As a consequence, between May 1975 and May 1976, the death-squads committed eighty-five attacks in Spain and thirty-five in France. They caused three deaths, left twenty people injured and not a single arrest was made in response.[38]

One crucial effect of this was to virtually guarantee that the co-operation of Basque civic society with the police would not be forthcoming in the effort to restore peace and stability. As a result, the revulsion that many felt towards the crimes of ETA could not be channelled effectively. It was widely felt that a protest against the activities of ETA—and only against the activities of ETA—would be a statement of support for others who were perpetrating equally unsavoury deeds. In the midst of these perceived 'injustices'—and with Spanish democracy still a 'work in progress'—few were prepared to make an appeal for peace on absolute grounds.

Against this background of ongoing violence, economic problems and concerns about the possible disintegration of Spain, the country's new democratic structures faced a final challenge from the Francoist 'old guard'. On 23 February 1981 a Lieutenant-Colonel in the Civil Guard, Antonio Tejero, entered the Spanish parliament with some two hundred men and attempted to seize power. Later in the evening military units in Valencia left their barracks and occupied the streets and similar incidents occurred in Madrid and other cities. Tejero's efforts, though, ended in failure. The 'co-conspirators' he had anticipated simply did not turn up. Once the King had broadcast a message describing the attempt to interfere with the democratic process as 'intolerable', the coup collapsed.

Even so, the abortive coup was not without consequence. Tejero had stormed parliament when it was forming a new government after the resignation of Suárez. The new Prime Minister, Leopoldo Calvo Sotelo, together with the Socialist opposition led by Felipe González, now agreed to a law to curtail the full extent of the autonomy that had been granted to Spain's regions (the 'Organic Law of Harmonisation of the Process of Autonomy'). Ultimately, this measure was not implemented as intended, but the threat of violence from the state's armed forces appeared, to some extent, to have succeeded in forcing politicians to alter course.

The failed putsch achieved something else too. Disputes within ETA-PM, between the group's 'politicians' and its more military-minded members, had been growing for some time. Already, in 1980, these tensions had reached a crescendo when the organisation's military wing decided to complement the political work of EE by killing Basque members of Suárez's UCD. Leaders of EE, like Mario Onaindia or Teo Uriarte, both of whom had been sentenced to death at the Burgos Trial, denounced such activities and began a process of engagement with the militants to convince them to stop. This process accelerated markedly after Tejero's attempted coup. They found an ally in the shape of the Minister of Interior, Juan José Rosón, who had already shown a genuine willingness to reform the security forces that were under his command.[39] When the politicians of EE contacted him to explore the possibility of a deal that could achieve the disbandment of ETA, he proved receptive. Together, they agreed on a plan of 'social reinsertion' for members of the group who renounced violence. Those who had blood in their hands were permitted to return after a period of five years. Those who had not actually killed anyone, it was decided, could return earlier. At the time of Tejero's attempted coup, ETA-PM had been holding the honorary consuls of Austria, El Salvador and Uruguay captive. After the coup had passed, ETA-PM immediately released the consuls and just seven days later it declared a ceasefire. In September 1982, with the 'social reinsertion' scheme having been agreed, the organisation then announced its disbandment. In the previous five years, during which democracy had returned to Spain, the group had murdered over 130 people and helped ensure that the nation's democratic transition would be far from peaceful.

However, not everyone within ETA-PM was persuaded by the new departure. While around one hundred members of the group followed their leadership and agreed to renounce violence, others—some estimates put the figure as high as two hundred people—continued to operate under the banner of 'ETA VIII'. Moreover, those that did disband handed their weapons over to those who did not.[40] This new formation itself later split and the bulk of its members now joined up with ETA-M—which was soon able to claim full ownership over the 'ETA' brand name.

5

TALKING TO ETA

The Long War and the French Connection: ETA re-evaluates, the state murders

In the October 1982 Spanish General Election, more than ten million people, nearly half of those who voted, gave their support to the Socialist Party (PSOE) and Felipe González became the new Prime Minister of Spain. Prior to the contest, the UCD, the former governing party had effectively disintegrated and it won less than 7% of the vote and returned only eleven deputies. Thereafter, the Catholic parties that comprised the main block within the UCD established a new coalition with the 'Popular Alliance' party that was led by Manuel Fraga, who had formerly been a Minister under Franco. Fraga now became the leader of the opposition. But with the PSOE having secured half of the votes and 202 of the 350 seats in the Cortes, Spain had a left-wing government—and one with an indisputable mandate to govern—for the first time since 1936.[1]

As had been the case in the 1930s, the Socialists were confronted by several major problems on coming to power. For one thing, the country was experiencing serious economic problems, as was the rest of western Europe in this period. Industrial and financial reforms pursued by the new government—as part of its effort to gain entry to the European Economic Community (EEC)—produced a fresh hike in unemployment from the already very high existing level of 16%. In the three years that followed, registered unemployment rose to account for 22.1% of the total workforce. Again, the industrial heartlands of the Basque region proved especially vulnerable. The Basque share of Spanish GNP had been 7.5% in 1960 and 7.8% in 1975. By 1985, though, it had fallen to 6.2%.[2] These economic difficulties continued to affect the young disproportionately. In the first fifteen years after the restoration of Spanish democracy, registered unemployment among Basque under-25 year olds multiplied eightfold.[3] By 1984, more than half of the unemployed in the region were under-25.[4] Once more, all of this helped endow ETA-M with a pool of willing recruits who were determined that its violent campaign should go on.

That campaign remained a major challenge for the Spanish state. Nevertheless, the progress and conclusion of the 'transición' had forced a re-evaluation of tactics on the part of radical Basque nationalists. The ceasefire and disbandment of ETA-PM served as the clearest indication of this. But there were also signs that ETA-M too was prepared to consider new approaches. Already in 1979, in the national parliamentary elections that followed the ratification of the Spanish constitution, a new coalition, *Herri Batasuna* ('Popular Unity', or HB), had been formed by parties and individuals inspired by ETA-M. When the results of that contest were announced, they showed that HB had secured three deputies in the Madrid parliament after receiving some 150,000 votes and the backing of 15% of the Basque electorate. Elections to the first regional Basque Parliament in 1980 brought victory to the PNV and saw the Socialists finish second; but HB again fared well. It won 16.6% of the vote and 11 deputies in the Parliament (out of a total of 75)—an assembly based on laws that they had rejected. What ETA-M (from 1982, the only 'ETA' and hereafter referred to simply as that) had effectively embraced was a 'Long War' approach (their own version of the 'Armalite and the ballot box' strategy espoused by Irish republicans). The aim was that ETA's electoral front should attempt to win local power in Basque towns and achieve representation in the regional Parliament, even as the military campaign against the Spanish state continued. The completion of the *transición* brought only the refinement, rather than the abolition of these tactics. Once the new framework of constitutional monarchy, coupled with regional autonomy for the Basque Country (and Navarre) had been put in place, ETA hoped to force the Madrid government to accede to its demands through a war of attrition, pursued by a combination of violence and political activism.

Despite this, the strategic reassessment and subsequent disbandment of ETA-PM did produce a marked decrease in the number of people killed by terrorism after this time. By the end of 1981, thirty people had been murdered by the organisation—a figure amounting to less than a third of those killed over the previous twelve months. This fall set a trend that would be continued in the years that followed.

To prosecute its ongoing war against the Spanish state, ETA relied on free movement across the Franco-Spanish border. The northern region of the traditional Basque homeland—*Iparralde*—which was within the borders of France, had proven invaluable to the organisation. A Basque- and French-speaking area of some three 3,000 sq km., with a population of 250,000, concentrated mainly in urban areas on the Atlantic coast, *Iparralde*, was home to the leaders of ETA, as well as many of the group's members. It was here that ETA held its assemblies, argued and split; and here too that it had its logistics base and published its statements. Militants from Spain would cross the border to meet with the group's leaders before being sent back to carry out operations. Commandos on the run would flee into France to rest and recuperate. Entrepreneurs who had received ETA's letter demanding payment of the 'revolutionary tax' were ordered to make contact with the group's collectors in *Iparralde*.

During the period of the 'transition', French President Valery Giscard d'Estaing had won the enmity of the Suárez government for his vetoing of Spanish accession to the EEC, as well as his apparent toleration of both branches of ETA within French borders. But Giscard was to some degree prevented from taking a tougher line on Basque terrorism by domestic constraints. When he tried to tighten the laws against both groups' members, he encountered significant resistance. The ethos of the French Republic and the spirit of *gaullisme*—of resistance to the Nazi occupation of France—remained a central component within French political culture. The notion that France should be prepared to offer political asylum to those who needed it was still a revered concept. And, in a legacy of the Franco era, many viewed ETA as a Basque resistance movement, fighting against repression from Madrid. Thus, while it was true that successive French governments had been prepared to either arrest, or expel from the border region, those suspects linked to offences committed in French territory, or against French citizens (and were also prepared to target those accused of particularly grave crimes), French efforts to rein in ETA had scarcely gone beyond such limits.

Giscard had signalled a willingness to begin to change policy in January 1979, in the aftermath of the approval of the Spanish constitution.

The French Department of Foreign Affairs announced that Spaniards living in France would no longer be granted official status as political refugees.[5] At the same time, two suspected members of ETA were detained under an international arrest warrant and sent to court for extradition. A few weeks later, the French Office for the Protection of Refugees and Stateless People (OFPRA) wrote to almost 1,000 Basques, informing them that the conduct of free elections in Spain meant that there was no justification for the extension of their refugee cards. Without the card, their residence and work permits were liable to be removed, because Spain was not then a member of the EEC. In response, a team of renowned lawyers that included the socialist Robert Badinter, brought a case against the proposed extraditions in Aix-en-Provence. The court there found that extraditions should not proceed. In this way, Giscard's halting efforts to curtail the activities of ETA seemed to have failed.

In May 1981, François Mitterrand won the French Presidential election—a development that appeared to herald little prospect for a change in policy. Mitterrand had previously voiced his opposition to the withdrawal of refugee cards and on the very day that he was sworn in as President, his Prime Minister, Pierre Mauroy, criticised the extradition of a suspected ETA member, as approved by a Paris tribunal.[6] Even more galling for the Spanish were the comments of the new Minister of the Interior, Gaston Defferre, that same July. In an interview with *Le Nouvel Observateur*, Defferre, a former member of the French resistance, was asked if he would permit extradition to Spain. His reply was unequivocal:

That is not possible, no. Perhaps because I know what it means to live clandestinely, I am firmly convinced that to allow extradition would be contrary to French tradition, especially when it is a question, as it is at present, of a political struggle.[7]

The uproar that his words provoked across the Pyrenees prompted the Minister to later state that he wanted to help the young Spanish democracy. Still, his reluctance to tackle ETA seemed evident.

In this context, it was significant that Defferre had another Basque problem. In the new French government he held both the Interior and Decentralisation portfolios. With regards to the latter, he was coming under pressure from members of his party who wanted to change the administrative structure of southwest France, to form a Basque Department. The Spanish decision to grant regional autonomy to the Basque

Country and Navarre had generated empathy on the other side of the border too. There, the French-Basque areas were part of the 'Atlantic Pyrenees' *département* (administrative unit), which had Pau as its capital. In 1981, elected councillors in the three Basque-French provinces had formed a lobby to break away from Pau and have their own administration. While still in opposition, the Socialist party of Mitterrand and Defferre had supported them and even introduced a bill in the National Assembly that provided for the creation of a Basque *département*. But once in power, Defferre had decided against following through with the policy. Opponents of the move had argued that a Basque *département* would pose a threat to French unity and the spirit of the Republic. Many asked whether it was sensible to create a unifying institution for French Basques at the precise moment when an upsurge in Basque identity politics on the other side of the Pyrenees had degenerated into a war for independence. The fact that a small number of French Basques had formed their own terrorist group, *Iparretarrak* (The 'ETA Northerners'), and occasionally bombed tourist resorts or government buildings, seemed merely to confirm the dangers. At the beginning of 1982, therefore, Defferre gradually announced a policy reversal: there would be no Basque *département*.

Given his disappointment of Basque nationalist sensibilities within France, Deferre was unwilling to interdict ETA's campaign against the Spanish state as well. Consequently, ETA members who had previously been exiled from the border region were now allowed to return.

It was clear, though, that the Spanish government needed French help. The truth of this was brought home to the administration of Felipe Gonzalez only a week after it took office, when an ETA commando unit, operating out of the French Basque Country, killed General Victor Lago, head of the Spanish Army's elite Brunete Armoured Division, which was stationed near Madrid. Around the same time, the incoming minister of Interior, José Barrionuevo, recalls that an inspection of the facilities available to him showed that his whole department had just three armour-plated vehicles.[8] This was the stark reality that confronted the new Spanish government. It therefore spent its first weeks in power reviewing comprehensive proposals to deal with the Basque situation. The 'Special Zone North' scheme (or ZEN plan as it was subsequently known), looked to an inter-locking programme of investment in security, legal reforms and political initiatives to counter ETA in the medium-to-long term. In addition, it had a section dedicated to the need for international cooperation, particularly with France. To this end, renewed diplomatic efforts were undertaken to convince the French government to adopt a harder line against ETA activists operating within its territory.

Madrid therefore welcomed the announcement that came just seven days after the murder of General Lago, when the French Council of Ministers announced that it was prepared to adjust asylum and extradition policy. France, it was emphasised, would not extradite people accused of political crimes and neither would it send suspects back to undemocratic countries. However, it would extradite those persons accused of 'such criminal acts (the taking of hostages, murder and violence causing serious injury or death) that the alleged political aim cannot justify the use of unacceptable means'.[9] The French Justice Minister, Robert Badinter, the man who had resolutely defended suspected ETA members against extradition three years earlier, now effectively conceded that such extradition might in fact be possible. This departure in French policy, which seemed to herald a new understanding between Madrid and Paris, came against a backdrop of ongoing violence, which appeared, for the first time, to impact upon France itself in a major way.

As has been described, much of the violent opposition to ETA in the late-Franco and 'transition' periods had been carried out by numerous 'uncontrolled' gunmen, operating under various names. Now, in the early 1980s, as the ETA campaign continued, the incoming Socialist government effectively launched a second 'dirty war' against Basque terrorism. This time, though, the focus was more on wider strategic objectives—particularly efforts to alter the outlook of the French government. This was to be done by effectively pursuing ETA across the border into France. The immediate context for this development was provided by the kidnapping of an army captain who worked as a chemist in Bilbao barracks, Alberto Martín, on 5 October 1983. The group responsible was a breakaway faction of the now defunct ETA-PM and it announced that it would kill Martín if Spanish state television did not broadcast a pre-prepared statement. The national Spanish television network subsequently announced on 17 October that it would consent to the statement being read and asked that the hostage be freed. Martín, however, was found dead the following day. The murder prompted major protest marches in Bilbao and Madrid. Yet, the public outcry against Basque separatist violence was not to be the only consequence arising out of the episode. The kidnapping had coincided with a major upsurge in ETA-M activity. Already, the group had killed two days prior to Martín's abduction and it murdered four other people while he was being held captive. On 15 October 1983, for instance, the group assassinated a Civil Guard in the Basque town of Oñate. That same day, though, two alleged ETA men disappeared in Bayonne, in southwest France. They were never heard of again, until their bodies were discovered buried in quicklime, in southeast Spain, twelve years later. It was to be the beginning of a pattern of reprisal abductions and killings carried out against suspected ETA militants by the forces of the state.

On the day that Spanish television had announced that it would concede to the demands regarding Captain Martín, a French *gendarme* intercepted and arrested four Spanish policemen who were in Bayonne and appeared to be on a mission to abduct the leader of the kidnappers. Then, on 4 December 1983, a French citizen of Spanish origin, Segundo Marey, was kidnapped in the border town of Hendaye. His captors claimed in a phone call that he was linked to ETA and demanded the release of the four Spanish policemen arrested fifty days earlier. When they were later acquitted, on 13 December, Marey was released. What these episodes had confirmed was that a new group was operating against ETA inside France: one that was prepared to kidnap and kill, with an acute sense of timing. On 19 December 1983, this new organisation revealed its name to the world when claiming responsibility for the murder of an ETA member: the Antiterrorist Groups of Liberation (GAL).[10]

The next day, 20 December 1983, François Mitterrand held a long meeting with Felipe González at the Élysée Palace. Jacques Attali, advisor to the French president, has stated that on that date an agreement on the extradition of suspected ETA members was reached.[11] This has been disputed by the then French ambassador in Spain, Pierre Guidoni, who claims that a deal had been reached earlier in the month.[12] Either way, the terms of the new accord were significant. It included provisions on police cooperation and a commitment from the French government that it would actively pursue ETA commandos operating within its territory. Those arrested and found guilty, it affirmed, would be extradited to Spain. For its part, according to the ambassador, the Spanish government promised to take forward certain domestic policies with regards to ETA. It committed itself, for instance, to facilitate the 'social reinsertion' of former members of the group. There were also assurances that the Spanish would, at some point, offer ETA the 'necessary procedures to allow it to abandon its arms, without a political negotiation' and endeavour to reach agreement with Basque nationalists as to the 'full development of the Statute of Autonomy'.[13] The agreement, however, did not lead to the first extraditions from France to Spain; instead the most that the French delivered was the expulsion of six Basque people to third-party countries and an order to another eleven to leave the border area. Neither did the accord put an end to the activities of the GAL. In the eight weeks that immediately followed, the GAL killed another five suspected members of ETA.

On 14 June 1984, the Spanish Interior Minister, José Barrionuevo signed a 'cooperation agreement' with his French counterpart, Gaston Defferre. Unlike the earlier accord, as described by the French ambassador, it did not include any clause that impinged on the domestic politics of Spain. At the time, Barrionuevo noted in his diaries the 'magnificent personal chemistry' that existed between him and Deferre. The latter was also said to have held a 'very affectionate' meeting with Felipe González.[14] Despite these personal ties, though, Deferre ultimately left office without signing a single extradition order that would have seen a prisoner transferred to Spain. He was replaced as French Interior Minister in July 1984 by the younger, Pierre Joxe. Yet, Defferre had set the trajectory and Joxe saw it through to its logical conclusion. In August of the same year, a court in Pau in southwest France, ordered the extradition of three suspected members of ETA. In protest, the prisoners started a hunger strike, but this proved futile and was abandoned (no member of ETA has ever carried a hunger strike to full-term). The Supreme Court confirmed the order, Joxe signed the extradition papers and the three prisoners were sent to Spain.

After these first extraditions, the French government later moved to introduce expulsion by the 'procedure of absolute urgency', based on a 1945 law. This allowed for the immediate transfer of suspected members of ETA to Spain. The first such handover occurred four days after a bomb attack on a bus in Madrid that killed twelve young civil guards on 14 July 1986. When the Conservatives returned to power in France later that same year, the new Interior Minister, Charles Pasqua, continued to apply the same policy. And with this process under way, the GAL ceased to commit murders inside French territory. After 29 assassinations, 27 of which had been committed in France, the undeclared objective of the GAL had been achieved.

The Spanish government's determination to secure the extradition of ETA suspects from France was not without controversy, especially among Basque nationalists. At the time of the first extraditions, for example, the PNV (then in government in the regional Basque Parliament) issued a statement asking Paris not to proceed. Its neighbour should, the PNV argued, 'maintain the historical policy that has made France a land of asylum for all those who, for political reasons, feel forced to search refuge in other countries'.[15] On this basis, Basque nationalists were often accused of being ambivalent on terrorism and of raising objections to every measure that put pressure on ETA. The most influential PNV leader at the time, Xabier Arzalluz, rejected such criticism in his autobiography, arguing that the Spanish parties always mistook disagreement on terrorist policy for a lack of resolve on the part of Basque nationalists.[16] And yet, even as he himself denied the existence of any ambiguity in the response of the Basque parties to terrorism, Arzalluz also appeared to confirm it. Within the same book— indeed, merely three pages later—he offered a portrait of Santiago Brouard, a paediatric consultant in Bilbao and ETA sympathiser, who was assassinated by the GAL in one of the few crimes the group committed inside Spain. In his account, Arzalluz told of how a member of ETA, who had been injured in a shoot-out with police found refuge in the house of two members of the PNV: 'A visit by a doctor was arranged and he was able to rest... One of us went to Brouard to tell him that we had the boy and that someone had to take charge of him'. In other words, it may be that Brouard and members of the PNV gave aid to a member of ETA who had recently been firing upon the police. This account came from the leader of a governing party that had overall control of those same forces of law-and-order—a man who also maintained that his party's position on terrorism was in no way ambiguous.

Still, it was not just within Basque nationalist circles that the rights and wrongs of the Spanish state's 'counter-terrorism' efforts in those years were questioned. Conservatives and some Socialists too raised political and ethical concerns about the steps taken in the battle against ETA. From 1988 until its demise in 1996, the administration of Felipe González was discredited by a series of media revelations and judicial trials that pointed to links between the government and the GAL. This culminated with the conviction and imprisonment of the Interior Minister, José Barrionuevo, together with some of his closest aides in

Madrid and the Basque Country, for involvement in the crimes of the AL. González has since argued repeatedly that his government actually worked to try to put a stop to a form of right-wing terrorism that had come into existence before he came to power. There are, however, a number of troubling facts arising out of the GAL affair. The assassinations perpetrated by BVE, ATE and various other 'pseudo-Francoist groups during the *transición* came to an end in 1981, just prior to the Socialists' first election victory. Moreover, these crimes had been committed in both France and Spain. By comparison, the GAL went into operation after a lapse of two and half years and after González had become Prime Minister. Furthermore, it killed, with only two exceptions, solely in France. It is clear too that people involved in the murders of the late 1970s, later killed and recruited for the GAL.[17] This continuity of personnel would seem to support the view of those who saw the death squads as an instrument of state policy. What changed was the strategy behind the killings. In the late 1970s, the death squads had aimed to create terror among members of ETA or the Basque population more broadly. In stark contrast, the actions of the GAL were designed specifically to change French policy towards ETA.

When later reflecting on the GAL and the conviction of Barrionuevo, Felipe González commented:

Every attempt to reflect on the facts stumbles immediately into an obstacle: it seems monstrous to put those events in their context, the hardest time of terrorist violence. But what is truly monstrous is not to do it...if you do not want to end up with a false view, as has happened with regards to the GAL nearly ten years after its disappearance. And everybody was complicit. Nobody, or nearly nobody, escapes.[18]

This is probably the closest the former Prime Minister of Spain has come, or may come, to admitting publicly the truth about the GAL; namely, that it engaged in a campaign of assassination against ETA that was planned by the Spanish government's security apparatus and carried out within the sovereign territory of a neighbouring country.

It is not merely the morality of the GAL campaign that is questionable, but also, the nature of its impact on ETA. For instance, in the same way that the right-wing death squads of the late 1970s appeared to reduce the willingness of many Basque people to express revulsion against ETA, so too the crimes of the GAL may have had a similar effect. In addition, they gave supporters of the group a further argument in favour of its resort to violence and damaged the image of the state. In both Basque and Spanish elections that followed the period of the GAL's activity, Herri Batasuna, the electoral wing of ETA, increased its share of the vote, from 14.7% in 1982 to 17.7% respectively in 1986. Significantly, this trend was not all one-sided. At the same time, it should be noted that the Socialists themselves continued to do well also, even at the level of the regional Basque parliament. Indeed, they became the largest party in that assembly after a split in the PNV—a development that allowed the Socialists to enter coalition government in Vitoria for the first time. Simultaneously, they lost only one Basque seat out of eight in the national Spanish parliament, when Felipe González, after national Spain had gained entry to the EEC, called for an election in 1986 and was returned to power with a very large majority.

In addition, what is undeniable about the period in which the GAL was active, is the fact that ETA members were forced to lead more secretive lives, a trend reinforced by the growing prospect of arrest by French police. Even if they avoided extradition or expulsion to Spain, prominent ETA leaders found themselves deported to Central and South American countries, or to Africa. Thus, the group's communications and command and control structures were seriously disrupted and it became far more difficult for it to wage its self-proclaimed 'war'. As a result, the number of attacks carried out by ETA decreased substantially. Florencio Domínguez Iribarren, the author of several well informed books on ETA, estimates that in 1985 and 1986, the number of ETA operations fell by 26% and 36% respectively, as compared with the organisation's previous level of activity.[19]

Moreover, if the reduction in the rate of attacks after 1980 had already signalled that ETA was considering a change in its approach (from an all-out attack against the Spanish state, to a slow war of attrition aimed at eventual negotiation), the closing off of the group's cross-border 'sanctuary' confirmed that the second option was the only viable one left open to it. The increased cooperation between French and Spanish police generated better intelligence and ETA suffered major reverses in the years that followed. For its part, meanwhile, ETA responded to this new, more difficult environment by making more frequent use of the car bomb—logistically simpler, but more indiscriminate and potentially of enormous damage politically.

The Algerian Connection: Killing and Talking

Dialogue between ETA and emissaries of the Spanish government had occurred at various points during the *transición*. As early as October 1976, ETA-PM had asked for talks with the government and the two sides had subsequently met in Geneva. There, the representatives of ETA-PM had explored the views of their interlocutor regarding a possible amnesty and the formation of a political party. Though the talks were inconclusive, the parties agreed to have a second meeting, to which ETA-M would also be invited. The result was a gathering in November, involving five members drawn from the two Basque separatist groups and three members of the intelligence services. A frank exchange of views reportedly followed, in which the KAS Alternative formed the basis of the programme put forward by both branches of ETA. Ultimately, however, the encounter proved fruitless.[20]

In late 1977–early 1978, the Spanish Interior Minister, Rodolfo Martín Villa, again attempted to engage ETA-M after intermediaries told the government that a ceasefire might be possible. Yet, by its own admission, the Basque group claimed that it was unwilling 'to negotiate in the strictest sense, since we are not ready to discuss the points of the ceasefire'; rather, it sought simply to 'pin them [the government] down and conversations are required to do just that'.[21] Furthermore, the negotiations stalled after ETA-M demanded that the talks should be held in public. Thereafter, further attempts to convince the leadership of ETA-M to declare a cessation failed, either because the group wanted negotiations to be conducted openly—or because it insisted that the KAS Alternative be implemented as a precondition for talks.

In January 1983, eight months prior to the emergence of the GAL and soon after the disbandment of ETA-PM, the President of the regional Basque government, Carlos Garaikoetxea, tried to set up a 'roundtable for peace' in which it was hoped that members of the PNV, the PSOE and Herri Batasuna (HB) would negotiate a political settlement and an end to the violence. Yet, echoing ETA's position, HB insisted that meetings be held openly, a demand deemed unacceptable by the other parties. An ETA bomb attack on the offices of the largest Basque bank, the BBV, in Bilbao, that killed three people and injured ten others on 2 February 1983, further poisoned the atmosphere and the proposed talks were aborted.

After the failure of this public initiative on the part of constitutional Basque nationalism, the Spanish government resolved to establish contact with ETA behind closed doors. Thus, a year later, in February 1984, a colonel in the Civil Guard, Enrique Rodriguez Galindo—a man later sentenced to 75 years in prison for his role in the first murder to be attributed to the GAL—travelled to Andorra to meet an ETA leader, Txomin Iturbe. In the months that followed, Spanish intelligence agents made contact with Iturbe three times, before a Jesuit priest, acting as an emissary for Prime Minister Felipe González, also met him in June 1984.[22] This latter encounter was followed up by the French ambassador in Spain, Pierre Guidoni, with the blessing of both governments. Guidoni's mission was to impress upon the leaders of violent Basque nationalism the shared resolution of the French and Spanish states that they would not concede to ETA's demands. The hope was that a blunt description of 'objective realities' might engender a rethink within ETA as to the likely success of the organisation's military campaign and that this, in turn, might encourage a new pragmatism among its leadership. Guidoni thus contacted HB leaders in September 1984 and emphasised the new determination of the French authorities to extradite members of ETA to Spain. At the same time, Guidoni held out the possibility of dialogue with ETA's representatives, on condition of a ceasefire. He then made arrangements for a meeting with ETA, but the group's representatives failed to turn up. They had rejected the 'carrot' and in keeping with Guidoni's message the 'stick' swiftly followed. The first extraditions of ETA suspects from France to Spain took place the day after the abortive talks.[23]

Further efforts to initiate dialogue proved unsuccessful and in the meantime, the killing went on. In September 1986 an ETA commando gunned down Dolores González Catarain, a former member of the organisation's own executive, who had left the group and lived in exile for a time, before returning home the previous year under the Spanish government's 'social reinsertion' scheme. The murder of Catarain was intended as a warning from the group to its own members, lest others consider abandoning 'the struggle'. There was no doubt that ETA was coming under increasing pressure. In November 1986, for example, French police discovered a secret cache of money and weapons, along with sensitive documents offering a wealth of information about ETA. This was merely the latest in a series of setbacks suffered by the group. Apparently in a position of weakness, it was at this time that ETA once more sent word, privately, that it wanted to talk with the Spanish authorities. Consequently, during the same month as the French raid, a fresh effort to initiate secret dialogue was launched by the Spanish government. The latter dispatched an envoy to the Algerian capital, Algiers, to talk with Iturbe, who was now in residence there after his expulsion from France. This was to be the start of the most prolonged attempt by the González government to negotiate an end to ETA's campaign.

At that initial meeting, Iturbe denied that ETA was weak or divided and rejected the notion that the group could follow the precedent set by ETA-PM and disband in exchange for social reintegration. Nevertheless, he made a distinction, according to the envoy, between 'negotiating the KAS Alternative' and what was necessary, 'to negotiate about the KAS Alternative'.[24] Iturbe declared that he was willing for the talks to move forward on this basis. Consequently, a higher level delegation was sent to Algiers in January 1987. It was composed of a former head of National Security (another man who was later imprisoned for GAL-related crimes), and two police officers (one of whom had been linked in court to a double murder committed in France that was claimed by the Basque Spanish Battalion, the BVE).[25] During the talks that followed, the Spanish representatives suggested that the government could offer individual pardons to those ETA prisoners who had not been convicted of 'blood crimes', in the event that there was a cessation of violence. Iturbe responded that a ceasefire would be possible only after political negotiations had been conducted on the granting of self-determination to the Basques. He also insisted on the union of Navarre with the Basque Autonomous Community.[26] Finally, Iturbe demanded that another ETA leader, Eugenio Etxebeste, be sent to Algiers from South America (where he had been exiled by the French government). From the outset, the gap between the two sides seemed unbridgeable, but the delegations nevertheless committed themselves to further talks and even dined together under the auspices of their Algerian hosts.

Iturbe did not long survive the meeting. In February 1987, he died in an accident and the leadership of the organisation changed. Iturbe's sudden death has been lamented by many as marking the last chance for a negotiated settlement with ETA. He has generally been portrayed as a man of straight-forward nationalist convictions, who was uncontaminated by the more 'revolutionary' jargon of other ETA leaders. In this respect, Iturbe stood in stark contrast to his successor, Eugenio Etxebeste, whose return from exile in South America Iturbe had requested in the earlier round of talks. According to the memoir of José Barrionuevo, Etxebeste liked to describe himself as a 'nationalist-communist', who was proud to be considered a hard-liner. He was alleged to have said that 'elections are worth nothing', that one of the main aims of ETA was to fragment the PNV and that the liberation of the Basque Country would require thousands of deaths.[27]

The immediate post-Iturbe period brought a cooling of contacts between the government and ETA. The situation was transformed again, however, by a new and devastating act of violence. In June 1987, ETA committed the single worst atrocity of the entire conflict when it left a car-bomb in the underground car-park of a supermarket in Barcelona. Twenty-one people were killed and hundreds injured. But if the aim of ETA had been to force the González government to return to Algiers, it achieved its objective. In the wake of the attack, the government took the decision to restart dialogue and made arrangements for Etxebeste to be sent to the Algerian capital. Thereafter, the two police officers who had previously held talks with Iturbe met Etxebeste in August and within a few days, Prime Minister González had announced to the press (having first briefed Francois Mitterrand at his holiday home in France) that even though any form of 'political negotiations' was unacceptable, the government believed that talks with ETA were necessary. Thereafter, the government's spokesman, Javier Solana, responded to media speculation as to the meaning of the Prime Minister's words by confirming that 'there has been, there is and there will be' dialogue with ETA.[28]

In parallel with this dialogue, though, the government also showed no signs of toning down its war of attrition against the organisation; ETA continued to be hit hard by the French and Spanish security services. On 30 September 1987, French police arrested the head of ETA's military office in Anglet. Already that year, the Spanish security forces had dismantled units in Madrid and Barcelona and now their French counterparts had delivered a critical blow to the backbone of ETA. The Anglet operation yielded a vast array of documents. In the days that followed the archives of the political office were also seized and some one hundred ETA members were arrested in France (58 of whom were later handed over to the Spanish authorities). At the same time, a similar number of activists were also seized in Spain, while the location of four safe houses and four weapons dumps were uncovered.[29]

In October 1987, Etxebeste met with Julen Elgorriaga, the most senior member of the central government's office in the Basque Country (and another man who was later imprisoned for his links to the GAL). Once again, the results of the dialogue proved inconclusive. Still, while these contacts were ongoing, other lines of communication were being pursued between the government and the representatives of radical Basque nationalism. Government emissaries met leaders of HB in both October and November 1987, for instance. According to Minister Barrionuevo, the HB emissaries were frank as to the unlikelihood of talks being successful for as long as Josu Urrutikoetxea remained head of ETA's political office. In their view, whilst Urrutikoetxea might opt for a ceasefire, such a move would only be the product of a tactical decision. The underlying motive would simply be to give ETA time to regroup and rebuild its capacity for war, after the damage caused by recent police operations.[30]

The end of 1987 brought a major new ETA atrocity, when the organisation's commandos planted a bomb at the Civil Guard barracks in Saragossa on 11 December. It killed eleven people: three guards, three family members, and five young girls aged between three and twelve years old. In the aftermath of the attack, the government immediately announced that all dialogue with ETA was being suspended. Nonetheless, the reality was that the Algiers dialogue continued behind-the-scenes. Only a week after the bomb, Spain's Director of State Security, Rafael Vera, travelled to Paris and from there to Algiers. Vera's publicly declared mission was to explain to the Governments of France and Algeria that talks were impossible and that the Spanish state could not engage with an organisation that murdered children. It was announced that he would ask his French colleagues to put more pressure on ETA within France, while he would also try to persuade the Algerians to send all members of ETA in residence there, including Etxebeste, back to South America. In reality, by the end of his short trip, Vera had himself engaged in indirect communication with Etxebeste. In the context of those exchanges, the Madrid emissary demanded a sixty-day truce from ETA, in return for a commitment from the Spanish government that it would form a 'mesa de negociación' (negotiating commission) in Algiers.[31]

Meanwhile, the Spanish Prime Minister, Felipe González, found himself under growing pressure as a result of the political and media debate that followed the Saragossa attack. As a consequence, he felt compelled to seek agreement with the other political parties, in order to shield his government from any further possible controversy arising out of the clandestine Algiers talks. The result was the 'Madrid Pact', signed by the main Basque and Spanish parties in December 1987, which rejected the possibility that ETA could be engaged in political negotiations. It instead called on the group to abandon violence and embrace democracy.[32] This was followed in January 1988, by the Ajuria-Enea Pact that the coalition Basque government signed with the opposition parties, with the notable exception of HB. This affirmed the principle of popular sovereignty in such a way as to deny ETA a role in any future negotiations about status of the Basque Country. It described the legal framework for Basque national aspirations as having been set by the Spanish constitution and the Statute of Autonomy (provided the latter was more fully developed). At the same time, the pact also expressed support, both for a policy of dialogue with ETA (provided 'adequate conditions' were put in place), and for a programme of social reinsertion for those who abandoned violence.[33]

In the wake of these developments ETA was under pressure to respond to the changing political dispensation. A month and half after the massacre in Saragossa and some fifteen days after the Basque parties had signed their pact, the organisation announced that it was willing to declare a sixty days 'cessation of military operations', provided that 'police hostilities ceased throughout the Basque Country' and the government agreed, in a preliminary meeting, to engage in dialogue with the Basque Movement of National Liberation (by which it meant representatives drawn from both ETA and HB). The purpose of such dialogue was said to be the establishment of a 'negotiating framework leading to a negotiated political solution to the conflict'. The ETA statement also expressed preference for 'the mediating role of the Algerian government' and declared, 'the only agreement which can lead to a [total] armistice is the signing of the KAS Alternative'.[34]

Despite the unpromising nature of what was on offer from ETA, which had given little indication of being imbued with a new pragmatism, the Spanish government dispatched Julen Elgorriaga once more to Algiers in February 1988. His meeting with Etxebeste proved acrimonious. The ETA leader demanded to know the names of the Spanish delegates who would attend future meetings and the proposed agenda for those meetings, neither of which Elgorriaga could provide. For his part, the government envoy asked for confirmation of an ETA ceasefire.[35] Four days later, ETA appeared to deliver its response, when it kidnapped a wealthy industrialist in Madrid. Once more, talks were suspended—supposedly for good. In July, though, after Prime Minister González had appointed José Luis Corcuera, a Basque member of the PSOE, as his Interior Minister, a new approach was made. Corcuera asked Rafael Vera to return to Algiers with a message for the Algerians to pass on to ETA: Madrid was willing to engage in dialogue, if the kidnapped industrialist was freed. In October, ETA freed their prisoner after he had spent eight months in captivity. Yet, rather than being a gesture of possible conciliation from the group, the reality was that his family had paid a hefty ransom. As if to underline the point, on the same day, a policeman was killed in Bilbao. In fact, the group appeared to be sending out mixed signals. Three days after the Bilbao murder, ETA released a communiqué offering a two-month truce, if the government engaged in dialogue.[36] But this was then followed by further acts of violence, including a car bombing in Madrid that killed two civil guards.

In the face of ETA's prevarications and the ongoing violence, government policy now hardened. Two policemen were sent back to Algiers, but only to ask the Algerians to expel Etxebeste. It was while they were there, however, that the Spanish emissaries were apprised of fresh developments: ETA was set to announce a two-month ceasefire in January 1989.[37] In the event, the statement actually released by ETA, on 8 January 1989, fell some way short of what the Algerians had led the Spanish government to expect. The ceasefire that the group declared had a two-week deadline, while the tone of the statement was belligerent and uncompromising. The sole aim of the truce was said to be the attainment of a 'democratic political alternative', which meant 'a political negotiation with the Spanish state about the dates for the implementation of the tactical KAS alternative'.[38] Despite this, the ceasefire served as a starting point for further contacts. Furthermore, prospects for meaningful progress appeared to have been boosted when the French police announced the arrest of Josu Urrutikoetxea—the man in charge of ETA's political office—who had been seen, even by some HB representatives, as a major obstacle to any settlement.

On 14 January 1989, Corcuera travelled to Algiers for talks at the head of a delegation that included Rafael Vera, and a Basque Socialist politician, Juan Manuel Eguigaray. For the Basque terrorist group, Ignacio Arakama and Belén González, both of whom were believed by the Spanish police to have been ETA commandos in Madrid, joined Etxebeste. The first meeting of what was to be known as the '*Mesa de*

Argel' (The Algiers Roundtable) produced an agreement for the extension of the existing ceasfire and an agenda for further meetings, or 'political conversations'.[39] Moreover, the statement subsequently released by ETA was softer in tone than usual. The initial discussions were described as 'a step forward in our willingness to search for avenues of dialogue that could lead to a negotiated political settlement'. And while ETA warned that nobody should expect quick and spectacular results, it also stated 'what has already been demonstrated is our responsibility and our spirit of armed dialogue, even when arms are silent'.[40] Thereafter, ETA's truce was extended until 26 March 1989—the day when the *Aberri Eguna*, or celebration of the Basque fatherland, was to be held that year. The sense that a breakthrough was at hand was further strengthened by the official response of the Interior Ministry, which declared itself 'ready to make an effort, maybe the last one, that could lead, through dialogue, to the final disappearance of violent acts'.[41] Four meetings between representatives of the Spanish government and the ETA delegation were held in Algiers in the weeks that followed. In the fourth of these, the two sides discussed the Spanish Statute of Autonomy. At this point, it seemed evident that, in spite of its claims to the contrary, the Spanish government was engaged in 'political discussions' with ETA—even if the purpose of these remained unclear. Discussions—involving an exchange of views— did not necessarily equate to negotiations; and in the government's view, the former were deemed acceptable while the latter were not.

Throughout the talks, Etxebeste argued that the Spanish constitution had to be reformed in order to accommodate the Basque right to self-determination. The government replied that an agreement on this matter with ETA was simply impossible. Ultimately, it was because of this impasse that the talks floundered. Etxebeste had aimed to open full-blown political negotiations, but the government consistently refused to countenance such a development. After their last meeting, the Spanish envoys left Algiers imbued with pessimism as to the continued viability of the talks and the likely durability of ETA's truce.[42] Subsequently, the two sides entrenched their positions. Etxebeste now demanded three concessions from the Spanish government so that ETA's ceasefire might be extended: a promise that there would be negotiations with regards to the political issues they had previously explored; a commitment that three ETA prisoners would be brought to Algiers, including the recently arrested Urrutikoetxea; and the creation of a parallel process of dialogue in Algiers between representatives of HB and the PSOE. As it became clear that no agreement could be reached on these three points, all discussions were brought to a halt. There followed a brief period in which ETA published an ultimatum and the Algerians attempted to salvage things, but they too failed. Finally, on 4 April 1989, an ETA statement announced emphatically, 'all fronts [are] open'. 'The truth is ethical and revolutionary', it declared.[43] Three days later the first in a wave of parcel bombs caused serious injuries to a schoolteacher in Vitoria.

ETA and its sympathisers argued that the Spanish side had withdrawn from an agreement reached at the talks, due to pressure from 'dark', right wing forces.[44] But most people realised that there were more straightforward explanations for the breakdown. In particular, proponents of further talks, who criticised the authorities in the wake of their collapse, were unable to answer how it was that the government could ever have abandoned its long standing policy towards ETA—as enshrined in public agreements with other political parties—in the wake of secret talks in Algeria. The reality was that the government was simply unwilling to concede to ETA's parameters as to the nature of a political settlement. Moreover ETA had again failed to force the Spanish state to accept its own precondition for negotiations: the implementation of the KAS Alternative.

After the halting of the Algiers talks, ETA sought to generate a new upsurge in violence. The number of attacks by the group now reached a level not seen since the early 1980s, as it made renewed and prolific use of the car bomb.[45] In this context, the group was particularly well served by a group of French citizens who had been recruited during the 1970s and found it easy to cross the border into Spain. This 'itinerant commando unit' was responsible for a string of high-profile strikes on Spanish cities.[46] ETA also directed its resources towards a new objective: an effort to launch attacks that coincided with major international events that Spain was due to host. Of particular significance in this regard was the fact that in 1992, Barcelona was scheduled to be the Olympic capital, while Seville was hosting the International Expo. ETA's calculation was that a government keen to secure its image in front of the world would be more vulnerable. On the one hand, it proved to be an accurate assessment. Faced with the renewed campaign of violence, the government sought to open new talks via Etxebeste, albeit unsuccessfully.[47] Yet, the pursuit of fresh dialogue was not the government's only response to the rising tide of ETA attacks. In May 1992, eight weeks before the Olympic Games' opening ceremony, a joint operation by French and Spanish police ended with the arrest in Bidart of the three-man Supreme Council of ETA. Never before had the group taken such a severe blow and further reverses followed as its capacity for violence appeared to wane. Throughout 1992, ETA was responsible for only 26 deaths; in 1993, the figure was 14; in 1994, it was 12. For the first time now, many speculated whether it might actually be possible to defeat ETA by force—a proposition previously deemed improbable.

The Irish Connection: Peace Processing or Slow Defeat?

In the early 1990s, following the failed Algiers talks and the serious setbacks that ETA suffered at the hands of the security services, the group also came under pressure from a new quarter: civil society. A protest movement against ETA violence now flourished in the Basque country. Assassinations were followed by silent demonstrations of disapproval in public squares. These displays took on a quasi-religious tone, even though their leading figures often pointed an accusing finger at the absence of the Basque clergy. The latter, it was sometimes alleged, found it easier to denounce human rights abuses against ETA detainees, than the crimes of ETA itself. Kidnappings became a particular focus for peaceful protest. A lengthy period of captivity for the victim helped spread the sense of popular indignation. In 1993, this grassroots civic movement adopted a blue ribbon in the shape of an 'A' as its emblem, as a symbol of the Basque word for 'free', askatu. ETA viewed the growth of these spontaneous protests as a serious threat, and it attempted to challenge their appeal. In towns and villages, people wearing the blue ribbon were intimidated or attacked. Rallies against ETA outrages were confronted by the counter-marches of ETA supporters, denouncing torture or the GAL. Nonetheless, the blue ribbon movement suggested that many Basques were now in revolt against ETA.

As it debated how to reverse its declining fortunes, there was deep disagreement within the radical Basque nationalist, or 'patriotic', movement (as it preferred to be known). Correspondence obtained by the police and leaked to the press showed the scale of the divisions between exiles like Etxebeste and others within the leadership of ETA on the best way forward for the group. One outcome of this debate on how ETA could overcome its political and military stagnation was the spread of '*kale borroka*', or street fighting. This looked to militant Basque youths to revive the movement's flagging fortunes, reflecting the changing composition of ETA membership over the decades. Whereas the earliest members of the organisation had largely been in keeping with Sabino Arana's ideals of a racially pure people, later recruits were frequently drawn more from urban areas and mixed or immigrant families.[48] Where the creators of ETA had often belonged to the professional classes, the new 'street fighting' members of the group comprised the sons and daughters of industrial and service workers; they were semi-skilled or unskilled youngsters from low-income backgrounds. The arrest of ETA's Supreme Council in 1992 enabled this new generation to steer the group in a more radical, nihilistic direction, apparently with less weight given to strategic imperatives.

Since the 1980s, a musical movement of 'Basque radical rock' that fused punk, ska and heavy metal had testified to the new spirit that now infused ETA. It was one of broken adolescent alienation, mixed with an ethos of resistance to oppression. In many ways, it formed a sub-culture of its own—one peppered with the high consumption of drugs and alcohol—and a world away from the ideals of ETA's founding fathers.[49] A former member of ETA, reflecting on the behaviour of the younger generation towards the end of the twentieth century, summed up their activities as follows:

To smash. To smash. To smash things for the sake of it. They take anything and just break it. Nothing had happened, there was nothing, the police was not hassling them...I don't know. Now all that is about drinking alcohol and smashing a phone box.[50]

Alongside this youth militancy, ETA continued to plan and attempt high-profile operations. Thus, a plot to assassinate the King was foiled in August 1995. Four months earlier, the group had attempted to kill the leader of the conservative opposition, José María Aznar, with a car bomb. In the public statement that claimed responsibility for the Aznar attack, ETA said that the failed assassination had 'brought to light the advancing political and institutional crisis in the Spanish state'.[51] Yet ETA itself was in a major crisis. In this period, over one hundred prisoners took advantage of the benefits available to those who distanced themselves from the group and entered the government's social reinsertion programme.[52] Significantly, too, a member of the ETA leadership triumvirate that had been arrested in 1992 experienced some kind of religious conversion while in jail and subsequently called for an end to the armed struggle on ethical grounds.

The group also faced a long-term recruitment problem in its efforts to replace those who were imprisoned or had abandoned the cause. In the decade since the PSOE had come to power in Spain, the Basque birth rate had dropped precipitately. Whereas 1982 had seen 39,282 Basques reach the age of eighteen—the highest number since records began—in 1996, only 15,987 children were born in the Basque Country.[53] A simple glance at such statistics alone, gave notice that ETA had lost almost 60% of its recruitment base—a fact that seemed to confirm perceptions as to the group's terminal decline. Moreover, by this period, the severe economic troubles that had characterised the early years of democratic Spain had eased in the context of a more expansive cycle and the country's accession to the EEC. As the following graph shows, there is a strong correlation between unemployment levels among under-25s in the Basque Country and the potency of the organisation:

All the while, ETA faced the growing rejection of its cause in the Basque Country and a sense of lost purpose. The impression was increasingly held that it could no longer make the same impact it once had. The reality was that Spanish society had become resigned to its

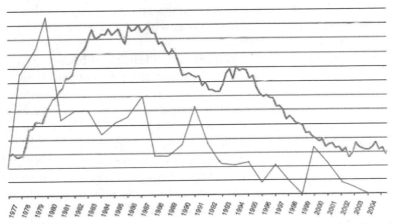

This graph shows a juxtaposition of the yearly figures for unemployed under 25 year olds in the Basque Country (Álava, Guipuzcoa and Biscay) (the line that is largely uppermost) and the number of killings by ETA (the predominantly lower line).

217

killings. They still had the capacity to cause damage and murder, but they could not threaten the underlying stability of the system.

In an effort to re-take the initiative, ETA announced in 1995 that it had updated the KAS Alternative after a period of internal debate. Those paragraphs, which had most obviously been made redundant, were now removed from the text. The revised 'Democratic Alternative' concentrated on the remaining points and laid out a map for its implementation. To give Basques their democratic rights, it argued, two strands for negotiation had to be established. The first was to be between ETA and the Spanish state, with the latter accepting three core principles: the territorial unity of the Basque Country and its right to self-determination; the legitimacy of whatever flowed from that act of self determination; and the necessity of an unconditional amnesty for all its prisoners. Once the Spanish state had endorsed all of this, the second strand of negotiation was to be opened. This was to be a process between Basques, involving political parties, but also 'trade unions, social movements and all kinds of institutions', to define both the 'formulation, methodology, options [and] times' of the right to self determination and the 'formulation of territorial unity and the process to build it'. Finally, after all of this had been achieved, the document provided for an ETA truce, by which the group would 'adapt its activity to the new juncture'. In reality, therefore, this new 'Democratic Alternative' was little more than a restatement of ETA's aims as they had existed over the previous four decades and the strategy outlined to achieve these aims ran counter to that which had been agreed by all the other parties to the conflict.

The attempt of ETA's electoral wing, HB, to publicise the new 'Democratic Alternative' during the campaign for the Spanish parliamentary elections of 1996, also brought a new departure from the state in its response to the Basque 'patriotic movement'. Tapes showing three men wearing white hoods topped with a traditional beret and sitting behind a table, on which three guns were laid, while reading fragments of the new programme, had been sent to radio and television stations. Twelve days before the broadcasts were due to be aired, ETA had killed a prominent Socialist in San Sebastián; five days before that it had murdered a former president of the Constitutional Court in Madrid. In response, the State Prosecutor successfully obtained a court order that banned the broadcast. Thereafter, all twenty-three members of the HB executive, who had taken the decision to send the tapes, were prosecuted for collaborating with an armed group.

At the March 1996 Spanish General Election, Felipe González and his Socialist party were finally defeated after three consecutive terms in office. The new Prime Minister, José María Aznar—the man whom ETA had attempted to assassinate the previous year—led his Popular Party (PP) to a narrow victory. To form a stable majority in parliament, he had to reach an agreement with Catalan and Basque nationalists, as well as other small parties. This, he duly did and the PNV committed itself to support Aznar's government in exchange for the transfer of more powers to the regional parliament in Vitoria and the renewal of the five year fiscal agreements that gave a high degree of independence to the Basque treasury. At the level of national government, meanwhile, Aznar put Jaime Mayor Oreja in charge of the Ministry of Interior. He was an experienced Basque politician and former member of the UCD who had seen his old party decimated by ETA killings and intimidation. Indeed, ETA had recently assassinated the leader of the PP in his hometown of San Sebastián. Such a background seemed to suggest that the Aznar government would most likely take a hard-line against ETA.

Prior to stepping down, Felipe González had passed to Aznar the details of his latest effort to engage ETA in dialogue, via emissaries. Interior Minister Mayor, though, rejected the notion that there should be any follow-up on these contacts. Instead, he signalled his intention to pursue a different approach against Basque terrorism. He thus succeeded in having Eugenio Etxebeste transferred to Spain from Santo Domingo in the Dominican Republic. After being deported from Algiers, Etxebeste had lived in the latter country to ensure any would-be Spanish peace envoys could easily reach him. Mayor was indicating that this would no longer be necessary. The gateway to talks with ETA was now firmly closed and the man who had served as the official representative of the group over the previous decade sent to jail.

Still, the government reacted cautiously to the ongoing crisis arising out of ETA's earlier kidnapping of a prison functionary, José Antonio Ortega Lara, in Logroño in January 1996. ETA had taken Ortega captive to highlight a hunger strike then underway by its prisoners, who were demanding transfer to jails near the Basque region. In an effort to defuse the situation, the new PP government announced that it would consider moving some prisoners; and later, a number of ETA inmates were indeed relocated to prisons in the north of Spain.

ETA then declared a one-week truce on 23 June 1996 and asked the government to state publicly its views on the right of the Basque Country to self-determination. In response, however, Minister Mayor said that ETA was just trying to sow divisions among the other parties.

In truth, such division was all too evident. In January 1997 the PNV issued a long statement that it heralded as offering a new departure for peace. It pointed to the existence of a 'permanent impasse', resulting from ETA's desire for direct negotiations with the Spanish government and the latter's unswerving refusal to countenance such a prospect. The statement went on to lament the way in which it felt that the 1988 Ajuria-Enea Pact among the Basque parties had been reduced to ittle more than an 'anti-terrorist pact'. For this reason, the PNV argued, it needed to be 'reformulated'. There was, it was said, 'a widely shared conviction, even among security forces', that the kind of conflict such as existed in the Basque Country 'cannot be solved exclusively by the police'. To support this argument, it pointed to events in Northern Ireland, where the faltering peace process (by this stage, the IRA had ended its first ceasefire) had at least generated the possibility that a seemingly intractable conflict could be brought to an end. In the hope of inaugurating a similar Basque 'peace process' the PNV declared its willingness to, 'move and take risks'. The statement concluded:

In view of other international experiences where more entrenched conflicts than ours are changing ...we do not renounce the effort to engage in contacts and initiatives [sic] with other parties, trade unions and associations, without exclusion.[54]

From the start, this PNV policy initiative sounded fundamentally incompatible with the views of Aznar and Mayor. And in an effort to exacerbate this disagreement, ETA tried to widen the gap between the Spanish and Basque nationalist parties by unleashing a campaign of assassination against supporters of the PP government. On 10 July 1997, ETA kidnapped Miguel Ángel Blanco, a twenty-nine year-old PP councillor in the Basque town of Ermua. It then released a statement that contained a 48-hour ultimatum: either the government transferred all of its prisoners to jails close to the Basque Country, or it would kill its hostage. There followed huge demonstrations across Spain, demanding Blanco's release. But after the ultimatum expired—and merely four hours after 100,000 people marched in Bilbao in protest against ETA—Blanco's body was found.

The episode prompted an outpouring of public anger against the Basque 'patriotic movement'. Spontaneous gatherings of people outside the offices of HB had to be contained by the police. The PNV was forced to put clear distance between itself and ETA. The regional Basque President, José Antonio Ardanza, read a statement signed by all parties (with the exception of HB) that read: 'We thought we knew how cruel ETA could be. But we never imagined to what appalling levels of degradation ETA was capable of descending'. He went on to label HB 'accomplices' in the crimes of ETA, with whom 'we cannot work together in the defence of any cause'. Ardanza finished by appealing for all those opposed to ETA's activities to register publicly their opposition with additional public demonstrations.[55] In the days that followed, an unprecedented number of people participated in marches across Spain. In Madrid, after a meeting which brought together all the parties represented in parliament, including the PNV, the Interior Minister Mayor declared that the murder of Councillor Blanco had confirmed 'that there is nothing to talk about with HB and the only way to normality in the Basque Country is through the political isolation of that party'.[56] Prime Minister Aznar went further still. He spoke to the media about the need for new legislation, to deal with the connection between HB and ETA, and urged Spain's political parties to forge an agreement to tackle this issue: one that he hoped would endure and not simply be changed 'in two or three weeks time'.[57] In speaking as he did, Aznar was perhaps particularly conscious of the PNV's ambiguous record as regards ETA and aware also that, just six months previously, the PNV had publicly announced its intention to 'move and take risks' for peace.

In the event, the disintegration of the united front erected by the constitutional parties did not take two or three weeks as Aznar had feared; it took six months. In the meantime, the condemnation to which it had been subjected after the Blanco murder had not altered ETA's approach and it continued to murder its political opponents. The group assassinated five PP local councillors in Spanish and Basque towns in the year after the killing of Blanco. ETA's message to the government appeared stark: it could kill any member of the party, anywhere in Spain. Faced with this fresh offensive, Aznar's administration increasingly focused its attention on a new security push against ETA and its surrogate entities. The twenty-three members of HB's executive who had been arrested prior to the 1996 General Election were sentenced to seven years in prison for collaborating with ETA in December 1997. The case, though initiated in the last weeks of Felipe González's third term in office, was widely interpreted as heralding the start of a new crackdown on the 'patriotic movement'. It soon became apparent that such a crackdown was one that the leaders of the PNV were unwilling to support, as Xabier Arzalluz's party moved away from its putative alliance with the Spanish government and towards a pan-Basque nationalist approach. When the sentences for the HB executive were handed down the PNV immediately criticised them as being politically motivated and of dubious legality.[58] The regional Basque President, Ardanza, then proposed a new 'peace process' based on an inclusive dialogue among all the Basque parties, including HB. Its aim would be an agreement on a constitutional settlement that could later be ratified by the Spanish parliament. To arrive at this point, Ardanza called for preliminary talks (to determine a start date for and the length of, substantive dialogue), to be followed by an ETA ceasefire before the onset of the actual negotiations.

The proposal was categorically rejected by Aznar and also by the Basque Socialists. The Socialists had previously served in a coalition government in the regional Basque parliament with the PNV, but now they resigned from the arrangement in protest. They were unwilling to acquiesce in the emergence of the new understanding between the PNV in government and the electoral representatives of ETA, whereby the latter offered support to the former to secure the passage of certain bills. Despite this, the PNV continued on its new trajectory and a significant gap seemed to have opened inside the political system. The parties holding power in Madrid and Vitoria respectively appeared to be pursuing markedly contradictory policies towards terrorism. Aznar and Mayor were set on the legal persecution of ETA and its various affiliates. The investigative judge, Baltasar Garzón, had already published his assessment as to the unitary nature of the 'ETA network', incorporating both legal and illegal bodies.[59] Now, in July 1998, he ordered the closure of the movement's newspaper *Egin*; its management team was arrested and charged with belonging to an organisation that was ultimately run by ETA.[60] Even as this new, tougher approach was being enacted by the national government, however, the PNV appeared to be converging with ETA and the broader Basque nationalist movement to create a new political platform that would seek a 'peace process' on the Irish model. The result was the 'Irish Forum' that took inspiration from events in Belfast, Dublin and London. This body debated the meaning of the Irish peace process and came to a set of conclusions, which were presented to the world in the Navarran town of Estella on 13 September 1998. The document that was put forward there drew a straight parallel between Northern Ireland and the Basque Country. It claimed that every participant in the Belfast Agreement, in April of that same year, had accepted the 'political nature' of the conflict and therefore recognised that 'its solution had to be political'. The British government and the IRA, it was argued, had realised that 'neither could win' and that 'the conflict could have gone on for a long time'. The Irish republican movement was said to have developed a strategy for conflict resolution based on an 'understanding of and respect for, all the traditions on the island [of Ireland]'. This had, in turn, been embraced, the authors of the document claimed, by those who had previously 'supported exclusive dialogues and the policies of isolation'. The result of all this had been the successful Northern Irish peace process. An additional conclusion read: 'Trust building gestures were made by both sides, so that nobody demanded unavoidable preconditions to start the dialogue'.[61]

On this reading of what had happened in Northern Ireland, the signatories to the Estella Agreement put forward a programme for a negotiated settlement to the Basque conflict, involving representatives of the Basque people together with the French and Spanish governments. It should start, they contended, with a multilateral dialogue 'without exclusion of those involved' and not be predicated upon 'insurmountable preconditions'. This dialogue, it was envisaged, would then lead to full negotiations, from which 'all violent expressions of the conflict would be permanently absent'. There could not be any 'specific impositions' as to what the eventual outcome of the process would be, but the two states 'should respect' the will of the Basque people. If the final, agreed framework had to be left 'open', then this was to be permitted, until such time as 'new formulas to respond to the traditions and wishes of sovereignty' among the people in the Basque Country could emerge. The Estella Agreement thus adhered to a Basque nationalist agenda in its analysis of the conflict and its prescriptions for the future in the Basque Country. The PNV, despite heading a regional government charged with raising taxes and running a police service, had *de facto* signalled its readiness to reach a profound bilateral understanding with HB and ETA, even as the 'patriotic movement' remained dedicated to the systematic killing of members of the Basque opposition.

Three days after the Estella Agreement was announced, ETA declared a 'general and indefinite' ceasefire. At the time, José María Aznar was visiting Peru, but he cautiously welcomed the move, stating his desire that 'hope would not become frustration'. Time would tell, he noted, whether 'what we are seeing is a tactical move' and if 'a price is being sought in return for peace'.[62] By comparison, his Interior Minister, Mayor, showed a more marked scepticism about developments from the start.[63] Significantly, ETA's ceasefire declaration had included a section entitled, 'What this step by ETA is not'. The duration of the truce, it said, would depend on the steps taken by the signatories of the Estella Agreement. The most important of these was to be 'the setting up of a unified and sovereign institution' for all seven of the historic Basques provinces in both France and Spain. This new authority was to be an assembly of 666 local councillors, drawn from across the Basque nationalist parties. Moreover, ETA's statement concluded by stating that all the parties to the Agreement 'should abandon forever all covenants with parties and institutions... which aim to destroy the Basque Country and uphold France and Spain'. As Mayor had noted, this appeared to be an ominous statement of the unchanging character of ETA's demands.

In October 1998, elections to the regional Basque parliament were held. The electoral wing of ETA took part under the name of *Euskal Herritarrok* ('Basque Citizens', or EH), so as to avoid prosecution on account of Judge Garzon's far-reaching investigation into the ETA network. It received more votes than ever previously (though its share of the overall vote was lower than that which it had achieved eight years earlier). Elsewhere, the PNV's share of the vote fell more than two points; while, the proportion of the votes cast for all the Basque nationalist parties amounted to only 53.8%—a lower figure than in any previous election to the Basque parliament. At the same time, the aggregate vote for the pro-Spanish parties—which together won 44.6% of the vote—had never been higher.[64] After the election, the PNV's Juan José Ibarretxe was elected as the new President of the regional Basque government, a position he only secured with the backing of EH, the electoral wing of ETA. Indeed, one of EH's elected parliamentarians, Josu Urrutikoetxea, had to be transported from prison in Madrid to the parliament in order that he might cast his vote in the critical debate, before being taken back to jail. As has been described, back in 1988, Urrutikoetxea's release from custody and transfer to Algiers had been demanded by Eugenio Etxebeste, as a precondition to further talks between the Spanish government and ETA. Nevertheless, in a powerful symbol of the apparent rehabilitation of ETA underway by late 1998, his parliamentary colleagues now named him to represent them on the regional parliament's human rights committee.

In the face of these developments, Prime Minister Aznar repeated his assertion that he would be prepared to engage in a peace process if ETA was genuine in its desire to end the conflict. In November 1998, he announced that he would send emissaries to meet ETA and 'assess the willingness of the terrorist group to take the necessary steps to start a peace process' by definitively renouncing violence.[65] Interior Minister Mayor's previously stated policy of refusing to have any contact with ETA—on the basis that it fuelled both a sense of government weakness and the inevitability of political negotiations—had been broken. A preliminary meeting was therefore held between representatives of Aznar and members of HB in Zurich. Seventeen days later, on 7 June 1999, just six days before the opening of polling stations in local, regional and European elections, both the Spanish president and ETA confirmed that the meeting had taken place.[66] Those present had discussed the situation in the Basque Country and exchanged comments on the Northern Ireland peace process. The Prime Minister's envoys sought to ascertain the willingness or otherwise of ETA to end its military campaign permanently. For their part, ETA's representatives expressed satisfaction at recent developments in the Basque Country. In particular they noted how the electoral wing of ETA had just signed an agreement to support the PNV-headed Basque regional government in Vitoria. Though inconclusive talks were also held around the issues of paramilitary prisoners and the question of Basque self-determination, the two sides agreed to meet again.

In the meantime, local elections were held. The share of the vote now recorded for the political representatives of ETA (operating again under the guise of EH), reached its highest ever level, as the party secured almost 20% of the overall vote. The PP and the Socialists also performed well. By comparison, the PNV did poorly and lost control, for the first time, of several major local authorities, including the City Council of the Basque capital, Vitoria.[67] What the election results had thus demonstrated was the extent to which a peace process based on the Estella Agreement was serving to polarise the political environment in the Basque Country (between the Spanish and Basque nationalist parties) and damaging the power base of the PNV.

For this reason, the results fuelled a growing reassessment within the PNV as to what the nascent peace process was about. In a meeting between representatives of ETA and the PNV in July 1999, there were angry exchanges between the two sides. The PNV delegates expressed concern about their party's declining electoral fortunes. In response, ETA rebuked them and claimed that such concerns were secondary to the task of building the Basque nation. What was required now, ETA argued, were fresh elections in all local authorities under nationalist control, in order to choose representatives for a new national assembly (as laid out in the Estella Agreement) that would produce a Basque constitution. In addition, ETA insisted that the PNV should boycott the Spanish general elections that were scheduled for the following year. Again, ETA demanded that the PNV should fulfil the programme outlined in its ceasefire statement and 'abandon forever' all institutions that purportedly aimed to 'destroy the Basque Country and uphold France and Spain'.[68] ETA's proposals were effectively a request that the PNV commit political suicide. The party was being asked to leave a Spanish parliament that had given the Basque Country significant regional powers—mainly exercised by the PNV—so that it could join with ETA in the holding of a voluntary election to an illegal assembly, for a parallel and virtual state. The PNV was being asked to renounce all of the gains it had won in the two decades since Franco's death and instead throw its lot in with ETA for an uncertain future. Unsurprisingly, the party's leadership baulked at such a prospect and the long-term viability of the Basque 'peace process' was critically undermined.

In the meantime, in an effort to keep the fledgling process going, the Spanish Prime Minister had offered fresh acts of rapprochement. The government moved over one hundred ETA prisoners to jails closer to the Basque Country. And Aznar also re-affirmed his willingness to send representatives for fresh talks with ETA; this, despite the fact that attacks with incendiary devices continued within the Basque Country throughout 1999, regardless of the alleged truce. When challenged about these, ETA's spokespeople had simply declared that they could not act as 'fire fighters', suppressing all violent episodes.[69]

Ultimately, though, the peace process was headed for eventual collapse. The moment of breakdown finally arrived towards the end of 1999. Already, ETA had announced that it wanted no further meetings with Aznar's representatives. Instead its sole focus was increasingly on whether the PNV would fulfil secret agreements it was alleged to have made with ETA. The PNV, for its part, had no intention of acting as ETA demanded. As a result, on 28 November 1999, the group announced the end of its fourteen-month ceasefire. The PNV's refusal to build on the Estella Agreement, it was claimed, was responsible for the return to 'armed struggle'. ETA's renewed campaign now reached an intensity not seen since 1992. Twenty-three people were killed in 2000, while some six hundred Basque policemen and innumerable private security guards had to be deployed to protect a wide range of people deemed to be under threat from what seemed to be a revitalised ETA.[70]

The Irish Connection Revisited: The Last Peace Process?

The Spanish General Election of 2000 saw Prime Minister Aznar secure a second victory, this time with an absolute majority in parliament. As a result, he no longer needed to forge alliances with other parties, as he had done during his first term. In addition, he had pledged to retire in 2004. There were, therefore, few constraints preventing Aznar from doing as he wished. On the opposition benches, meanwhile, the PSOE elected a new leader after their defeat, José Luis Rodriguez Zapatero. In the context of ETA's revived campaign, he proposed a new agreement that would unite the parties against the terrorist threat. Though Aznar initially rejected this offer, he eventually signed a new 'Pact for Freedom and Against Terrorism' in December 2000.[71] This rejected the possibility that any understanding could be reached with the Basque nationalist parties, unless they 'formally and definitely abandoned the Estella Agreement and all its institutions'. At Estella, ETA had demanded that the PNV sever all links with the Spanish parties. Now, it seemed, the Spanish parties had decided to break all links with the PNV, at least until it renounced its de facto alliance with ETA. In addition, under the terms of the new pact, the PP and the socialists promised to try to reach agreement on new policies dealing with prisons and counter-terrorism strategy. The aim of the accord, according to its signatories, was 'the elimination from legitimate political or electoral confrontation, [those] policies that were pursued to end terror-ism'. As such, it sought to open the way towards the emergence of a bi-partisan consensus among the Spanish parties in their response to the ETA threat.

In the meantime, there were significant political developments within the Basque Country itself. With elections due to be held there for the regional Basque Parliament in 2001, Aznar's Interior Minister, Jaime Mayor Oreja, resigned his post and resolved to lead a 'constitutional front' that would unite the Basque branches of the PP and PSOE par-ties. His aim was to dislodge from power the PNV and President Ibar-retxe and to take control of the autonomous government. More broadly, Mayor talked of shifting the central tenets of Basque culture. Until that point, he argued, the Basque education system, public broad-casting system and political discourse had all helped to promote a nationalist culture that was based on a powerful sense of grievance towards Spain. The effect of this had been to make nationalism the only meaningful political force in the Basque Country, creating an ideological 'sea' in which ETA could swim. The reality, according to Mayor, was that Basques had a greater degree of autonomy than almost any other European region. Nationalists might denounce Span-ish oppression, he claimed, but Basque income *per capita* compared favourably with the other regions of Spain. In conclusion, Mayor pointed to the synergy between constitutional and radical Basque nationalism, with the former exploiting the threat of violence from the latter, to promote peace negotiations in which they could pursue their shared goal of independence. The PNV, said Mayor, needed to do what other parties had done since the advent of Spanish democracy. Over the course of the previous three decades, he asserted, Francoists had become democrats, Socialists had abandoned Marxism; but the PNV had not changed. Mayor wanted to bring about that change now by removing the PNV from power in Vitoria.

Against this background, the election brought an unprecedented turnout. The share of the vote won by EH, the electoral wing of ETA, fell by more than 7% as compared to its performance at the previous regional election. But contrary to what the former Interior Minister, Mayor, had hoped, nationalists rallied to the PNV standard. Not only did the party win the election, but Ibarretxe was now held up as the saviour of constitutional Basque nationalism; the loser, Mayor, was widely judged to be a spent force.

After the contest, the question of how best to deal with ETA re-emerged once more to sow fresh disagreement. The catalyst was the suggestion from the leader of the PNV, Xabier Arzalluz, that an all-inclusive approach to negotiations should be adopted, similar to that taken in Northern Ireland. In response, Aznar said that he was unwilling to negotiate over Basque self-determination. With regards to this objective, he said, 'some pursue it by steps, in the long-term, while others want it straight away, by immediate surrender, and that is why they kill and extort'—a pointed reference to what he saw as PNV-ETA collaboration.[72] The PSOE leader, though, did not endorse Aznar's stance. Zapatero instead criticised what he termed Aznar's 'intransigence' and demanded that the Prime Minister seek an understanding between the PNV and the PP.[73] Already, the solemn 'Pact for Freedoms and Against Terrorism' that had been signed just five months earlier seemed brittle.

Yet irrespective of such criticism, Aznar's government was determined to press ahead with a raft of new policies that aimed at the repression of ETA and its support networks. Thus, in June 2002, the Spanish parliament approved a new Political Parties Act, which was designed to give the courts the power to ban the electoral wing of ETA—known successively as *Herri Batasuna, Euskal Herritarrok* and now reincarnated as *Batasuna*. The wide-ranging ninth article of the new Act proscribed any political party that: publicised the statements of terrorist organisations; engaged in activities that gave 'public or tacit support' to terrorism; attempted to 'foment a culture of confrontation'; or included 'on its board or its electoral lists, persons who have been sentenced for crimes of terrorism'. Once the Supreme Court had declared a party illegal on such grounds, it was meant to cease all activity and official liquidators were permitted to dispose of its assets. In the wake of the bill's passage, parliament immediately brought a case before the Supreme Court that sought the banning of *Batasuna*. While the tribunal considered the case, Judge Garzón ordered that the party suspend all activities. He also sent instructions to Vitoria calling on the regional Basque parliament to suspend the party's 'assembly group' of elected representatives, though their individual rights, as parliamentarians, were to remain the same. In the event, the nationalist presiding officers within the Basque parliament refused to accede to Garzón's request and they themselves were later prosecuted for disobeying the court's orders.

In March 2003, the Supreme Court banned *Batasuna*. In July of the same year, the Spanish parliament also made changes to some articles of the penal code. It had been a long held aim of the PP to introduce stiffer sentencing and harsher prison conditions for those found guilty of terrorism. The reformed articles extended the maximum custodial period for those guilty of terrorist crimes from twenty to forty years; it also restricted rights of remission and prospects for parole. In order to qualify for a sentence in an open prison, or to stand a chance of being granted parole, it was decreed that a prisoner would have to pay financial compensation to the victims of his crimes and cooperate fully with the authorities in counter-terrorism efforts.

Such measures appeared to confirm the complete breakdown in relations between the PNV and the PP—the two parties having once been allies in the Spanish parliament. Further testament to this followed the announcement by regional Basque President Ibarretxe that he would introduce a new bill of Autonomy into the Basque parliament. If the bill was approved, he declared, he would then hold a referendum on the proposals within the Basque Country (a step that he was not legally empowered to take). Predictably, the move was denounced by the PP—but also by the PSOE.[74] The Basque nationalists and the main Spanish parties, it seemed, had never been further apart.

In March 2004, a new General Election was held in Spain. The country had experienced a long period of economic growth and a general feeling of optimism prevailed. Nevertheless, the natural erosion of support, caused by eight years in government, together with the particular leadership style of Prime Minister Aznar, and his backing for the US-led invasion of Iraq, had dented the popularity of the PP. Even so, it was widely expected that it would win a third term in office. Three days before voting, however, Madrid was hit by coordinated bomb attacks on the capital's commuter trains that killed 191 people and injured more than 1,700 others. Aznar's government immediately blamed ETA, even though arrests and the previous year's banning of Batasuna had dramatically weakened the organisation. In 2003, ETA had killed only three people—its lowest level of activity (in a year when it was not on ceasefire) since the return of democracy to Spain. In the first three months of 2004, ETA had failed to carry out a single serious attack (though it had attempted to drive a van bomb into Madrid). Despite this, the government seemed reluctant to follow alternative lines of inquiry, even as the evidence gathered by the police began to suggest that the bloodiest terrorist attack ever committed in Spain was not the work of ETA, but of radical Islamist terrorists. Amid an atmosphere of growing public recrimination between the PP and the PSOE, over the nature of the government's response to the bombings, a higher-than-predicted turnout gave the PSOE an unexpected victory.

The new Prime Minister, José Luis Rodríguez Zapatero, had become head of the Spanish government at his first attempt. Once in office, he began by fulfilling his manifesto pledge to withdraw Spanish troops from Iraq and to realign the country's foreign policy towards the Franco-German axis in the European Union. It was a symbolically neat departure from Aznar's alliance with the English-speaking powers.

In the Basque Country, meanwhile, Zapatero was faced by President Ibarretxe's proposals for a unilateral Autonomy Statute. The preamble to the 'Ibarretxe Plan', as it became known, began by claiming self-determination on behalf of the Basque territories in both France and Spain. More modestly, further down the text, the bill provided for greater autonomy for the three provinces under Ibarretxe's direct leadership. But sovereignty was now to be moved from the Spanish to the Basque parliament, in a direct challenge to the Spanish constitution. A new relationship was to be established between Vitoria and Madrid; henceforth, the Basque Autonomous Community was to exist in 'free association' with the Spanish state. In this way the 'Ibarretxe Plan' was indicative of the way in which the failed peace process, based on the convergence of democratic and violent nationalism, had tilted the balance of power inside the PNV towards its more radical faction. As if to confirm the apparent synergy of constitutional and violent Basque nationalism, on grounds favourable to the latter, when the bill was eventually debated in the Basque Parliament in December 2004, it was only passed with the assistance of deputies from *Batasuna*. Inevitably, when it was then brought before the Spanish Congress of Deputies in February 2005, it was resoundingly rejected, by 331 votes to 29.

While such political manoeuvrings were ongoing, ETA had largely remained quiet. The group did not perpetrate a single attack between March, when Al Qaeda had struck in Madrid, and August 2004. In the latter month it reappeared, claiming responsibility for a number of small bombs that were detonated at various locations in northern Spain. These were followed by further attacks on state offices in the Basque Country and military facilities in the Pyrenees. Still, it was clear that ETA's capacity for action had been dramatically reduced. Spain now faced a form of 'minimalist' domestic terrorism that paled in comparison with the mass casualty atrocities of international radical Islamism.

In November 2004, newspapers published a letter that had been sent to the head of ETA's political office, Mikel Albizu, by six prominent ETA prisoners. One of the authors was a member of the organisation's three-man leadership council that had been arrested in 1992. French police had recently arrested Albizu and the document leaked to the press. In the letter, the prisoners rejected suggestions that they start a campaign of protest in jail and instead asked ETA's leadership to consider whether the 'armed struggle' was failing. The group, they claimed, had never been so vulnerable. For this reason, they proposed that ETA should invest its 'political capital' in what they called 'the institutional and mass struggle'.[75] The ETA leadership formally rejected the ideas contained within the prisoners' letter. But, a few days after its publication, on 14 November 2004, ETA's electoral wing, *Batasuna*—an illegal party according to the Spanish courts—was allowed to organise a rally in San Sebastián, at which it put forth a new political programme. At the Anoeta Velodrome, the group's most prominent leader, Arnaldo Otegi, called for the 'building [of] a peace process that would overcome forever the scenario of political and armed confrontation in our country'. 'The priority is now peace', said Otegi and he argued that there needed to be two 'distinct spaces for dialogue and agreement'. One was to be reserved for 'political, social and trade union agents' and would seek a 'political transition' to a constitutional framework that could then be put to the people in a referendum. The other 'space' was to comprise a dialogue between, on the one hand, the Spanish and French states, and on the other ETA. They were to discuss three main issues: 'demilitarisation, prisoners and refugees [and] victims'.[76]

This 'Anoeta Declaration' was a departure from previous ETA policy, which for nearly thirty years had insisted that only ETA could negotiate the path to Basque independence. Now the group was saying that it was for 'political agents' to negotiate the political and legal framework for the future, while ETA engaged with the French and Spanish governments on what it termed 'technical' matters. It seemed as if ETA, inspired by the IRA at the moment of its birth, was once more committing itself to following in the footsteps of the Irish republican organisation. Yet, two immediate question marks hung over the plan: first, it called for political dialogue outside existing parliamentary channels; and, second, it did not spell out the timeframe for these two 'spheres' of negotiation. More broadly, many wondered whether the example of the Irish peace process was a viable 'model' that could be enacted in the Basque Country.

In January 2005, *Batasuna* sent a letter to the Spanish Prime Minister confirming the substance of the Anoeta Declaration. This time, it said, the Basque 'patriotic movement' was not looking for the peace process to bring about the formation of a nationalist front, or Basque independence. Zapatero responded at a public meeting of the Socialist party in San Sebastián a few days later. 'Peace', he said, 'has to be reached by the application of reason, as we will soon demonstrate'.[77] The speech was interpreted as a declaration of intent to open dialogue with ETA and its affiliates. Confirmation of this came in May, when Zapatero's government introduced a motion into the Spanish parliament asking for support for the embryonic peace process. It endorsed a 'process of dialogue' between the Spanish state and those who were ready to abandon violence, provided that a 'clear will to end' such violence was demonstrated. Talks, the motion stated, could only occur on the basis of 'democratic principles that cannot be renounced'. Two such democratic principles were then laid out: one, that there had to be an acceptance that 'political questions should be solved only by legitimate representatives of the popular will'; and two, an acknowledgement that 'violence can have no political price'.[78] The motion also stated that the Spanish state had been successful against terrorism in the past through a combination of three policies: the pursuit of terrorists by the security forces; the building of international cooperation; and the maintenance of domestic unity among the political parties, around the assertion that terrorism had no place in politics. Ironically, this third 'leg' of policy was sacrificed in the passage of the motion. Though it was approved by a margin of 192–147 votes, the PP voted against the government after an angry debate.

The bitterness between government and opposition now reached unprecedented levels. Relations had been soured anyway by Zapatero's announcement of a bill to compensate the victims of Franco and the enactment of measures to erase the eulogies and monuments to the dictator on public buildings and streets. Conservatives accused him of breaking the '*pacto de olvido*'—the unspoken pact, by which the leaders of the *transición* had agreed not to re-open the wounds of the Franco era. When the Barcelona assembly approved the draft of a new Statute of Autonomy for Catalonia, things went from bad to worse. Zapatero had promised in his election manifesto to support greater autonomy for Catalonia and this he duly did. In response, the PP launched a case against the Act at Spain's Constitutional Court. The unity of the country was at risk, the conservatives argued, because Zapatero was intent on appeasing nationalist sentiment and building a new set of relationships with the regions, based on mutual sovereignty. In the minds of the PP, moreover, the biggest threat to the unity of Spain came from the emerging Basque peace process.

Only days after the parliamentary motion supporting that peace process had gained the backing of a divided Spanish Congress, the head of the Basque branch of the Socialist party, Jesús Eguiguren held the first in a series of meetings with Josu Urrutikoetxea, the ETA veteran and former HB deputy in the regional Basque parliament. The two men met in Geneva; further talks followed in Norway in November 2005. The original conception of the peace process had been for ETA to be involved in dialogue on purely technical matters only. But from the beginning Urrutikoetxea was being engaged by a politician and not by members of the security forces. These meetings produced a preliminary agreement outlining future steps. ETA would declare a permanent ceasefire and the government would respond by inaugurating a six-month 'verification' period. Once it had been confirmed that violence had genuinely been brought to an end, formal dialogue with ETA would then begin. It was this that paved the way for the 'permanent ceasefire' that was declared in March 2006. The purpose of the initiative, ETA claimed, was 'to stimulate a democratic process' that could achieve 'the political change that the Basque Country needs through dialogue, negotiation and agreement'. It was possible to finally end the conflict, they averred, 'here and now'.[79]

In response, the Spanish Prime Minister, Zapatero, gave a long interview to *El País* in which he claimed to detect a difference between this latest statement and previous ETA pronouncements. The use of the word 'permanent', he said, was a key change (the 1998 ceasefire had used the word 'indefinite'). Zapatero then announced the commencement of a verification period—to establish ETA's 'will to abandon arms definitively'. Though acknowledging that the process would be 'long, hard and difficult', the Prime Minister also said that he thought the 'decisive' moment would come when the government entered talks with ETA, indicating that he thought such a development was likely. When asked about the parallels with Northern Ireland and the risk that a Basque peace process could generate a Spanish version of the Canary Wharf bomb, Zapatero replied by referring to what he claimed to have learned from the British Prime Minister, Tony Blair: '[The British] always kept a channel of communication open'.[80] To many, it seemed as if the Prime Minister had opened this latest chapter in the Spanish state's engagement with ETA by effectively telling the organisation that even if it killed again, dialogue would not be broken off.

Nevertheless, Zapatero had also emphasised that the process required a genuine abandonment of violence by ETA. In addition, he had used his interview to affirm the enduring validity of the Political Parties Act that had banned Batasuna. 'The most logical way is to promote a new political formation that could leave behind the justifications for violence', he declared. Thus, what he actually offered was the integration of the political representatives of the 'patriotic movement' into the mainstream—on terms set by that mainstream—rather than a capitulation to their objectives. Such a peace process required ETA to abjure half a century of history, having gained nothing more than the better treatment of its prisoners and the integration of its political wing into constitutional politics.

ETA's unhappiness with a peace process founded on these principles quickly manifested itself. In April, the newspaper *Gara*, the successor to the now defunct *Egin*, published a long interview in which the group accused the Basque Socialists of surrendering the lead role in the peace process to Zapatero. In 1998, ETA had sought to drive a wedge between Basque nationalist parties of all hues and their Spanish counterparts; now it seemed as if it wanted to do the same between Basque Socialists and Spanish Socialists. More ominously, the ETA interviewees, in a convoluted application of logic, described the notion that a 'permanent' ceasefire should be 'irreversible', as 'nonsense'.[81] Furthermore, events on the ground signalled that ETA remained active during the ceasefire. The group had stolen weapons and car number plates in France, just prior to the ceasefire announcement and after the cessation it continued to extort money from Basque businesses (albeit by softening its letters demanding payment, so that rather than pay a 'revolutionary tax', those targeted were invited to contribute to the peace process).

Meanwhile, the security forces continued to apply pressure to ETA. Arnaldo Otegi was briefly sent to prison as part of the ongoing investigation by the Spanish courts into the links between *Batasuna* and ETA. Police in France and Spain arrested several people accused of being members of, or collaborating with, ETA. The biggest coup for the authorities came in June, when a network of mediators and collectors of the revolutionary tax in the Basque Country was broken up.

Despite all of this, on 29 June 2006, Zapatero announced to the Spanish parliament that he was ready to initiate direct dialogue with ETA. He added, though, that 'democracy will never pay a political price for peace' and that 'the government will respect the decisions taken freely by Basque citizens'. In addition, the Prime Minister again confirmed that the Political Parties Act would remain in place. A month later, a meeting was held between representatives of ETA and emissaries of the government. Almost immediately, however, the talks faltered when ETA refused to discuss 'technical' matters such as weapons decommissioning or prisoner releases, until negotiations between political parties had begun.[82] Then, in August 2006, as the process continued to stall, ETA released a menacing statement, which stressed 'the gravity of the political situation' and claimed that the other parties were not fulfilling the agreements that had been reached before the ceasefire. ETA also made reference to what it saw as the continued persecution of its movement and criticised 'attempts to identify recent developments as heralding the end of ETA'.

The PNV and PSOE responded to these latent ETA threats in September 2006, by engaging with *Batasuna* in a trilateral dialogue in Loyola. There, the parties exchanged drafts about a 'road map' for the political process and the desired final destination. The 'patriotic movement' wanted a commitment from the Basque Socialists and the PNV to incorporate Navarre into the Basque Autonomous Community and to guarantee that the new entity would have the right of self-determination. The Basque Socialists rejected the proposal. So too did the PNV—now led by Josu Jon Imaz, who had repeatedly rejected the notion that there could be any deal while there remained the threat of a resumption of violence from ETA. The meeting thus broke up in disagreement.

The peace process was approaching breakdown. While the parties were meeting in Loyola, three hooded members of ETA fired weapons into the air at a gathering of the radical Basque nationalist movement and read a statement 'reaffirming our firm commitment to retaining our weapons until we reach independence and socialism'. Then, in October, ETA stole a quantity of explosives in France after kidnapping the employees of a depot. And the tense atmosphere was heightened by the hunger strike of Iñaki De Juana, an ETA prisoner who had previously distanced himself from the group. After serving eighteen years in jail for the murder of 25 people, De Juana had been sentenced to a further twelve years imprisonment, on the eve of his scheduled release, for publishing two articles in 2004 that were deemed by the courts to be 'terrorist threats'.[83]

Finally, only days after government representatives had met again with ETA and reported back that the ceasefire was not in peril, a massive bomb exploded on 30 December 2006 in the car park of the new Madrid airport terminal in Barajas. Two Ecuadorian immigrants, sleeping in their cars while they waited for their families' arrival, were killed among the rubble. ETA immediately issued a statement claiming that it had not broken its ceasefire. Yet, this statement was to prove to be a defining moment in the collapse of the moral authority of the group. If the Estella Agreement had broken down when ETA had demanded that the PNV sacrifice itself and surrender the leadership of Basque nationalism to ETA, the 2006 peace process had collapsed because it had failed once more to induce the Spanish government to begin constitutional negotiations. With the December 2006 bombing, ETA had attempted to submit Spanish Socialists and Basque nationalists to its will, by the strength of a one-off attack. It was a failure.

And yet, new talks between *Batasuna*, the PNV and the Basque branch of the PSOE were held under the watchful eyes of a representative of Sinn Fein and international mediators in early 2007. The Socialists attended after the Spanish government accepted the advice of both Tony Blair and Sinn Fein leader Gerry Adams, who counselled that Zapatero had to 'listen to ETA'.[84] The dialogue achieved little. The final collapse of the peace process was confirmed in a statement released by ETA on 5 June 2007, hours after the Socialist party of Zapatero agreed to support a regional minority government in the Navarre parliament led by the Union of the Navarran People (UPN), a party linked to the PP. 'The masks have fallen', ETA declared, 'we the citizens lack democracy. The minimal democratic basis for a negotiating process does not exist'.[85] The ceasefire was formally abandoned and armed actions 'on all fronts' resumed.

In response, the Spanish judiciary reactivated all cases connected with ETA and its political front. Soon after, Otegi, the most visible leader of *Batasuna*, was imprisoned and this was followed by the arrest and imprisonment of the party's entire executive. The Basque President, Ibarretxe, and Basque Socialist leaders were also now prosecuted in court for meeting Otegi. At the same time, the security forces successfully degraded ETA's capabilities still further. In the face of this, the organisation retained the capacity to inflict isolated acts of murder and destruction—as demonstrated when it murdered a former Socialist councillor in Mondragon two days before the 2008 General Election.

Nevertheless, by mid-2008, the inability of ETA to destabilise the Spanish political system had been made apparent. And with the path to political negotiations closed, many now believe that the future of ETA will be decided by the commitment and efficiency of the Spanish and French security forces. With regards to the latter, it is striking that more than twenty years after the French altered their asylum policy and the two governments began to cooperate more closely in the suppression of ETA, all of the group's senior structures and personnel continue to be located in France.[86] Nonetheless, security breakthroughs continue. On 20 May 2008, five days after a car bomb had killed a civil guard in the Basque town of Legutiano, French police arrested four members of the political apparatus of ETA in Bordeaux; those detained included the man who had represented ETA in the last round of talks the organisation held with the Spanish government.[87] In November of that same year, French police arrested the man alleged to be the head of the organisation's military and logistical apparatus.[88]

With such Franco-Spanish security co-operation delivering sustained dividends, the outlook for ETA looks bleak. In the long-term, it is likely that much will depend on, above all, the trajectory of constitutional Basque nationalism. Hitherto, those who adhere to such beliefs have remained divided between, on the one hand, those who wish to sever sentimental ties with the violent 'patriotic movement' and instead join the Spanish Socialist party in a consensual accommodation within Spain, and on the other, those who still hope to form a pan-nationalist political front with links to ETA and its followers in pursuit of Basque independence. This has long been the unresolved dilemma that fed the political ambitions of ETA. The path that is chosen will do much to determine the future of Basque nationalism in the twenty first century.

CONCLUSION

Talking to Terrorists set out to examine the two longest-running violent conflicts in western Europe over the last forty years. The aim was to illustrate the distinct regional, historical, socio-economic and political factors that have shaped the course of events in Northern Ireland and the Basque Country throughout this period. Inevitably, there are similarities between the two cases. Yet alongside these, there are also important points of contrast and divergence. What follows in this concluding chapter is an attempt to synthesise some of the key themes of these two conflicts, as highlighted in the respective narratives. It should be reiterated that what follows is not intended to provide a rigid 'model' or template. There are no prescriptive 'lessons' which can simply be applied elsewhere. Nonetheless, it is possible to identify several factors that shaped these conflicts and attempts to solve them peacefully.

(i) Terrorist hinterlands—Ideological and Territorial

In the first years of its existence, the Provisional IRA rooted itself in the Catholic-nationalist communities of Northern Ireland, particularly in the highly-segregated urban centres of Belfast and Londonderry. This provided members of the organisation with a safe haven and logistical base—especially in the early years of the conflict when many of these 'ghettos' literally became 'no-go areas' for the security services. This was supplemented by the existence of rural republican 'heartlands', such as South Derry, South Armagh and the border regions of Fermanagh and Tyrone in the south west of Northern Ireland, which shared a land frontier of some 150 miles with the Irish Republic.[1] In each instance, a partially sympathetic 'host' community allowed the IRA to operate with relative impunity, away from the control of the central security apparatus.

239

Of even greater strategic importance was the IRA's capacity to cross the border into the Irish Republic. From the British perspective, the Irish government's commitment to a common security approach was found wanting for much of the conflict. Furthermore, British attempts to pursue republican terrorists into Irish territory proved highly controversial, as with the SAS incursion of 1976. In part, the republican movement was able to exploit the degree of ideological congruity which existed between its aims and those of the Irish state. For historical reasons, there was an overlap between the aims of Irish republicans and the intellectual and emotional rationale that underpinned the Republic of Ireland. Significantly, Ireland had achieved independence after an armed campaign against British rule, led by an earlier incarnation of the IRA. Furthermore, the republican goal of Irish unity was one that the southern state continued to share with the Provisional IRA throughout the conflict. Despite the fact that only a small minority within the Irish Republic ever gave explicit support to IRA violence, the Irish constitution of 1937 enshrined a territorial claim to the north of Ireland. It was not until the 1990s that the Irish state appeared ready to abandon this irredentist objective, modifying articles two and three of its constitution after a referendum, in line with its commitments under the Belfast Agreement.

In the Basque Country, ETA has also been able to draw upon the historical legitimacy of Basque nationalist aspirations. ETA was born out of the perceived failures of the PNV in the late 1950s. That party's apparent passivity and inability to deliver progress on the question of Basque nationhood, in the face of Franco's dictatorship, had encouraged the growth of militancy among a younger and more impatient generation. This umbilical relationship between the peaceful and violent strains of Basque nationalism generated a loose, but enduring sympathy for ETA among the broader Basque population. Even among those who oppose its values and methods, ETA's campaign has often been perceived as a potent symbol of the oppression of the Basque people by the central Spanish state—the group's very existence reaffirming a sense of shared national struggle.[2] One product of this sentiment was the ambivalence with which many Basque people viewed Spain's transition towards democracy in the years after Franco's death. More recently, it has been manifested in the affinity apparently felt by some sections of the PNV for the political supporters of ETA.

Alongside this loosely defined ideological 'support system' for ETA within the Basque Country, the organisation could also draw on its own cross-border territorial hinterland. The historical region of the Basque Country includes a significant portion of southern France. This alone ensured that the Basque separatist family extended beyond the reach of Spanish sovereignty. Moreover, in the 1960s and 1970s, French opposition to Franco's regime allowed ETA to exploit a broader empathy for its activities. The group was often seen as an anti-fascist 'resistance movement', comparable to the French Resistance to Nazi occupation during the Second World War. This perception endured even after Spain's 'transition' to democracy and fed into the reluctance of successive French governments to take decisive action against ETA. Thus, French territory became a key logistical base for ETA's war against the Spanish state. It was only in the mid-1980s that this began to change due, in significant part, to the activities of the GAL.

Within the last two decades, the evolution of an undeniably democratic Spain has forced the French state to adjust its position and define a new relationship with its southern neighbour. The two countries' shared EEC membership proved particularly important in this regard. Since the 1990s, Madrid and Paris have cooperated successfully in the prosecution of a counter-terrorism strategy against ETA. This persisted even when tensions between the two states emerged on other issues, such as over Prime Minister José María Aznar's support for the US-led invasion of Iraq in 2003. Indeed, some of the most spectacular security defeats inflicted on ETA have occurred within French territory. In 1992, the organisation's three-man Supreme Council was arrested in the town of Bidart; more recently, in May 2008, the head of ETA's political wing was arrested along with several others in Bordeaux. And in November 2008, the alleged head of the organisation's military and logistical wing was also arrested in France. Still, notwithstanding these successes and even after twenty years of close cooperation, it is noteworthy that the top structures of ETA's apparatus continue to reside within France.

(ii) How the state shapes the conflict

One of the central—and most misguided—mantras of Irish republicanism was the notion that it was the nefarious, 'colonial' interference of the British state in Ireland that was at the root of the conflict in Ulster.

The existence of Northern Ireland—as a product of British imperial design—was assumed to be the main obstacle to Irish unity and a harmonious co-existence for all peoples on the island, whatever their creed or origin.[3] Where those who supported the Union with the United Kingdom fitted into the IRA's analysis was something that the republican movement never satisfactorily resolved. As Henry McDonald has written, in trying to get the British to act as 'persuaders for Irish unity' in the early 1990s, the IRA were 'delivering the message to the wrong address'.[4] The reality was that the British state had no serious long-term geopolitical or strategic interest in maintaining a presence on Irish shores, north or south. During the mid-1970s, it is true that some civil servants had objected to an immediate withdrawal from Northern Ireland, on the grounds that this was likely to destabilise the Irish state, and could lead to the establishment of an openly hostile regime in Dublin. Nevertheless, this was not a widely held concern at the time and one which had all but disappeared by the late 1970s. As the Northern Ireland Secretary of State, Peter Brooke, famously affirmed in 1990— one year after the fall of the Berlin Wall—Britain had 'no selfish strategic or economic interest in Northern Ireland'. This stance was then explicitly written into the Downing Street Declaration of 1993, which formed a critical foundation stone for the later peace process.

There is little evidence to support the view that the 'real lesson' of Ulster is that, over a number of administrations, the British government successfully transformed itself from colonial overlord into lead partner in the search for a solution; or that the real achievement of the Blair government was that 'it behaved as a democratic state rather than a colonial master'.[5] Neither does it seem accurate that, to borrow Gerry Adams's formulation, British policy shifted from out and out repression, to 'trying to find some accommodation with republicanism'; nor is it true that this shift was the crucial 'part of the jigsaw which allowed and which created the space for the type of compromises which underpin the Good Friday Agreement'.[6] Rather, it is the case, as Paul Dixon has stated, that British policy between 1972 and 1998, with some important adjustments, was largely characterised by continuity. At its core lay the pursuit of a compromise settlement, resting on power-sharing within Northern Ireland and an 'Irish dimension' of cross-border co-operation with the Republic.[7]

Theoretically, the fact that the British government saw itself, to some extent, as a disinterested broker should have augured well for its chances of ending the violence. But in the event it took thirty years to find a working solution to the conflict. Why was this? Part of the explanation lies in the existence of an internal sectarian dynamic within Northern Ireland, which did much to fuel the conflict. State policy could do little to shape or ameliorate this, at least in the short term. But it is also the case that, at a critical point, the British state's failure to establish clear constitutional red lines during the onset of the Troubles, proved hugely destabilising. It was this absence of a long-term strategy which was to be one of the key contributory factors to the sharp increase in violence from 1969 to 1975–6. The rapid oscillation of policy in these years proved particularly damaging: from an 'ostrich-like' policy of neglect as the province spiralled towards collapse, to full-blown intervention and 'Direct Rule', to negotiations with the IRA in 1972, to an abortive attempt at power-sharing with moderate parties in 1973–4, only to return to more exploratory talks with terrorists in 1975.[8] What characterised this era was the inability of the state to recognise how its own behaviour could exacerbate the situation. The lack of a consistent approach or over-arching vision—not to mention periodic flirtations with the possibility of a complete withdrawal from Northern Ireland—heightened suspicion of British intentions and undermined those moderate voices who were the most likely partners for peace (including the Irish government). As one commentator has noted, such behaviour was indicative, not so much of 'high minded imperialists', but rather 'late colonialists', whose first instinct was not domination, but extrication.[9]

From the mid-1970s, as violence spiralled out of control, the British government—with some reluctance—came to the decision that it needed to establish a 'long haul' commitment to Northern Ireland, in order to end the instability upon which the terrorist campaigns (both loyalist and republican), had thrived. By focusing their energies on 'normalising' the security situation and prioritising economic regeneration over constitutional experiments, the British effectively abandoned the hope that they might reach a peaceful settlement in the near future. Yet in taking this new path, they also wrested the initiative away from those violent groups that were prepared to use spectacular attacks to influence political events at important junctures. It was this change of tactics that forced the IRA to adopt its own 'long war' strategy—effectively a tacit admission of weakness on the part of republicans and a marked departure from the 'one last push' philosophy which had prevailed in their ranks until that point.

The shift in approach by the British state helped forge a closer relationship with the Irish government—something that proved crucial in undermining the terrorist campaign. During the first years of the conflict, both the Irish and British governments held unrealistic expectations about what the other could deliver as a partner for peace. After the collapse of the Sunningdale Agreement, for example, the Irish accused the British of lacking the resolve to stand up to unionist opponents of the deal. For the British, meanwhile, the failure of their Irish counterparts to take decisive action against the IRA was an enduring source of criticism in the early years of the violence. From 1976, the British adoption of a 'long haul' approach helped place Anglo-Irish relations on a firmer footing. On the surface, this may seem surprising, given that it entailed a long-term presence for the British in Northern Ireland. Certainly, it caused tensions with the Irish government, which believed that it represented a shift to a more unilateral approach to the crisis from London. But the truth was that this commitment to a sustained period of Direct Rule actually paved the way towards a more stable future relationship. The Irish government was now reassured that the British would not simply withdraw from the province. For its part, the British state publicly accepted full responsibility for the political, financial and security situation—something which it had previously seemed reluctant to do. Eventually, this relationship yielded greater results, particularly in relation to security matters. And it was upon this foundation that the warm personal rapport between Bertie Ahern and Tony Blair in the 1990s could be built. Reflecting on the Northern Ireland peace process, President Bush's former Special Envoy to Northern Ireland has correctly identified the importance of 'unity among key stakeholders'.[10]

The nature of the Spanish state—as well as its behaviour—has also been central to the shaping of the conflict in the Basque Country, albeit in different ways. First, as has been described, ETA was created and rose to prominence, partly as a response to the dictatorship of General Franco. The founders of ETA drew legitimacy from a number of sources: from Basque cultural and ethnic distinctiveness within Spain; from the precedent set by the semi-independent institutions that had governed the territory in the past; and from the brutal suppression of Republican democracy and regional autonomy by Franco in the aftermath of the Spanish Civil War. The latter ensured that elements of the wider Basque nationalist community and opponents of Franco were sympathetic towards the activities of ETA. At the same time, Franco's repressive regime did restrict ETA's capacity to operate, and it remained a relatively small organisation—even after enjoying major publicity coups (such as the 'Burgos Trial' of 1970) and military successes (including the murder of Prime Minister Carrero Blanco in 1973). It was only after Franco's death and during Spain's transition to democracy that ETA emerged as a much stronger and more deadly paramilitary force. It is no coincidence that the years from 1975 to 1982 marked the high-point of the organisation's military campaign, as it turned its energies against the nascent democratic Spanish state. The instability and fragility of that state during the *transición* provided the ideal context for ETA to intensify its violence. Furthermore, the economic problems that Spain faced in the late-Franco to early-democratic period—which were particularly pronounced in the Basque Country—helped ensure that ETA was supplied with a ready pool of recruits from which to replenish its ranks. By the same token, the slow improvement of the country's economic fortunes—in the wake of Spanish accession to the EEC in 1986—and the dramatic fall in the birth rate in this period, helped deplete ETA's recruitment base. In this regard, it is interesting to note a synergy with events in Northern Ireland, where economic factors likewise played a role. For example, unemployment increased steadily from the beginning of 'the Troubles' until the mid-1980s—rising particularly sharply after the 1973 and 1979 oil crises.[11] In both conflicts, the worst periods of violence tended to coincide with marked economic downturns and high levels of unemployment.

Once the Spanish state had passed through the *transición* and a functioning democratic system had been successfully established—including an autonomous parliament and government in the Basque Country—this also affected ETA's capacity to achieve its ends. Crucially, it soon became clear that the unitary nature of Spain was as central to the self-image of the newly democratic state as it had been to Franco's regime. The Basque Country was still regarded as an integral component of the modern Spanish nation (in a way that was not the case with the British commitment to Northern Ireland). While the extent of regional autonomy remains an open question, no post-Franco Spanish government has ever countenanced a withdrawal from the region and the granting of full independence to the Basque Country.

As a consequence of this, all the main Spanish political parties have a serious presence in the Basque Country and elected representatives from the region have often played a key role in the making and breaking of governments in Madrid. At the time of writing, for instance, the parliamentary majority of Socialist government of José Luis Rodriguez Zapatero rests on an understanding that the PSOE reached with regional nationalist parties. By contrast, the main British political parties—with occasional exceptions—have largely refrained from organising in Northern Ireland (until recently). One result of this has been that the local population has been left with a choice of local political parties, which entrench existing divisions. Another consequence, particularly during the years of Direct Rule, was that it fed the destabilising perception that Northern Ireland was somehow 'semi-detached' from the British state as a whole. The Spanish state never allowed the evolution of such a view with regards to the relationship between itself and the Basque Country. Neither has it shown a willingness to concede ETA's central demand: constitutional concessions in exchange for peace.

(iii) The impact of hard power

The extent to which the IRA was defeated by the British will be debated for many years. Nonetheless, as Peter Taylor has observed, one crucial variable which has frequently been lost from sight in recent years is the fact 'the Brits were not prepared to let the IRA win'.[12] There has been a growing tendency to see the 1990s peace process in Northern Ireland as something entirely removed from the war that preceeded it. But such a view is highly misleading. By the late 1980s, the IRA had been heavily infiltrated by informers and it was subject to a successful strategy of containment by the British security services. While retaining the ability to mount the occasional 'spectacular' attack, the IRA's operational capacity had been steadily undermined. The result of this was that it was the IRA who came to the British seeking negotiations, not *vice versa*.

It is therefore necessary to re-evaluate the oft-repeated notion that the military conflict ended in a 'stalemate', which set the stage for a peace process as both sides realised they could not win. As Thomas Hennessey has neatly put it, 'It was true that the IRA were not defeated militarily; but the British only needed a draw to win'.[13] The British

Army's own official report of its struggle with the IRA appears to support the 'stalemate' thesis.[14] Yet, what this report does not take into account is the highly effective unofficial war against the republican movement that was being carried out by the intelligence services. This had a decisive impact on what occured subsequently. As Lord Guthrie, the former Chief of the General Staff of the British Army has recently described:

People are now saying it was soft power that really won in Northern Ireland: it was not soft power; it was a mixture of both. It was the security services who created the atmosphere in which Gerry Adams and Martin McGuinness realised they couldn't win by the bullet. Government after government, both Conservatives and Labour, were resolute in not being frightened out of Northern Ireland. That created a much more stable atmosphere; then people were prepared to get together and talk.[15]

Again, this is not to dismiss altogether the importance of engaging in dialogue. But it is to underscore the need for a more accurate understanding of the context in which that dialogue took place.

Similarly, the 'dirty war' between ETA and the Spanish security services—particularly the use of the GAL—cannot be ignored if events in the Basque Country are to be properly understood. Whatever the profound and complex political consequences arising out of the GAL controversy—not to mention the important moral implications of the fact that that organisation was recruited, financed and managed by high-ranking officials in the Spanish government—it is hard to escape the conclusion that this group fundamentally altered the balance of the conflict. In great part, this was because the activities of the GAL prompted the French government to cooperate more closely with their Spanish counterparts on key issues such as extradition.

More transparent manifestations of Spanish (and French) 'hard power' have also had a significant impact on the fortunes of ETA. The tough line promoted by the Aznar government, for instance, served to constrict the political prospects of violent Basque nationalism, with the successful legal prosection of those parties and organs with links to ETA. At the same time, since the 1990s, the security forces on both sides of the Pyrenees have inflicted a series of major reverses on the organisation, including the arrest of several senior leadership figures. As a result, it has become possible to raise the prospect that ETA might actually be defeated by security measures alone. Here, even more starkly than was the case in Northern Ireland, the importance of 'hard power' cannot be overlooked.

(iv) The wider democratic context

It is one thing to acknowledge the importance of the military and intelligence aspects of the respective states' counter-terrorism campaigns in Northern Ireland and the Basque Country. However, this is not the same thing as advocating the primacy of military 'solutions', above all others. Interpretations based entirely around the importance of the 'dirty war' share the same fundamental flaw as those which hold that 'dialogue with the extremes' is the only way to achieve peace. Both also encourage the creation of a false dichotomy between 'hawks' and 'doves' and give rise to the misleading impression that the only forces in the conflict that really mattered were those of the state and the terrorists respectively. One of the recurring themes of previous chapters has been the emphasis on the wider democratic context, as represented by legitimate political parties and the governments involved.

It is impossible to understand the transition from the Downing Street Declaration of 1993 to the Belfast Agreement of April 1998 without fully grasping the significance of this dynamic. Peter Mandelson, a former Secretary of State for Northern Ireland, has argued that the key to the 1998 deal was 'constitutional innovation'. In his words, the 'failure to get the institutions right' and the 'failure to guarantee political inclusion' had previously been 'literally a matter of life and death'.[16] Mandelson was right in so far as constitutional innovation played an important part in 1998; it is easy to lose sight of the fact that the elaborate structures of the Agreement represented a major achievement, albeit one vulnerable to challenge and revision.[17] At the same time, what was truly unique about the Good Friday Agreement—what made it different from other initiatives, such as the Sunningdale Agreement of 1973–4 or the Anglo-Irish Agreement of 1985, and what entrenched it irrevocably on the political landscape—was the fact that it was endorsed by a majority of the population in Northern Ireland. As has been described, the basic outline of the 1998 accord had been agreed over the preceding years by the British and Irish governments, together with those parties (the UUP and the SDLP) that, at that point, represented the majority of people in their respective communities in Northern Ireland. 'Even in April '98', as David Trimble has since commented, for the UUP 'the deal was [with] the SDLP' and not with Sinn Fein.[18] It was therefore an agreement constructed explicitly on the moderate constitutional centre ground. Moreover, the settlement that the parties finally arrived at was then ratified by a referendum in Northern Ireland. South of the border, another referendum bolstered that verdict by expressing overwhelming support for the amendment of articles two and three of the Irish constitution. Thus, the question of whether the British government pursued an 'inclusive' or 'exclusive' approach with regards to republicans rests on 'too crude' an understanding of the complexities of the deal.[19] Most importantly, it ignores the assertion of a democratic imperative that was central to what transpired.

The commonplace assumption that the Northern Ireland peace process was a process of bi-lateral negotiation between terrorists and the British government is a product of the period after 1998. It represents a confusion of the post-Agreement negotiations over 'guns and government', with an understanding of what it was that had brought Northern Ireland to that point. As has been argued, the concerns of unionists—the majority community within Northern Ireland—were prioritised repeatedly at key moments in the talks process that led to the Agreement. From the notion of 'sufficient consensus' to the production of the 'Heads of Agreement' document in January 1998, through to the final days of the talks, when the British government forced its Irish counterpart to renegotiate 'North-South' relations in order to meet the concerns of Trimble, Tony Blair adhered to the 'consent principle' as the bed-rock of the process. It is striking how the eventual deal signed in 1998 was more favourable to unionism than most observers—within both governments and across the political spectrum in Northern Ireland—would have predicted ten years earlier as the likely framework of the settlement; it was certainly nothing approaching the 'Joint Authority' (between the British and Irish governments) which the Sinn Fein leadership had intimated would be the minimum that it would be willing to accept. In other words, the Good Friday Agreement reflected the core democratic reality of unionist political power—a power that imposed certain limits on the nature of any accord.

This was not the simple majoritarianism which had blighted the Stormont regime before Direct Rule. What made the difference in 1998 was that the SDLP was also a central participant in the Good Friday Agreement, bringing with it a majority of the nationalist community. As the driving force behind the deal, along with the UUP, it ensured that the 1998 settlement was a triumph for moderation over extremism. Even though these 'moderate' parties were later eclipsed by the DUP and Sinn Fein, the latter have broadly operated within the parameters set for them by Hume and Trimble in 1998.

Initially, Sinn Fein was welcomed into the post-Agreement dispensation, insofar as it signed up to and delivered on the fundamentals of the accord. Indeed, many of the problems that emerged after 1998 occurred because the governments shifted their focus from shoring up the moderate consensus to the need to 'bring the terrorists on board'. Alistair Crooke, the former British intelligence officer, has asserted that 'history teaches us' that we will 'end up having to talk with those who possess legitimacy and credibility within their own constituencies'.[20] The potential problem with such an attitude is that it can generate a self-fulfilling prophecy. In prioritising Sinn Fein's continued participation after 1998, it is arguably the case that the two governments lost sight of the essential basis of the Agreement. Certainly, this is a view with which many in the SDLP would agree. Constitutional nationalists have argued, not only that they were marginalised for the sake of Trimble, but also (and more critically) that their concerns were deemed secondary to those of Sinn Fein and the IRA.[21]

In the Basque Country, ETA has been singularly unable to dictate the political agenda, despite the violent threat it has posed to the democratic system. Crucially, its decision to stay aloof from Spain's *transición* to democracy left it isolated and rudderless. The fact that the rest of Basque society, including the PNV, came to accept the legitimacy of democratic Spain confirmed ETA's marginalisation. Symptomatic of this, the group has, at the outset of peace negotiations with the Spanish government, repeatedly wanted to re-engage in retrospective debates about the transition. As Spanish politics have moved on, ETA has often seemed to be searching for a post-dated justification for its 1977 decision to opt out of the political process.

At various points since the mid-1970s, the group and its supporters have attempted to build alliances within the broader Basque nationalist family. The closest that it came to success in this regard was the Estella Agreement of 1998. This was based on a flawed and self-interested analysis of the factors that had brought peace in Northern Ireland. But it led to a ceasefire that began in September 1998 and lasted for just over a year. The assumption was that the 'pan-nationalist front' flowing from the accord (involving ETA and the PNV) would allow ETA to achieve its goals through peaceful means—a conscious echo of the alliance assumed to have been forged between the IRA, the SDLP and

Irish government in the early 1990s. In truth, the 'pan-nationalist alliance' in Northern Ireland was more imagined than real. The SDLP and the Irish government did not adopt a 'republican' posture during the peace process. Both were willing to assist Sinn Fein's entry into that process, but—following the rejection of the 'Hume-Adams' initiative in 1993—they largely operated within the terms set by successive British governments. Furthermore, in the Basque case, the agreement reached between the PNV and ETA did not look towards negotiations with other parties, but rather a series of unilateral steps in which Basque nationalists would build the institutions of independent statehood. In reality, the PNV were never committed to this vision. After poor results in local elections, the party refused to move forward with an agenda determined by ETA. With its political strategy undermined, ETA responded by terminating its ceasefire and going back to war. Thus, as on all previous occasions, the Basque terrorists had not been able to define the terms upon which the conflict might be settled.

ETA's inability to set the agenda was also apparent during the most recent attempt to inaugurate a Spanish peace process, which lasted from 2005 to 2007. This is best understood as a failed attempt by Prime Minister José Luis Rodríguez Zapatero to respond to the peace initiative devised jointly by Basque Socialists and members of ETA's political wing. Zapatero had hoped to elicit a ceasefire and then engage ETA in a protracted dialogue that would diminish its military readiness and force it to scale down its political ambitions. ETA, by contrast, pressed for a Northern Ireland-type peace process, based on all-party talks aimed at producing a settlement, with a parallel dialogue on disarmament. Ultimately, the Spanish government refused to move along that path and ruled out the possibility that any constitutional change could result from dialogue with ETA's political front. Once more, ETA had failed in its attempt to determine the parameters for a resolution to the conflict; for this reason it returned again, despite its own increasing fragility, to a violent campaign.

Constitutional dialogue remains within the gift of the PNV, of the other Basque parties and of the Spanish government. In the last few years a sizeable rift has emerged between the governments in Vitoria and Madrid over the issue of sovereignty. Supporters of ETA present this rift as marking the validity of their own political analysis. They portray it as the product of the PNV's recognition that the constitutional settlement reached at the time of the *transición* is flawed and does not satisfy Basque nationalist aspirations. As a result, ETA continues to hope that a new political agreement on the status of the Basque Country might still emerge—one into which they will have a critical input. In reality, however, ETA has persistently failed to entice the forces of mainstream Basque nationalism into a common political front. This seems ever less likely now given the apparently terminal state of ETA's military capabilities and the erosion of sympathy for it within Basque nationalist circles. The group's most recent activities have been seen increasingly as redundant, deprived of any moral or political justification and causing only further damage to the reputation of Basque nationalist political culture. As in Northern Ireland, therefore, the power to shape future political developments would appear to lie, as it has in the past, with the democratic parties, rather than with the terrorists.

(v) Talking to Terrorists

At the outset of this book it was observed that some governments have talked to terrorists and that others will likely do the same in the future. From this startpoint, the subsequent chapters attempted to examine the successive episodes by which this process has occurred in Northern Ireland and Spain. In the final analysis, it is possible to conclude that what was most important was not the act of talking to terrorists itself, but a whole range of factors, relating to the context in which that act occured. In this regard, there are a number of key questions to consider. When does it take place? What are the motives behind it, on both sides? Does it fit into a wider strategy? When does the act of establishing lines of communication become an officially sanctioned process of negotiation?

In endeavouring to provide a response to these and other questions, the first thing to note is that it is not always 'good to talk'. In 1972, Willie Whitelaw's decision to meet the IRA provided the backdrop to a huge escalation of the conflict in Northern Ireland. In the short-term, it fuelled the republican perception that violence had brought the British to the negotiating table and that more violence might force them out of the province. Over a longer period, it fed into a sense of constitutional instability—arising out of a belief that the British had no bottom line—which bedevilled attempts to build sufficient moderate support for the Sunningdale Agreement of 1973-4. It is highly

CONCLUSION

significant that the former Irish Taoiseach Garret FitzGerald—whose
direct involvement with Northern Ireland spans both the Sunningdale
period and the later Anglo-Irish Agreement—has specifically criticised
Jonathan Powell's assertions that 'it is always right to talk to your
enemy, however badly they are behaving' and that governments should
not 'refuse to talk to them without pre-conditions'. As FitzGerald
pointed out, Powell's experience is 'limited to the period after it had
become clear that the IRA was already seeking to initiate a peace process' and was 'prepared to consider throwing in the towel'.[22] The situation confronted by Powell was therefore markedly different from that
faced by earlier British and Irish governments. Prior to the 1990s, there
is evidence to suggest that the pursuit of dialogue had exacerbated the
conflict by encouraging the IRA's belief that it could pursue negotiations and violence in tandem. Intriguingly, Powell has himself criticised
John Major's government for resuming contacts with the IRA after the
bombing of Canary Wharf in 1996. On that occasion, he noted, 'The
government response should have been that they would never deal
with the IRA again until they had put violence aside for good'. Their
failure to take such a firm stance, according to Powell, merely 'made
Republicans believe the British government had no position of principle on the subject and helped convince them to continue with their
dual strategy of violence and politics together'.[23]

Similarly, the dialogue which occurred between ETA and the Spanish government in Algeria in the mid-1980s did little to encourage the
former to modify, or abandon, its violent campaign. On the contrary,
the worst attack ever carried out by ETA—the bombing of a Barcelona
supermarket car-park that killed twenty-one people in June 1987—
took place amidst the ongoing talks. In this instance the Spanish government decided to continue the discussions—only for ETA to launch
another huge attack in December 1987 when it bombed a Civil Guard
barracks building in Saragossa, killing eleven people. A decade later,
during the abortive 1998–9 'peace process', ETA effectively tested
the solidity of the alliance it had reached with the PNV by killing
politicians from rival parties to see whether the relationship could
survive such actions; and in the run-up to the ceasefire it did. Furthermore, when ETA's cessation was later terminated, the organisation's
level of activity reached a height not seen since the early 1990s. A
comparable trend was in evidence during and after the events of
2005–7. Prior to its 2006 ceasefire, ETA had not carried out a lethal

attack since 2003, but the collapse of that ceasefire brought a return to killing once again.

One of the constant aims of ETA over the last four decades has been the desire to shift the position of the Spanish government, which had long claimed that it would never negotiate on political matters with the organisation. Again, the group has enjoyed some success on this issue. In 1998, for example, Prime Minister Aznar appeared to abandon the policy of his Interior minister, Jaime Mayor Oreja, who had earlier closed all channels for communicating with ETA that had been inherited from the previous government. Even as Aznar had publicly reaffirmed that no political concessions to ETA were possible, he had sent a delegation of three personally-selected aides to talk with the group's representatives. Prime Minister Zapatero acted in similar fashion in 2006, when he authorised leading members of his Socialist Party to engage in talks with ETA—even as he was telling the organisation through intermediaries that no political negotiations were possible. These conflicting signals, sent by both Socialist and PP governments alike have thus fed the hopes of ETA that it could finally force a negotiating process, from which it might secure political gains to retrospectively justify the violence of the previous decades. In this way, 'talking' has been no more of a simple panacea in the Basque context than it has in Ulster. And in some respects it might actually have served to stimulate further violence.

The second thing to emerge from both the Spanish and British experiences of 'talking to terrorists' is that the distinction between 'direct negotiation' and 'back-channel communication' can easily become blurred in the minds of the interlocutors. Obviously, there is a logic behind the maintenance of such unofficial contacts. Away from the glare of publicity, where the respective sides might be tempted to stake out hard-line positions to appeal to their support bases, they can provide better opportunites for compromise. However, the cultivation of secret links is not without significant risks. One example of this was provided by the management of the 1981 hunger strike. The Thatcher government, having previously been adamant that it would offer no concessions to the protestors, suddenly offered a 'deal' in July 1981. Whereas the IRA's prison leadership had earlier resolved to abandon the strike after the death of four hunger strikers (on the grounds that it was achieving little), this offer encouraged them to continue. The republican leadership outside the prison now effectively engaged in a brinkmanship exercise, in the belief that further concessions could be won; it badly miscalculated. The hunger strike continued and a further six prisoners also starved themselves to death. Although it was an unintended consequence, the British intervention arguably prolonged the strike by encouraging the prisoners to believe that the government was prepared to bend. Garret FitzGerald has suggested that this 'ham-handed approach' unintentionally undermined a Catholic Church move to end the crisis. Again, FitzGerald's longer-term perspective is useful here. 'Over a period of more than 20 years', he has claimed, 'it was the consistent view of successive Irish governments that such contacts could only buoy the terrorists' hopes that, if they kept on, they would finally force a "cave-in" by the governments'. For the Irish government, throughout the 1970s and 1980s, 'any contact, direct or indirect' was avoided, because such approaches 'encouraged the IRA to believe that some British government would eventually give them what they wanted'.[24] The possibility this raises is that a willingness to engage with extremes can actually create and bolster an 'incentive structure' for violence.[25]

In the same way, the back-channel communications of the early 1990s led the IRA to believe that there was a gap between the British government's public and private position. Here, the danger of relying on intermediaries to exchange messages was made apparent. In March 1993, the IRA bomb attack on Warrington was immediately followed by a secret meeting between the IRA and the 'British government Representative', in which the latter appeared to suggest that the British viewed withdrawal from Northern Ireland as an inevitability. The proximity of the two events can have done little to dispel the notion in republican minds that violence on the British mainland was eroding London's will to remain in the province. Further major acts of violence followed in swift succession, including the attack on the Baltic Exchange in London in April 1993.

A third key point to draw from recent British and Spanish experiences is the extent to which there is a crucial qualitative difference between talking to terrorists who are on the crest of a wave—in terms of propaganda, confidence and momentum—and talking to terrorists who have been made to realise that their aims are unattainable by violent means (but who have also, been induced to believe—whether it is true or not—that an alternative path might lead them towards these objectives).[26] Thus, on the one hand, the British state made it clear to

Irish republicans that they could be part of the solution in Northern Ireland, if they so chose. At the same time, the IRA's failing military campaign had, by the late 1980s and early 1990s, generated new pragmatism within the republican leadership. A critical mass of that leadership began to look for a way out.

Here it should be stressed that the personality, temperament, and idiosyncratic nature of key participants fed into this process. The particular configuration of republican leaders during this period meant that they were amenable to a peace process—to 'cash in the chips' and avoid total defeat. In this sense, Jonathan Powell is right to assert that an important part of what occurred in Northern Ireland was the 'generational shift' that brought 'mould-breaking political leaders' to the fore on all sides.[27] Indeed, one of the unusual aspects of the Northern Ireland experience—which is not commonly replicated elsewhere—is the continuity of leadership on the republican side. Adams and McGuinness had been identified as key players, with whom 'business could be done', as early as the mid-1970s, despite their ostensibly hard-line positions. The contrast with the high turnover of personnel within ETA's leadership is striking.

The unity of Sinn Fein-IRA and strength of Adams and McGuinness as politico-military leaders inside the republican movement has had no parallel in the Basque Country. In part this is because of the internal structures of the Basque 'patriotic movement'. After its split with ETA Political-Military in the 1970s, ETA Military maintained a separate and clandestine military and political structure in France and Spain. This hidden apparatus of ETA continues to control the strategy of the movement. The successive electoral platforms of ETA—*Herri Batasuna*, *Euskal Herritarrok* and *Batasuna*—have remained subservient to the secret networks. At the same time, the successes of the security forces against ETA on French territory have had two further effects on the organisation that are worth considering. The first is that it has left ETA in the hands of younger and more inexperienced recruits, who, having reached the higher echelons of the group, are reluctant to give up their arms and their status. Second (and perhaps more fundamentally), ETA has been so weakened in recent years that it is very difficult to conceive of the kind of 'happy ending' to the organisation's campaign, of the sort afforded to the IRA by Sinn Fein's involvement in the peace process. Without this incentive, it is hard to imagine how the kind of pragmatism that asserted itself among the IRA leadership could also emerge within ETA.

CONCLUSION

In Northern Ireland, the republican pragmatism of the late 1980s and early 1990s derived from a reassessment of the long-term viability of the IRA's 'armed struggle'. Yet for many years, such a deep-seated rethink had been unimaginable. Recently published private correspondence between the senior IRA figure, Brian Keenan, and a member of the Communist Party of Great Britain, dating from November 1987—in the wake of the IRA's Remembrance Day Enniskillen bombing—shows how even at that point Keenan remained totally committed to 'armed struggle'. Despite the suggestion that Enniskillen might prove to be a turning point for the IRA, he insisted that Sinn Fein was not 'shifting its ground on the armed struggle' and stated that he did not believe it 'remotely possible that, even given its history, the republican movement will edge into reformism—now, or any time'.[28] Twenty years later, Jonathan Powell has explained how integral Keenan was to the peace process and the final stages of IRA decommissioning. Though he described Keenan as 'at one stage the biggest single threat to the British state', he also noted how he was 'instrumental' to the final denouement of the IRA's military campaign: 'If he had been against it, it would not have happened'.[29]

Strategic realities had therefore clearly impressed themselves upon the republican leadership—even upon as intransigent and determined a man as Keenan. While it maintained an ideological commitment to Irish unity, there is no question that the British government was increasingly faced with an IRA whose immediate political aims had become much more modest. Notably, recent republican accounts of the conflict have been marked by a shift in emphasis. To give but one example, Gerry Adams used a September 2007 interview to make the remarkable claim that 'the use of armed actions was never about building the united Ireland, they were always about protesting or standing up to British policy'.[30] This statement seemed to mark a clear departure from the IRA's rationale of the previous four decades. Republicans seemed no longer willing to justify past actions on the basis that they had carried them out in the first place.

Of course, one should perhaps not underestimate the importance here of self-delusion on the part of the IRA leadership. The current generation of leading republicans had, in the mid-to-late 1970s, criticised their predecessors for believing British suggestions that military withdrawal was likely in the short-term.[31] It was this criticism that underpinned their preference for a 'long war' of attrition. But, in the

257

late 1980s and early 1990s, the IRA again bought into a peace process in which it was apparently persuaded to believe that history was moving in a republican direction. Whether it was officially sanctioned or not, the republican leadership seemed to set great store in the 1993 message from the SIS agent 'Fred' that the 'final solution' would be a united Ireland and that the 'historical train' entailed defeat for unionism. It is possible that this was a deliberate feature of government policy, with republicans encouraged to believe that major concessions were always just around the corner. After 1997, for instance, Peter Mandelson has argued that Tony Blair kept the IRA in the peace process by periodically making promises that could not be kept.[32] More striking still, is the extent to which republicans appeared willfully to take such promises at face value and anticipate additional, substantial political gains. Even after the deal of 1998, for instance, when Jonathan Powell suggested to republicans that there would be further concessions in return for IRA decommissioning, the republican leadership responded by asking if this would mean something to do with a united Ireland.[33] That such a conversation could have occurred so far into a peace process, at a time when the settlement was so obviously in place, perhaps offers the clearest evidence, as to the extent of the republican capacity for self-deception.

In Northern Ireland, participation in the peace process did not come cost-free for republicans. Whatever was being said in private, the terms of trade had been set by the British government, in the form of the pre-conditions that were placed on IRA involvement during the 1990s. It has been argued that an insistence on pre-conditions held up the development of talks and contributed to the stuttering progress of the early years of the peace process. There is no doubt that it frustrated the IRA and contributed to tensions between the organisation and the British government. Ultimately, however, an insistence on these pre-conditions—albeit with a certain degree of 'constructive ambiguity' as to their implementation—provided a more stable context for negotiations. Moderate parties were the chief beneficiaries of this insistence on fundamental democratic 'norms'. With these norms in place, several key participants were willing to adopt bolder, more imaginative positions in the run up to the Belfast Agreement. Rather than a warning against setting pre-conditions, it might instead be argued that the lesson here 'is not that electoral success and political participation moderate terror groups, but that robust insistence on democratic norms is a prerequisite to introducing terror groups into democratic dialogue'.[34] Or, as one key participant in the Northern Irish peace process put it, while some degree of 'constructive ambiguity' can be useful in allowing flexibility on preconditions, there is likely to be a time when 'core issues can no longer be deferred, denied or drafted around'.[35]

Conventional wisdom is fast coalescing around the idea that talking to terrorists is *the* pre-requisite for a solution to violent conflicts in which a terrorist organisation is a key protagonist. The interlinking notions of 'inclusiveness', 'bringing in the extremes' and 'talking to one's enemies' continue to be fetishised in many quarters. Often, such activities are portrayed as self-contained and ameliorative in their own right. They are removed from the many other ingredients which feed into violent conflict, as well as those which are required to bring it to an end. What this book has shown is that a variety of other factors can be decisive in determining when and how governments talk to terrorists—and with what result. Inclusive dialogue with terrorists has been a feature of government policy in the Basque Country and Northern Ireland on several occasions over the last thirty years. But it has not, in itself, provided a magic solution to either conflict, particularly in the Basque Country where ETA is yet to renounce violence. Ultimately, if talking to terrorists can be said to have had some success in Northern Ireland, this was only when the terrorists had come to accept the rules of the game and agreed to abide by them in the search for a settlement.

NOTES

INTRODUCTION

1. R. Soans, *Talking to Terrorists*, London: Royal Court, 2005, p. 28, 90. The script for this play was based on genuine interview material.
2. P.R. Neumann, 'Negotiating with Terrorists', *Foreign Affairs*, vol. 86, no. 1, January-February, 2007.
3. For a classic example, see J. McGarry (ed.), *Northern Ireland and the Divided World: Post-Agreement Northern Ireland in Comparative Perspective*, Oxford: Oxford University Press, 2001.
4. P. Hain, *Peacemaking in Northern Ireland: A model for conflict resolution?*, speech made at Chatham House, 12 June 2007, published by the Northern Ireland Office.
5. Quoted on 7 July 2003, speaking at the University of Ulster, <http://news.ulster.ac.uk/releases/2003/850.html>.
6. E. McCann, 'How Hilary saved us when no one else could ... honest', *Belfast Telegraph*, 24 January 2008.
7. 'Statement on 10-year anniversary of Belfast Agreement', from *States News Service*, 9 April 2008. See also, J. Barrett, 'Obama: North peace process is key', *Daily Mail*, 16 February 2007.
8. 'McCain hails inspirational NI', *BBC News Online*, 23 September 2008, <http://news.bbc.co.uk/1/hi/northern_ireland/7630614.stm>.
9. D. Frum, 'The Irish Model', National Review Online, 11 April 2008, <http://frum.nationalreview.com/post/?q=NDYwYjM0MmE3NGVlMjgw Yzk2ZWYyNDE2ZmFmNWU1ODE>.
10. J. Powell, *Great Hatred, Little Room: Making Peace in Northern Ireland*, London: The Bodley Head, 2008, p. 4.
11. Ibid., p. 310.
12. Ibid., p. 312.
13. Ibid.
14. Ibid.
15. Ibid.
16. Ibid., p. 317.
17. Ibid.
18. Ibid., pp. 321–2.

19. Ibid., p. 322.
20. Interview in *GQ Magazine*, January 2002.
21. 'Mowlam: 'We must talk to al-Qaeda'', *BBC News Online*, 8 April 2004, <http://news.bbc.co.uk/1/hi/uk_politics/3611805.stm>.
22. Interview in *The Times*, 15 July 2003.
23. J. Powell, 'What I learned in Belfast', *Prospect*, no. 146, May 2008.
24. I. Katz, 'Top Blair aide: we must talk to al-Qaida', *The Guardian*, 15 March 2008. For a receptive response to Powell, see R. Whelan, 'Talking with Islamists is the only route to a lasting peace', *Irish Times*, 4 April 2008.
25. V. Dodd, 'Time to talk to al-Qaida, senior police chief urges', *The Guardian*, 30 May 2008.
26. L. Clarke, 'Peace building expertise sought world-wide', *The Sunday Times* (Irish edn), 1 July 2007.
27. J. Perera, 'Inclusiveness is the path to peace', *UPI Asia online*, 4 June 2008, <http://www.upiasiaonline.com/Politics/2008/06/04/inclusiveness_is_the_path_to_peace/5499/>.
28. See Irish Department of Foreign Affairs website, <http://www.dfa.ie/home/index.aspx?id=42628>.
29. 'NI figures boost Iraq peace talks', *BBC News Online*, 4 September 2007, <http://news.bbc.co.uk/1/hi/northern_ireland/6977190.stm>.
30. 'Martin McGuiness will lead Iraq peace mission', *Daily Telegraph*, 30 April 2008. See also, D. McKittrick, 'Conquering sectarianism: Can Ulster be a model for Iraq?', *The Independent*, 24 February 2008.
31. J. Hilder, 'McGuinness arrives in Baghdad with furniture dealer on mission of peace', *The Times*, 5 July 2008.
32. D. Godson, 'Lessons from Northern Ireland for the Arab-Israeli Conflict', *Jerusalem Viewpoints*, no. 523, October 2004.
33. J. Doward, 'MI5 chief told agents: 'Call me Bob'', *The Observer*, 11 March 2007.
34. The service was held on 10 September 2008. Quotation from Bishop of London available at Ministry of Defence website, <http://www.mod.uk/defenceinternet/defencenews/historyandhonour/northernirelandvetstheirday.htm>.
35. C. Freeman, 'I will talk to those with blood on their hands, says British general', *The Sunday Telegraph*, 11 November 2007.
36. Quoted in D. Godson, 'The real lessons of Ulster', *Prospect*, no. 140, November 2007.
37. T. Shipman, 'The Brits have lost Basra. What they are doing there is of no value', *The Sunday Telegraph*, 19 August 2007.
38. D. Haynes and M. Evans, 'Secret deal kept Army out of battle for Basra', *The Times*, 5 August 2008.
39. Quoted in, 'SAS courage hailed after victory over al-Qaeda bombers', *The Times*, 11 August 2008.
40. For further discussion of this question, see Z. Evrony (Israel's ambassador to Ireland), 'Hamas is not the IRA', *International Herald and Tribune*,

31 August 2007; M. Phillips, 'Engaged to Hamas', *Jerusalem Post*, 15 September 2007; Godson, 'The real lessons of Ulster'.
41. See, for example, D. Trimble, *Misunderstanding Ulster*, pamphlet published by Conservative Friends of Israel, London, 2007 and, D. Trimble, 'Ulster's lessons for the Middle East: don't indulge extremists', *The Guardian*, 25 October 2007. See also S. Farry, 'Northern Ireland: Prospects for Progress in 2006?', *United States Institute of Peace: Special Report*, no. 173, November 2006, available at <http://www.usip.org/pubs/special-reports/sr173.pdf> and P. Taylor, 'Sinn Fein has hijacked the history of Ulster', *The Sunday Times*, 5 August 2007.
42. 'British official arrested in Afghanistan', *Daily Telegraph*, 26 December 2007, <http://www.telegraph.co.uk/news/main.jhtml?xml=/news/2007/12/25/wafg125.xml>. 'Afghanistan: A First Step Toward "Turning" Moderate Taliban?', Radio Free Europe, 9 January 2008.
43. *The Phoenix*, 22 February 2008.
44. H. McDonald, 'Ulster peace process inspired aid workers', *The Observer*, 30 December 2007.
45. R. Sylvester, 'We must talk to the Taliban, says Des Browne', *Daily Telegraph*, 31 March 2003.
46. See, for example, J. Freedland, 'The Transformation of the IRA shows why Israel should talk to Hamas', *The Guardian*, 24 January 2007. For an academic discussion of some of these themes, see J. Moore, 'Irish Republicanism and the Peace Process: Lessons for Hamas', in R. Miller (ed.), *Ireland and the Middle East*, Dublin: Irish Academic Press, 2007, pp. 101–112.
47. C. Strenger, 'Applying lessons from Northern Ireland', *Haaretz*, 3 July 2007, <http://haaretz.com/hasen/spages/877080.html>. See also, 'An Irish lesson for Palestinians', *Gulf Daily News*, 18 May 2008, <http://www.gulf-daily-news.com/1yr_arc_Articles.asp?Article=182530&Sn=BNEW&IssueID=30059&date=5-18-2007>.
48. Quoted in G. Brock, 'Who really brought peace to Belfast?', *The Times Literary Supplement*, 27 February 2008.
49. Cited in B. Maddox, 'Confident Blair sells his step-by-step Middle East remedy', *The Times*, 6 June 2008.
50. A. Crooke, 'From conflict to politics', *The Guardian*, 28 July 2005. For the Conflict Forum, see <http://conflictsforum.org>. For a critique of Crooke's interpretation, see D. Godson, 'Gone native', *Prospect*, no. 124, July 2006.
51. G. Rifkind, 'What Lies Beneath Hamas's Rhetoric: What the West Needs to Hear', *Oxford Research Group*, March 2006, <http://www.oxford-researchgroup.org.uk/publications/briefing_papers/online/hamasonline.php>.
52. *Forward Thinking*, <http://www.forwardthinking.org/>.
53. Quoted in T. Shipman, 'Blair 'will fail unless he talks to Hamas"', *The Sunday Telegraph*, 22 July 2007.

54. J. Greenstock, 'Why Fatah is not the answer', *Newsweek*, 13 August 2007, <http://www.msnbc.msn.com/id/20123385/site/newsweek/>.

55. 'Powell: Thinning US Resources will require pullout', National Public Radio, 18 July 2007, <http://www.npr.org/templates/story/story.php?storyId=12067170>.

56. Quoted in C. Simpson, 'What If Israel Talked to Hamas?', *The Wall Street Journal*, 1 August 2007.

57. Interview in *The Sunday Telegraph*, 15 July 2007. After the release of Alan Johnston—the BBC journalist held captive in Gaza for four months—Hamas leader, Ismail Haniyeh, claimed that contact between Hamas and British representatives of 'high rank' had taken place. However, officials at the Foreign Office and British Consulate in Jerusalem moved to deny the existence of 'political' links with Hamas and said that contact had been 'humanitarian and consular'. They added that Mr Haniyeh may have mistaken non-governmental groups as representatives the British state. For details, see C. Urquhart, 'Hamas leader claims UK has widened links', *The Guardian*, 26 July 2007, <http://www.guardian.co.uk/international/story/0,,2134598,00.html>.

58. Lord Malloch Brown, Middle East debate, House of Lords, 22 January 2008, <http://www.publications.parliament.uk/pa/ld200708/ldhansrd/text/80122-0015.htm>.

59. Hain, *Peacemaking in Northern Ireland*.

60. Lord Judd, Middle East debate, House of Lords, 22 January 2008, <http://www.publications.parliament.uk/pa/ld200708/ldhansrd/text/80122-0013.htm>.

61. M. Ancram, 'To succeed, Blair must dance with wolves', *The Sunday Telegraph*, 1 July 2007. See also <http://conflictsforum.org/2007/talking-to-terrorists-audio/print/>; M. Ancram, 'Why we should be talking to Hamas', Conservative Home, 5 July 2007, <http://conservativehome.blogs.com/platform/2007/07/michael-ancram-.html>.

62. Details of the conversation are available at <http://conflictsforum.org/briefings/Usamah_Hamdan_meeting_June_19.pdf>.

63. 'The EU and the Middle East peace Process', 2 vols, House of Lords European Union Committee (26th Report of Session 2006–7), published on 24 July 2007. For the spokesman's statement, see J. Paul, 'UK parliamentarians soften on Hamas', *The Jerusalem Post*, 24 July 2007.

64. H. McDonald, 'Derry to host centre for world peace', *The Observer*, 13 April 2008.

65. A. Sens (a US diplomat who served as a member of the Independent International Commission on Decommissioning, set up by the British and Irish governments in 1997 to facilitate the disposal of paramilitary arms), 'Lessons from Northern Ireland's Peace Process', *Foreign Service Journal*, September 2007, pp. 53–5.

66. M. Burleigh, *Blood and Rage: A Cultural History of Terrorism*, London: Harper Press, 2008.

67. M. Goldring, *Renoncer à la terreur*, Paris: Éditions du Rocher, 2005, p. 288.

68. P. Unzueta, *La historia de ETA*, Madrid: Temas de Hoy, 2000, p. 427, and E. Gallastegi, 'Gudari', in *Por la libertad vasca (Orreaga)* Tafalla: Txalaparta, 1993, pp. 11–5, 202–6.

69. *Batasuna* delegates have regularly attended Sinn Fein's annual conference (*ard fheis*), while leading Sinn Fein politicians have often visited the Basque Country. See S. Morris, 'IRA's links with FARC and ETA revealed', *The Guardian*, 25 August 2001; and F. Mercado, 'El IRA aporta a ETA material e información técnica para realizar atentados' *El País*, 8 January 1990.

70. 'ETA calls for positive response to ceasefire', *The Guardian*, 23 March 2006.

71. G. Keeley, 'Spanish PM announces peace talks with ETA', *The Times*, 29 June 2006.

72. *El País*, 26 March 2006.

73. A. Daniels, '"Meddling" by Adams angers families of Eta's victims', *The Sunday Telegraph*, 11 June 2006.

74. D. Sharrock and G. Keeley, 'The Irish priest who brought Eta killers to peace', *The Times*, 17 June 2006.

75. P. Woodworth, 'The Spanish-Basque Peace Process: How to Get Things Wrong', *World Policy Journal*, vol. XXIV, no. 1, Spring 2007, pp. 65–73.

76. G. Keeley and M. Campbell, 'Spain goes on terror alert as Eta calls off ceasefire', *The Sunday Times*, 10 June 2007.

77. Interview in *El País*, 1 May 2008.

78. *Noticias de Alava*, 20 January 2007.

79. R. Alonso, *Irlanda del Norte: Una historia de guerra y la búsqueda de la paz*, Madrid: Editorial Complutense, 2001. Also, see Alonso's 'Pathways Out of Terrorism in Northern Ireland and the Basque Country: The Misrepresentation of the Irish Model', in *Terrorism and Political Violence*, vol. 16, no. 4, Winter 2004, pp. 695–713, and 'The Ending of ETA Terrorism: Lessons to learn and mistakes to avoid from Northern Ireland', *Análisis Del Real Instituto Elcano*, 31 May 2006, <http://www.realinstitutoelcano.org/analisis/987.asp>. For comparisons between the two conflicts, see M. Keating, 'Northern Ireland and the Basque Country', in McGarry (ed.), *Northern Ireland and the Divided World*, pp. 181–208; and Goldring, *Renoncer à la terreur*.

80. For important exceptions, see: D. Conversi, *The Basques, the Catalans and Spain*, London: Hurst and Co., 1997; R. P. Clarke, *The Basque insurgents: ETA 1952–1980*, Reno, NA: University of Nevada Press, 1984; and R.P. Clarke, *Negotiating with ETA: Obstacles to peace in the Basque Country, 1975–1988*, Reno, NA: University of Nevada Press, 1990.

81. See, for example, H. Keinon, 'Why the N. Ireland comparison doesn't fit', *Jerusalem Post*, 14 August 2007.

82. *Operation Banner: An Analysis of Military Operations in Northern Ireland* (prepared under the direction of the Chief of General Staff) p. i, released on the website of the Pat Finucane Centre, <http://www.serve. com/pfc/misc/opbanner.html>.
83. R. Debray, *Praise Be Our Lords: A Political Education*, London: Verson, 1997, pp. 296–7.

1. INTERVENTION AND OSCILLATION: BRITISH POLICY, 1968–1974

1. S. Prince, *Northern Ireland's '68: Civil Rights, Global Revolt and the Origins of the Troubles*, Dublin: Irish Academic Press, 2007; T. Hennessey, *Northern Ireland: The Origins of the Troubles*, Dublin: Gill and Macmillan, 2005; M. Mulholland, *Northern Ireland at the Crossroads: Ulster Unionism in the O'Neill Years, 1960–9*, Basingstoke: Palgrave Macmillan, 2000; N.O. Dochartaigh, *From Civil Rights to Armalites: Derry and the Birth of the Irish Troubles*, Cork: Cork University Press, 1997.
2. R. Bourke, *Peace in Ireland: The War of Ideas*, London: Pimlico, 2003, pp. 1–20, 198–9.
3. M. Mulholland, 'Why Did Unionists Discriminate?' in S. Wichert (ed.), *From the United Irishmen to Twentieth-Century unionism: A Festschrift for A.T.Q. Stewart*, Dublin: Four Courts Press, 2004, pp. 187–206.
4. R. Ramsay (senior civil servant in Northern Ireland), *Ringside Seats: An Insider's View of the Ulster Crisis*, forthcoming, Dublin: Irish Academic Press, 2009.
5. F. Wright, *Two Lands on One Soil: Ulster Politics before Home Rule*, Dublin: Gill and Macmillan, 1996.
6. H. Patterson, *Ireland Since 1939: The Persistence of Conflict*, Dublin: Penguin Ireland, 2006, pp. 185–91.
7. Interview in the *Belfast Telegraph*, 10 May 1969.
8. O'Neill in the *Belfast Newsletter*, 12 January 1969.
9. Patterson, *Ireland Since 1939*, pp. 191–3.
10. For a fuller discussion of Paisley's emergence in opposition to O'Neill, see E. Moloney, *Paisley: From Demagogue to Democrat?*, Dublin: Poolbeg Press, 2008, pp. 101–71.
11. See E.P. Kaufmann, *The Orange Order: A Contemporary History*, Oxford: Oxford University Press, 2007, pp. 5, 21–48.
12. See J. Bew, 'Introduction' to D.W. Miller, *Queen's Rebels: Ulster Loyalism in Historical Perspective* [first published, 1978], University College Dublin Press, 2007, pp. vii–xxiv.
13. For the civic tradition within unionist thinking, see J. Bew, *The Glory of being Britons: Civic unionism in Nineteenth-Century Belfast*, Dublin: Irish Academic Press, 2009.
14. The Portland Trust, *Economic Lessons from Northern Ireland*, May 2007, pp. 6–11, <http://www.portlandtrust.org/Economics%20in%20Peacemaking%20-%20Lessons%20from%20Northern%20Ireland.pdf>.

15. Bourke, *Peace in Ireland*, p. 50.
16. Prince, *Northern Ireland's '68*.
17. L. Baxter, B. Devlin, M. Farrell, E. McCann, 'Discussion of the strategy of People's Democracy', *New Left Review*, no. 55, May–June 1969, pp. 3–19.
18. *Belfast Telegraph*, 12 November, 1968. For the liberal stewardship of the newspaper in this period, see A. Gailey, *Crying in the Wilderness: A Liberal Editor in Ulster, 1939–69*, Belfast: Institute of Irish Studies, Queen's University, 1995.
19. Mulholland, *Northern Ireland at the Crossroads*.
20. Patterson, *Ireland Since 1939*, pp. 204–9.
21. *Belfast Telegraph*, 13 December 1968.
22. Ibid., 16 December 1968.
23. Ibid., 27 December 1968.
24. Ibid., 30 December 1968.
25. Patterson, *Ireland Since 1939*, pp. 208–9.
26. Baxter, Devlin, Farrell, McCann, 'Discussion of the strategy of People's Democracy'.
27. A. Green, 'Why civil rights report was naive and hasty', *Belfast Telegraph*, 13 September 1999.
28. For the impact of Burntollet in Derry, see D. Murphy, *To Establish the truth: Essays in Revisionism: Derry 1960–9*, Derry: Aileach Press, 1996, pp. 26–9.
29. Ramsay, *Ringside Seat*.
30. Patterson, *Ireland Since 1939*, pp. 209–10.
31. Prince, *Northern Ireland's '68*, p. 211.
32. Patterson, *Ireland Since 1939*, pp. 222–5. See also T. Hennessey, *The Evolution of the Troubles, 1970–2*, Dublin: Irish Academic Press, 2007. Hennessey argues that the presence of the British in Northern Ireland 'distorts the core [religious] division [within Northern Ireland] somewhat', pp. 342–9.
33. M. Cunningham, *British Government Policy in Northern Ireland, 1969–2000*, Manchester: Manchester University Press, 2001, p. 2.
34. Patterson, *Ireland Since 1939*, pp. 193–210.
35. K. Bloomfield, *A Tragedy of Errors: The government and Misgovernment of Northern Ireland*, Liverpool: Liverpool University Press, 2007, p. 18.
36. See G. Warner, 'Putting Pressure on O'Neill: The Wilson Government and Northern Ireland, 1964–9', *Irish Studies Review*, vol. 13, no. 1, 2005, pp. 13–21. For a critique of Warner and an emphasis on the 'fissiparous tendencies' within unionism as a causative factor in O'Neill's defeat, see G.K. Peatling, 'Unionist Divisions, the Outset of the Northern Ireland Conflict and "Pressures" on O'Neill reconsidered', *Irish Studies Review*, vol. 15, no. 1, 2007, pp. 17–36.
37. Baxter, Devlin, Farrell, McCann, 'Discussion of the strategy of People's Democracy'.

38. Hennessey, *Evolution of the Troubles*, pp. 45–8.
39. R. English, *Armed Struggle: A History of the IRA*, London: Palgrave Macmillan, 2003, pp. 81–108.
40. Hennessey, *Evolution of the Troubles*, p. 7.
41. Ibid., pp. 28–37.
42. C. de Baroid, *Ballymurphy and the Irish War*, London: Pluto Press, 2nd edn, 2000, p. 54.
43. Ibid., p. 33, 39, 54.
44. Ibid., p. 49.
45. E. Moloney, *A Secret History of the IRA*, London: Penguin, 2nd edn, 2007, pp. 91–2.
46. See T. Parker, 'Fighting an Antaean Enemy: How Democratic States Unintentionally Sustain the Terrorist Movements They Oppose', *Terrorism and Political Violence*, vol. 19, 2007, pp. 155–79.
47. Patterson, *Ireland Since 1939*, p. 21.
48. M. Dewar, *The British Army in Northern Ireland*, London: Weidenfeld Military, 2nd edn, 1996, pp. 228–9.
49. De Baroid, *Ballymurphy and the Irish War*, p. 55.
50. A. McIntyre, 'Modern Irish Republicanism: The Product of British State Strategies', *Irish Political Studies*, vol. 10, 1995, pp. 97–122.
51. *Operation Banner*, pp. 2–7.
52. *The Sunday Times* 'Insight Team', *Ulster*, London: Penguin, 1972, pp. 260–1.
53. Ramsay, *Ringside Seat*.
54. *The Sunday Times* 'Insight Team', *Ulster*, pp. 252–68.
55. For details see B. Anderson, *Joe Cahill: A Life in the IRA*, Dublin: O'Brien Press, 2002, pp. 228–231.
56. S. Halper and J. Clarke, *America Alone: The Neo-Conservatives and the Global Order*, Cambridge: Cambridge University Press, 2004, p. 284.
57. *Operation Banner*, pp. 2–7.
58. G. Warner, 'The Falls Road Curfew Revisited', *Irish Political Studies*, vol. 14, no. 3, 2006, pp. 325–42. We would also like to express thanks to the author of this article for discussing the findings of his research in more detail.
59. Hennessey, *Evolution of the Troubles*, pp. 120–51.
60. Ibid., pp. 103–7.
61. Ibid., 130–45.
62. Moloney, *Secret History of the IRA*, p. 102.
63. P. Taylor, *Brits: The War against the IRA*, London: Bloomsbury, 2nd edn, 2001, p. 68.
64. Ibid., pp. 68–73.
65. *Ireland v. United Kingdom, 1976 Y.B. European Convention on Human. Rights, 512, 748, 788–94*, European Commission of Human Rights, 1976.
66. *Ireland v. United Kingdom—5310/71 [1978] ECHR 1*, European Court of Human Rights, 18 January 1978.

67. *Operation Banner.*
68. Bloomfield, *Tragedy of Errors*, p. 21.
69. Ramsay, *Ringside Seat.*
70. Author interview with 'Charlie Longrass' (senior officer in British Army in Northern Ireland), 17 September 2006.
71. Bloomfield, *Tragedy of Errors*, p. 22, 26.
72. Hennessey, *Evolution of the Troubles*, p. 346.
73. Bloomfield, *Tragedy of Errors*, p. 20.
74. Ramsay, *Ringside Seat.*
75. Ibid.
76. L. Clarke and K. Johnston, *Martin McGuinness: From Guns to Government*, London: Mainstream Publishing, 2001, pp. 74–7.
77. Anderson, *Joe Cahill*, pp. 244–8.
78. Clarke and Johnston, *Martin McGuinness*, pp. 74–7.
79. Ibid.
80. P. Bishop and E. Mallie, *The Provisional IRA*, London: Heineman, 1987, pp. 175–7.
81. D. McKittrick and D. McVea, *Making sense of the Troubles*, Belfast: Blackstaff Press, 2000, pp. 83–7.
82. W. Whitelaw, *The Whitelaw Memoirs*, London: Aurum Press, 1989, pp. 101–2.
83. B. Faulkner, *Memoirs of a Statesman*, J. Huston (ed.), London: Weidenfeld and Nicolson, 1978, pp. 170–1.
84. Clarke and Johnston, *Martin McGuinness*, pp. 74–7.
85. Moloney, *Secret History of the IRA*, p. 117.
86. McKittrick and McVea, *Making Sense of the Troubles*, p. 87.
87. M. Dillon, *25 Years of Terror: The IRA's war against the British*, London: Bantam Books, revised edn, London, 1999, pp. 153–4.
88. Patterson, *Ireland Since 1939*, p. 223.
89. G. FitzGerald, 'Powell Wrong about Talking in the Midst of Terror campaign', *Irish Times*, 29 March 2008.
90. P. Taylor, *Loyalists*, London: Bloomsbury, 1999, pp. 88–90.
91. C. Hirst, *Religion, Politics and Violence in Nineteenth-Century Belfast: the Pound and Sandy Row*, Dublin: Four Courts, 2002.
92. Faulkner, *Memoirs of a Statesman*, p. 164.
93. Whitelaw, *The Whitelaw Memoirs*, pp. 101–2.
94. Faulkner, *Memoirs of a Statesman*, pp. 170–2.
95. Bloomfield, *Tragedy of Errors*, pp. 30–1.
96. Cunningham, *British Government Policy*, pp. 13–4.
97. Patterson, *Ireland Since 1939*, pp. 239–41.
98. For an interesting perspective on this argument, see B. White, 'Thinking of future—not back to '74', *Belfast Telegraph*, 9 May 2007.
99. John K. Hickman from the British Embassy to 'Bill' Harding, 29 October 1975, *State Papers*, NRA, FCO 87/450.
100. P. Devlin, *The Fall of the Northern Ireland Executive*, Belfast: Paddy Devlin, 1975, p. 32.

101. P. Bew, *Ireland: The Politics of Enmity, 1789–2006*, Oxford: Oxford University Press, 2007, pp. 512–3.

102. Ibid., p. 513.

103. McKittrick and McVea, *Making Sense of the Troubles*, pp. 100–1.

104. Patterson, *Ireland Since 1939*, p. 270; Taylor, *Loyalists*, pp. 125–6.

105. Copy of a note from Robert Armstrong to Wilson on 31 May 1974 (in response to the latter's 'Doomsday document' of the previous day), in *Donoughue Papers*, Churchill Archives Centre, Cambridge University, DNGH 1/1/2. Thanks to Patrick Gregory of the BBC for passing on this information.

106. For a fuller discussion on the significance of the Convention, see D. Godson, *Himself Alone: David Trimble and the Ordeal of Unionism*, London: Harper Collins, 2004, pp. 50–64.

107. M. Rees, *Northern Ireland: A Personal Perspective*, London: Methuen, 1985, p. 318.

108. R. Fisk, *The Point of No Return: The Strike which Broke the British in Ulster*, London: Andre Deutsch, 1975.

109. Bew, *Ireland*, p. 515.

110. Anderson, *Joe Cahill*, pp. 250–2.

111. Letter by Michael Oatley to *Prospect*, 22 July 2006.

112. Powell, *Great Hatred, Little Room*, pp. 66–7.

113. E. Mallie and D. McKittrick, *Endgame in Ireland*, London: Hodder and Stoughton, 2001, pp. 98–9; Clarke and Johnston, *Martin McGuinness*, pp. 86–7.

114. Mallie and McKittrick, *Endgame in Ireland*, pp. 98–99; Clarke and Johnson, *Martin McGuinness*, pp. 86–7.

115. 'Labour in Contact with the Provisional IRA', *The Guardian*, 1 January 2005.

116. Powell, *Great Hatred, Little Room*, p. 68.

117. Note of a meeting between the Secretary of State and Mr Vivian Simpson MP at Stormont Castle, 7 May 1973, *State Papers*, NRA, FCO 87/221.

118. Ibid.

119. Document by M.C Oatley, 25 April 1973, *State Papers*, NRA, FCO 87/221.

120. 'Labour in contact with the Provisional IRA', *The Guardian*, 1 January 2005.

121. Note by Secretary of State for the Prime Minister, 26 September 1974, *State Papers*, NRA, PREM 16/151.

122. Proscription of Sinn Fein and Ulster Volunteer Force/Political Matters, 30 April 1973—17 December 1975, *State Papers*, NRA, CJ4/862.

123. Moloney, *A Secret History of the IRA*, pp. 138–42.

124. Author interview with Sean O'Callaghan, 12 January 2008.

125. R. O'Rawe, *Blanketmen: An Untold story of the H-Block Hunger Strike*, Dublin: New Island Books, 2005, pp. 72–3.

126. Seanna Walsh, in conversation with Sean O'Callaghan (author interview with O'Callaghan, 12 January 2008).

127. Moloney, *A Secret History of the IRA*, pp. 142–6; Bishop and Mallie, *The Provisional IRA*, p. 269; O'Rawe, *Blanketmen*, pp. 72–5.
128. Cited in P. Taylor, *Provos: The IRA and Sinn Fein*, London: Bloomsbury, 1997, p. 171.
129. Ibid.
130. Quoted in P. Bew and H. Patterson, *The British State and the Ulster Crisis: From Wilson to Thatcher*, London: Verso, 1985, pp. 80–1.
131. Taylor, *Provos*, pp. 177–181.
132. Moloney, *A Secret History of the IRA*, pp. 165–6; Taylor, *Provos*, pp. 174–5.
133. Taylor, *Provos*, p. 176, 186.
134. Bishop and Mallie, *The Provisional IRA*, p. 254; 'Obituary: Brian Keenan', *Daily Telegraph*, 21 May 2008.
135. Dillon, *25 Years of Terror*, pp. 176, 188–90.
136. Ibid., p. 192.
137. Bishop and Mallie, *The Provisional IRA*, p. 271.
138. T. Harnden, *'Bandit Country': The IRA and South Armagh*, London: Hodder and Stoughton, 1999, p. 15; Moloney, *A Secret History of the IRA*, pp. 146–7.
139. Report on Sectarian Assassinations, January to June 1975, *State Papers*, NRA, CJ4/830; Sectarian and Interfactional Policy as Statistics, *State Papers* (1975), NRA, CJ4/829.
140. Dillon, *25 Years of Terror*, pp. 198–209.
141. Top Secret document, Merlyn Rees to Prime Minister, 29 November 1975, *State Papers*, NRA PREM 16/958.
142. Taylor, *Provos*, pp. 186–7.
143. Ibid., pp. 189–90.
144. Michael Daly from the Dublin Embassy to Julian Hartland-Swann, 24 November 1975, *State Papers*, NRA, FCO/87/446.
145. Ibid., p. 188.
146. J. Bew, 'British tried to distance themselves', *Irish Times*, 29 December 2005.
147. John K. Hickman from the British Embassy to 'Bill' Harding, 29 October 1975, *State Papers*, NRA, FCO 87/450.
148. Top Secret document, Merlyn Rees to Prime Minister, 29 November 1975, *State Papers*, NRA, PREM 16/958.
149. R.W. White, *Ruairí Ó'Bradaigh: The Life and Politics of an Irish Revolutionary*, Indiana: Indiana University Press, 2006, p. 225.
150. A. Morgan, *Harold Wilson*, London: Pluto, 1992.
151. Copy of a note from Robert Armstrong to Wilson on 31 May 1974 (in response to the latter's 'Doomsday document' of the previous day) in *Donoughue Papers*, Churchill Archives Centre, Cambridge University, DNGH 1/1/2,
152. B. Donoughue, *Downing Street Diary: With Harold Wilson in No. 10*, London: Jonathan Cape, 2004, pp. 129–30, 380.

153. Taylor, *Provos*, pp. 190–3.
154. Harold Wilson, 'Apocalyptic Note for the Record', 10 January 1976, *State Papers*, NRA, CJ4/1358.
155. Ibid.
156. Meeting between Airey Neave and NIO (following Neave's meeting with OUP representatives), 15 September 1976, *State Papers*, NRA, CJ4/1351.
157. Memo on British Policy Towards Northern Ireland (rejecting withdrawal), 17 October 1975, *State Papers*, NRA, FCO/87/446.
158. Michael Daly from the Dublin Embassy to Julian Hartland-Swann, 24 November 1975, *State Papers*, NRA, FCO/87/417.
159. Sir Frank Cooper to Sir John Hunt, 15 January 1976, *State Papers*, NRA, CJ4/1358.
160. G. FitzGerald, *All in a Life: An Autobiography*, Dublin: Gill and Macmillan, 1991, pp. 258–9.
161. Bew, 'British tried to distance themselves', *Irish Times*, 29 December 2005.
162. Rees, *Northern Ireland*, pp. 346–9.
163. P. Bew and G. Gillespie, *Northern Ireland: A Chronology of the Troubles, 1968–1993*, Dublin: Gill and Macmillan, 1993.
164. 'Next Steps in Northern Ireland' (memo by the Secretary of State), 12 December 1975, *State Papers*, NRA, CAB 134/3921.
165. Annex to Cabinet Committee discussions on Northern Ireland, 7 May 1976, *State Papers*, NRA, CAB 134/4040.
166. Memo on British Policy Towards Northern Ireland (rejecting withdrawal), 17 October 1975, *State Papers*, NRA, FCO/87/446.

2. THE LONG WAR, 1975–1990

1. NIO Briefing before the visit of Liam Cosgrave to the British Prime Minister, which took place on 5 March 1976, *State Papers*, NRA CAB 133/464.
2. Rees, *Northern Ireland*, p. 354.
3. Report of British officials on meeting the Irish Ambassador in London, 28 October 1976, *State Papers*, NRA, CJ4/1354.
4. Faulkner, *Memoirs of a Statesman*, p. 279.
5. Patterson, *Ireland Since 1939*, p. 250.
6. Merlyn Rees, draft note, 10 October 1975, Papers on Provisional IRA, *State Papers*, NRA, CJ4/859.
7. Secretary of State to Prime Minister, 30 October 1975, Security Policy on Northern Ireland, *State Papers*, NRA, FCO 87/446.
8. Taylor, *Provos*, p. 196.
9. G. Ellison and J. Smyth, *The Crowned Harp: Policing in Northern Ireland*, London: Pluto Press, 1999, p. 90. See also Cabinet Committee on Northern Ireland, 12 May 1976, *State Papers*, NRA CAB 134/4040.

10. Dewar, *The British Army in Northern Ireland*, p. 147. See also, Frank Cooper, NIO, to Sir John Hunt at the Cabinet office, 5 November 1975, *State Papers*, NRA, FCO/87/442; Annex to Cabinet Committee discussions on Northern Ireland, 7 May 1976, *State Papers*, NRA CAB 134/4040.

11. Cabinet Committee on Northern Ireland, 19 October 1976, *State Papers*, NRA, CAB 134/4040.

12. Top Secret document, Merlyn Rees to Prime Minister, 29 November 1975, *State Papers*, NRA, PREM 16/958.

13. Report by M. Hodge, Republic of Ireland Department, 24 January 1975, *State Papers*, NRA, FCO 87/484.

14. Top Secret document, Merlyn Rees to Prime Minister, 29 November 1975, *State Papers*, NRA, PREM 16/958.

15. Annex to Cabinet Committee discussions on Northern Ireland, 7 May 1976, *State Papers*, NRA, CAB 134/4040.

16. *Report of the Committee of Inquiry into Police Interrogation Procedures in Northern Ireland*, London, 1979.

17. J. Newsinger, *British Counterinsurgency: From Palestine to Northern Ireland*, Basingstoke: Palgrave Macmillan, 2002, pp. 179–80.

18. Annex to Cabinet Committee discussions on Northern Ireland, 7 May 1976, *State Papers*, NRA, CAB 134/4040.

19. Harnden, *Bandit Country*, p. 134.

20. Message from Prime Minister to Taoiseach (official records suggest that this was actually written by Jim Callaghan, Wilson's successor), 6 January 1976, *State Papers*, NRA, PREM 16/958.

21. R. Rapple, 'British Misled Irish on SAS', *The Sunday Business Post*, 31 December 2006.

22. For a discussion of Irish and American reactions to this in January 1976, see *State Papers*, NRA, FCO/852.

23. FitzGerald, *All in a Life*, p. 277–8.

24. R. Mason, *Paying the Price*, London: Robert Hale, 1999, pp. 168–9.

25. *State Papers*, NRA, PREM 16/1339.

26. Account of a meeting between Airey Neave and Mr John Biggs-Davison at HQNI, with the army GOC, 29 March 1976, *State Papers*, NRA, CJ4/1351.

27. G. Wheatcroft, 'A Happy 80th Birthday to the IRA's Deadly Foe', *The Daily Telegraph*, 18 April 2004.

28. Donoughue, *Downing Street Diary*, p. 622.

29. Mason, *Paying the Price*, pp. 160–5.

30. Ibid., pp. 166–72; see also Cunningham, *British Government Policy in Northern Ireland*, pp. 17–9.

31. Thanks to Bernard Donoughue for this information, which is contained in his recently published *Downing Street Diary, vol. 2: With James Callaghan in No. 10*, London: Jonathan Cape, 2008.

32. Mason, *Paying the Price*, pp. 166–72.

33. For Mason's report to the Prime Minister, *State Papers*, 1977, NRA, PREM 16/1344. See also NRA, CJ4/1567/1.
34. Mason, *Paying the Price*, pp. 166–72.
35. Ibid.
36. D. Hamill, *Pig in the Middle: The Army in Northern Ireland, 1969–1985*, London: Methuen, 2nd edn, 1986, p. 220.
37. Mason, *Paying the Price*, p. 251.
38. Article from *New Hibernia*, 21 January 1977, contained in *State Papers* (1977), NRA, FCO 87/682.
39. Mason, *Paying the Price*, p. 205.
40. Patterson, *Ireland Since 1939*, p. 253.
41. Moloney, *A Secret History of the IRA*, pp. 149–50.
42. P.R. Neumann, 'Winning the "War on Terror"? Roy Mason's Contribution to Counter-Terrorism in Northern Ireland', *Small Wars and Insurgencies*, vol. 14, no. 3, Autumn 2003, pp. 45–64.
43. FitzGerald, *All in a Life*, pp. 277–8.
44. Roy Mason to Jim Callaghan, 9 February 1977, *State Papers*, NRA, PREM 16/1343.
45. Note of Roy Mason's meeting with deputation from Ballylumford, 6 May 1977, NRA, *State Papers*, CJ4/1567/2.
46. Roy Mason to Jim Callaghan, 9 February 1977, *State Papers*, NRA, PREM 16/1343.
47. J. Bew, 'IRA sent message to London seeing talks', *Irish Times*, 30 December 2008. The IRA leadership from the time has since disputed the validity of this message.
48. J. Bew, 'UK Officials Felt They Were Succeeding Against the IRA', *Irish Times*, 31 December 2007.
49. Memo, 1 August 1977, *State Papers*, NRA, FCO 87/682.
50. Author interview with Brian Cubbon (Permanent Under Secretary of State of the Northern Ireland Office from 1976 to 1979), 1 May 2008.
51. M. Dillon, *The Dirty War*, London: Hutchinson, 1988, p. 479.
52. Moloney, *A Secret History of the IRA*, p. 149.
53. Visit of British Officials to Northern Ireland, conversation with HQNI, 9 April, *State Papers*, NRA, FCO 87/484; PIRA Ceasefire, *State Papers* (1975), NRA, FCO 87/461.
54. Moloney, *A Secret History of the IRA*, pp. 142–60.
55. Ibid.
56. J. Bowyer Bell, *IRA Tactics and Targets: an Analysis of Tactical Aspects of the Armed Struggle, 1969–1989*, Dublin: Poolberg, 1990.
57. Clarke and Johnston, *Martin McGuinness*, pp. 97–99; Moloney, *A Secret History of the IRA*, pp. 155–7; Bishop and Mallie, *The Provisional IRA*, pp. 322–3. The Green Book is reproduced in full as an appendix to Dillon's, *25 Years of Terror*.
58. Moloney, *A Secret History of the IRA*, p. 154.
59. Ibid., p. 170.

60. J. Drumm, 'Annual Commemoration of Wolfe Tone, Bodenstown Oration 1977', *Republican News*, 18 June 1977, p. 7.
61. Author interview with Sean O'Callaghan, 12 January 2008.
62. McKittrick and McVea, *Making Sense of the Troubles*, pp. 116–7.
63. Taylor, *Provos*, pp. 211–2.
64. Ibid., pp. 215–6.
65. J. Moore, 'Irish Republicanism and the Peace Process: Lessons for Hamas', in Miller, *Ireland and the Middle East*, pp. 101–12.
66. Harnden, *Bandit Country*, pp. 120–1.
67. R. Bourke, 'Digging in For Long Haul of Direct Rule', *Irish Times*, 4 January 2005.
68. Rees, *Northern Ireland*, pp. 346–9.
69. Bew, *Ireland*, p. 509.
70. State of Security Assessment: Republic of Ireland (produced by British Embassy in Dublin for Security Department of the Foreign and Commonwealth Office), 28 October 1976, *State Papers*, NRA, FCO/87/536.
71. 'Republic of Ireland's Policy Towards Northern Ireland', 11 December 1975, *State Papers*, NRA, FCO/87/460.
72. L. Branney, FCO Research Department, note on the prospect of 'Negotiated Independence', 28 August 1975, *State Papers*, NRA, FCO/87/445.
73. Republic of Ireland Department, briefing for Cabinet Committee on Northern Ireland, 4 July 1975, *State Papers*, NRA, FCO/87/440.
74. FitzGerald, *All in a Life*, pp. 278–9.
75. IRA activities in the Republic of Ireland, 6 January 1976, *State Papers*, NRA, FCO 87/513.
76. Bishop and Mallie, *The Provisional IRA*, p. 254.
77. FitzGerald, *All in a Life*, p. 282.
78. Author interview with Brian Cubbon, 1 May 2008.
79. See discussion of various approaches, late July 1976, *State Papers*, NRA, CJ4/1060.
80. Internal memo on Irish government's Security Package, 16 August 1976, *State Papers*, NRA, CJ4/1059.
81. R. Rapple, 'Assassination of suspect named', *The Sunday Business Post*, 31 December 2006.
82. Cabinet Committee on Northern Ireland, 19 October 1976, *State Papers*, NRA, CAB 134/4040.
83. State of Security Assessment: Republic of Ireland (produced by British Embassy in Dublin for Security Department of the Foreign and Commonwealth Office), 28 October 1976, *State Papers*, NRA, FCO 87/536.
84. Report from the British Embassy in Dublin on Lynch's first press conference after the election, 7 July 1977, *State Papers*, NRA, PREM 16/1337.
85. NIO briefing, 16 September 1977, NRA, PREM/16/1337.
86. A. McIntyre, 'A Quarter Of a Century Ago', *The Blanket*, 24 August 2004, <http://www.phoblacht.net:80/quartercentam.html>.
87. Bloomfield, *A Tragedy of Errors*, p. 53.

88. A. Cooke (former advisor to Neave), 'The Victory of Ulster's Extremists', *The Salisbury Review*, vol. 26, no. 1, Autumn 2007, pp. 13–4.
89. Patterson, *Ireland Since 1939*, pp. 253–5.
90. A. Wilson, *Irish America and the Ulster Conflict, 1968–1995*, Belfast: Blackstaff, 1995, pp. 126–34, 152–60.
91. Ibid., pp. 136–7.
92. Ibid., pp. 152–165.
93. M. Thatcher, *The Downing Street Years*, London: Harper Collins, 1993, p. 387.
94. Wilson, *Irish America*, p. 163.
95. Ibid., p. 164.
96. P. Bew, P. Gibbon and H. Patterson, *Northern Ireland, 1921–1996: Political Forces and Social Classes*, London: Serif, 2nd edn, 1996, p. 207.
97. Bew, *Ireland*, pp. 499–500.
99. Thatcher, *Downing Street Years*, p. 100.
99. Bew, Gibbon and Patterson, *Northern Ireland*, p. 207.
100. Ibid.
101. Taylor, *Provos*, pp. 203–4.
102. Bishop and Mallie, *The Provisional IRA*, pp. 349–50.
103. Ibid., p. 351.
104. Cabinet committee on Northern Ireland, 25 March 1977, *State Papers*, NRA, CAB 134/4150.
105. Bishop and Mallie, *The Provisional IRA*, pp. 351–2.
106. McKittrick and McVea, *Making Sense of the Troubles*, pp. 137–41.
107. Taylor, *Provos*, p. 229.
108. Ibid., pp. 232–3.
109. Bishop and Mallie, *The Provisional IRA*, p. 360.
110. Patterson, *Ireland Since 1939*, pp. 255–6.
111. For more on this see R. Kearney, *Myths and Motherland*, Derry: Field Day, 1984.
112. Taylor, *Provos*, pp. 233–4.
113. Powell, *Great Hatred, Little Room*, p. 70; Bishop and Mallie, *The Provisional IRA*, pp. 360–1
114. Cited in Taylor, *Provos*, p. 234.
115. Ibid., p. 235.
116. O'Rawe, *Blanketmen*, p. 92.
117. Ibid., p. 114.
118. Patterson, *Ireland Since 1939*, p. 256.
119. Moloney, *A Secret History of the IRA*, pp. 211–4.
120. Patterson, *Ireland Since 1939*, p. 256.
121. Taylor, *Provos*, p. 243; Moloney, *A Secret History of the IRA*, p. 209.
122. Taylor, *Provos*, p. 243.
123. Ibid., pp. 244–5.
124. O'Rawe, *Blanketmen*, p. 133.

125. Ibid., p. 161.
126. Ibid., p. 165.
127. Taylor, *Provos*, p. 246.
128. O'Rawe, *Blanketmen*, p. 173.
129. Taylor, *Provos*, p. 246.
130. O'Rawe, *Blanketmen*, pp. 176–91.
131. Ibid.
132. Taylor, *Provos*, p. 247.
133. O'Rawe, *Blanketmen*, pp. 199–203.
134. Moloney, *A Secret History of the IRA*, p. 213.
135. O'Rawe, *Blanketmen*, pp. 248–59.
136. McFarlane cited in S. McCaffrey, 'Former comrades' war of words over hunger strike', *Irish News*, 26 May 2006.
137. McKittrick and McVea, *Making Sense of the Troubles*, p. 144.
138. Patterson, *Ireland Since 1939*, p. 258.
139. Prior cited in Taylor, *Provos*, p. 251.
140. McKittrick and McVea, *Making Sense of the Troubles*, p. 157.
141. J. Prior, *A Balance of Power*, London: Hamish Hamilton, 1986, p. 197.
142. Crooke, 'The Victory of Ulster's Extremists'.
143. Moloney, *A Secret History of the IRA*, p. 203.
144. Bloomfield, *Tragedy of errors*, pp. 58-66; Bew, Gibbon and Patterson, *Northern Ireland*, p. 211.
145. Patterson, *Ireland Since 1939*, p. 396.
146. Bishop and Mallie, *The Provisional IRA*, p. 386.
147. Bloomfield, *Tragedy of Errors*, p. 58.
148. Ibid.
149. D. Hurd, *Memoirs*, London: Little, Brown, 2003, p. 303.
150. Private information.
151. Ibid.
152. Entry for 13 August 1985 in A. Clarke, *Diaries*, London: Weidenfeld and Nicolson, 1993, p. 177.
153. Bloomfield, *Tragedy of Errors*, p. 66.
154. Crooke, 'The Victory of Ulster's Extremists'.
155. Author interview with Sir Nicholas Fenn, 21 July 2007.
156. Wilson, *Irish America and the Ulster Crisis*, p. 249.
157. We are grateful to Dr Sydney Elliott for this information.
158. Bloomfield, *Tragedy of Errors*, p. 60.
159. A. Aughey, *Under Siege: Ulster Protestants and the Anglo-Irish Agreement*, London: Hurst, 1989.
160. Bew, *The Glory of Being Britons*.
161. H. Patterson and E. Kaufmann, *Unionism and Orangeism in Northern Ireland Since 1945: the Decline of the Loyal Family*, Manchester: Manchester University Press, 2007, pp. 219–60.
162. McKittrick and McVea, *Making Sense of the Troubles*, pp. 165–6.
163. Ibid., p. 327.

164. Ibid., p. 166.
165. Thatcher, *The Downing Street Years*, pp. 393–402.
166. N. Lawson, *The View from No. 11: Memoirs of Tory Radical*, London: Bantam, 1992, pp. 670–2.
167. Thatcher, *The Downing Street Years*, pp. 402–6.
168. Cited in H. Patterson, 'The IRA and sectarianism revisited', *Terrorism and Political Violence* (forthcoming). We are grateful to the author of this article for providing us with an advance copy of it.
169. Moloney, *A Secret History of the IRA*, pp. 20–4.
170. J. Lees-Milne, *Diaries, vol. 3, 1984–1997*, introduction by M. Bloch, London: John Murray, 2008, entry for 15 November 1987, p. 151.
171. Thatcher, *The Downing Street Years*, pp. 406–15.

3. THE PEACE PROCESS

1. H. Patterson, 'The IRA and sectarianism revisited'. See also, Patterson's, 'War of National Liberation or Ethnic Cleansing: IRA Violence in Fermanagh during the Troubles', in B. Bowden and M. Davis (eds), *Terror: From Tyrannicide to Terrorism*, Brisbane: University of Queensland, 2006.
2. Adams cited in T. Hennessey, *The Northern Ireland Peace Process: Ending the Troubles?* Dublin: Gill and Macmillan, 2000, p. 39.
3. Moloney, *A Secret History of the IRA*, p. 350.
4. McKittrick and McVea, *Making Sense of the Troubles*, p. 325.
5. Adair, cited in C. Crawford, *Inside the UDA: Volunteers and Violence*, London: Pluto Press, 2003, p. 167.
6. Crawford, *Inside the UDA*, p. 35.
7. Taylor, *Loyalists*, p. 215.
8. Mallie and McKittrick, *Endgame in Ireland*, pp. 143–7; McKittrick and McVea, *Making Sense of the Troubles*, pp. 192–4.
9. The claim that there would be 'no more ceasefires' was made by Martin McGuinness, *Bodenstown Oration*, 1988, Linenhall Library Belfast, Political Collection; for the IRA ceasefire declaration, see 'IRA Ceasefire Statement 31 August 1994', CAIN, <http://cain.ulst.ac.uk/events/peace/docs/ira31894.htm>.
10. Taylor, *Loyalists*, pp. 227–34.
11. See, for example, J. Smyth, 'A Discredited Cause? The IRA and Support for Political Violence', in A. O'Day and Y. Alexander (eds), *Ireland's Terrorist Trauma: Interdisciplinary Perspectives*, Basingstoke: Palgrave Macmillan, 1989, pp. 101–23.
12. Taylor, *Brits*, p. 254.
13. Author interview with 'Charlie Longrass', 29 August 2006.
14. Moloney, *A Secret History of the IRA*, pp. 318–9.
15. 'Veteran Republican's Spy Statement', *BBC News Online*, 16 December 2005, <http://news.bbc.co.uk/1/hi/northern_ireland/4536896.stm>; 'Sinn

Fein man admits he was an agent', *BBC News Online*, 16 December 2005, <http://news.bbc.co.uk/1/hi/northern_ireland/4536826.stm>; N. Mackay, 'Why this man *is* Stakeknife', *Sunday Herald*, 18 May 2003; R. Cowan, 'Ex-spy handler fears for Stakeknife's life', *The Guardian*, 19 May 2003.

16. 'Obituary: Denis Donaldson', *The Daily Telegraph*, 7 April 2006.

17. 'Veteran Republican's Spy Statement', *BBC News Online*, 16 December 2005, <http://news.bbc.co.uk/1/hi/northern_ireland/4536896.stm>.

18. See, for example 'Spy claims nonsense—McGuinness', *BBC News Online*, 30 May 2006, <http://news.bbc.co.uk/1/hi/northern_ireland/5029768.stm>; S. Breen, 'The Tale of Two Martins', *Sunday Tribune*, 5 June 2006.

19. J. Holland and S. Phoenix, *Phoenix: Policing the Shadows: The Secret War Against Terrorism in Northern Ireland*, London: Hodder and Stoughton, 1996, p. 391.

20. Ibid., p. 393.

21. Author interview with Sean O'Callaghan, 22 November 2005.

22. S. O'Callaghan, *The Informer*, London: Bantam Press, 1998, p. 337.

23. D. Morrison, *Then the Walls Came Down: A Prison Journal*, Dublin: The Mercier Press, 1999, p. 241.

24. 'Our day will come: Interview with Danny Morrison', *Sunday News*, 16 November 1986.

25. Moloney, *A Secret History of the IRA*, pp. 339–40.

26. Author interview with Danny Morrison, Belfast, 21 August 2003.

27. For further details on this see D. Bloomfield, *Political Dialogue in Northern Ireland: The Brooke Initiative, 1989–92*, London: Palgrave Macmillan, 1998, pp. 11–63.

28. Morrison, *Then the Walls Came Down*, p. 240.

29. See, for example, the debate within the prisoner-run journal, *An Glor Gafa/Captive Voice*, in 1991, which discussed the republican movement's political problems at length: 'Ten Years On', *An Glor Gafa/Captive Voice*, 3, 2, Summer 1991; M. O Treasaigh, 'Organise for Changing Times—A Reply to "Ten Years On"', *An Glor Gafa/Captive Voice*, 3, 3, Winter 1991.

30. The article was eventually printed in Morrison, *Then the Walls Came Down*, pp. 288–92.

31. For a fuller discussion on this, see M. Frampton, *The Long March: The Political Strategy of Sinn Fein, 1981–2007*, Basingstoke: Palgrave Macmillan, 2008, pp. 74–88.

32. Moloney, *A Secret History of the IRA*, pp. 269–72. A full copy of the letter can be found in the appendix to the book, pp. 615–30.

33. Ibid., p. 277.

34. Letter from Fr. Alec Reid to Charles Haughey 11 May 1987, available in Moloney, *A Secret History of the IRA*, pp. 615–630.

35. Ibid.

36. For a fuller discussion on this, see Frampton, *The Long March*, pp. 58–65.

37. Moloney, *A Secret History of the IRA*, pp. 274–9.

38. For more, see Frampton, *The Long March*, pp. 58–65.

39. Mallie and McKittrick, *Endgame in Ireland*, pp. 124–2.
40. Moloney, *A Secret History of the IRA*, pp. 246–9.
41. Ibid., pp. 252–4.
42. Ibid.
43. Ibid.
44. Ibid., pp. 255–7.
45. Hennessey, *The Northern Ireland Peace Process*, pp. 67–70.
46. *Setting the record straight: A record of communication between Sinn Fein and the British government October 1990–November 1993*, Belfast: Sinn Fein Publicity Department, 1994, p. 3.
47. Powell, *Great Hatred, Little Room*, p. 70; Clarke and Johnston, *Martin McGuinness*, p. 185. See also, *Setting the Record Straight*, p. 3.
48. Statement from Martin McGuinness in *Setting the Record Straight*, pp. 11–2.
49. Ibid., pp. 11–2, 17.
50. For a flavour of this see Danny Morrison's reaction to Thatcher's resignation in November 1990: 'Oh, what a beautiful day! Thatcher, the bad bastard, the biggest bastard we have ever known, has been ousted!', in Morrison, *Then the Walls Came Down*, p. 120.
51. A. Bevin, 'IRA has an ethical dimension', *The Observer*, 28 November 1993.
52. Taylor, *Provos*, pp. 320–1.
53. 'Fred' produced a letter signed by Brooke to verify his credentials. See *Setting the Record Straight*, p. 17; Powell, *Great Hatred, Little Room*, p. 71.
54. Powell, *Great Hatred, Little Room*, p. 70.
55. *Setting the Record Straight*, pp. 19–20.
56. Ibid.
57. Ibid., pp. 20–1.
58. Ibid., p. 24. See also, Taylor, *Provos*, p. 330.
59. *Setting the Record Straight*, p. 24.
60. Powell, *Great Hatred, Little Room*, p. 72.
61. Clarke and Johnston, *Martin McGuinness*, p. 196.
62. Cited in Mallie and McKittrick, *Endgame in Ireland*, p. 89.
63. A. Seldon (with L. Baston), *Major: A Political Life*, London: Weidenfeld and Nicholson, 1997, p. 415.
64. Clarke and Johnston, *Martin McGuinness*, p. 197.
65. Ibid.; *Setting the Record Straight*, p. 25.
66. *Setting the Record Straight*, pp. 26–7.
67. Ibid.
68. Dillon, *25 Years of Terror*, p. 291.
69. M. Holland, 'Meeting Held Two Days After Warrington Bomb', *The Observer*, 28 November 1993.
70. *Setting the Record Straight*, p. 28.
71. Screened on BBC One, 26 March 2008. For some of Taylor's interview with Duddy, see 'Disobeyed orders and a dangerous message', *The Guardian*,

18 March 2008, <http://www.guardian.co.uk/politics/2008/mar/18/north-ernireland.past1>.
72. Cited in Mallie and McKittrick, *Endgame in Ireland*, p. 93.
73. Dillon, *25 Years of Terror*, pp. 264–99.
74. Ibid.
75. Seldon, *Major*, pp. 412–7.
76. *Setting the Record Straight*, pp. 13–4, 31–2.
77. Ibid., pp. 31–2.
78. Ibid., pp. 32–4.
79. Ibid., pp. 34–5. For an additional account of this internal debate, see Mallie and McKittrick, *Endgame in Ireland*, pp. 95–7.
80. *Setting the Record Straight*, p. 30.
81. Ibid., p. 40.
82. Ibid., p. 29.
83. Ibid.
84. Mallie and McKittrick, *Endgame in Ireland*, pp. 132–3.
85. Ibid., p. 134.
86. The June 1993 document is 'Draft 11' in the appendixes to E. Mallie and D. McKittrick, *The Fight for Peace: The Secret History of the Irish Peace Process*, London: Mandarin, 2nd edn, 1997, p. 420.
87. Seldon, *Major*, p. 425.
88. Mallie and McKittrick, *Endgame in Ireland*, pp. 141–8.
89. Ibid., pp. 148–50.
90. Seldon, *Major*, p. 425.
91. 'Joint Declaration on Peace: The Downing Street Declaration, Wednesday 15 December 1993', Conflict Archive in Northern Ireland (CAIN) Web Service, <http://cain.ulst.ac.uk/events/peace/docs/dsd151293.htm>.
92. Mallie and McKittrick, *Endgame in Ireland*, p. 166.
93. F. Finlay [advisor to Dick Spring], 'Under the Gun', *The Sunday Times (News Review)*, 14 December 1997.
94. Quoted in Seldon, *Major*, p. 423.
95. Moloney, *Paisley*, pp. 339–40.
96. Seldon *Major*, p. 427.
97. For a full account of this see J. Cusack and H. McDonald, *UVF*, Dublin: Poolbeg, 2nd edn, 2000, pp. 290–320.
98. Ibid. See also, Taylor, *Loyalists*, pp. 220–34.
99. Taylor, *Loyalists*, pp. 225–6.
100. 'Joint Declaration on Peace'.
101. M. Mansergh, 'From conflict to consensus: the legacy of the Good Friday Agreement and the role of the two governments', address given on 3 April 2008 at the Institute for British-Irish Studies, University College Dublin.
102. See, for instance, Sinn Féin, *Speech by Martin McGuinness to the 1994 Sinn Féin Ard Fheis* (1994), Linenhall Library Belfast, Political Collection.
103. This document appears in the appendix to Moloney, *A Secret History of the IRA*, pp. 598–601. For a discussion of this, see also, Patterson, *The*

Politics of Illusion: A Political History of the IRA, London: Serif, 2nd edn, 1997, pp. 254–69.

104. For an indication of the extent to which the security services had established a grip over the IRA, see Holland and Phoenix, *Phoenix: Policing the Shadows*, pp. 389–95.

105. John Major, 31 August 1994, cited in P. Bew and G. Gillespie, *The Northern Ireland Peace Process, 1993–1996: A Chronology*, London: Serif, 1996, p. 64.

106. Michael Ancram, 21 August 1994, cited in Bew and Gillespie, *The Northern Ireland Peace Process*, p. 61.

107. Patrick Mayhew, 31 August 1994, cited in ibid., p. 65.

108. Ibid.

109. 'Combined Loyalist Military Command (CLMC) Ceasefire Statement, 13 October 1994', Conflict Archive in Northern Ireland (CAIN) Web Service, <http://cain.ulst.ac.uk/events/peace/docs/clmc131094.htm>.

110. Cusack and McDonald, *UVF*, pp. 308–14.

111. H. McDonald, *Gunsmoke and Mirrors: How Sinn Fein dressed up defeat as victory*, Dublin: Gill and Macmillan, 2008, p. 95.

112. John Major, 21 October 1994, cited in Bew and Gillespie, *The Northern Ireland Peace Process*, p. 74.

113. Ibid.

114. Dick Spring, 21 November 1994, cited in ibid., pp. 75–6.

115. Michael Ancram, 9 December 1994, cited in ibid., p. 78. For more on this issue, see Trimble, *Misunderstanding Ulster*, pp. 10–2.

116. Mitchel McLaughlin, 27 October 1994, cited in Bew and Gillespie, The *Northern Ireland Peace Process*, p. 75.

117. Bew and Gillespie, *The Northern Ireland Peace Process*, pp. 81–8.

118. Ibid.

119. Ibid., pp. 87–8.

120. Gerry Adams, 4 July 1993, cited in Bew and Gillespie, *The Northern Ireland Peace Process*, p. 12.

121. Moloney, *Paisley*, p. 342.

122. Godson, *Himself Alone*, pp. 146–55.

123. John Major, 20 December 1994 and 30 December 1994, cited in Bew and Gillespie, *The Northern Ireland Peace Process* p. 79.

124. See for example, John Major, 10 May 1995, cited in ibid., p. 100.

125. John Major, 13 October 1995, cited in ibid., p. 124.

126. IRA spokesperson, 1 September 1995, cited in ibid., p. 117.

127. Martin McGuinness, 20 June 1995, cited in ibid., p. 105.

128. Gerry Adams, 21 September 1995, cited in ibid., p. 120.

129. Gerry Adams, 14 June 1995, cited in ibid., p. 105.

130. Gerry Adams, 14 July 1995, cited in ibid., pp. 110–1.

131. P. Dixon, '"The Usual English Doubletalk": The British Political Parties and the Ulster Unionist 1974–95', *Irish Political Studies*, vol. 9, no. 1, 1994, pp. 25–40.

132. Gerry Adams, 14 June 1995, cited in Bew and Gillespie, *The Northern Ireland Peace Process*, p. 105.
133. Cited in E. O'Kane, 'Decommissioning and the peace process: where did it come from and why did it stay so long?', *Irish Political Studies*, vol. 22, no. 1, March 2007, pp. 81–101.
134. Dick Spring, 15 December 1993 and Gerry Adams, 14 June 1995, cited in Bew and Gillespie, *The Northern Ireland Peace Process*, p. 35.
135. Dick Spring, 1 June 1994, cited in ibid., p. 54.
136. Gerry Adams, 8 January 1994, cited in ibid., p. 41.
137. S. Duignan, *One Spin on the Merry-Go-Round*, Dublin: Blackwater Press, 1996, p. 151.
138. Albert Reynolds, 20 April 1995, cited in Bew and Gillespie, *The Northern Ireland Peace Process*, p. 97.
139. Dick Spring, 27 September 1995, cited in ibid., p. 121.
140. John Bruton, 11 November 1995, cited in ibid., p. 129.
141. John Major, 12 November 1995, cited in ibid., p. 129.
142. Bew and Gillespie, *The Northern Ireland Peace Process*, pp. 133–6.
143. Ibid., p. 119.
144. 'Report of the International Body on Arms Decommissioning, 22 January 1996', Conflict Archive in Northern Ireland (CAIN) Web Service, <http://cain.ulst.ac.uk/events/peace/docs/gm24196.htm>.
145. Author interview with David Trimble, 11 September 2007.
146. Gerry Adams, 26 January 1996 and 24 January 1996, cited in Bew and Gillespie, *The Northern Ireland Peace Process*, pp. 152–5.
147. Fergus Finlay, 'Under the Gun'.
148. Bertie Ahern, 11 January 1996, cited in Bew and Gillespie, *The Northern Ireland Peace Process*, p. 148.
149. Godson, *Himself Alone*, p. 277.
150. Ibid., p. 246.
151. Powell, *Great Hatred, Little Room*, p. 14.
152. See F. Millar, 'Ireland: the Peace Process', in A. Seldon (ed.), *Blair's Britain: 1997–2007*, Cambridge: Cambridge University Press, 2007, pp. 509–28.
153. Godson, *Himself Alone*, pp. 263–6.
154. Ibid., pp. 243–9.
155. P.R. Neumann, 'Bringing in the Rogues: Political Violence, the British Government and Sinn Fein', *Terrorism and Political Violence*, vol. 15, no. 3, Autumn 2003, pp. 154–71.
156. T. Blair, 'Labour committed to finding settlement for North', *Irish Times*, 28 April 1997.
157. Powell, *Great Hatred, Little Room*, p. 14.
158. Hennessey, *The Northern Ireland Peace Process*, pp. 107–14.
159. 'Prime Minister's Speeches—1997—Royal Ulster Agricultural Show', website of 10 Downing Street, <http://www.number-10.gov.uk/output/Page948.asp>.

160. Mallie and McKittrick, *Endgame in Ireland*, p. 245. See also, M. Mowlam, *Momentum: The Struggle for Peace, Politics and the People*, London: Hodder and Stoughton, 2002; and J. Langdon, *Mo Mowlam*, London: Little Brown, 2000.
161. Mallie and McKittrick, *Endgame in Ireland*, p. 245.
162. For the importance of this concept during this period see D. Trimble, 'Antony Alcock Memorial Lecture', at the University of Ulster, 24 April 2007, <http://www.davidtrimble.org/speeches_alcock.pdf>.
163. Finlay, 'Under the Gun'.
164. Author interview with David Trimble, 11 September 2007.
165. Sinn Fein, *Speech by Pat Doherty, Sinn Féin Vice-President, for 80ᵗʰ Anniversary of 1916 Rising, Belfast, 7 April 1996*, Linenhall Library Belfast, Political Collection. See also, '"No return to Stormont"—IRA: Easter Message from Óglaigh na hÉireann', *An Phoblacht*, 4 April 1996; G. Kelly, 'There can be no return to Stormont', *An Phoblacht*, 16 May 1996.
166. Author interview with David Trimble, 11 September 2007.
167. Molloy cited in T. Harnden, 'Talks Under Threat as IRA is Primed', *Daily Telegraph*, 17 November 1997.
168. Author interview with David Trimble, 11 September 2007.
169. Adams cited in J. Clarity, 'In Ulster Drama, a U.S. Player is Hopeful About Peace', *New York Times*, 25 July 1997.
170. P. Bew, 'Can Blair's Plan at Last Bring Peace?', *The Times*, 12 January 1998.
171. Mallie and McKittrick, *Endgame in Ireland*, p. 263.
172. Godson, *Himself Alone*, p. 329.
173. A. Campbell (with R. Stott ed.), *The Blair Years: Extracts from the Alistair Campbell Diaries*, London: Hutchinson, 2007, pp. 287–8.
174. Powell, *Great Hatred, Little Room*, p. 95.
175. Campbell, *The Blair Years*, p. 291.
176. From an interview given by Ahern, 'For Compromise Not Victory', in *Parliamentary Brief*, vol. 5, no. 4, March 1998, pp. 8–11.
177. Cited by Steven King in *Parliamentary Brief*, vol. 11, no. 10, April 2008. For a fuller account of this episode see Godson, *Himself Alone*, pp. 326–37.
178. Godson, *Himself Alone*, pp. 333, 346–7.
179. Mallie and McKittrick, *Endgame in Ireland*, p. 271.
180. Cited in Campbell, *The Blair Years*, p. 293.
181. Mallie and McKittrick, *Endgame in Ireland*, p. 295.
182. Ibid.
183. Ibid.; see also, Godson, *Himself Alone*, pp. 347–9.
184. Mallie and McKittrick, *Endgame in Ireland*, p. 272.
185. Mansergh, 'From Conflict to Consensus'.
186. Anthony Alcock cited in Godson, *Himself Alone*, p. 330.
187. See, for instance, Hennessey, *The Northern Ireland Peace Process*, pp. 145–9, 153; G. Murray and J. Tonge, *Sinn Féin and the SDLP: from*

Alienation to Participation, London: Hurst and Co., 2005, p. 199, 213; Mallie and McKittrick, *Endgame in Ireland*, pp. 272–7.

188. Godson, *Himself Alone*, pp. 348–9.
189. Mallie and McKittrick, *Endgame in Ireland*, pp. 278–9.
190. 'The Agreement: Agreement reached in the multi-party negotiations 10 April 1998', Conflict Archive in Northern Ireland (CAIN), <http://cain.ulst.ac.uk/events/peace/docs/agreement.htm>.
191. Mallie and McKittrick, *Endgame in Ireland*, pp. 281–2.
192. Godson, *Himself Alone*, p. 351.
193. Ibid., pp. 351–5.
194. Powell, *Great Hatred, Little Room*, p. 17.
195. For aggregate results of the referendums in the Republic and Northern Ireland respectively, see 'The 1998 Referendums', ARK, Northern Ireland: Social and Political Archive, <http://www.ark.ac.uk/elections/fref98.htm>. For estimates of the breakdown of the results, according to community, see 'Results of the Referenda in Northern Ireland and Republic of Ireland, Friday 22 May 1998', see CAIN, <http://cain.ulst.ac.uk/issues/politics/election/ref1998.htm>.
196. S. Wolff, 'Context and Content: Sunningdale and Belfast Compared', in R. Wilford (ed.), *Aspects of the Belfast Agreement*, Oxford: Oxford University Press, 2001, pp. 11–25.
197. Frampton, *The Long March*, pp. 121–31.
198. Trimble, 'Antony Alcock Memorial Lecture'.
199. 'Tony Blair's pledge to the people of Northern Ireland on 20 May 1998' CAIN, <http://cain.ulst.ac.uk/events/peace/docs/tb20598.htm>
200. 'Hearts and Minds Poll: The Details', *BBC News Online*, 17 October 2002, <http://news.bbc.co.uk/1/low/northern_ireland/2335861.stm>.
201. *A New Beginning: Policing in Northern Ireland*, The Report of the Independent Commission on Policing for Northern Ireland, CAIN, <http://cain.ulst.ac.uk/issues/police/patten/patten99.pdf>.
202. This debate has been revisited by Lord Robin Eames, former Archbishop of Armagh. See B. Rowan, 'Eames: State Allowed Innocent People to Die', *Belfast Telegraph*, 29 May 2008.
203. Godson, *Himself Alone*, pp. 470–93.
204. F. Millar, *David Trimble: The Price of Peace*, Dublin: The Liffey Press, 2nd edn, 2008, p. 66.
205. R. MacGinty and J. Darby, *Guns and Government: The Management of the Northern Ireland Peace Process*, Basingstoke: Palgrave Macmillan, 2002.
206. Godson, *Himself Alone*, p. 412.
207. Powell, *Great Hatred, Little Room*, p. 142
208. Ibid., p. 149. For a statement of Sinn Fein's position in this period, see G. Adams, 'We must now find a way to break the cycle of mistrust', *Irish Times*, 5 July 1999.
209. M. Oatley, 'Forget the weapons and learn to trust Sinn Fein', *The Sunday Times*, 31 October 1999.

210. Godson, *Himself Alone*, pp. 550–91.
211. Figure based on information collated from 'Conflict-related Deaths in Northern Ireland since the 1994 Ceasefires', British Irish Rights Watch, <http://www.birw.org/Deaths%20since%20ceasefire/deaths%20 since%201994.html>.
212. Powell, *Great Hatred, Little Room*, p. 210.
213. 'Prime Minister's Speeches—Harbour Commissioners' Office, Belfast, October 2002', Northern Ireland Office, <http://www.nio.gov.uk/ speech_by_pm_at_harbour_commissioners_office.pdf>.
214. Ibid.
215. S. Sexton, 'Low Surrender', *Magill*, 2, 2008, p. 18.
216. Author interview with David Trimble, 11 September 2007.
217. Powell, *Great Hatred, Little Room*, p. 25.
218. This message was delivered to the British Ambassador in Dublin by Father Alec Reid. See Powell, *Great Hatred, Little Room*, p. 167.
219. Ibid., pp. 147–8, 149, 155, 193, 216, 226
220. 'Carrots and Capitulation—Mandelson on Blair', *The Guardian*, 14 March 2007.
221. Powell, *Great Hatred, Little Room*, p. 274.
222. Moloney, *A Secret History of the IRA*, pp. 504–30.
223. Private information.
224. M.B. Reiss, 'The Troubles We've Seen', *The American Interest*, vol. III, no. 6, July–August 2008.
225. Blair interview with Noel Thompson on BBC Northern Ireland television programme, *Hearts and Minds*, on 20 April 2008.
226. Powell, *Great Hatred, Little Room*, p. 24.
227. S. Sexton, 'The Last Chuckle', *Magill*, May 2008.
228. Cited in Hennessey, *The Northern Ireland Peace Process*, p. 108.
229. P.R. Neumann, 'The Imperfect Peace: Explaining Paramilitary Violence in Northern Ireland', *Low Intensity Conflict and Law Enforcement*, vol. 11, no. 1, Spring 2002, pp. 116–38.
230. H. Patterson, 'From Insulation to Appeasement: the Major and Blair Governments Reconsidered', in Wilford (ed.), *Aspects of the Belfast Agreement*, pp. 166–83.
231. N. Watt, P. Wintour, O. Boycott, 'Blair Guilty of Capitulating to Sinn Fein—Mandelson', *The Guardian*, 13 March 2007.
232. 'Carrots and Capitulation—Mandelson on Blair'.
233. Kaufmann, *Orange Order*, pp. 202–35.
234. Bew, *Ireland*, p. 552.
235. P. Bew, 'A pyrrhic victory in the polls: Direct rule tinged with green', *The Sunday Times*, 30 November 2003.
236. 'Four admit city centre abduction', *BBC News Online*, 13 December 2005, <http://news.bbc.co.uk/1/hi/northern_ireland/4526270.stm>.
237. H. Patterson, 'A Conspiracy of Agreement', *Parliamentary Brief*, 9, 5, October 2004, p. 5.
238. 'IRA Statement', *An Phoblacht*, 9 December 2004.

239. *Third Report of the Independent Monitoring Commission*, October 2004, <http://cain.ulst.ac.uk/issues/politics/docs/imc/imc041104.pdf>.
240. 'IRA plc turns from terror into biggest crime gang in Europe', *The Times*, 25 February 2005.
241. See, for instance, A. McIntyre, 'Burdens Unbearable', *The Blanket*, 4 February 2005, <http://lark.phoblacht.net/am0402058g.html>; A. Chrisafis, 'Brutal killing turns republicans against IRA', *The Guardian*, 9 February 2005; S. Breen, 'They'll never vote Sinn Féin again', *Sunday Tribune*, 13 February 2005.
242. Referred to in Reiss, 'The Troubles we've seen'.
243. McDowell cited in T. Brady and S. Molony, 'McDowell: These men are leaders of the IRA', *Irish Independent*, 21 February 2005.
244. W. O'Dea, 'Now is the time for "the truth, justice and freedom from fear"', *Sunday Independent*, 20 February 2005.
245. 'Prime Minister warns IRA to give up criminality to allow return of power sharing', Northern Ireland Office, <http://www.nio.gov.uk/media-detail.htm?newsID=10846>.
246. 'Stop acting like a child, says Ahern in response to Adams', *Irish Independent*, 12 February 2005.
247. 'IRA Offer Withdrawn', *An Phoblacht*, 3 February 2005.
248. T. Brady and G. McKenna, 'Now Provos put a gun to our heads', *Irish Independent*, 4 February 2005.
249. *Irish Independent*/Millward Brown IMS Opinion Poll, cited in J. Cusack and J. O'Malley, 'McCartney/heist backlash rocks SF despite core vote', *Sunday Independent*, 27 February 2005; *Irish Times*/TNS MRBI Opinion Poll, cited in M. Brennock, 'Two-thirds of voters believe Sinn Féin must split from IRA', *Irish Times*, 5 March 2005.
250. 'IRA Statement in full', *BBC News Online*, 28 July 2005, <http://news.bbc.co.uk/1/hi/northern_ireland/4724599.stm>.
251. De Chastelain cited in, 'IRA "has destroyed all its arms"', *BBC News Online*, 26 September 2005, <http://news.bbc.co.uk/1/hi/northern_ireland/4283444.stm>.
252. Reiss, 'The Troubles We've Seen'.
253. 'Sinn Fein Ard Fheis 2006—Policing: Going on the offensive on policing issue', *An Phoblacht*, 23 February 2006.
254. P. Sherwell, 'I'll never deal with Adams again, says Bush', *Sunday Telegraph*, 13 March 2005. See also, M. Evans and H. Rumbelow, 'US calls halt to Sinn Fein fundraising in IRA backlash', *The Times*, 14 March 2005.
255. See 'Reiss's peace: Bush's envoy issues "report card" on North', *Irish Echo Online*, 21–27 December 2005, <http://www.irishecho.com/archives/archivestory.cfm?newspaperid=17605&issueid=446>; 'Gerry Adams challenges Mitchell Reiss attack on Sinn Fein policing position', Sinn Fein, 1 January 2006, <http://www.sinnfein.ie/news/detail/12473>; 'The Northern Ireland Peace Process: A Status Report', Mitchell B. Reiss, Testimony Before the House International Relations Committee Subcom-

mittee on Africa, Global Human Rights and International Operations, US Department of State, 15 March 2006, <http://www.state.gov/p/eur/rls/rm/65817.htm>; F. Millar, 'Issue of policing is capable of being resolved, says Adams', *Irish Times*, 11 May 2006.
256. F. Millar, 'Bush's envoy sees policing as key issue for Sinn Fein', *Irish Times*, 10 June 2006.
257. Speech by Peter Hain, then Secretary of State for Northern Ireland, to the Magill Summer School, Glenties, County Donegal, 16 July 2006, CAIN, <http://cain.ulst.ac.uk/issues/politics/docs/nio/ph160706.htm>.
258. P. Hain, 'It's time for reality', *Belfast Newsletter*, 31 July 2006.
259. 'Butter Not Guns', *The Times*, 5 March 2007.
260. 'Sir Reg vows to prevent carve-up "axis"', *Belfast Telegraph*, 8 May 2007.
261. S. Jenkins, 'Bigotry and violence made Paisley and Adams the Taliban of Europe', *The Guardian*, 7 March 2008.
262. It has been suggested that ethnic divisions and segregation are as prominent as ever. See, for example, C. Gouverneur, 'Northern Ireland's apartheid', *Le Monde diplomatique*, July, 2006.
263. Farry, 'Northern Ireland: Prospects for Progress in 2006?'.
264. M. O'Doherty, 'Selling peace to the world', *The Belfast Telegraph*, 29 April 2008.

4. BIRTH, RESISTANCE AND THE ASSAULT ON LIBERTY

1. S. Oppenheimmer, *The Origins of the British: A Genetic Detective Story*, London: Constable and Robinson, 2006, and A. Uriarte, in *Historia del clima de la tierra*, Gastiez: Servicio Central de Publicaciones del Gobierno Vasco, 2003. See also <http://antonuriarte.blogspot.com/>.
2. For more on this narrative, see R. Collins, *The Basques*, Oxford: Basil Blackwell, 2nd edn, 1990, and J. Caro Baroja (ed.), *Historia General del País Vasco*, Bilbao-San Sebastian: Editorial La Gran Enciclopedia Vasca y Luis Haranburu-Editor, 1980.
3. J. Caro Baroja, *Introducción a la Historia Social y Económica del Pueblo Vasco*, San Sebastian: Editorial Txertoa, 1986, p. 90.
4. J. Corcuera Atienza, *Orígenes, ideología y organización del nacionalismo vasco, 1876–1904*, Madrid: Siglo Veintiuno Editores, 1979, p. 65.
5. S. de Pablo and L. Mees, *El péndulo patriótico, Historia del Partido Nacionalista Vasco (1895–2005)*, Barcelona: Critica, 2005, pp. 46–50, 320–4.
6. Ibid., pp. 46–50.
7. J. Antonio Aguirre, *Freedom was Flesh and Blood*, London: Victor Gollancz, 1945, p. 285.
8. Excerpt from E. Hobsbawm's *War of Ideas* as published in *The Guardian*, 17 February 2007.
9. G. van Hensbergen, *Guernica, The Biography of a Twentieth-Century Icon*, London: Bloomsbury, 2004, pp. 107–8.

10. N. Rankin, *Telegram from Guernica*, London: Faber and Faber, 2003; J. Ángel Etxaniz and V. del Palacio, 'Los muertos del bombardeo', *El Correo*, 25 April 2004.

11. G.L. Steer, *The Tree of Guernica, A Field Study of Modern War*, London: Hodder and Stoughton, 1938, pp. 365–6. See also, Aguirre, *Freedom was Flesh and Blood*, p. 288.

12. Aguirre, *Freedom was Flesh and Blood*, p. 288.

13. G. Brenan, *The Face of Spain*, London: Harmondsworth, 1987, p. 79.

14. S.G. Payne, *Franco*, Madrid: Espasa-Calpe, 1992, pp. 163–4.

15. J. María Garmendia in A. Elorza (ed.), *La historia de ETA*, Madrid: Temas de Hoy, 2000. See also, Payne, *Franco*, p. 78

16. P. Unzueta in Elorza (ed.), *La historia de ETA*, p. 427.

17. Ibid.

18. E. Gallastegi, *Por la libertad vasca*, Txalaparta: Orreaga, 1993, p. 15.

19. Unzueta in Elorza (ed.), *La historia de ETA*, p. 426.

20. *El Correo*, 19 September 2000.

21. F. de Arteaga, *ETA y el proceso de Burgos*, Madrid: Editorial E. Aguado, 1971, pp. 270–1.

22. *Terrorismo y justicia en España*, Madrid: Centro Español de Documentación, 1975, pp. 111–2.

23. J. Luis de Villalonga, *El Rey, Conversaciones con D. Juan Carlos I de España*, Barcelona: Plaza and Janés, 1993, p. 86.

24. A. Carreras and X. Tafunell, *Historia Económica de la España Contemporánea*, Barcelona: Crítica, 2003, pp. 380–1.

25. M. Herrero de Miñón, *Memorias de estío*, Madrid: Temas de Hoy, 1993, p. 144.

26. This version of the KAS Alternative was published in July 1976 and recorded, among others, by Iñaki Egaña. See I. Egaña, *Diccionario histórico-político de Euskal Herria*, Tafalla: Txalaparta, 1996. The programme was modified later as recorded by Robert P. Clark. See R.P. Clark, *Negotiating with ETA*, Reno, NA: University of Nevada Press, 1990, p. 82.

27. De Pablo and Mees, *El péndulo patriótico*, pp. 383–90.

28. I. Camaño, 'Treinta años de Txiberta', *Deia*, 3 April 2007.

29. 'Todos apoyaron la amnistía', *El País*, 15 October 2008.

30. E. Malefakis, 'Lo que falta para terminar la Guerra Civil', *El País*, 31 December 2006.

31. G. Morán, 'Evocación sarcástica del impostor, Sabatinas intempestivas', *La Vanguardia*, 29 October 2005.

32. F. Domínguez Iribarren, *ETA: Estrategia, Organización y Actuaciones, 1978–1992*, Bilbao: Servicio Editorial de la Universidad del País Vasco, 1998, pp. 222–3.

33. E. Fuentes Quintana, *De los Pactos de la Moncloa a la entrada en la Comunidad Económica Europea*, Información Comercial Española, no. 826, 2005, p. 40.

34. G. Caprio and D. Klingebiel, 'Episodes of Systemic and Borderline Financial Crises', World Bank Datasets, <http://econ.worldbank.org>.

35. C. Alonso Zaldívar and M. Castells (eds), *España, fin de siglo*, Madrid: Alianza Editorial, 1992, pp. 75–7.
36. Author's figure based on 'Población según sexo y edad desde 1900 hasta 2001', Instituto Nacional de Estadística, 2007, <www.ine.es/inebase>.
37. M. Salvo, 'Profesionales del Derecho piden que se analice qué pasó en Sanfermines del 78', *Diario de Noticias*, 26 June 2008.
38. J. María Portell, cited in L. Rincón, *ETA (1974–1984)*, Barcelona: Plaza & Janés, 1985, p. 37.
39. F. Reinares in J.F. Tezanos et al. (eds), *La transición democrática española*, Madrid: Sistema, 1989, p. 638.
40. J. María Lizundia Zamalloa, 'La paz de 1982 con ETA p-m', *Diario de Avisos*, 5 December 2006.

5. TALKING TO ETA

1. J. Hooper, *The New Spaniards*, London: Penguin, 1995, pp. 116–25.
2. B. Bilbao Vizcaya, 'Participación en porcentaje del PIB español, por comunidades autónomas', in Zaldivar and Castells (eds), *España*, p. 161.
3. Author's figure based on 'Población según sexo y edad desde 1900 hasta 2001', Instituto Nacional de Estadística, 2007, <www.ine.es/inebase>.
4. E. Morán Aláez, *Análisis sociológico del paro en la Comunidad Autónoma de Euskadi*, Ekonomiaz N° 1, 1985, pp. 34–5.
5. P. Cassan, *Francia y la cuestión vasca*, Tafalla: Txalaparta, 1998, p. 145.
6. Ibid., p. 163.
7. L. Núñez Astrain, translated by M. Stephens, *The Basques: Their Struggle for Independence*, Cardiff: Welsh Academic Press, 1997, p. 101.
8. J. Barrionuevo, *2001 Días en Interior*, Barcelona: Ediciones B, 1997, p. 39.
9. Cassan, *Francia y la cuestión vasca*, p. 170.
10. For an English language history of the GAL, see P. Woodworth, *Dirty War, Clean Hands: ETA, the GAL and Spanish Democracy*, Cork: Cork University Press, 2001.
11. J. Attali, *Verbatim*, Paris: Fayard, 1992, p. 526.
12. P. Guidoni, 'Una página de historia', *El País*, 23 January 1995.
13. Ibid.
14. Barrionuevo, *2001 Días en Interior*, pp. 155–6.
15. T. Etxarri, 'El PNV pide a Francia que siga siendo tierra de asilo y que no ratifique la decisión', *El País*, 13 September 1984.
16. X. Arzalluz, *Así fue*, Madrid: Foca, 2005, pp. 261–5.
17. E. Cedri, *Le GAL ou Le terrorism d'Etat dans l'Europe des démocraties*, Bern: CEDRI, 1989, p. 55.
18. F. González and J. Luis Cebrián, *El futuro no es lo que era*, Madrid: Aguilar, 2001, pp. 154–5.
19. P. Unzueta in A. Elorza (ed.), *La historia de ETA*, p. 427.
20. Á. Ugarte, *Espía en el País Vasco*, Barcelona: Plaza & Janés, 2005, pp. 209–71.

21. F. Domínguez Iribarren, *De la negociación a la tegua ¿El final de ETA?*, Madrid: Taurus, 1998, p. 49.
22. Núñez Aristrain and Stephens, *The Basques*, pp. 61–2.
23. Domínguez Iribarren, *De la negociación a la tegua*, pp. 53–6.
24. A. Pozas, *Las conversaciones secretas Gobierno-ETA*, Barcelona: Ediciones B, 1992, p. 60.
25. Woodworth, *Dirty War Clean Hands*, pp. 45–6.
26. Clark, *Negotiating with ETA*, pp. 183–214.
27. Barrionuevo, *2001 Días en Interior*, p. 415.
28. Ibid., p. 410.
29. Domínguez Iribarren, *ETA: Estrategia, Organización y Actuaciones*, p. 202.
30. Barrionuevo, *2001 Días en Interior*, p. 436.
31. Clark, *Negotiating with ETA*, p. 213.
32. Pozas, *Las conversaciones secretas Gobierno-ETA*, pp. 235–7.
33. Ibid., pp. 253–64
34. Clark, *Negotiating with ETA*, pp. 212–6.
35. Ibid., p. 219
36. Pozas, *Las conversaciones secretas Gobierno-ETA*, p. 127.
37. Ibid., p. 128.
38. Ibid., pp. 265–7.
39. Ibid., p. 140.
40. Ibid., pp. 269–74.
41. Ibid., p. 144.
42. Ibid., p. 157.
43. Ibid., pp. 293–4.
44. Núñez Aristrain, *The Basques*, pp. 67–9.
45. Domínguez Iribrarren, *De la negociación a la tegua*, p. 83.
46. F. Domínguez, *Josu Ternera*, Madrid: La Esfera de los Libros, 2006, p. 174.
47. I. Sánchez-Cuenca, *ETA contra el Estado*, Barcelona: Criterios Tusquets Editores, 2001, pp. 134–8.
48. F. Reinares, *Patriotas de la muerte*, Madrid: Taurus, 2001, pp. 39–49.
49. For a sympathetic description of the Basque patriotic youth movement, see E. Ó Broin, *Matxinada: Basque Nationalism and Radical Basque Youth Movements*, Belfast: Left Republican Books, 2004.
50. Reinares, *Patriotas de la muerte*, p. 46.
51. J. Luis Barbería, 'ETA asume el atentado contra Aznar y advierte que seguirá matando si no hay autodeterminación', *El País*, 27 April 1995.
52. F. Domínguez Iribarren in A. Elorza (ed.), *La historia de ETA*, p. 357.
53. 'Thematical statistical series', Basque Statistics Office, <http://www.eustat.es>.
54. Documentos EBB, 27 January 1997, <www.eaj.pnv.eu>.
55. 'Public Declarations: Communiqué of the Committee of Ajuría-Enea', 13 July 1997, <www.euskadi..net>.
56. J. Duva, 'El Pacto de Madrid decide aislar a HB y reformas legales para combatir los apoyos al terrorismo', *El País*, 15 July 1997.

57. L.R. Aizpeolea, 'Aznar propone que se imponga una cuarentena social y política a la coalición independentista', *El País*, 15 July 1997.

58. R. Herreo, 'El PNV denuncia «síntomas de descomposición» en el Poder Judicial', *El Mundo*, 4 December 1997.

59. Morán Blanco, *ETA entre España y Francia*, Madrid: Editorial Complutense, 1997, pp. XXII–XXXV.

60. F. Lázaro and A. Yanel, 'Garzón ordena el cierre de «Egin» por su implicación en la red financiera de ETA', *El Mundo*, 16 July 1998.

61. Lizarra Agreement, <www.vascodocuteca.org/documentos/pdf/Otros_partidos_politicos_nacionalistas_vascos/Lizarra.pdf>.

62. I. San Sebastián, *Jaime Mayor Oreja*, Madrid: La Esfera de los Libros, 2001, p. 247.

63. Ibid., p. 248.

64. Department of Political Science, University of the Basque Country, <*http://www.ehu.es/cpvweb/pags_directas/euskobarometroFR.html*>.

65. L.R. Aizpeolea, 'Aznar anuncia contactos con el entorno de ETA', *El País*, 4 November 1998.

66. F. Garea and M. Cruz, 'Zarzalejos y Fluxá se reunieron en Bélgica con el "jefe político" de ETA, Mikel "Antza"', *El Mundo*, 8 June 1999.

67. J. Rivas, 'La victoria de la coalición nacionalista no frena el ascenso de EH y los partidos opuestos a Lizarra', *El País*, 14 June 1999.

68. Domínguez, *Josu Ternera*, pp. 274–81.

69. 'Interview with ETA', *Euskal Irratí Telebista*, 29 March 1999.

70. J. Luis Barbería and P. Unzueta, *Cómo llegamos a esto*, Madrid: Taurus, 2003, p. 44.

71. <www.libertaddigital.com/index.php?action=desanoti&cpn=12762 15416>.

72. C. Remirez de Ganuza, 'Aznar cree que «la vía irlandesa» es el intento de conseguir la autodeterminación a plazos', *El Mundo*, 18 May 2001.

73. A. Díez, 'Zapatero critica la intransigencia de Aznar y reclama diálogo entre PNV y PP', *El País*, 19 May 2001.

74. A. Díez, 'Los socialistas anuncian que votarán con el PP contra el proyecto nacionalista', *El País*, 30 September 2003.

75. *Diario de Noticias*, 2 November 2004.

76. <http://www.gees.org/documentos/Documen-01956.pdf>.

77. Speech by J.L. Rodríguez Zapatero, reproduced in *El País*, 16 January 2005.

78. Boletín Oficial Cortes Generales: Congreso de los Diputados, series D, no. 204, 17 May 2005, pp. 54–5.

79. <http://es.wikinews.org/wiki/ETA_anuncia_un_alto_el_fuego_permanente>.

80. J. Moreno, J. Ceberio and L.R. Aizpeolea, 'La democracia debe a las víctimas un pacto de memoria y apoyo', *El País*, 26 March 2006.

81. J. Juaristi, 'Si desaparecen los ataques, estamos dispuestos a asumir compromisos firmes con un escenario sin violencia', *Gara*, 14 May 2006.

82. L. Rodríguez Aizpeolea, 'Así fue el diálogo con ETA', *El País*, 10 June 2006.

83. 'De Juana, condenado a doce años por denunciar el sistema carcelario', *Gara*, 9 November 2006.

84. L.R. Aizpeolea, 'El Gobierno llegó al borde del precipicio en el proceso con ETA', *El País*, 6 April 2008.

85. 'Texto del communicado de ETA', *BBC News Online*, 5 June 2007, <http://news.bbc.co.uk/hi/spanish/international/newsid_6721000/6721 877.stm>.

86. F. Iturribarria, 'Sarkozy condecora al jefe de la unidad anti-ETA de la Policía francesa', *El Correo*, 25 March 2008.

87. F. Iturribarria, 'Detenidos en Burdeos el jefe de ETA que rompió la tregua y otros tres terroristas', *El Correo*, 21 May 2008.

88. F. Iturribarria, 'Cae en Francia "Txeroki", el etarra más buscado', *El Correo*, 18 November 2008.

CONCLUSION

1. Patterson, 'The IRA and sectarianism revisited'.

2. A. Maskaliunaite, 'Role of (ETA) violence in the construction of nationalism in Spain and Basque country', paper given at 17th annual ASEN Conference, *The Dark Face of Nationalism: Violence, Extremism and the Nation*, at the London School of Economics, 18 April 2007.

3. Patterson, *The Politics of Illusion*. See also R. English, *Armed Struggle: The History of the IRA*, Oxford: Oxford University Press, 2003.

4. McDonald, *Gunsmoke and Mirrors*, p. 92.

5. C. Lucey, 'The real lessons of Ulster', *Magill*, December 2007–January 2008, pp. 20–2.

6. N. Stadlen, 'Interview with Gerry Adams Part I', *The Guardian*, 12 September 2007.

7. P. Dixon, '"A Tragedy Beyond Words"; Interpretations of British Government Policy and the Northern Ireland Peace Process', in A. Edwards and S. Bloomer (eds), *Transforming the Peace Process in Northern Ireland: From Terrorism to Democratic Politics*, Dublin: Irish Academic Press, 2008, pp. 175–92.

8. T.E. Utley, *The Lessons of Ulster*, London: Dent, 1975.

9. Godson, 'The real lessons of Ulster'.

10. M.B. Reiss, 'Lessons of the Northern Ireland Peace Process', paper given at the British Irish Association conference, Emmanuel College, Cambridge, 9 September 2005, <http://www.state.gov/p/eur/rls/rm/54869.htm>.

11. The Portland Trust, *Economic Lessons from Northern Ireland*.

12. Taylor, 'Sinn Fein has hijacked the history of Ulster'.

13. Hennessey, *The Northern Ireland Peace Process*, p. 220.

14. 'Army paper says IRA not defeated', *BBC News Online*, 6 July 2007, <http://news.bbc.co.uk/1/hi/northern_ireland/6276416.stm>.

15. Cited in M. Lancaster, '"Shooting from the Hip": Interview with General the Lord Guthrie', *The House Magazine*, no. 1241, vol. 33, 10 December 2007.

16. P. Mandelson, 'How should we elect our MPs?', in *Peter Mandelson MP's Lecture on the Northern Ireland peace process and the renewal of British politics* (pamphlet), London, 2000.
17. B. O'Leary, 'The Character of the 1998 Agreement: Results and Prospects', in Wilford, *Aspects of the Belfast Agreement*, pp. 49–83. For a critique of aspects of the Agreement and consociational theory, see Farry, 'Northern Ireland: Prospects for Progress in 2006?'.
18. Millar, *David Trimble*, p. 54.
19. Dixon, '"A Tragedy Beyond Words"', pp. 175–92.
20. Quoted in I. Black, 'Terror talks: would contacting al Qaeda be a step too far?', *The Guardian*, 15 March 2008.
21. See review of Powell's *Great Hatred, Little Room*, by Mark Durkan (SDLP leader). M. Durkan, 'Primadonna of peace', *The House Magazine*, 12 May 2008. For the moderate unionist perspective on Powell, see D. Trimble, 'Agreeing to differ', *The Guardian*, 5 April 2008.
22. FitzGerald, 'Powell wrong about talking in the midst of terror campaign'.
23. Powell, *Great Hatred, Little Room*, pp. 85–6.
24. FitzGerald, 'Powell wrong about talking in the midst of terror campaign'.
25. D.M. Tull and A. Mehler, 'The hidden costs of power-sharing: reproducing insurgent violence in Africa', *African Affairs*, vol. 104, no. 416, 2005, pp. 375–98.
26. For a more detailed exposition of this argument, see J. Bew and M. Frampton, 'Talking to Terrorists: The Myths, Misconceptions and Misapplication of the Northern Ireland Peace Process', *Jerusalem View Points*, no. 566, August–September 2008. See also, A. Edwards, 'Talking to Terrorists: Political Violence and Peace Process in the Contemporary World', in Edwards and Bloomer (eds); *Transforming the Peace Process in Northern Ireland*, pp. 195–211; and Neumann, 'Negotiating with Terrorists'.
27. Powell, *Great Hatred, Little Room*, pp. 309–11.
28. Brian Keenan to Jack Conrad, 19 November 1987, Communist Party of Great Britain website, <http://www.cpgb.org.uk/theory/keenancorresp.html>.
29. Powell, *Great Hatred, Little Room*, pp. 2–3.
30. Stadlen, 'Interview with Gerry Adams Part I'.
31. Moore, 'Irish Republicanism and the Peace Process'.
32. 'Carrots and capitulation—Mandelson on Blair', *The Guardian*, 14 March 2007.
33. P. Bew, 'The Long Good Friday', *Literary Review*, May 2008.
34. 'Why Hamas is not Sinn Fein' (revised Autumn 2007 edition), Paper for Britain Israel Communications and Research Centre, <http://www.bicom.org.uk/background/research-and-analysis/israeli-palestinian-arena/why-hamas-is-not-sinn-fein-revised-autumn-2007->.
35. Reiss, 'Lessons of the Northern Ireland Peace Process'.

BIBLIOGRAPHY

PRIMARY SOURCES

Manuscript Sources
Churchill Archives Centre, Cambridge University Donoughue
  Papers—DNGH
Linen Hall Library, Belfast
  Political Collection
National Register of Archives (NRA), Kew, Richmond
  Cabinet Files, 1974–8—CAB
  Foreign and Commonwealth Office, 1974–8—FCO
  Northern Ireland Office Files, 1974–8—CJ
  Prime Minister Files, 1974–8—PREM

Official Publications
European Commission of Human Rights: *Ireland v. United Kingdom, 1976
  Y.B. European Convention on Human. Rights, 512, 748, 788–94*
European Court of Human Rights: *Ireland v. United Kingdom—5310/71
  [1978] ECHR 1*
Operation Banner: An Analysis of Military Operations in Northern Ireland
'The EU and the Middle East peace process', 2 vols, House of Lords European
  Union Committee, 26th Report of Session 2006–7, published on 24 July
  2007
Report of the Committee of Inquiry into Police Interrogation Procedures in
  Northern Ireland, London, 1979

Interviews
Sir Brian Cubbon, London, 1 May 2008
Sir Nicholas Fenn, 21 July 2007
Danny Morrison, 21 August 2003
Sean O'Callaghan (1), 22 November 2005
Sean O'Callaghan (2), 12 January 2008
Lord Trimble, 11 September 2007

BIBLIOGRAPHY

Newspaper, Magazines and Political Journals
An Glor Gafa/Captive Voice
An Phoblacht
Belfast Newsletter
Belfast Telegraph
Daily Mail
Daily Telegraph
Deia
Diario de Avisos
Diario de Noticias
El Correo
El Mundo
El País
Foreign Service Journal
GQ Magazine
Gara
Gulf Daily News
Haaretz
Independent
International Herald and Tribune
Irish Independent
Irish News
Irish Times
Jerusalem Post
La Vanguardia
Le Monde diplomatique
Magill
New Hibernia
New Left Review
Newsweek
New York Times
Noticias de Alava
Parliamentary Brief
Prospect
Sunday Business Post
Sunday Herald
Sunday Independent
Sunday News
Sunday Telegraph
Sunday Times
Sunday Times (Irish edition)
Sunday Tribune

296

BIBLIOGRAPHY

The American Interest
The Guardian
The House Magazine
The Observer
The Phoenix
The Times
The Times Literary Supplement
Wall Street Journal

Memoirs

Aguirre, Jose Antonio, *Freedom was Flesh and Blood*, London: Victor Gollancz, 1945.

Arzalluz, Xabier, *Así fue*, Madrid: Foca, 2005.

Barrionuevo, José, *2001 Días en Interior*, Barcelona: Ediciones B, 1997.

Bloomfield, Kenneth, *Political Dialogue in Northern Ireland: The Brooke Initiative, 1989–92*, London: Palgrave Macmillan, 1998.

———, A Tragedy of Errors: The government and Misgovernment of Northern Ireland, Liverpool: Liverpool University Press, 2007.

Campbell, Alistair (with R. Stott ed.), *The Blair Years: Extracts from the Alistair Campbell Diaries*, London: Hutchinson, 2007.

Clarke, Alan, *Diaries*, London: Weidenfeld and Nicolson, 1993.

Devlin, Paddy, *The Fall of the Northern Ireland Executive*, Belfast: Paddy Devlin, 1975.

Dewar, Col. Michael, *The British Army in Northern Ireland*, London: Weidenfeld Military, 2nd edn, 1996.

Donoughue, Bernard, *Downing Street Diary: With Harold Wilson in No. 10*, London: Jonathan Cape, 2004.

———, *Downing Street Diary, vol. 2: With James Callaghan in No. 10*, London: Jonathan Cape, 2008.

Duignan, Sean, *One Spin on the Merry-Go-Round*, Dublin: Blackwater Press, 1996.

Faulkner, Brian, *Memoirs of a Statesman*, John Huston (ed.), London: Weidenfeld and Nicolson, 1978.

FitzGerald, Garret, *All in a Life: An Autobiography*, Dublin: Gill and Macmillan, 1991.

Herrero de Miñón, Miguel, *Memorias de estío*, Madrid: Temas de Hoy, 1993.

Hurd, Geoffrey, *Memoirs*, London: Little, Brown, 2003.

Lawson, Nigel, *The View from No. 11: Memoirs of Tory Radical*, London: Bantam, 1992.

Lees-Milne, James, *Diaries, vol. 3, 1984–1997*, introduction by Michael Bloch, London: John Murray, 2008.

Mason, Roy, *Paying the Price*, London: Robert Hale, 1999.

Morrison, Danny, *Then the Walls Came Down: A Prison Journal*, Dublin: The Mercier Press, 1999.

Mowlam, Marjorie, *Momentum: The Struggle for Peace, Politics and the People*, London: Hodder and Stoughton, 2002.

O'Callaghan, Sean, *The Informer*, London: Bantam Press, 1998.

O'Rawe, Richard, *Blanketmen: An Untold story of the H-Block Hunger Strike*, Dublin: New Island Books, 2005.

Powell, Jonathan, *Great Hatred, Little Room: Making Peace in Northern Ireland*, London: The Bodley Head, 2008.

Prior, Jim, *A Balance of Power*, London: Hamish Hamilton, 1986.

Ramsay, Robert, *Ringside Seats: An Insider's View of the Ulster Crisis*, Dublin: Irish Academic Press, 2009.

Rees, Merlyn, *Northern Ireland: A Personal Perspective*, London: Methuen, 1985.

Thatcher, Margaret, *The Downing Street Years*, London: Harper Collins, 1993.

Whitelaw, William, *The Whitelaw Memoirs*, London: Aurum Press, 1989.

Lectures, Papers and Speeches

Hain, Peter, 'Peacemaking in Northern Ireland: A model for conflict resolution?', speech made at Chatham House, 12 June 2007, published by the Northern Ireland Office, June 2007.

Mandelson, Peter, 'Lecture on the Northern Ireland peace process and the renewal of British Politics', London, 2000.

Mansergh, Martin, 'From conflict to consensus: the legacy of the Good Friday Agreement and the role of the two governments', address given on 3 April 2008 at the Institute for British-Irish Studies, University College Dublin..

Reiss, Mitchell B., 'Lessons of the Northern Ireland Peace Process', paper given at the British Irish Association conference, Emmanuel College, Cambridge, 9 September 2005, <http://www.state.gov/p/eur/rls/rm/54869.htm>.

———, 'The Northern Ireland Peace Process: A Status Report', Testimony Before the House International Relations Committee Subcommittee on Africa, Global Human Rights and International Operations, US Department of State, 15 March 2006, <http://www.state.gov/p/eur/rls/rm/65817.htm>.

Trimble, David, 'Antony Alcock Memorial Lecture', at the University of Ulster, 24 April2007, <http://www.davidtrimble.org/speeches_alcock.pdf>.

———, *Misunderstanding Ulster*, pamphlet published by Conservative Friends of Israel, London, 2007.

BIBLIOGRAPHY

Other Printed Primary Sources

Boletín Oficial Cortes Generales: Congreso de los Diputados.

Le GAL ou Le terrorism d'Etat dans l'Europe des démocraties, Bern: CEDRI,1989.

González, Felipe, and Juan Luis Cebrián, *El futuro no es lo que era,* Madrid: Aguilar, 2001.

Setting the record straight: A record of communication between Sinn Fein and the British government, October 1990–November 1993, Belfast: Sinn Fein Publicity Department, 1994.

The Portland Trust, *Economic Lessons from Northern Ireland,* May 2007.

Terrorismo y justicia en España, Madrid: Centro Español de Documentación, 1975.

INTERNET RESOURCES

ARK, Northern Ireland: Social and Political Archive, <http://www.ark.ac.uk/ elections/fref98.htm>.

Basque Statistics Office, <http://www.eustat.es>.

BBC News Online, <http://news.bbc.co.uk>.

British Irish Rights Watch, <http://www.birw.org>.

Department of Political Science, University of the Basque Country, <http:// www.ehu.es/cpvweb/pags_directas/euskobarometroFR.html>.

Hansard—House of Lords Debates, <http://www.parliament.the-stationery-office.co.uk/pa/ld/ldhansrd.htm>.

Instituto Nacional de Estadística 2007, <www.ine.es/inebase>.

Irish Department of Foreign Affairs website, <http://www.dfa.ie/home/index. aspx?id=42628>.

Ministry of Defence website, <http://www.mod.uk/DefenceInternet/home>.

National Public Radio, <http://www.npr.org>.

National Review Online, <www.nationalreview.com>.

Northern Ireland Office, <http://www.nio.gov.uk>.

Prime Minister's Speeches, <http://www.number-10.gov.uk>.

Radio Free Europe website, <http://www.rferl.org>.

States News Service, <http://www.highbeam.com/States+News+Service>.

The Blanket, <http://lark.phoblacht.net>.

University of Ulster website, <http://www.ulster.ac.uk>.

US State Department, <www.state.gov>.

World Bank Datasets, <http://econ.worldbank.org>.

SECONDARY LITERATURE

Alonso, Rogelio, *Irlanda del Norte: Una historia de guerra y la búsqueda de la paz,* Madrid: Editorial Complutense, 2001.

BIBLIOGRAPHY

————, 'Pathways Out of Terrorism in Northern Ireland and the Basque Country: The Misrepresentation of the Irish Model', in *Terrorism and Political Violence*, vol. 16, no. 4, Winter, 2004.

————, 'The Ending of ETA Terrorism: Lessons to learn and mistakes to avoid from Northern Ireland', *Análisis Del Real Instituto Elcano*, 31 May 2006, <http://www.realinstitutoelcano.org/analisis/987.asp>.

Anderson, Brendan, *Joe Cahill: A Life in the IRA*, Dublin: O'Brien Press, 2002.

Attali, Jacques, *Verbatim*, Paris: Fayard, 1992.

Aughey, Arthur, *Under Siege: Ulster Protestants and the Anglo-Irish Agreement*, London: Hurst, 1989.

Bew, John, 'Introduction' to David W. Miller, *Queen's Rebels: Ulster Loyalism in Historical Perspective*, first published, 1978, University College Dublin Press, 2007, pp. vii–xxiv.

————, *The Glory of being Britons: Civic unionism in Nineteenth-Century Belfast*, Dublin: Irish Academic Press, 2009.

Bew, Paul, *Ireland: The Politics of Enmity, 1789–2006*, Oxford: Oxford University Press, 2007.

Bew, Paul, and Gordon Gillespie, *Northern Ireland: A Chronology of the Troubles, 1968–1993*, Dublin: Gill and Macmillan, 1993.

————, *The Northern Ireland Peace Process, 1993–1996: A Chronology*, London: Serif, 1996.

Bew, Paul, and Henry Patterson, *The British State and the Ulster Crisis: From Wilson to Thatcher*, London: Verso, 1985.

Bew, Paul, Peter Gibbon and Henry Patterson, *Northern Ireland, 1921–1996: Political Forces and Social Classes*, London: Serif, 2nd edn, 1996.

Bishop, Patrick, and Eamonn Mallie, *The Provisional IRA*, London: Heineman, 1987.

Bourke, Richard, *Peace in Ireland: The War of Ideas*, London: Pimlico, 2003.

Bowyer Bell, James, *IRA Tactics and Targets: an Analysis of Tactical Aspects of the Armed Struggle, 1969–1989*, Dublin: Poolberg, 1990.

Brenan, Gerald, *The Face of Spain*, London: Harmondsworth, 1987.

Burleigh, Michael, *Blood and Rage: A Cultural History of Terrorism*, London: Harper Press, 2008.

Carreras, Albert, and Xavier Tafunell, *Historia Económica de la España Contemporánea*, Barcelona: Crítica, 2003.

Caro Baroja Julio, (ed.), *Historia General del País Vasco*, Bilbao-San Sebastian: Editorial La Gran Enciclopedia Vasca y Luis Haranburu-Editor, 1980.

————, *Introducción a la Historia Social y Económica del Pueblo Vasco*, San Sebastian: Editorial Txertoa, 1986.

Cassan, Patrick, *Francia y la cuestión vasca*, Tafalla: Txalaparta, 1998.

BIBLIOGRAPHY

Clarke, Liam, and Kathryn Johnston, *Martin McGuinness: From Guns to Government*, London: Mainstream Publishing, 2001.
Clarke, Robert P., *The Basque insurgents: ETA 1952–1980*, Reno, NA: University of Nevada Press, 1984.
———, *Negotiating with ETA: Obstacles to peace in the Basque Country, 1975–1988*, Reno, NA: University of Nevada Press, 1990.
Collins, Roger, *The Basques*, Oxford: Basil Blackwell, 2nd edn, 1990.
Conversi, Daniele, *The Basques, the Catalans and Spain*, London: Hurst and Co., 1997.
Cooke, Alistair, 'The Victory of Ulster's Extremists', *The Salisbury Review*, vol. 26, no. 1, Autumn 2007, pp. 13–4.
Corcuera Atienza, Javier, *Orígenes, ideología y organización del nacionalismo vasco, 1876–1904*, Madrid: Siglo Veintiuno Editores, 1979.
Crawford, Collin, *Inside the UDA: Volunteers and Violence*, London: Pluto Press, 2003.
Cunningham, Michael, *British Government Policy in Northern Ireland, 1969–2000*, Manchester: Manchester University Press, 2001.
Cusack, Jim, and Henry McDonald, *UVF*, Dublin: Poolbeg, 2nd edn, 2000.
de Arteaga, Frederico, *ETA y el proceso de Burgos*, Madrid: Editorial E. Aguado, 1971.
de Baroid, Ciaran, *Ballymurphy and the Irish War*, London: Pluto Press, 2nd edn, 2000.
de Pablo, Santiago, and Ludger Mees, *El péndulo patriótico, Historia del Partido Nacionalista Vasco (1895–2005)*, Barcelona: Critica, 2005.
de Villalonga, José Luis, *El Rey, Conversaciones con D. Juan Carlos I de España*, Barcelona: Plaza & Janés, 1993.
Debray, Régis, *Praise Be Our Lords: A Political Education*, London: Verso, 1997.
Dillon, Martin, *The Dirty War*, London: Hutchinson, 1988.
———, *25 Years of Terror: The IRA's war against the British*, London: Bantam Books, revised edn, 1999.
Dixon, Paul, '"The Usual English Doubletalk": The British Political Parties and the Ulster Unionist 1974–95', *Irish Political Studies*, vol. 9, issue 1, 1994, pp. 25–40.
———, '"A Tragedy Beyond Words"; Interpretations of British Government Policy and the Northern Ireland Peace Process', in Aaron Edwards and Stephen Bloomer (eds), *Transforming the Peace Process in Northern Ireland*, Dublin: Irish Academic Press, 2008, pp. 175–92.
Dochartaigh, Niall, *From Civil Rights to Armalites: Derry and the Birth of the Irish Troubles*, Cork: Cork University Press, 1997.
Domínguez Iribarren, Florencio, *ETA: Estrategia, Organización y Actuaciones, 1978–1992*, Bilbao: 'Servicio Editorial de la Universidad del País Vasco, 1998.

———, *De la negociación a la tegua ¿El final de ETA?*, Madrid: Taurus, 1998.

———, *Josu Ternera*, Madrid: La Esfera de los Libros, 2006.

Edwards, Aaron, 'Talking to Terrorists: Political Violence and Peace Process in the Contemporary World', in Aaron Edwards and Stephen Bloomer (eds), *Transforming the Peace Process in Northern Ireland*, Dublin: Irish Academic Press, 2008, pp. 195–211.

Egaña, Iñaki, *Diccionario histórico-político de Euskal Herria*, Tafalla: Txalaparta, 1996.

Ellison, Graham, and Jim Smyth, *The Crowned Harp: Policing in Northern Ireland*, London: Pluto Press, 1999.

Elorza, Antonio (ed.), *La historia de ETA*, Madrid: Temas de Hoy, 2000.

English, Richard, *Armed Struggle: A History of the IRA*, London: Macmillan, 2003.

Farry, Stephen, 'Northern Ireland: Prospects for Progress in 2006?', *United States Institute of Peace: Special Report*, no. 173, November 2006, available at <http://www.usip.org/pubs/specialreports/sr173.pdf>.

Fisk, Robert, *The Point of No Return: The Strike which Broke the British in Ulster*, London: Andre Deutsch, 1975.

Frampton, Martyn, *The Long March: The Political Strategy of Sinn Fein, 1981–2007*, Basingstoke: Palgrave Macmillan, 2008.

Fuentes Quintana, Enrique, *De los Pactos de la Moncloa a la entrada en la Comunidad Económica Europea, Información Comercial Española*, no. 826, 2005.

Gailey, Andrew, *Crying in the Wilderness: A Liberal Editor in Ulster, 1939–69*, Belfast: Institute of Irish Studies, Queen's University, 1995.

Gallastegi, Eli, 'Gudari', in *Por la libertad vasca (Orreaga)* Tafalla: Txalaparta, 1993.

Gillespie, Gordon, *Years of Darkness: The Troubles Remembered*, Dublin: Gill & Macmillan, 2008.

Godson, Dean, *Himself Alone: David Trimble and the Ordeal of Unionism*, London: Harper Collins, 2004.

———, 'Lessons from Northern Ireland for the Arab-Israeli Conflict', *Jerusalem Viewpoints*, no. 523, October 2004.

Goldring, Maurice, *Renoncer à la terreur*, Paris: Éditions du Rocher, 2005.

Halper, Stefan, and Jonathan Clarke, *America Alone: The Neo-Conservatives and the Global Order*, Cambridge: Cambridge University Press, 2004.

Hamill, Desmond, *Pig in the Middle: The Army in Northern Ireland, 1969–1985*, London: Methuen, 2nd edn, 1986.

Harnden, Toby, *'Bandit Country': The IRA and South Armagh*, London: Hodder and Stoughton, 1999.

Hennessey, Thomas, *Northern Ireland: The Origins of the Troubles*, Dublin: Gill and Macmillan, 2005.

————, *The Evolution of the Troubles, 1970–2*, Dublin: Irish Academic Press, 2007.

————, *The Northern Ireland Peace Process: Ending the Troubles?*, Dublin: Gill and Macmillan, 2000.

Hirst, Catherine, *Religion, Politics and Violence in Nineteenth-Century Belfast: the Pound and Sandy Row*, Dublin: Four Courts, 2002.

Holland, Jack and Susan Phoenix, *Policing the Shadows: The Secret War against Terrorism in Northern Ireland*, London: Hodder and Stoughton, 1996.

Hooper, John, *The New Spaniards*, London: Penguin, 1995.

Kaufmann, Eric, P., *The Orange Order: A Contemporary History*, Oxford: Oxford University Press, 2007.

Kearney, Richard, *Myths and Motherland*, Derry: Field Day, 1984.

Langdon, Julia, *Mo Mowlam*, London: Little, Brown, 2000.

Luis Barbería, José and Patxo Unzueta, *Cómo llegamos a esto*, Madrid: Taurus, 2003.

Mallie, Eamonn, and David McKittrick, *The Fight for Peace: The Secret History of the Irish Peace Process*, London: Mandarin, 2nd edn, 1997.

Maskaliunaite, Asta, 'Role of (ETA) violence in the construction of nationalism in Spain and Basque country', paper given at 17th annual ASEN Conference, 'The Dark Face of Nationalism: Violence, Extremism and the Nation', at the London School of Economics, 18 April 2007.

MacGinty, Roger, and John Darby, *Guns and Government: The Management of the Northern Ireland Peace Process*, Basingstoke: Palgrave Macmillan, 2002.

McDonald, Henry, *Gunsmoke and Mirrors: How Sinn Fein dressed up defeat as victory*, Dublin: Gill and Macmillan, 2008.

McDonald, Henry and David McKittrick, *Endgame in Ireland*, London: Hodder and Stoughton, 2001.

McGarry, John (ed.), *Northern Ireland and the Divided World: Post-Agreement Northern Ireland in Comparative Perspective*, Oxford: Oxford University Press, 2001.

McKittrick, David, and David McVea, *Making sense of the Troubles*, Belfast: Blackstaff Press, 2000.

McIntyre, Anthony, 'Modern Irish Republicanism: The Product of British State Strategies', *Irish Political Studies*, vol. 10, 1995, pp. 97–122.

Millar, Frank, *David Trimble: The Price of Peace*, Dublin: The Liffey Press, 2nd edn, 2008.

————, 'Ireland: the Peace Process', in Anthony Seldon (ed.), *Blair's Britain: 1997–2007*, Cambridge: Cambridge University Press, 2007, pp. 509–28.

————, *Northern Ireland: A Triumph of Politics*, Dublin: Irish Academic Press, 2009.

Miller, Rory (ed.), *Ireland and the Middle East*, Dublin: Irish Academic Press, 2007.

Moloney, Ed, *A Secret History of the IRA*, London: Penguin, 2nd edn, 2007.

———, *Paisley: From Demagogue to Democrat?*, Dublin: Poolbeg Press, 2008.

Moore, Jonathan, 'Irish Republicanism and the Peace Process: Lessons for Hamas', in Rory Miller (ed.), *Ireland and the Middle East*, Dublin, pp. 101–12.

Morán Aláez, Enrique, *Análisis sociológico del paro en la Comunidad Autónoma de Euskadi*, Ekonomiaz, no. 1, 1985, pp. 34–5.

Morán Blanco, Sagrario, *ETA entre España y Francia*, Madrid: Editorial Complutense, 1997.

Morgan, Austin, *Harold Wilson*, London: Pluto, 1992.

Mulholland, Marc, *Northern Ireland at the Crossroads: Ulster Unionism in the O'Neill years, 1960–9*, Basingstoke: Palgrave Macmillan, 2000.

———, 'Why Did Unionists Discriminate?' in Sabine Wichert (ed.), *From the United Irishmen to Twentieth-Century Unionism: A Festschrift for A.T.Q. Stewart*, Dublin: Four Courts Press, 2004, pp. 187–206.

Murphy, D., *To Establish the truth: Essays in Revisionism: Derry 1960–9*, Derry: Aileach Press, 1996.

Murray, Gerard, and Jonathan Tonge, *Sinn Féin and the SDLP: from Alienation to Participation*, London: Hurst and Co., 2005.

Neumann, Peter, 'The Imperfect Peace: Explaining Paramilitary Violence in Northern Ireland', *Low Intensity Conflict and Law Enforcement*, vol. 11, no. 1, Spring 2002, pp. 116–38.

———, 'Winning the "War on Terror"? Roy Mason's Contribution to Counter-Terrorism in Northern Ireland', *Small Wars and Insurgencies*, vol. 14, no. 3, Autumn 2003, pp. 45–64.

———, 'Bringing in the Rogues: Political Violence, the British Government and Sinn Fein', *Terrorism and Political Violence*, vol. 15, no. 3, Autumn 2003, pp. 154–71.

———, 'Negotiating with Terrorists', *Foreign Affairs*, vol. 86, no. 1, January–February 2007.

Newsinger, John, *British Counterinsurgency: From Palestine to Northern Ireland*, Basingstoke: Palgrave Macmillan, 2002.

Núñez Astrain, Luis, translated by Meic Stephens, *The Basques: Their Struggle for Independence*, Cardiff: Welsh Academic Press, 1997.

Ó Broin, Eoin, *Matxinada: Basque Nationalism and Radical Basque Youth Movements*, Belfast: Left Republican Books, 2004.

O'Haplin, Eunan, '"A poor thing but our own": The Joint Intelligence Committee and Ireland, 1965–72', *Intelligence and National Security*, vol. 23, no. 5, October 2008, pp. 658–80.

O'Kane, Eamonn, 'Decommissioning and the peace process: where did it come from and why did it stay so long?', *Irish Political Studies*, vol. 22, no. 1, March 2007, pp. 81–101.

O'Leary, Brendan, 'The Character of the 1998 Agreement: Results and Prospects', in Richard Wilford (ed.), *Aspects of the Belfast Agreement*, Oxford: Oxford University Press, 2001, pp. 49–83.

Oppenheimmer, Walter, *The Origins of the British: A Genetic Detective Story*, London: Constable and Robinson, 2006.

Payne, Stanley, G., *Franco*, Madrid: Espasa-Calpe, 1992.

Parker, Tom, 'Fighting an Antaean Enemy: How Democratic States Unintentionally Sustain the Terrorist Movements They Oppose', *Terrorism and Political Violence*, vol. 19, 2007, pp. 155–79.

Patterson, Henry, *Ireland Since 1939: The Persistence of Conflict*, Dublin: Penguin Ireland, 2006.

——, 'From Insulation to Appeasement: the Major and Blair Governments Reconsidered', in Richard Wilford (ed.), *Aspects of the Belfast Agreement*, Oxford: Oxford University Press, 2001, pp. 166–83.

——, 'The IRA and sectarianism revisited', *Terrorism and Political Violence* (forthcoming).

——, *The Politics of Illusion: A Political History of the IRA*, London: Serif, 2nd edn, 1997.

——, 'War of National Liberation or Ethnic Cleansing: IRA Violence in Fermanagh during the Troubles', in Brett Bowden and Michael Davis (eds), *Terror: From Tyrannicide to Terrorism*, Brisbane: University of Queensland, 2006.

Patterson, Henry, and Eric Kaufmann *Unionism and Orangeism in Northern Ireland since 1945: The Decline of the Loyal Family*, Manchester: Manchester University Press, 2007.

Peatling, Geoffrey K., 'Unionist Divisions, the Outset of the Northern Ireland Conflict and "Pressures" on O'Neill reconsidered', *Irish Studies Review*, vol. 15, no. 1, 2007, pp. 17–36.

Pozas, Alberto, *Las conversaciones secretas Gobierno-ETA*, Barcelona: Ediciones B, 1992.

Prince, Simon, *Northern Ireland's '68: Civil Rights, Global Revolt and the Origins of the Troubles*, Dublin: Irish Academic Press, 2007.

Rankin, Nicholas, *Telegram from Guernica*, London: Faber and Faber, 2003.

Reinares, Fernando, *Patriotas de la muerte*, Madrid: Taurus, 2001.

Rincón, Luciano, *ETA (1974–1984)*, Barcelona: Plaza & Janés, 1985.

San Sebastián, Isabel, *Jaime Mayor Oreja*, Madrid: La Esfera de los Libros, 2001.

Sánchez-Cuenca, Ignacio, *ETA contra el Estado*, Barcelona: Criterios Tusquets Editores, 2001.

Seldon, Anthony (with Lewis Baston), *Major: A Political Life*, London: Weidenfeld and Nicholson, 1997.

Smyth, James, 'A Discredited Cause? The IRA and Support for Political Violence', in Alan O'Day and Yonah Alexander, (eds), *Ireland's Terrorist Trauma: Interdisciplinary Perspectives*, Basingstoke: Palgrave Macmillan, 1989, pp. 101–23.

Soans, Robin, *Talking to Terrorists*, London: Royal Court, 2005.

Steer, George L., *The Tree of Guernica, A Field Study of Modern War*, London: Hodder and Stoughton, 1938.

Taylor, Peter, *Brits: The War against the IRA*, London: Bloomsbury, 2nd edn, 2001.

———, *Loyalists*, London: Bloomsbury, 1999.

———, *Provos: The IRA and Sinn Fein*, London: Bloomsbury, 1997.

Tezanos, José F., Ramón Cotarelo, and Andrés. Deblas (eds), *La transición democrática española*, Madrid: Sistema, 1989.

The Sunday Times Insight Team, *Ulster*, London: Penguin, 1972.

Thomas, Hugh, *The Spanish Civil War*, London: Eyre & Spottiswoode, 1961.

Tull, Denis, and Andrea Mehler, 'The hidden costs of power-sharing: reproducing insurgent violence in Africa', *African Affairs*, vol. 104, no. 416, 2005, pp. 375–98.

Ugarte, Ángel, *Espía en el País Vasco*, Barcelona: Plaza & Janés, 2005.

Unzueta, Patxo, *La historia de ETA*, Madrid: Temas de Hoy, 2000.

Uriarte, Antón, *Historia del clima de la tierra*, Gastiez: Servicio Central de Publicaciones del Gobierno Vasco, 2003.

Utley, Tom E., *The Lessons of Ulster*, London: Dent, 1975.

van Hensbergen, Gijs, *Guernica: The Biography of a Twentieth-Century Icon*, London: Bloomsbury, 2004.

Warner, Geoffrey, 'Putting Pressure on O'Neill: The Wilson Government and Northern Ireland, 1964–9', *Irish Studies Review*, vol. 13, no. 1, 2005, pp. 13–21.

———, 'The Falls Road Curfew Revisited', *Irish Political Studies*, vol. 14, no. 3, August 2006, pp. 325–42.

White, Robert W., *Ruairi O'Bradaigh: The Life and Politics of an Irish Revolutionary*, Indiana: Indiana University Press, 2006.

Wilson, Andrew, *Irish America and the Ulster Conflict, 1968–1995*, Belfast: Blackstaff, 1995.

Wolff, Stefan, 'Context and Content: Sunningdale and Belfast Compared', in Richard Wilford (ed.), *Aspects of the Belfast Agreement*, Oxford: Oxford University Press, 2001, pp. 11–25.

Woodworth, Paddy, *Dirty War, Clean Hands: ETA, the GAL and Spanish Democracy*, Cork: Cork University Press, 2001.

———, 'The Spanish-Basque Peace Process: How to Get Things Wrong', *World Policy Journal*, vol. XXIV, no. 1, Spring 2007.

Wright, Frank, *Two Lands on One Soil: Ulster Politics before Home Rule*, Dublin: Gill and Macmillan, 1996.

Zaldívar, Alonso C., and Manuel Castells (eds), *España, fin de siglo*, Madrid: Alianza Editorial, 1992.

INDEX

2003), 229–30, 235; dialogue
with (1980s), 206, 210, 211;
electoral politics, 196, 205; as
Euskal Herritarrok (EH), 224,
225, 228–9, 256; peace initiative
(2005–07) and, 232, 233, 236;
prosecution of leaders (1996–7),
218, 221–2; Sinn Fein and, 14, 237
BBV Bank attack (Bilbao, 1983), 206
Belfast Agreement (1998), 2–3,
109, 144–7, 148, 154–65,
242–3, 248–9; decommissioning
of weapons and, 147–8, 149,
151–3; IRA ceasefire transgressions (1998–2002), 153–4; Irish
constitution and, 148, 240;
Northern Ireland Act (2000) and,
152; post-Agreement negotiations, 154–66, 249, 250; prisoner
releases and, 146–7, 149; referenda to ratify, 148–9, 150, 240,
249; resemblance to Sunningdale
Agreement, 45, 142, 149, 166;
review of (February 2004), 159;
SDLP and, 144, 148, 248, 249,
250; suspensions of institutions
of, 152–3, 158; unionist opponents of, 6, 150–1, 153, 155, 158
Belfast Telegraph, 25–6, 131; Bell,
Ivor, 40, 52, 73
Beñarán, José Miguel, murder of
(1975), 192
Bennett, Charles, 154
Bennett Report (1979), 83
bin Laden, Osama, 5, 14
Birmingham public house bombings
(1974), 54
Bishopsgate bombing (April 1993),
121, 123
Blair, Tony: administration of
(1997–2007), 138–48, 149–50,
154, 155–60, 162–3, 164, 242;
Bertie Ahern and, 244; Belfast
Agreement (1998) and, 144–6,
147–8, 150, 154–5, 156, 249;

Harbour Commissioners' speech
(October 2002), 154–5, 158–9;
'Quartet' Middle East peace envoy, 9, 10; republican movement
and, 138–40, 144, 145–6, 154,
156, 157–8, 161, 258; Royal
Ulster Agricultural Show speech
(1997), 140–1; Spanish government and, 15, 16, 235, 237;
David Trimble and, 139, 147–8,
156, 158, 249; Ulster unionism
and, 139, 140–1, 150
Blanco, Miguel Angel, 220–1
'blanket protests' against criminalisation, 86–7
Bloody Friday (July 1972), 42
Bloody Sunday (January 1972), 33,
37, 42
Bloomfield, Ken, 37, 95, 101
border, French/Spanish, 170,
181–2, 197, 199, 200, 201, 202,
205, 214, 241
border, Irish, 66, 67–8, 76, 77, 82,
239–40
'Border Poll' (8 March 1973), 44,
100
Bradley, Father Denis, 50, 115, 118
Bridges, Lord, 50
British army in Northern Ireland:
Bloody Sunday (January 1972)
and, 33, 37, 42; British public
support for withdrawal, 61;
casualties/fatalities, 7, 81–2, 108;
Catholic-nationalist communities and, 30–5, 66; containment
of IRA, 52, 72, 109–12, 246–7;
deployment (August 1969),
29–30; Falls Curfew (July 1970),
32–3, 34–5; Government policy
problems and, 36–7; intelligence
war, 34, 35, 52, 55, 67, 109–10,
129, 247; internal appraisal of
operations, 17, 33, 34, 36, 104,
246–7; Internment and, 33–4,
35–6; IRA, infiltration of, 109,

INDEX

INDEX

INDEX

Northern Ireland Labour Party
(NILP), 22–3
Nugent, Ciaran, 86–7

O Fiaich, Tomas, 87
Oatley, Michael, 50, 51, 52, 88, 91,
115, 116, 117, 152
Obama, Barack, 2–3
O'Bradaigh, Ruairi, 53, 58
O'Brien, Connor Cruise, 78
O'Callaghan, Sean, 111
O'Conaill, Daithi, 39, 40, 42, 51, 54
O'Dea, Willie, 161
O'Hara, Patsy, 90
O'Loan, Nuala, 6
Omagh bombing (August 1998),
156
O'Malley, Padraig, 6
Onaindia, Mario, 194
O'Neill, Captain Terence, 22–4,
25–9, 30
O'Neill, 'Tip', 83–4
'Operation Motorman' (1972), 42,
66Orange Order, 23, 158
O'Rawe, Richard, 89, 90, 91, 92
Orde, Sir Hugh, 5, 159
Organic Law of Harmonisation of
the Process of Autonomy (1981),
193
Ortega Lara, José Antonio, 219
Otegi, Arnaldo, 232, 236, 238
Oxford Research Group, 10

'Pact for Freedom and Against Terrorism' (December 2000), 227–8,
229
'pacto de olvido' (pact of forgetting), 188, 234
Pacts of Madrid (1953), 175
Paisley, Reverend Ian, 23, 69, 126,
132, 155, 158, 160, 165
Pasqua, Charles, 202
'Peace People' movement, 74
peace process in Northern Ireland:
1990–93 period, 112–23; all-

party talks (September 1997–
April 1998), 139–40, 141–4;
assumptions about, 12–13, 249,
259; ceasefire (IRA, July 1997),
109, 128–9, 130, 133, 136, 137,
138; ceasefires (1994) and, 109,
126, 128–30, 133, 136, 137,
138; Comprehensive Agreement
(2004), 163–4; as conflict resolution 'model', 1–17, 166, 232–3;
consent principle, 45, 97, 101,
119, 124, 125, 128, 131, 139,
140, 148, 249; 'cross-borderism'
and, 45, 102–3, 131, 142, 143,
144–6, 148; democratic context,
135–6, 148–50, 248–50, 258–9;
dominant narratives, 8, 13,
116, 249, 259; Downing Street
Declaration (1993), 125–8, 133,
138, 242, 248; 'Frameworks for
the Future' documents (1995),
131–2; 'Heads of Agreement'
document (January 1998), 143–4,
249; Hume-Adams process, 113–
14, 123–5, 127–8, 251; Jonathan
Powell on, 3–4, 5, 117, 148,
151–2, 154, 156, 157, 253, 256,
257; Leeds Castle talks (2004),
159–60; long-term impact, 166;
Mitchell Commission, 135–7,
138, 139–40; Post-Agreement
negotiations, 154–66, 249, 250;
St Andrews Agreement (October
2006), 163; 'sufficient consensus'
concept, 141, 143, 249; 'twin
track' approach, 134–5, 136;
'Washington 3' criteria (March
1995), 132, 142; see also Belfast
Agreement (1998)
People's Democracy movement,
24–5, 26, 27, 29
Perera, Dr Jehan, 5
Petraeus, General David, 7, 8
Phoenix, Ian, 110
Picasso, Pablo, 174–5

321

Statutes of Autonomy, Basque, 173, 184–5, 190, 202, 211, 213
Steele, Frank, 39–40, 50
Steer, George, 175
Stormont government, 21, 22, 37–8, 63
'Stormont-gate' spy-ring affair, 154
Strand Road holding centre (Londonderry), 66
street fighting, ETA, 216
Suárez, Adolfo, 183–4, 186, 197
'sufficient consensus' concept, 141, 143, 249
Sunningdale Agreement (1973–4), 44–9, 53, 59, 64, 68, 77, 142, 149, 166, 244, 248, 252–3

Taliban, 8–9
Tamil Tigers, 5–6
Taylor, Peter, 91, 120, 246
Tejero, Antonio, 193–4
Thatcher, Margaret, 85, 86, 93, 94, 95, 96, 104–5; administration of (1979–90), 82–6, 87–92, 93–105, 116, 117; on Anglo-Irish Agreement (1985), 103–4; republican hunger strikes and, 87, 116; Thomas, Quentin, 133
The Times newspaper, 7–8, 49, 131, 175
Timor-Leste, 6
Tohill, Bobby, 159
tourism, Spanish, ETA targeting of, 191
trade unions, Spanish, 189, 218
Trimble, David, 47, 132, 136, 142, 143, 151, 152, 153, 156, 250; Belfast Agreement (1998) and, 145, 146, 147–8, 149, 150, 158, 159, 248, 249, 250; Tony Blair and, 139, 147–8, 156, 158, 249; decommissioning issue and, 149, 151, 152–3
'The Troubles' in Northern Ireland: assumptions about, 30; background to, 21–8; British Government policy failure, 36–8, 39;

deployment of British army (August 1969), 29–30; internationalisation of conflict, 83–4, 98; violence and civil disorder (1969–72), 28, 29–30, 31–2, 36, 39, 40, 41–3; violence and civil disorder (1972–75), 52, 55, 56, 64, 73, 252; violence and civil disorder (1976), 59, 67, 72, 74, 79–80, 87; violence and civil disorder (1977–84), 72, 81–3, 92, 96–7; violence and civil disorder (1985–95), 103, 104, 107–11, 120, 121, 123, 124, 129–30, 255, 257; violence and civil disorder (1996–2005), 136, 137, 138, 139, 153–4, 159, 160–1, 235, 253
Truce Incident Centres, 55–6
Truman, Harry S., 175
'TUAS' document (IRA, 1994), 128–9
Tuzo, Harry, 33–4
'twin track' approach to peace process, 134–5, 136
Twomey, Seamus, 40, 51, 53, 56, 75

Ulster Defence Association (UDA), 42–3, 126, 129–30
Ulster Defence Regiment (UDR), 65, 108
Ulster Freedom Fighters (UFF), 43, 108, 109, 129–30
Ulster Unionist Council (UUC), 153
Ulster Unionist Party (UUP), 21, 22–4, 44, 47, 84, 102, 131–2, 141, 158; Belfast Agreement (1998) and, 144, 145, 147–8, 153, 158, 248, 249; Downing Street Declaration (1993) and, 125, 126; Sunningdale Agreement and, 44, 46; *see also* unionism in Ulster
Ulster Volunteer Force (UVF), 109, 126–7, 129–30
Ulster Workers' Council (UWC), 47, 48, 49, 53, 57